HARVARD STUDIES IN INTERNATIONAL DEVELOPMENT

INDUSTRIALIZATION AND THE STATE

THE CHANGING ROLE OF THE TAIWAN GOVERNMENT IN THE ECONOMY, 1945–1998

Li-min Hsueh, Chen-kuo Hsu, and Dwight H. Perkins

Harvard Institute for International Development
Harvard University

and Chung-hua Institution for Economic Research

Distributed by Harvard University Press

Published by Harvard Institute for International Development
Distributed by Harvard University Press

Editorial management: Gretchen O'Connor
Copyediting and indexing: Hope Steele
Design and production: Digital Design Group, Newton, MA

Library of Congress Cataloging-in-Publication Data

Industrialization and the state : the changing role of the Taiwan government
in the economy, 1945–1998 / edited by Li-min Hsueh, Chen-kuo Hsu, and
Dwight H. Perkins.
    p. cm. -- (Harvard studies in international development)
    Includes bibliographical references and index.
    ISBN 0-674-00252-0 (cloth) -- ISBN 0-674-00253-9 (paper)
    1. Industrial policy -- Taiwan. I. Hsueh. Le-min. II. Hsu, Chen-kuo.
        III. Perkins, Dwight
    Heald. IV. Series.

HD3616.T283 I53 2000
338.95124'9--dc21   00-040687

TABLE OF CONTENTS

Preface

A number of years ago, the Chung-hua Institution for Economic Research (CIER) and the Harvard Institute for International Development (HIID) undertook a joint, multi-volume study of the economic development experience of Taiwan's economy. This monograph is the first to be published in that planned series. It has been a collaborative effort between researchers in the two institutions in every sense of the word. Collaborative efforts between scholars separated by thousands of miles is never easy, but in this case, through travel and e-mail, the collaboration has worked.

As this volume goes to press, it is not clear whether there will be any subsequent volumes on Taiwan's economy published in the Harvard Studies in International Development series. HIID no longer exists as an independent body within Harvard University, although many of its functions have been transferred to the teaching faculties, notably the Kennedy School of Government. Changes in CIER have also contributed to the delay in getting research on the subsequent volumes completed. Any future volumes are therefore likely to be published elsewhere.

The chapters in this study that do not have listed authors were written in collaboration by the three main authors of this monograph. The chapters with listed authors were those written by individuals who were not responsible for the book as a whole. In this regard, it should be noted that the untimely death of Michael Roemer made it impossible for him to participate in the ultimate revisions of Chapter 5, but we acknowledge his central contribution to that chapter by listing him as co-author.

We wish also to acknowledge the contribution of several people to this volume. Our two outside readers, Professor Gustav Ranis and Dr. Joseph Stern, each read the whole manuscript with care. They made many suggestions for revision and improvement, and we have tried our best to take advantage of their insight. The volume is much improved by their help, although they bear no responsibility for its continued shortcomings.

The manuscript was ably edited by Hope Steele, and the book was designed and produced by Marc Kaufman at Desktop Publishing and Design Co. for the Harvard series. Gretchen O'Connor played a central role in overseeing the process that brought this effort to fruition.

Li-min Hsueh
Chen-kuo Hsu
Taipei, Taiwan

Dwight H. Perkins
Cambridge, Massachusetts
January, 2001

1 FOUR DECADES OF CHANGE

For nearly four decades, Taiwan's economy has been one of the Asian tigers. As such there has been much written about it both by specialists on the economy of Taiwan and by those trying to draw general lessons from the experience of the East Asian tigers. Most of these studies have looked at Taiwan's experience at a particular moment in time or have concentrated on those aspects of the experience that are similar to the experiences of Korea, Hong Kong, and Singapore or to the high-performing Asian economies in general. Other studies, like most works in economics, have focused on a single aspect of Taiwan's economy.

INTRODUCTION

This study is different in that it attempts to trace the history of Taiwan's efforts to develop the modern sector of its economy from the 1950s to the present. The underlying premise behind this approach is that the policies and development efforts undertaken can be fully understood only in their historical context. There was no single Taiwan model or set of policies that was pursued unchanged throughout the four decades. The major shift in policy in the early 1960s is well understood, but there were important changes in the approach to development in the 1970s and even more dramatic changes in the mid 1980s. When the history of the 1990s is written with the benefit of a decade or more of hindsight, it is likely to be seen as another major period of transition to a new approach to development. In fact, one of the most important lessons one can learn from Taiwan's development experience is that rapid growth requires equally rapid changes in approach as the context in which policies are implemented changes. Taiwan's unquestioned economic success is not the result of that country's leaders having discovered a successful development model and sticking to it, but rather the result of having found several models and being willing to jettison one for another when circumstances required it.

The focus of this study is on Taiwan's modern sector, by which we mean industry and business and financial services. We do not attempt to review the history of policies toward agriculture nor explore issues of income distribution and the impact on human welfare of the policies pursued. The focus instead is exclusively on how these development efforts influenced the growth and efficiency of the production of industrial products and business and financial services. Important as these welfare and distribution issues are, where others have not already definitively studied them, they are left to subsequent volumes in this series.

THE HISTORICAL APPROACH

Any effort to present history in a coherent fashion must be selective to be understandable. The approach in this study divides the Taiwan modern sector development experience into several reasonably distinct periods and focuses on key turning points in policy. The starting point for this history is the economic scene of the 1950s, which was itself largely a reflection of the intellectual and experience baggage that the Mainlanders of the Kuomintang government brought with them when they came to Taiwan in the late 1940s. This early period had to deal with ending the hyperinflation, with settling 1.6 million immigrants from the mainland, and with land reform, among other things. Industrial policy, reflecting the approach pursued on the mainland, was unrelentingly oriented toward import substitution. Foreign exchange requirements, to a large degree, were met by relying on large inflows of U.S. aid.

The first major turning point in policy took place in 1960 when the Taiwan government promulgated The Nineteen-Point Program for Economic and Financial Reform. This program was by no means a call for laissez-faire economic policies, but it did lay the groundwork for what soon became a dramatic rise in the export of manufactures. The most important policies actually implemented under this program involved the unification and devaluation of the exchange rate and a long series of other export incentives that ranged from import duty rebates to export processing zones. Imports not used in exported products continued to be highly restricted by high tariffs, quotas, and outright bans. It is this set of policies that has often been described as mercantilist even though, like South Korea, at the time Taiwan faced very large balance of payments deficits. These deficits made import restrictions of this sort almost inevitable, particularly given the dominant intellectual currents of that period with their emphasis on the desirability of active government intervention in the economy.

The second turning point in Taiwan's industrial policies involved changes that have received much less attention, at least outside of Taiwan itself. This turning point involved the decisions in the late 1960s and the early 1970s to develop heavy industries, notably petrochemicals, steel, and shipbuilding, along with an effort to build passenger automobiles that never really got off the ground. The policy initiative associated with this effort went under the title The Ten Major Development Projects. This program had many features in common with the well-known and frequently studied Korean Heavy and Chemical Industry Drive that occurred at roughly the same time, but there were also important differences. The Taiwan heavy industry program, for example, was carried out almost entirely by state-owned enterprises, whereas the Korean program was designed by the government but then turned over to the private sector for implementation, at least in most cases. The Taiwan effort was also oriented mainly toward import substitution and retained that orientation for some time thereafter; the Korean program was export oriented from the start and heavy industry products came to dominate Korean exports by the 1980s.

The Taiwan heavy industry drive was successful at least in some sectors, but soon ran head on into an unexpected obstacle: the large price increases for imported petroleum instituted by the Organization of Petroleum Exporting Countries (OPEC) in 1973 and 1979. By the late 1970s, emphasis among government policy makers was beginning to shift toward "technology-intensive" industries rather than heavy industries, and the first science and technology research plan was drawn up to cover the years 1979 to 1981. The decision to establish the Hsinchu Science-based Industrial Park was made in 1980. These and many other efforts, described in Chapter 3, were to bear fruit in the late 1980s and early 1990s when electronic and information products plus machinery came to dominate Taiwan's exports.

The heavy industry program, and even the early efforts to promote technology-intensive industry, fit reasonably comfortably into the mercantilist framework put together in the 1960s. The very success of that early framework, however, made its continuation untenable. By the mid-1980s, Taiwan was under great pressure from both economic and political forces to reject the mercantilist approach with its emphasis on high barriers to imports. The OPEC price increases in the 1970s had temporarily obscured the longer term economic forces at work, but by the mid-1980s there was nothing obscure about these forces as Taiwan's balance of payments surplus and its accumulated reserves of foreign exchange soared. Pressures to liberalize the economic system and to rely mainly on market forces rather than government intervention built up both inside and outside Taiwan. By 1986, Taiwan was formally committed to a policy of liberalization. Major steps to implement that policy followed, although Taiwan was still far from a laissez-faire economy driven mostly by market forces.

The final phase of Taiwan's development policy and performance that is studied here was still not fully integrated into government policy and strategy even by the late 1990s. The economic change that required both a government and a private-sector response was the sharp decline in the growth of industry and the continued rapid growth of the service sector, leading services to rise to over 60 percent of GDP. Whereas Taiwan succeeded in building a formidable exporting machine for manufacturing that could compete with anyone in the world, no one would describe its service sector in those terms. Taiwan's service sector lagged far behind that of neighboring Hong Kong and Singapore; the financial sector in particular was in no position as of the mid-1990s to face open international competition, but it was on this service sector, including the financial sector, that Taiwan depended to sustain continued rapid growth. One vision of the future sees Taiwan becoming a Regional Operations Center for all of East and Southeast Asia, an achievement that would come about in large part through the full liberalization and globalization of the Taiwan economy in general and the service sector in particular. The other vision sees Taiwan following something closer to the Japanese model, which retained a highly protected and inefficient service sector even as its per capita GDP approached US$30,000 a year.

POLITICAL AND ECONOMIC INFLUENCES

This study's history of Taiwan's efforts to develop its modern industrial and service sectors attempts to get beyond simple historical description to an understanding of the primary forces at work that led to the shifts in policy and performance over time. Attention is paid to three quite different kinds of influences. To begin with, there are the macroeconomic changes over time in Taiwan that played such a central role in virtually forcing changes in policy. The balance of payments problems and heavy dependence on foreign aid in the 1950s was central to the decision to try to promote exports, for example. The balance of payments surpluses of the 1980s had an equally profound influence, and the marked slowdown in industrial growth after 1987 helped push changes as well.

Political influences are also readily observable in the policy turning points and in the evolution of policy following these turning points. Some of these political influences were external to Taiwan. The most important such influence that has been there since the late 1940s was the fact that Taiwan's very existence as an autonomous government depended on having a strong economy. Anything less and Taiwan risked immediate incorporation into the People's Republic of China. The realization of this fact, together with the authoritarian nature of the Taiwan government in the 1960s and 1970s, kept economic policy making largely in the hands of technocrats rather than politicians during these critical early decades. The issue of relations with the Chinese mainland is also important to major economic policy initiatives in the 1990s. The effort to make Taiwan a center for multinational corporate headquarters and a service center supporting the entire East and Southeast Asian region is probably a viable concept only if Taiwan's relations with the mainland become substantially closer than they are today.

Other important external political influences on economic policy in Taiwan include those emanating from the United States. The critical role of U.S. foreign aid in the 1950s made U.S. aid officials important players in the debates that led up to the 1960 policy reforms. Actions by the U.S. Executive Branch of Government and pressures from the U.S. Congress also played an important role in Taiwan's exchange rate and trade liberalization decisions in the 1980s.

Internal political forces were equally important in the shaping of policies toward industry. Taiwan in the 1950s and 1960s was a society where recent immigrants from the Chinese mainland largely controlled government, whereas the private sector was largely in the hands of those born and raised on Taiwan; relations between the two groups were not close. The two groups had to work together, but their divergent interests had more than a little to do with why government retained such an active involvement in the economy, even to the extent of relying mainly on state-owned enterprises when the decision was made to promote

heavy industry. By the late 1980s and early 1990s, this division between Mainlanders and Taiwanese was no longer greatly significant
for economic policy, but numerous other interest groups emerged
as the island became increasingly democratic. Large factories of actual or potential damage to the environment, from nuclear power plants
to petrochemical complexes, became increasingly difficult to build as
localities mobilized politically to prevent such factories from being located in their backyards. The rise of industry itself created other powerful interest groups that played important roles on both sides of the
debates over economic liberalization. By the late 1980s and 1990s, as a
result, economic decision making was no longer in the hands of a small
group of technocrats reporting to an all-powerful chief executive.

Economic policy, however, is not just the outcome resulting from
contending economic pressures and internal and external interest
groups. In the final analysis, it is individuals who must make decisions
about how to respond to these external pressures and how to translate
those decisions into implementable rules and regulations. The intellectual perspective that these individuals bring to the process, a perspective based on their education and experience, matters; never is this
truer than when policy is largely in the hands of technocrats rather
than politicians. In Taiwan's case, two small groups of individuals played
central roles in the formulation of policy. One group was largely educated to be engineers and scientists and rose to positions of influence
through the government bureaucracy and state-owned enterprises,
notably the China Petroleum Corporation. The other, outside government for the most part, was a group of economists trained in the West
who regularly challenged the intellectual assumptions of the economic
ministers, most of whom came from the first group. Ultimately it was
politicians trained neither as engineers or economists who made the
decisions, but it was the debates between these two groups that helped
shape the choices.

STUDY ORGANIZATION

In the historical chapters that follow, an attempt is made to describe
the economic, political, and intellectual forces that lay behind the major policy decisions and to put them in their proper historical context.
For the most part this analysis concentrates on national-level policy
rather than on how particular policies have played out in each sector.

For those interested in how these policies worked at the sector level, we have included Appendixes A through C. These three appendixes go into more depth on how policies were implemented in three industries, each of which represents a different period in Taiwan's industrial development. The first group of industries selected is textiles and apparel (Appendix A). These industries represent the early period of industrial development on Taiwan when manufactured exports depended most importantly on easily trained and inexpensive labor. Textiles and apparel also illustrate how Taiwan firms responded to rising wages either by introducing labor-saving technology (textiles) or by shifting operations abroad to low-wage countries such as Vietnam, Indonesia, and the Chinese mainland. The second industry studied is petrochemicals (Appendix B). Petrochemicals were at the center of Taiwan's heavy industry drive and, in later years, the experience of this sector provides examples of some of the new forces that influenced development as Taiwan became more democratic. Appendix C deals with electronics and information technology. These sectors have dominated the technology-intensive development of the 1980s and 1990s. These sectors have also required a very different kind of supportive industrial policy than those that characterized the earlier periods of industrial development on Taiwan.

Three sets of issues require analysis in some depth that does not lend itself well to the historical approach of Chapters 2 and 3. The historical chapters concentrate on how policy was made, who made it, and how those policies played out in individual industrial sectors. But it was individual firms and their managers that had to actually produce the goods and sell them at home or abroad. How were these firms organized and who were the managers who ran them? These issues are the subject of Chapter 4. One distinguishing feature of the Taiwan industrial landscape was that many of the largest firms, particularly in the earlier decades, were state-owned enterprises and, even in the 1990s, efforts to privatize these enterprises proceeded slowly. Manufactured exports, however, were largely produced in the private sector. The most widely known feature of this sector was that most firms were quite small, particularly when one compares them with the *chaebol* conglomerates of Korea. But what was true in the 1960s and 1970s was less true in the 1980s and 1990s, as Taiwan's own conglomerates or relationship (*kuan-hsi*) firms rose to prominence. Furthermore, Taiwan's small firms do not fit the textbook definition of a firm well. These were not fully independent entities responding to impersonal market forces. Most were nested in a network of subcontracting relationships, often with only a single dominant firm at the top of the network pyramid. At other times, these small subcontractors worked for several firms, but on a long-term basis. Personal relations between the subcontractors and prime contractors were close. The large conglomerates, with a few exceptions, were also loosely knit organizations based on overlapping boards of directors made up of family members and a few other close associates. Few of Taiwan's corporations fit the image of the American or European large corporation with its professional management overseen by a board of directors that, in principle at least, represents the interests of the majority stockholders who have few if any personal ties to the managers. Another feature of Taiwan's business organizations was that, for the first two or three decades, they were mainly owned and managed by individuals born and educated on Taiwan during the Japanese colonial period. Yet they were able to work effectively with an interventionist government made up of people almost none of whom, at the higher levels, shared this background. These distinctions were less and less relevant as Taiwan entered the 1980s and 1990s, as new firms arose and the sons and daughters of the older firms took over, individuals who shared a common educational experience in Taiwan and often in the United States as well. This study does not try to answer why this set of relationships between individuals and firms seems to have worked so well. Social cleavages between the governed and those governing, as in the ethnic cleavages found so often in Africa and even Southeast Asia, frequently distort economic policies in directions that undermine economic development. State-owned enterprises are notorious for their inefficiencies. Social cleavages and large numbers of state-owned enterprises, however, don't appear to have undermined Taiwan's development efforts to any significant degree.

The economic influences that most shaped Taiwan's changing development strategy over the four decades were those that occurred at the aggregate or economy-wide level. An understanding of these macroeconomic forces is critical to a complete picture of why trade and other industrial policies changed so much in the 1980s and 1990s. Macroeconomic policies also played an important role in the 1950s through the 1970s, but this history is much studied and well understood, and so will be considered only briefly here.

There were a number of dramatic and closely related changes in the macroeconomic sphere on Taiwan in the 1980s. The change most apparent to even casual observers was Taiwan's expanding balance of payments surplus and it's rapidly rising foreign exchange reserves. Less obvious but closely related was a rise in Taiwan's rate of gross savings that peaked at 40 percent of GDP in the late 1980s. This rise in savings was accompanied by an equally pronounced fall in the rate of gross domestic investment, which began declining in 1982 and did not bottom out until 1987. As suddenly as this large savings investment gap appeared, it began to disappear. By 1989, the rate of savings was on the way down and the investment rate had recovered, although not back to the levels of the 1970s. The current account surplus in the balance of payments also fell in the 1990s, although it did not disappear altogether. The macro trends in the first half of the 1980s triggered a major real revaluation of the NT dollar after 1985. The revaluation of the NT dollar, when combined with the rapid rise in real wages that had been going on for over a decade, brought an end to Taiwan as an exporter of labor-intensive manufactures. Even with the shift to technology-intensive exports, the Taiwan export engine slowed markedly. In quantity terms, the rate of growth of exports fell to 6.1 percent per year in the seven years from 1991 through 1997, down from an annual rate of 10.6 percent in the 1980s. A large jump in the unit value of exports in 1995 meant that the value of Taiwan's exports grew considerably more rapidly than their quantity in the 1990s, but all the indications pointed to Taiwan's era of manufactured export-led growth having come to an end. A description of these macro trends is the main subject of Chapter 5. The chapter also attempts to understand the degree to which these macro trends simply happened because of events largely out of the control of Taiwan's economic policy makers. Or were the trends in some sense the result of deliberate policy initiatives of the Taiwan government?

A central question that is asked about all economic policy initiatives is whether the initiatives were a success. Were people better off as a result of the policies studied, or were they worse off? At one level, Taiwan's trade, macro, and other industrial policies have to be considered a success. Taiwan's GDP grew at double-digit rates for nearly three decades and slowed to a still very respectable rate of 6.2 percent per year during the 1990s. Furthermore, for the first three decades of rapid GDP growth at least, it was industry that led the way and it was manufactured exports that made possible this rapid industrial growth. Given that most industrial sectors were able to export their products within a few years of starting up, and that these exports did not depend on continuing subsidies, it would appear that most of Taiwan's industrial sectors were managed at least as successfully as similar industries found elsewhere in the world in countries at a similar stage of development as Taiwan. There were numerous individual firm and even industry-wide exceptions to this general conclusion, and a number of these are noted in the relevant chapters, but the overall picture is one of success.

If the overall picture is one of success, the question of which policies and pressures actually were central to that success remains. Did Taiwan's economic leaders, for example, come up with a fundamentally different pattern of structural change in industry in order to achieve this sustained rapid industrial growth? As the figures presented in Chapter 6 indicate, the answer to that question would appear to be no. Structural change in Taiwan's industry followed a pattern much like that found elsewhere in East and Southeast Asia, and deviations from the more general pattern appear to be explained by Taiwan's comparative advantage, vis-à-vis the more natural-resource rich countries of Asia, for example. Taiwan, like the other rapid developers of East Asia, does deviate significantly from the worldwide pattern of structural change in that exports as a share of GDP grew much more rapidly than is true in much of the world. That, however, has been a well-known component of the East Asian experience for some time.

One can also ask whether GDP, industry, and modern sector services have grown rapidly in Taiwan primarily because of high rates of investment or because of high rates of total factor productivity growth. Is the story that can be told about these trends the same for all periods during which Taiwan was growing rapidly and for all sectors of the economy? Recent studies have been interpreted as showing that Taiwan's experience is mostly a story about rapid capital accumulation. This study will attempt to demonstrate that that conclusion is an oversimplification at best. Although capital accumulation is an important part of the story, it does not follow that the only policies that mattered were those that facilitated a high rate of investment in capital. The capital still had to be used efficiently to achieve high rates of growth. An even more important issue is whether high rates of capital formation caused high growth or the management of Taiwan's economy created high-return investment opportunities that led to a higher rate of investment. We cannot answer that question definitively, but Taiwan's investment experience in the 1980s and 1990s provides some hints as to an answer.

The main objective of this study is to understand better the experience of Taiwan's actual industrial and service sector growth over the past four remarkable decades. A better understanding of how Taiwan got to where it is today, however, can also be one foundation from which we can think about the future.

2 THE POLICY FRAMEWORK: THE EARLY YEARS

Seen from the perspective of the end of the 20th century, Taiwan's economic policies have been models worthy of emulation around the world. In the late 1940s and early 1950s, in contrast, Taiwan's economy was in a shambles, heavily dependent on large inflows of U.S. foreign aid. China regained control over Taiwan in 1945, ending fifty years of Japanese colonial rule—a rule that most residents of the island saw as having been relatively benign. The Kuomintang government on the mainland brought many of their troubles with them when they reoccupied the island.

In addition to inflation and military insecurity, the Kuomintang government brought with it an ideology that was itself a major obstacle to Taiwan's economic recovery and development in this initial stage. There were, for example, serious conflicts over economic ideology and policy between the first Nationalist governor-general Ch'en Yi and Taiwanese elites. With a large number of confiscated properties, Ch'en Yi made an effort to create a state-dominated economic system based on "four public pillars," which were "production, transportation, foreign trade, and the monetary system," and a large monopolistic business sector. In addition, Ch'en Yi planned to promote cooperativization in small private businesses and farms. Ch'en Yi frequently stressed his faith in Sun Yat-sen's Doctrine of Livelihood and aspired to realize this idea in Taiwan. Yet what he saw in Sun's ideology was egalitarianism and statism. He also frequently used the principle of "restriction of private capital and development of national capital" to justify his policy.[1]

In an effort in these early years to limit the spread of hyperinflation from the Chinese mainland to Taiwan, the government had issued a separate Taiwan currency, the *taipi*. That effort achieved only limited success. Prices on Taiwan still rose by 603 percent in 1947 and 620 percent in 1948, a rate that looked good only in comparison with that of Shanghai and the Chinese mainland as a whole, where price increases in those two years were 1,223 percent and 141,800 percent, respectively.[2] With the move of the Kuomintang government to Taiwan, however, this hyperinflation was brought quickly to an end. From 1953 through 1960, consumer price increases averaged only 10 percent a year; during the 1960s the average was only 3 percent per year. The government had learned a painful lesson from the era of hyperinflation, and fiscal and monetary conservatism had become the order of the day. This conservatism characterized macroeconomic policy throughout the remainder of the century.

On the real side of the economy, Taiwan under Japanese colonial rule had become a major supplier of sugar and rice to the Japanese home islands in exchange for industrial products from Japan. This pattern continued in the 1950s, although by then imports of industrial products came as much from the United States as from Japan. The industry and infrastructure that did exist on Taiwan during the Japanese colonial period had been badly damaged by war, with industrial output in 1945 at only one-third of its previous peak.[3] Full recovery of industrial production to previous peak levels did not occur until 1951.

Even after prices had stabilized and real output had recovered, the economy faced major challenges. Exports throughout the remainder of the 1950s grew at only 4.4 percent a year in current price terms, and total exports averaged only US$116 million in the 1952 to 1956 period. In fact, from 1952 to 1956 exports did not grow at all and Taiwan ran an annual balance of trade deficit of US$81 million, financed entirely by U.S. aid inflows that averaged US$101 million per year (1951–1956).[4] On top of all this, the government had the problem of resettling 1.6 million mainland Chinese who had moved with it to Taiwan in 1949, as well as finding new management staff for the many public enterprises it had taken over from the Japanese.

The Kuomintang government's initial approach to these large structural adjustment problems was heavily influenced by the ideological baggage that it brought with it from the Chinese mainland. From the middle of the 1930s right through the end of the war with Japan in 1945 and beyond, the government attempted to create what it called a "planned economy," a "total economy," or even a "war economy." State power in the management of the economy had clear priority over the private autonomy of a market-based economic system. The ideas behind this approach were based in China's own intellectual traditions, notably the writings of Sun Yat-sen and the much earlier essays of Confucian and Legalist scholars.[5] The Kuomintang Party itself, with the help of Soviet advisors in the 1920s, had been organized along authoritarian Leninist lines. In the system that evolved from these ideas operating in a war and civil war context, Party cadres, government bureaucrats, and military officers were seen as the major actors in promoting social change and extracting resources in the name of mobilization. Those who promoted this vision had little trust in markets in general and foreign trade in particular. The approach was in many ways a right-wing version of what the Chinese Communists were trying to achieve on the Chinese mainland from the left wing of the political spectrum.

But the ideology of a state-led planned economy did not have the field entirely to itself even in the 1940s. If it had, the economic reforms that were to come in Taiwan in the late 1950s would be much harder to explain. Even in the 1940s, President Chiang Kai-shek began to invite professional economists as either consultants or special assistants to help in the formulation of economic and financial policies. Prominent among this group was Ho Lian (Franklin Ho), an economist trained at Yale University. Ho became President Chiang's close assistant and was given the title of Deputy Minister of the Department of Economic Affairs. Ho and the other economists in government gained credibility by the way they handled specific tasks such as food crises and textile shortages. Instead of using coercive extraction through administrative channels to achieve their ends, the preferred method of the Party bureaucrats, they relied instead on marketlike incentives in production and processing.[6]

Debates between the Party bureaucrats and the economists over the appropriate role of the public and private sectors were common in the early 1940s. These debates came to the fore near the end of the war with Japan when Chiang Kai-shek built up the Central Planning Bureau (*Chung-yang-chi-hua chu*) and made Ho Lian the deputy chief of the new organization (the head of the organization was Hsiung Shih-hui). In direct confrontation with Weng Wen-hau, the Minister of Economic Affairs, Ho Lian won a majority of the seven-person standing committee of the Central Planning Bureau for a new policy guideline called the "planned free economy."[7] This new guideline was approved by the National Defense High Commission in 1944 and declared by President Chiang in a national broadcast on the anniversary of Double Ten (October 10) in 1945. The Ho view of industrial development was also included in the draft five-year plan.

The core ideas in this document dealt with the appropriate division between the role of the public and private sector and the respective contributions to be expected from public, private, and foreign capital formation. Government was to be responsible for postal and telegraph services, military supplies, mining, creation of money and its substitutes, railroads, and large-scale producers and distributors of electric power. All other businesses were to be managed by the "people," that is, the private sector. In the context of the 1990s, this document does not appear to be particularly liberal. But in the Chinese context of 1945 it definitely was.

Conditions on the Chinese mainland in the late 1940s were not conducive to the actual implementation of this policy. But the ideas behind the "planned free economy" continued to be developed and promulgated, notably in "The Act of Economic Reform" of 1947. In essence, this document stated that it was essential first to raise the standard of living of people by relying on the profit-oriented motivation of private entrepreneurs operating through the free market. The "restriction of capital," the Sun Yat-sen term used by the bureaucratic planners, could wait until a greater level of prosperity had been achieved.[8]

The importance of this shift to a planned free economy cannot be overstressed. There was a similar debate on the Chinese mainland three and four decades later within the Chinese Communist Party. The term that evolved from that debate was a *socialist market economy*. That term represented the acceptance by the Chinese Communist Party of the goal of a full market economy. The debate over terminology in the 1980s was not itself the major contributor to the changes in policy, however. The market economy had been expanding for over a decade as a result of a series of pragmatic measures. The new terminology legitimated what was already happening on the Chinese mainland.

On Taiwan, however, the 1940s debate over basic principles came before most of the changes in policy that created a vital market economy on the island and laid a critical foundation for some of the policy changes that were to occur. When challenged by Party conservatives, the more liberal-minded technocrats frequently referred back to these 1945 and 1947 documents. The term *planned free economy* remained in active use to describe the government's overall approach for nearly four decades.

POLICIES IN THE 1950S

Economic policies in the 1949 to 1952 period are sometimes referred to as the *whatsoever* policies. Whatsoever was necessary to stop inflation, resettle 1.6 million new immigrants from the mainland, and bring about economic recovery was given a try. With the recovery and the end of inflation, however, the government set out to promote industrialization with the first four-year development plan (1953–1956).

The policies from the period through 1957 designed to promote industry fit readily within a fairly strong version of the import substitution approach. Exports, especially exports of manufactures, received little attention. The basic goal of industrial policy was to develop domestic industries that could produce basic necessities to replace the dependence on imports evident at that time. The promoted industries included cement, glass, fertilizer, textiles, and several others. Only sugar, tea, and canned pineapple, along with rice—all commodities built up during the Japanese colonial period—were encouraged to export.

The government's approach to achieving import substitution was interventionist to an extreme degree. To begin with, the government identified promising investment opportunities, drew up plans, and invited particular private entrepreneurs to carry them out, arranging low-interest loans and foreign aid funds for those who did. Since government owned the banks and directly controlled the allocation of aid funds, directing resources to the favored sectors and firms was easily managed.

The key industry in the first four-year plan was textiles. China had developed a large textile industry based in Shanghai and Tianjin in the 1920s and 1930s, and a number of Shanghai firms moved their operations to Taiwan, while still others went to Hong Kong. To ensure the success of this move, the government on Taiwan in 1951 to 1953 provided cotton and other materials to the factories and then bought the finished product. All the firm had to do was produce. With most risks removed, the textile industry grew rapidly and soon saturated the domestic market for yarn and fabric.

To back up these import-substituting measures, the government instituted a wide variety of measures. Luxury goods and goods already produced domestically faced outright import bans. Nominal import tariff rates were high and the effective rate of protection for domestic producers was, as is usually the case, even higher. The median nominal tariff rate was a bit below 30 percent in 1948, but rose above 30 percent by 1955 (see Table 2-1), and the average rate was 38.2 percent. There was also a wide dispersion in the rates, resulting in a domestic price structure that bore little relation to international prices.

Exchange rate controls were initially quite simple, and those exchanging foreign for domestic currency received part in cash and part

TABLE 2-1
Distribution of Import Tariff Rates in Taiwan by Year and Month of Promulgation

Tax Rate Bracket (%)	1948, August		1955, January		1959, August		1965, September		1973, August	
	Number of items	Distribution (%)	Number of items	Distribution (%)	Number of items	Distribution (%)	Number of items	Distribution (%)	Number of items	Distribution (%)
Free	10	0.90	13	1.22	22	2.00	31	2.72	129	3.23
1–15	166	15.80	157	14.73	219	19.89	260	22.77	350	8.77
16–30	388	36.95	327	30.68	384	34.88	379	33.19	1,110	27.81
31–45	156	14.86	238	22.33	160	14.53	178	15.59	658	16.46
46–60	139	13.24	132	12.38	145	13.17	142	12.43	701	17.56
61–75	36	3.43	38	3.56	26	2.36	23	2.01	252	6.31
76–90	49	4.67	41	3.85	56	5.09	62	5.43	212	5.31
91–105	45	4.29	46	4.32	65	5.90	64	5.60	267	6.69
106–120	21	2.00	22	2.06	3	0.27	3	0.26	37	0.93
121–135	—	—	—	—	—	—	—	—	206	5.16
136–150	18	1.72	11	1.03	—	—	—	—	—	—
151–165	—	—	41	3.85	21	1.91	—	—	69	1.73
166–180	—	—	—	—	—	—	—	—	—	—
181–195	—	—	—	—	—	—	—	—	—	—
196–210	22	2.10	—	—	—	—	—	—	—	—

Source: Tsiang and Chen (1984).

"—" designates no rates in this tax bracket.

in "exchange settlement certificates," but both cash and the certificates were exchanged at the same rate, and the certificates were freely negotiable on the market. By 1951, however, demand for foreign exchange outstripped supply and the government responded by both devaluing the currency and introducing multiple exchange rates. Public sector imports and important raw materials and intermediate inputs needed by the private sector were able to use a lower official exchange rate.[9] The exchange rate, it was widely believed, was also overvalued. Certainly it was overvalued relative to the level it was to reach after devaluation at the end of the decade.

THE FOREIGN TRADE REFORMS OF 1958 TO 1960

It was in this context that Taiwan introduced two important policy changes that were to transform its economy, turning it from a slow-growth, import-substituting regime into the engine of rapid export growth for which the island would eventually become famous. The two key policy changes were the Foreign Exchange Reform of 1958 and the Nineteen-Point Program for Economic and Financial Reform of 1960.

The leading government figure behind these reforms was Yin Chung-long (K.Y. Yin). The leading intellectual forces behind the reforms were Tsiang Suo-chieh (S.C. Tsiang) and Liu Ta-chung (T.C. Liu), both economists with the International Monetary Fund.

Yin Chung-long, like many of the government officials who led Taiwan's economic development, was an engineer by training, and had graduated from Nanyang University in 1925. From then until he transferred to Taiwan nearly a quarter of a century later, Yin had acquired wide-ranging experience in business and economic affairs as well as in his specialty, electrical engineering. The business and economic posts included work with China Silver Construction Company—then the largest private company in China—for five years in New York and Washington, purchasing materials and equipment for the wartime government, as well as various other posts with both central and local government. Early on, Yin had become a part of the group around T.V. Soong, and when Soong became Premier of the Executive Yuan in 1945, he made Yin secretary in charge of confidential affairs in economic administration. Yin left that position when Soong stepped down as Premier.[10]

In 1949, Ch'en Ch'eng, then the provincial governor of Taiwan and later the vice president of the Republic of China, made Yin the vice-chairman of the Taiwan Production Board. Ch'en Ch'eng himself was chairman. The Board in 1949 had twenty-eight members, at least fifteen of whom had studied abroad, including six who had received PhDs abroad. Most were mainlanders and had held important government positions on the Chinese mainland before coming to Taiwan. The largest number of this group had majored in engineering or science, but five had studied economics or finance.[11] The makeup of this board is illustrative of the background of the people who were to be in charge of economic and industrial policy in the next decades. Yin subsequently was made Minister for the Economy. A lawsuit sidetracked his career temporarily, but he soon returned to a leadership position as Chairman of the Foreign Exchange and Foreign Trade Council. It was in this latter post that Yin initiated the foreign exchange reform.[12]

Yin Chung-long did not come to his first economic posts with much knowledge of the way an economic system works, although he understood business and hence many aspects of economics at the micro level. He also understood engineering planning. During the 1950s, however, in part through exposure to a number of able economists, he was to acquire an in-depth understanding of how an economic system must be put together if it is to work efficiently. One of the first economics books he read was by James E. Meade, later the winner of the Nobel Prize in Economics, titled *Planning and the Price Mechanism.* The book was given to him by S. C. Tsiang after they first met, and it reflected Meade's considerable practical experience as well as his theoretical knowledge, the former derived from his work with the government in wartime Britain.[13] Yin not only read this book himself, but also circulated it widely to his subordinates. During the period when Yin's career was sidetracked by a lawsuit, he made a further effort to study economics. Two other local economists, Wang Tso-yun and Hsing Mo-huan, also helped Yin in his understanding of economics.[14]

During his first years in office, Yin's greatest concern was with Taiwan's chronic shortage of foreign exchange. To help solve this problem, he had asked USAID in 1953 to send out an economic advisory group. To work with this advisory group, he asked the International Monetary Fund to assign two Chinese staff economists, S. C. Tsiang and T. C. Liu, to work with the advisory group temporarily. The recommendations of the foreign advisory group were cautious and called only for some devaluation of the Taiwan dollar (NT$) and greater effort to balance the government's budget. Tsiang and Liu, dissatisfied with this paper, decided to write one of their own calling for a major devaluation of the NT$ and the elimination of the multiple exchange rate system. These suggestions, together with ideas about related matters to control capital flight, were presented to the government in 1954.[15] The then finance minister and chairman of the Foreign Exchange and Foreign Trade Council, Hsu Po-yuan, was the architect of the multiple exchange rate system. He and most other economic officials, with the notable exception of Yin, strongly opposed the recommendations of Tsiang and Liu.[16] When Yin's career was temporarily sidetracked by the lawsuit, the issue of foreign exchange reform was shelved. It was Yin's return to power in 1958 that reactivated the issue.[17] In 1958 the NT$ was devalued from NT$24.7 to US$1 to NT$36.1 to US$1; the buying rate then further devalued to NT$40.0 to US$1. This latter rate was then maintained unchanged until the early 1970s. Of equal importance, the multiple exchange rate system was abolished and replaced by a single exchange rate.

Exchange rate management in the late 1950s on Taiwan was seen as mainly a technical issue to be decided by economic technicians. Decades later businessmen and politicians had become somewhat more sophisticated about the power of exchange rate changes to alter fundamentally the behavior of an entire economy, but this was not the case in the 1950s. As Chairman of the Foreign Exchange and Foreign Trade Council, K. Y. Yin had formal responsibility over exchange rate management and he pushed the changes through. Once the decision to change was made, implementation was not difficult. In essence, all that has to be done is to order the Central Bank to begin buying and selling foreign exchange at the new rate. Complications usually arise only when the exchange rate decided upon has no relation to the rate that would have been set by market forces if such forces had been allowed to set the rate. When there is a large discrepancy between the official and the market rate, black markets quickly develop. Government efforts to control illegal exchange transactions then lead to numerous measures that further complicate the process.

The 40:1 exchange rate finally settled upon was the result of the best judgment of the economists and Yin as to what the market rate was. To call this a *market equilibrium rate*, however, is to overstate the case. Taiwan's economy in the 1950s was in a state of major disequilibrium. War and overvaluation of the exchange rate had profoundly depressed exports, far below what they would have been under more normal circumstances. Taiwan needed an exchange rate that would push exports and reduce the demand for imports until a more normal trading pattern had been established. The sharply devalued 40:1 rate gave it just that.

Although changes in the exchange rate were seen as a primarily technical issue, the other reforms of the 1958 to 1960 period were considered less so. The key document that was to guide reform for the next decade and more was The Nineteen-Point Program for Economic and Financial Reform promulgated in 1960. This document, together with the exchange rate reform, marks a major break with the import substitution policy. The Nineteen-Point Program did not come as an entirely new idea. Even the second four-year plan (1957–1960), basically still an import substitution document, called for greater effort to expand exports, and some concrete export promotion measures were introduced at the time. Furthermore, there was increasing recognition by the government that import-substituting industries were saturating the local market, and their growth, as a result, was slowing down. The annual rate of growth of private manufacturing, for example, fell from 19.4 percent per year during the first four-year plan (1953–1956) to 11.1 percent per year in the second four-year plan period (1957–1960). Thus the Nineteen-Point Program was in part drawn up in response to the government's perception that Taiwan's economy was not doing particularly well.

Taiwan's relations with the United States also played a central role in the Kuomintang government's approach to economic development. President Chiang Kai-shek's primary goal throughout his life was to restore his government to power on the Chinese mainland. As early as 1951, President Chiang had recognized the importance to this goal of developing Taiwan as a model province. That goal was secondary, however, to the importance of maintaining a large defense budget, made necessary in part by President Chiang's decision to hold onto the islands of Quemoy and Matsu close to the Chinese mainland. A purely defensive posture would not have required such a large defense budget since the American Seventh Fleet effectively made any successful attack on Taiwan by the Chinese Communists impossible. Without U.S. aid it is unlikely that Taiwan could have sustained both large defense expenditures and a program of economic development for the island. Gross capital formation, which was only 16 percent of the gross domestic product (GDP) in the 1950s, would have to have been cut substantially. The cuts in imports, as the data in Table 2-2 make clear, would have been even more drastic.

The United States, therefore, had considerable leverage over what Taiwan could or could not accomplish, and the United States had no interest in supporting President Chiang's goal of recovering the Chinese mainland. On October 23, 1958, the American Secretary of State,

TABLE 2-2

U.S. Aid and Government Defense Expenditures

| Years | Total U.S. Aid Received | | | | Government Administration and Defense Expenditures | |
	Million US$	Million NT$ at official exchange rate	As % of GDP	As % of Imports	Million NT$	As % of GDP
1951–1954	375.2	5,834	7.2	49.0	—	—
1955	132.0	2,845	9.5	65.7	4,153	13.8
1956	101.6	2,507	7.3	52.4	4,472	12.9
1957	108.1	2,668	6.6	51.0	5,507	13.6
1958	81.6	2,944	6.6	36.1	6,661	14.8
1959	128.9	4,651	9.0	55.8	—	—
1960	101.1	4,044	6.5	34.0	7,371	11.7
1961	94.2	3,768	5.4	29.3	8,563	12.2
1962	65.9	2,636	3.4	21.7	9,100	11.7
1963	115.3	4,612	5.3	31.9	9,759	11.1
1964	83.9	3,356	3.3	19.6	10,795	10.5
1965	56.5	2,260	2.0	10.1	12,055	10.6
1966	4.2	168	0.1	0.7	14,619	11.5

Source: Data were derived from the *Taiwan Statistical Data Book, 1974* (1974), pp. 17, 146, 164, and 197. The government expenditure figures are for the fiscal year; the GDP figures are for the calendar year. Years designated "—" indicate data not available.

John Foster Dulles, visited Taipei and signed a mutual defense agreement with the Republic of China government. Secretary Dulles pushed President Chiang to change policy for recovery of the mainland from one stressing the military to an approach based on developing Taiwan's economy. A new director of the China division of USAID, Wesley Haraldson, took office in February 1959 and began vigorously pushing for economic policy changes in Taiwan in accordance with what was called for in the mutual defense agreement.

The concern of the new aid director, however, was not mainly with how to develop an export-led growth strategy. Consistent with the dominant thinking about economic development at that time, his focus was on getting government military expenditures down and the investment rate up. He also called for control of inflation, reform of the exchange rate, privatization of public enterprises, and the creation of a stock market. In a meeting with most of the senior economic officials in Taiwan's government in December 1959, the USAID director offered to increase American assistance if the Taiwan government went along with his suggestions.

Negotiations with USAID on the Taiwan side included all of the major economic figures of the government at that time: Yen Chia-kan, Minister of Finance (and later President); Yang Chi-cheng, Minister of Economics; Yin Chung-long; and General Secretary of the USAID Council, Li Kuo-t'ing (K.T. Li). Ultimately, in a meeting at the end of December, Vice President Ch'en Ch'eng also became involved. The result on the Taiwan side was the drafting, by staffer Wang Tso-lung (T.Y. Wang), of The Nineteen-Point Program for Economic and Financial Reform, which was written as a response to the USAID director's eight-point proposal. This Nineteen-Point Program was then presented to President Chiang on January 8, 1960, by Minister of Finance Yen in the presence of several other senior officials, including Vice President Ch'en and K.T. Li. After listening to the proposal and raising several questions, President Chiang gave it his approval and the program, for all practical purposes, was law then and there.[18]

The Nineteen-Point Program accepted the main points put forward by the USAID director in essence, but there were subtle differences in emphasis, particularly in the way that many of the points were actually implemented. Minister of Finance Yen had already modified the defense expenditure proposal to make it more palatable to President Chiang. In the January 8 meeting, Yen had simply argued that defense expenditures should be maintained at their current level instead of being reduced as in the original eight-point proposal of the USAID Director.[19]

The first part of the Nineteen-Point Program dealt with efforts to achieve overall economic development. This part included efforts to promote savings and to develop Taiwan's capital markets so as to raise the overall rate of investment. Probably of greater importance in practice in this section were the measures designed to create a more favorable climate for the private sector. The proposal did talk about turning public enterprise over to the private sector, although little was in fact done in this regard at that time. The government's promise to study ways of lightening the licensing and regulatory burden on the private sector did lead to significant changes in these areas.[20] Overall this part of the Nineteen-Point Program was a far cry from laissez-faire economics. Government was expected to make demonstration investments, to make low-interest loans and allocations of USAID finance to favored activities, and to take over and restructure failing private businesses, among other things. But the proposal did make clear that the private sector, not the public sector, was to be the leading edge of the overall economic development program. For a government whose economic officers had, in many cases, come up through a career in public enterprises, that was a real concession. State-owned enterprises in 1960 still accounted for a third of all output in manufacturing, over half of all transport, and all of electricity, gas, and water (see Chapter 4).

The second component of the Nineteen-Point Program involved getting better control over the government's budget. The key provisions involved a call for a revision of the tax system, charging fees for certain public services, and eliminating some subsidies while making others more transparent in the budget. This section also dealt with the military expenditure issue that had been such a central part of the negotiations with USAID. Whatever the intent of the drafters of the Nineteen-Point Program, military and administrative expenditures in nominal terms grew by 12 percent per year, a rate undoubtedly far higher than the rate USAID had in mind.

The third category of proposals dealt with reform of the banking system. These proposals treated such issues as clearly separating commercial banking activities from the role of the central bank. There was also a call for better bank supervision to ensure the stability of the system. The banking system, however, was firmly in state-owned hands and this was not challenged either in 1960 or for decades thereafter.

The eighteenth and nineteenth points, which made up the fourth part of the proposal, called for the establishment of a single exchange rate, a process already underway as pointed out above. These points also stated the goal of introducing measures to encourage exports. The need for more exports in the context of the years 1959 to 1960 was obvious, so this nineteenth point could not have been controversial. It is doubtful, however, that anyone on either the Taiwan or the USAID side realized with what extraordinary vigor this nineteenth point was to be implemented.

The Nineteen-Point Program for Economic and Financial Reform was not, therefore, a detailed blueprint followed faithfully by Taiwan's economic policy makers in the 1960s. Many of the specific proposals did not lead to important changes in the system. Several, such as the call for privatization of state-owned enterprises, were largely ignored; others, notably the provision about defense spending, were countermanded in practice. For all of these caveats, however, the Nineteen-Point Program was what launched the drive toward export-led growth.

The Program did at least two things. First, it provided a framework that legitimized a wide range of reform activities that were designed to promote more rapid growth of income and of exports. Several of the proposals were broad enough to encompass most of the policy and systems changes that were introduced over the next decade.

Second, the process of drawing up the Nineteen Points helped focus the minds of all of the senior economic policy makers and ultimately of President Chiang himself on the strategic economic challenge facing Taiwan. Government ministers, like most lower-level personnel, are usually caught up in day-to-day administration and political maneuvering. It is not easy to look up from these daily demands to focus on the long-term picture, but the negotiations with USAID and the need to sell the program to President Chiang brought strategic issues to the fore. More specifically, President Chiang had been concerned for some time that his government had become too dependent on USAID. The economic reformers were able to persuade President Chiang that systematic reform would make it possible to use USAID in the short run to eliminate that dependence over the long run. The goal was "self sufficiency,"[21] not in the sense of reducing dependence on foreign trade but in the sense of eliminating the need for foreign grants.

This emphasis on self-sufficiency and independence from aid also helps explain which of the Nineteen Points really mattered. The most important input supplied by foreign aid was the foreign exchange that allowed Taiwan to import twice what its own export earnings would have allowed. If an alternative source of foreign exchange could be found to pay for these imports, aid would no longer be required. The only realistic alternative source of foreign exchange in 1960 was to increase exports.

EXPORT PROMOTION IN THE 1960S

The single most important export promotion policy was the devaluation of the NT dollar and the unification of the exchange rate, and these changes were fully implemented by 1960. But export promotion did not stop there. There were several other initiatives designed to promote exports. They included:

- Import tax rebates
- Low-interest export loans
- Export processing zones
- The Statute for Encouraging Investment

Import Tax Rebates

Tax rebates actually began to be used in the 1950s, but it was in the 1960s that their use expanded and they became an essential part of the export promotion strategy. In essence, the tax rebate system returns the duty on imported inputs that are used in goods that are exported. Because import tariffs were high, rebates had a substantial impact on the cost of exports and hence on their competitiveness worldwide. From the mid-1950s when the rebate system was first introduced, the kinds of taxes that could be rebated and the scope of export goods included in the rebate scheme were steadily broadened. At first only customs duties could be rebated. Then in 1955, the commodity tax and the defense surcharge were rebated. In 1958 the harbor tax was added, and in 1960 and 1964 the salt tax and slaughter tax were rebated for meat products. The eligibility rules for tax rebates were also broadened. At first, products had to be exported within three months after importing materials. In 1958, the period was extended to six to twelve months. In 1961, it was extended to twelve to eighteen months.

The administration of tax rebates gradually became very complicated and costly. To prevent tax evasion, government announced rebate standards for different kinds of export products. At the end of 1968, it had accumulated more than 7,000 standards, of which only 1,200 standards were applicable to more than one product.[22] In 1968, the system of bonded factories, where all the products were for export, and bonded warehouses, where all imported materials were for producing export goods, was established to simplify the administration of tax rebates and to prevent tax evasion.

The amount of tax waived increased very fast in the 1960s. In 1955 NT$21 million in duties were waived; in 1960, the amount increased to NT$457 million; in 1965, NT$1,795 million; and in 1968, NT$4,234 million. The rebate system continued to exist into the 1990s, but the total amount of the rebates by 1996 had fallen to NT$4,978 million, one-sixth of the amount of 1980.[23]

Low-Interest Export Loans

In the 1950s, only government and public enterprises could get low-interest loans from banks that were primarily publically owned. The private sector not only had to pay much higher interest rates, but even at the higher rates it often could not borrow all it required. To get credit, therefore, private business usually had to go outside of the banking system. In 1957, the Bank of Taiwan started a program of export loans.

The interest rate was 6 percent for loans returned with foreign currency and 11.88 percent for loans returned with local currency. The rate for local currency was about the same level as the rates for public enterprises, whereas the usual interest rates for private enterprises were 16.2 to 22.3 percent. The interest rate difference between export loans and secured loans for private enterprises was narrowed throughout the years. In the 1960s, the difference was between 8.7 and 5.1 percent; in the 1970s, it was between 2.5 and 4.5 percent; it was narrowed to 3 to 0.25 percent in the first half of 1980s; and the export loan policy was terminated 1989. The evolution of the rate structure for the export loans, private enterprises and public enterprises is shown in Table 2-3.

At first, the export loan was applicable only to products that were ready for shipment. It was gradually relaxed to apply to all stages of production, and was granted based on a letter of credit. In addition, between 1964 and 1974, exporters could also apply for loans according to their previous year's export performance and their current year's planned exports. In the whole banking system, however, the proportion of loans granted to exporters was quite small. They reached 5.93 percent in 1972 and their share declined steadily thereafter (see Table 2-4).

TABLE 2-3

Interest Rate Structure of the Bank of Taiwan (Annual Interest Rates in %)

Years	Export Loans Returned in Foreign Currency	Export Loans Returned in NT$	Private Enterprise Loans	Public Enterprise Loans
1956–1960	6.0	11.88	16.2–22.3	10.8–11.9
1962–1966	7.5	7.5	13.3–18.7	10.8–11.9
1970–1972	7.5	—	11.3–12.6	—
1973–1974	8.5–13.0	—	12.0–16.5	—
1975–1977	6.5–9.5	—	11.0–13.3	—
1980–1981	10.5–11.0	—	13.5–16.8	—
			(Loans of one year or less)	(Medium- and long- term loans)
1981–1982	8.25–12.25	—	9.0–18.0	9.5–18.0
1983–1985	6.25–8.0	—	6.25–10.25	6.75–11.0
1989	6.5	—	6.5–12.0	7.25–13.0

Source: *Financial Statistics Monthly for Taiwan Republic of China* (various, 1967–1993).

Rates designated "—" indicate no interest rates in that category.

Export Processing Zones

The Statute for Export Processing Zones (EPZ) was enacted in 1965. The purpose of establishing the zones was to facilitate the investment in export industries. Physically, an EPZ looked like an industrial park that provided standard factory space and good public facilities. All the red tape—notably the investment application process, import and export documents, and buying and remitting foreign exchange—was

TABLE 2-4
Share of Export Loans in Total Banking System Loans

Year	Loans for Export (million NT$)	Total (million NT$)	Share (%)
1971	5,196	92,152	5.64
1972	6,544	110,334	5.93
1973	8,742	179,784	4.86
1974	7,470	244,540	3.05
1975	8,000	319,596	2.50
1976	8,857	369,050	2.40
1977	11,108	426,835	2.60
1978	12,947	470,186	2.75
1979	12,398	544,650	2.28
1980	13,367	693,599	1.93
1981	15,972	760,369	2.10
1982	20,339	903,567	2.25
1983	30,468	1,035,334	2.00
1984	19,252	1,146,106	1.68
1985	19,195	1,221,461	1.57
1986	16,455	1,354,803	1.21
1987	13,615	1,613,071	0.84
1988	18,570	2,215,397	0.84
1989	14,482	2,857,725	0.51
1990	18,047	3,141,678	0.57
1991	19,506	3,881,184	0.50
1992	20,324	4,916,134	0.41
1993	18,151	5,652,069	0.32

Source: *Financial Statistics Monthly for Taiwan Republic of China* (various, 1971–1973).

Note: These loans began in 1964 and were particularly important in the 1960s, but data for loans before 1971 are not available.

greatly simplified in the zone. Firms in the zone could also enjoy more favorable tax treatment. Since all products produced in the zone were meant to be exported, all the imported intermediates, including machinery, were exempted from taxes in the first place, rather than having to apply for rebates later.

The first EPZ was inaugurated in 1966, near Kaoshiung Harbor, Taiwan's biggest harbor. Both domestic and foreign investors welcomed this zone, and within two years it was full. In June 1969, 102 firms had started operation and were employing 40,000 workers. Annual export value of these 102 firms was US$177 million. Two other EPZs were subsequently established, both opening in 1971—one in Nantze, a suburb of Kaoshiung City, the other in Tantze, Taichung County, in the central part of Taiwan. In effect, when government could not improve the investment environment in general, it sought instead a point breakthrough by creating a favorable environment in designated special areas.

Firms in the EPZs were mostly labor intensive, because a cheap and abundant labor supply existed in the areas surrounding them. These firms were very prosperous until the early 1980s, when labor shortages and wage rate increases reduced their export competitiveness. It was at that point that firms started to withdraw from the EPZs.

The data in Table 2-5 show that throughout the 1970s, the number of enterprises operating in the three EPZs continued to increase until 1979, when the highest number of 272 firms was reached. The number of workers employed by the firms in EPZs increased from 49,000 in 1971 to 78,000 in 1981, and continued to its height in 1987 when 91,000 persons worked in the EPZs. The figures of accumulated investment by different sources indicate that foreign capital had the biggest investment share throughout these years, followed by joint ventures, domestic capital, and finally overseas Chinese capital. The EPZs thus effectively served the purposes of attracting foreign investment.

Exports from the zones rose from US$163 million in 1971 to US$1,589 million in 1981 and US$3,991 million in 1991. The share of electronics within these EPZ exports rose steadily, from 49.8 percent in 1981 to 73.1 percent in 1991. These exports, however, do not really capture the full significance of these special zones. Exports from the zones accounted for only 3 to 4 percent of all exports from Taiwan in the 1970s and 1980s. The zone share in the critical electronics sector was much higher, but even there a much larger share of output and exports came from outside the zones. The zones played an important role in attracting foreign direct investors who did not have the patience, the knowledge,

TABLE 2-5

Number of Enterprises, Employed Workers, and Accumulated Investment in the EPZs

Year	Number of Export Enterprises in Operation	Approved Accumulated Investment by Source (US$000s)				Average Number of Employees
		Domestic	Overseas Chinese	Foreign	Joint Ventures	
1971	177	9,120	7,947	31,116	14,994	48,966
1972	193	11,588	10,481	35,849	19,944	59,685
1973	222	15,992	15,303	68,014	41,498	75,557
1974	—	—	—	—	—	62,562
1975	263	20,346	18,300	106,947	30,947	66,115
1976	267	22,496	18,665	128,947	38,748	74,930
1977	267	24,206	19,278	143,751	42,414	70,814
1978	267	27,324	15,525	163,856	48,711	77,389
1979	272	33,038	17,674	180,482	50,498	80,166
1980	270	36,597	17,985	199,586	54,399	79,126
1981	272	37,981	20,263	230,371	58,350	77,663
1982	270	39,473	2,053	245,700	59,923	73,078
1983	263	39,894	19,064	257,810	66,160	73,828
1984	257	38,911	14,611	196,245	167,778	81,241
1985	247	40,713	10,972	182,787	163,137	77,640
1986	239	46,448	11,084	219,313	182,638	82,437
1987	248	51,115	7,116	297,523	197,193	90,807
1988	244	69,454	5,016	324,987	225,750	86,863
1989	237	84,788	5,016	351,451	265,266	77,214
1990	225	116,317	5,623	352,477	322,412	68,196
1991	234	173,264	737	338,815	373,158	66,151
1992	229	175,838	737	349,531	397,194	60,747
1993	221	185,637	737	324,445	403,521	53,189

Source: Export Processing Zones Essential Statistics (1971/12 – 1994/11).

"—" indicates data not available.

or the connections needed to wend their way through the maze of rules and regulations that faced anyone trying to start up a new business on Taiwan. Foreign direct investment, however, in or out of the zones, was not central to the success of Taiwan's development effort in the 1960s and 1970s. Foreign direct investment in this period never amounted to more than 10 percent of gross domestic investment nationwide and was usually much less.[24]

The real significance of the EPZs was that they were models of what could be achieved in the way of deregulation of the economy. By initially confining deregulation to a limited geographic area, those benefiting from the myriad of restrictions that existed would not feel threatened. Over time, however, it was inevitable that questions would be raised about why something that worked so well in one location couldn't be applied elsewhere, and why something that was clearly so beneficial to foreigners couldn't be applied to domestic investors as well. Partly as a result of the example set by the EPZs, the whole island of Taiwan over the course of the 1960s and 1970s became an export processing zone. The slow growth of the EPZs after 1980 and their absolute decline in the late 1980s was not a reflection of the fact that the industries in these zones had become less competitive. In the environment of the 1980s, those that were more competitive could have replaced less competitive industries. The decline of the EPZs in the 1980s mainly reflected the fact that special zones were no longer needed. Although the statute governing EPZs still existed, the rules that governed them were widely applicable throughout Taiwan as well as inside the zones.

The Statute for Encouraging Investment

The umbrella law that was central to Taiwan's efforts to promote more rapid growth of exports and of GDP on an islandwide basis was the Statute for Encouraging Investment. The law was enacted in September 1960, only seven months after the government announced the Nineteen-Point Program for Economic and Financial Reform. In effect, the Nineteen-Point Program had outlined the policy changes required. The Statute for the Encouraging Investment merely provided the legislative authority for changes in the laws and regulations so as to make these policies a reality.[25] The statute was much more than just an export promotion document: its purpose was to foster across-the-board industrial development. The statute existed for thirty years, until 1990, when it was replaced by the Statute for Promoting Industrial Upgrading.

At the outset, the main contents of the statute provided for investment that promoted tax exemptions and deductions and dealt with procedures to facilitate the acquisition of plant sites. During the thirty years of its existence, the statute was revised many times. Originally, its goal was to encourage investment and saving, to promote export, and to increase production. In the 1970s, its goal expanded to accelerate equipment renewal, to encourage mergers of enterprises to gain economies of scale, and to encourage research and development. In the 1980s, the goal expanded again to encourage energy saving, pollution control, international marketing, strategic industries, and high-tech industries.[26] Measures of tax encouragement included tax holidays, tax ceilings, deductions of sales taxes, the stamp tax, and custom duties. Accelerated depreciation was added in the 1970s, and an investment tax credit was added in the 1980s.

Industries eligible for tax deductions were expanded gradually. Toward the end of the thirty-year period, almost all manufacturing industries were included, but to qualify, firms in the manufacturing industries had to meet certain requirements with respect to quantity, quality, their local content ratio, and their export ratio.

The tax deducted amounted to 2 to 5 percent of total tax revenue in the 1960s; it increased to 6 to 9 percent in the 1970s and the first half of 1980s, but declined to 5 to 6 percent in the second half of 1980s. The business income tax, sales tax, and stamp tax were the three biggest items in terms of the amount of tax deducted (see Table 2-6).[27]

Due to the stringent regulation on land use conversion, it had been very difficult to obtain land for factory sites, and this had become one of the major obstacles to attracting domestic and foreign investment in the 1950s. To solve this problem, the Statute for Encouraging Investment facilitated the conversion of farmland to industrial use by empowering the government to expropriate private farmland for industrial use. Between 1963 and 1988, 21,884 hectares of land were designated for industrial use, and 73.6 percent of that land was developed into industrial parks by the government. Until 1981, the Statute also allowed industrialists to locate their factories in farmland they owned or purchased, thus further facilitating the conversion of land to industrial use. Between 1963 and 1985, 7,186 hectares of land were used by 9,584 factories through this method.[28]

BOOMING EXPORTS: THE FIRST STAGE

There are several general points that one can make about these economic reforms in the 1960s. To begin with, their main purpose was to promote exports. No one with decision-making authority was trying to move Taiwan toward a free trade regime. Imports that were not used as inputs for products to be exported were and remained subject to high protective tariffs and other barriers. It would be premature, how-

TABLE 2-6
The Amount and Share of Different Kinds of Tax Deduction

Fiscal Year	Business Income Tax		Sales Tax		Stamp Tax		Other Taxes		Total		Tax Deductions as a Percentage of Total Tax Revenue
	Amount (million NT$)	%	Amount (million NT$)	%	Amount (million NT$)	%	Amount (million NT$)	%	Amount (million NT$)	%	
1961	24	15.85	33	22.26	93	61.80	0	0.09	150	100.00	2.07
1962	175	43.71	53	13.15	129	32.21	44	10.93	400	100.00	5.41
1963	193	61.53	59	18.63	62	19.57	1	0.26	314	100.00	3.79
1964	196	56.14	63	18.02	89	25.43	1	0.41	348	100.00	3.50
1965	235	47.88	134	27.36	104	21.18	18	3.59	490	100.00	4.10
1966	274	42.74	74	11.58	274	42.74	19	2.94	642	100.00	4.72
1967	322	43.07	89	11.95	316	42.35	20	2.66	747	100.00	4.89
1968	346	36.50	212	22.35	371	39.17	19	1.99	948	100.00	4.84
1969	372	33.17	302	26.96	438	39.07	9	0.80	1,120	100.00	4.10
1970	518	34.36	388	25.69	587	38.92	15	1.02	1,509	100.00	4.92
1971	610	23.68	975	37.84	977	37.92	14	0.56	2,576	100.00	7.52
1972	926	34.77	771	28.94	945	35.46	22	0.83	2,664	100.00	6.49
1973	1,232	26.01	2,287	48.28	1,182	24.96	36	0.75	4,730	100.00	8.92
1974	3,027	47.40	1,679	26.29	1,628	25.50	54	0.83	6,386	100.00	7.89
1975	2,003	27.68	3,327	45.98	1,842	25.47	63	0.87	7,235	100.00	8.57
1976	2,805	33.59	3,182	38.51	2,160	26.14	116	1.40	8,262	100.00	7.72

1977	2,862	32.77	3,081	35.28	2,660	30.47	129	1.48	8,732	100.00	7.12
1978	4,067	40.91	3,681	37.03	2,145	20.58	48	0.49	9,941	100.00	6.67
1979	4,703	44.38	3,776	35.63	1,901	17.94	218	2.06	10,598	100.00	5.32
1980	5,280	36.14	6,872	47.03	2,375	16.26	84	0.57	14,611	100.00	6.16
1981	5,616	39.17	6,161	42.97	2,239	15.62	322	2.25	14,338	100.00	5.10
1982	14,963	56.19	7,805	29.31	3,547	13.32	316	1.19	26,631	100.00	8.86
1983	10,827	50.52	6,993	32.63	3,028	14.13	583	2.72	21,431	100.00	7.09
1984	18,118	54.34	10,400	31.19	3,948	11.84	874	2.62	33,340	100.00	9.71
1985	12,626	43.78	10,441	36.20	5,066	17.56	710	2.46	28,843	100.00	8.17
1986	18,972	54.84	9,437	27.28	4,271	12.35	1,913	5.53	24,593	100.00	9.69
1987	19,133	95.79	592	2.96	30	0.15	219	1.09	19,973	100.00	4.81
1988	27,880	99.21	0	0.00	0	0.00	221	0.79	28,102	100.00	5.49
1989	36,501	97.98	0	0.00	0	0.00	735	2.02	36,336	100.00	5.77
1990	31,787	67.83	0	0.00	0	0.00	15,075	32.17	46,862	100.00	5.90
1991	41,303	98.91	0	0.00	0	0.00	456	1.09	41,759	100.00	5.58
Total:	267,896	64.40	82,867	19.99	42,407	10.23	22,354	5.39	404,611	100.00	

Source: Adapted from Ke-Nan San (1993).

ever, to describe these 1960s policies as mercantilist in spirit. That term could aptly be applied to the 1970s and 1980s, but in the 1960s Taiwan was mainly trying to overcome a major foreign exchange shortage that made the country highly dependent on foreign aid.

The second general point is that the export promotion policies of the 1960s were applied generally. Almost anyone who exported was able to obtain at least some of these benefits. The exchange rate devaluation clearly did not discriminate between one exporter and another. The tax exemptions and land conversion provisions were also widely available. The 1960s policies were not primarily oriented toward promoting particular industries, and they were certainly not designed to favor individual companies. If the policies of the 1960s had been targeted to individual sectors or firms, the results might have been quite different. Most of the export boom that followed was carried out by firms owned by individuals native to Taiwan, whereas the government was dominated by mainlanders who, given a choice, in the 1960s at least, were apt to favor fellow mainlanders.

The general applicability of trade policy changes is very similar to the applicability of trade policy changes in South Korea in the 1960s, except that the South Korean effort began three years later (in 1963) than the Taiwanese effort. Korean industrial policy that involved targeting of individual sectors and firms did not really get underway until the heavy and chemical industry drive of the 1970s.

The last general point is that there is no question that Taiwan's export promotion policies had the desired effect. A quantitative analysis of Taiwan's changing industrial structure is the subject of a later chapter. A few summary tables are presented here to make the point that the policies introduced did indeed have the intended result.

The principal data that demonstrate the results of the policies are presented in Table 2-7. As the data in that table make clear, export growth in general and export of manufactures in particular took off after 1960. By 1970, manufactured exports in current international prices were twenty times the minuscule level of 1960, and the increase in constant prices was almost as large. This boom in manufactured exports also largely accounted for the acceleration in the growth rate of GNP. The 2 percentage point increase in the growth rate of GNP between the 1950s and 1960s, however, understates the impact of policy changes on GNP growth. Growth in the 1950s depended heavily on U.S. aid–financed imports. Growth by the latter half of the 1960s did not depend on foreign aid to any significant degree.

TABLE 2-7

Growth Rates of GNP and Exports (Annual Rate of Increase)

	GNP	Exports	Industrial Product Exports	
Years	Real increase (%)	Nominal value increase in US$ (%)	Nominal value increase in US$ (%)	Absolute value (million US$)
1952–1960	7.6	4.4	24.0	(1952) 9.5
1961–1970	9.6	24.6	36.2	(1960) 53.0
1971–1980	9.7	29.6	31.5	(1970) 1,164.7
				(1980) 17,989.7

Source: *Taiwan Statistical Data Book, 1995.*

Accelerated growth was accompanied by rapid structural change of both exports and industry. In 1952, sugar, rice, bananas, and tea accounted for 85 percent of all exports (see Table 2-8). By 1961, these products still made up 43 percent of exports, but by 1971 they accounted for only 6.1 percent. Textile exports rose from negligible amounts in 1952 to 15.1 percent of all exports in 1961 and 35.4 percent in 1971. The other major exports in the 1960s and very early 1970s were consumer electronic products, canned food, and plywood.

Data on manufacturing employment tell the story of what was happening in industry as a whole. Food processing made up 21.8 percent of all manufacturing employment in 1961 but only 11.3 percent in 1971. Textiles and wearing apparel went from 20.9 percent in 1991 to 25.2 percent of a much larger total employment figure in 1971. Consumer electronics employment rose from 0.3 percent to 10.6 percent.

By 1971, therefore, Taiwan had basically accomplished the transition from an economy based mainly on agriculture and food processing to one based on labor-intensive manufactures of light consumer products. Employment in agriculture in a single decade had fallen from 49.8 percent of the total workforce to 35.1 percent, an extraordinarily steep decline for such a short period. Industrial employment rose from 20.9 to 29.9 percent. This growth in labor-intensive light manufacturers was to continue into the 1970s and in some sectors—such as leather, wood products, and consumer plastics—even into the 1980s. By the early 1970s, however, the attention of the government had turned elsewhere. The export promotion policies remained in place and some were extended further, but the focus turned to heavy industry.

TABLE 2-8

Value and Percentage Share of Principal Exports (by CCC Code)

	1952	1956	1961	1966	1971	1976	1981
Total value (million US$)	116	118	195	536	2,060	8,166	22,611
Share (%)							
Bananas	5.25	2.32	4.90	9.03	2.10	0.23	0.11
Rice	15.26	14.05	4.80	5.54	0.22	0.00	0.12
Canned Food	1.91	4.95	6.14	10.48	4.66	2.30	0.96
Sugar	58.87	52.23	28.85	9.83	3.11	1.91	0.62
Tea	5.79	4.20	4.57	1.85	0.66	0.22	0.12
Fishery Products	0.00	0.03	0.08	0.56	1.51	2.72	1.63
Textile Products	0.75	3.89	15.08	17.79	35.43	27.52	22.25
Plywood	0.00	0.10	3.66	6.21	4.62	2.33	1.77
Wood & Products	0.07	0.14	0.60	3.14	3.09	4.36	3.60
Cement	0.20	0.00	2.05	3.49	0.75	0.15	0.29
Refined Petroleum Products	0.14	0.00	0.65	0.50	0.39	1.58	1.95
Glass & Products	—	0.03	0.40	0.48	0.49	0.43	0.50
Rubber & Products	—	0.00	0.83	0.66	1.15	0.94	1.38
Plastic Articles	—	—	—	—	2.23	6.48	7.15
Chemicals	3.75	6.07	5.43	4.09	1.86	1.83	2.39
Basic Metals	0.48	2.25	4.67	3.88	2.86	1.64	2.23
Metal Manufactures	0.00	0.82	0.65	1.59	1.88	2.97	4.65
Machinery	0.07	0.07	0.42	2.21	3.18	3.56	4.16
Electrical Machinery & Apparatus	0.27	0.00	0.82	4.84	12.90	15.64	18.45
Others	7.19	8.85	15.39	13.83	16.92	23.18	25.68
Total Shares	100.00	100.00	100.00	100.00	100.00	100.00	100.00

Source: *Taiwan Statistical Data Book* (1989).

"—" indicates level of exports negligible or not available.

Heavy Industry Development in the 1970s

With the export and light industry program well launched, economic policy makers began in the late 1960s and early 1970s to take steps to promote such industries as steel, petrochemicals, and shipbuilding. The program these policy makers developed, or important parts of it at least, even acquired a name: The Ten Major Development Projects. The

Ten Major Development Projects, it should be noted, also included a number of major infrastructure investments that do not belong in a discussion of heavy industry. The motivations behind the program were related to both economic and security issues. On the economic front, demand on Taiwan for certain intermediate inputs was rising and the government wanted to ensure a stable source of supply. Shortages of petrochemicals, for example, arose during the OPEC-generated oil shortages of the 1970s.

On the security front, heavy industries also had a role. Guaranteeing sources of supply was as much a security as an economic issue, and Taiwan's security situation appeared increasingly fragile in the 1970s. First there was Taiwan's loss of its seat in the United Nations in October 1971, followed shortly thereafter by President Nixon's trip to China in February 1972. Full normalization of relations between Washington and Beijing occurred in 1979. Not only did the United States reduce its diplomatic ties with Taiwan, but it also began withdrawing American military personnel from the island after 1972: the total going from 10,000 in 1972 to only 750 in 1978 on the eve of full normalization. The United States did continue to sell arms to Taiwan, but they also took steps to aid Taiwan's own arms industry, notably with the agreement to have the Northrup Corporation co-produce the F5E fighter plane with Taiwan.

The incentives to push an import substitution program for heavy industries, therefore, were strong ones. They were reinforced by the fact that key economics ministers at the time (Li Ta-hai, for example) had come up through government companies in the heavy industry sector, notably the China Petroleum Corporation.

The heavy industry program that unfolded had many features in common with a similar effort undertaken by South Korea at almost the same time and for similar reasons. Both Taiwan and South Korea targeted particular industries for development, and both governments chose the firms to carry out the construction and operation of the individual plants within those industries. But South Korea turned to private firms for this purpose, with some notable exceptions, while Taiwan turned mainly to state-owned enterprises. Taiwan did not always start with the assumption that enterprises in particular sectors would be publicly owned, but the government was unwilling to provide the subsidies necessary to attract the private sector. In the absence of subsidies, Taiwan's private sector, dominated as it was by small firms, did not have the financial capacity to take on plants with large economies of scale. South Korea, in contrast, had many large conglomerates (the *chaebol*) and the Korean government provided those charged with implementing the heavy and chemical industry drive with low-interest loans, favored access to imports, low-price land in special industrial parks, and much else.

Whether to develop by means of private enterprises or public enterprises had long been an ideological issue for the Republic of China (ROC) policy decision makers. In the 1950s and the period of forming the Nineteen-Point Program, K.Y. Yin, with the support of Vice-President Ch'en Ch'eng, tended to support private enterprise. K.T. Li, as a major economic decision maker in the 1960s, also followed this tendency. There was a significant change, however, when Chiang Ching-kuo took over economic policy decision making. With his experience of a long stay in the Soviet Union plus the experience of striking capitalists and speculators in Shanghai, Chiang Ching-kuo retained some preference for supporting public enterprises, although he started to appreciate the merit of capitalism and accumulated some knowledge of modern economics. The major economic officials in the 1970s appointed by Chiang, Sun Yun-hsuan (Economics Minister and then Premier) and Li Ta-hai (Economics Minister), with careers as engineers and heads of major public enterprises, respectively, exhibited a strong tendency toward supporting public enterprises. In this new atmosphere, K.T. Li turned to improving the efficiency of public enterprises and had them organized in the form of corporations.

Chiang's preference for government-run business was fully displayed in the Ten Major Development Projects. The petrochemical industry and steel mill, the two major projects for building heavy industry, had at K.T. Li's direction originally been assigned to private management. As it turned out, however, these two major efforts, plus the shipyard, were created and run by the men appointed by Chiang Ching-kuo.

It is unlikely that it is just the personalities and preferences of Chiang Ching-kuo and several of his principal advisors that accounts for the very different ways that Taiwan and South Korea went about their heavy industry programs. The fact that South Korea already had several fairly large conglomerates or *chaebol* by the 1970s whereas Taiwan did not is also part of the story. The question then becomes one of why South Korea had these large conglomerates capable of taking on large-scale heavy industry projects while Taiwan did not? The immediate reason is that South Korea provided all kinds of support for the creation of these *chaebol* in the form of targeted low-interest loans and other kinds of subsidies. Targeted subsidies to individual private firms were not a characteristic of the way Taiwan's government provided support.

The existence of targeted subsidies to private *chaebol* in South Korea and their absence in Taiwan is only a partial explanation. The question of why this was the case remains. The full explanation is probably a political one. The Korean *chaebol* were led by Koreans who had close ties to government and over time came to be major supporters and financiers of the governing party and its president. Private businessmen in Taiwan, in contrast, were mainly Taiwanese, most of whom had only weak ties to the mainlander-dominated Kuomintang government. Particularly in the 1960s and 1970s, the mainlander elite relied mainly on its own economic resources together with an army whose officer corps was completely dominated by mainlanders. Although there were mainlanders in the private sector, the principal business of the mainlanders was government. The expansion of the public enterprise sector, in that context, was thus also an expansion of mainlander power over the economy and polity. It is possible or even likely that those who decided to create new public enterprises never explicitly articulated their reasons in this way. Proof that this was the underlying motivation, therefore, may not exist. All one can say with confidence is that the hypothesis is a plausible one.

The Taiwan government's efforts to build public-sector heavy industries were focused in the 1970s on petrochemicals, steel, and shipbuilding. Later the government began to lay plans to develop a domestic auto industry. In addition, the Ten Major Development Projects included a nuclear power plant and six transport infrastructure projects. Other heavy industry sectors also began expanding during the 1970s, but with little help from the government. Each of the government-promoted heavy industries will be described in more detail. The history of the petrochemical component of the heavy industry drive is also presented in more detail in Appendix B.

Petrochemicals

In the 1950s and 1960s, downstream producers of textiles and plastic products had expanded rapidly, creating enough domestic demand for basic chemicals to justify building plants that could achieve the necessary economies of scale. In 1968, the China Petroleum Corporation, a state-owned enterprise, built and put into operation the first upstream naphtha cracking plant. This plant produced 54.5 thousand tons of ethylene annually and required an investment of NT$300 million. Three related midstream plants required the investment of another NT$1,100 million. Downstream demand for synthetic fibers and plastic materials, however, was growing at an annual rate of 80 and 25 percent, respectively, and hence the demand quickly outstripped the supply capacity of this first group of plants.

The first energy crisis of 1973 led to shortages of domestic supplies of petrochemicals and reinforced the government's desire for self-sufficiency in petrochemicals. Major emphasis was given to this task in the Sixth Four-Year Economic Plan (1973–1976). The China Petroleum Corporation continued to hold a government-granted monopoly over upstream naphtha cracking plants. The government also coordinated the development of the related midstream projects, but the China Petroleum Corporation was not given a monopoly of these as well. Instead the government created two new public enterprises, the China Petrochemical Development Corporation and Chung-Tai Chemicals. Later, in 1982, these two public enterprises were merged into one. In addition, the government allowed private firms, both domestic and foreign, to build and own midstream plants.

China Petroleum Corporation completed two large naphtha cracking plants, one in 1975 and the other in 1978, each producing 230,000 tons of ethylene annually.[29] Sixteen different firms were involved in 20 midstream projects, with 61 percent producing intermediates for synthetic fibers, 31 percent intermediates for plastic products, and the remainder for rubber and detergent materials. Of a total investment of NT$29 billion, public enterprises accounted for 43 percent of the total (all of the naphtha cracking and half of the synthetic fiber projects).

The policy of government led development of the petrochemical industry was maintained in the Six-Year Economic Plan (1976–1981) that followed the Sixth Four-Year Plan. The China Petroleum Corporation completed second and third aromatics extraction plants and a xylene separation plant in 1976, 1978, and 1980, respectively. To accommodate these petrochemical plants, government also developed three new industrial complexes, totaling 894 hectares in the Kaoshiung area.

Under government arrangement, marketing orders were established between upstream and midstream firms by long-term contracts guaranteeing the supply of a fixed amount of materials from the upstream plants. This system guaranteed the sale of the China Petroleum Corporation's products, and also provided protection for midstream firms by preventing them from competing with each other. This scheme created an industrial structure within this industry where the upstream was monopolistic, and the midstream was divided into several steps of production, each firm producing only one or two intermediate products, and each product being produced by only one or a few firms.

This structure created a conflict of interest between upstream, midstream, and downstream firms. After the second energy crisis, when the international price of petrochemical products fell, this conflict started to appear. To reconcile the conflict and to protect domestic industries, the government strongly intervened to coordinate the interests of upstream, midstream, and downstream firms. It strictly regulated the import and export of materials and coordinated the prices between firms. In 1981, the government decided that the China Petroleum Corporation should supply its petrochemical products at international prices regardless of their cost in order to increase the competitiveness of midstream firms. Midstream producers were also ordered to supply downstream users at international prices. This policy was maintained until the mid-1980s, when the economic liberalization policy changed the situation.

In the early 1980s, due to the energy crisis and the domestic anti-pollution movement, the government decided not to expand the energy-consuming and highly polluting petrochemical industry any further. In the Eighth Four-Year Economic Plan (1982–1985), it was decided that after the completion of the fourth naphtha cracking plant,[30] the government would not further expand upstream capacity, and shortages would be made up through imports.

By the mid-1980s, this government-dominated petrochemical sector had become very important in Taiwan's industrial structure. In 1976, chemical materials, chemical products, and plastic products combined were 10.22 percent of total manufacturing GDP, rising to 12.4 percent in 1981 and 15.4 percent in 1986, its highest point. If all downstream industries were to be counted, probably about 25 percent of total manufacturing GDP was petrochemical-related.[31]

Steel

Due to the strategic position of the steel industry in industrial development, the planning agency of the government had studied the feasibility of establishing a large-scale steel mill for many years before the establishment of China Steel Corporation. Different foreign consultants drew up several feasibility studies during the 1950s and 1960s.[32] Government did not decide to invest because the huge capital requirements for a steel mill were seen as being beyond the financial capacity of the economy. Not only would it be difficult to raise the capital, but government also worried that the huge investment would cause inflation.

In the 1960s, the domestic demand for steel began to expand very rapidly. In 1972, there were about 50 mini steel mills in Taiwan; total steel production was about 1,497 thousand tons, which was not sufficient to meet domestic demand either in terms of quantity or quality (see Table 2-9). In 1967, based on a feasibility study by the Arthur G. McKee Corporation of the United States, the government formally set up a team for preparing the establishment of a large scale integrated steel mill.

China Steel Corporation was formally set up in 1971. At first, the Taiwan government invested 45 percent, First Steel of Austria invested 20 percent, the domestic private sector invested 35 percent, and Krupp of West Germany was chosen as the engineering consultant. First Steel withdrew in 1973, and China Steel decided to change the engineering consultant. It chose U.S. Steel to redraw the plan, and that new plan enlarged the production capacity to 1.5 million tons per year. The mill began construction in September 1974 and was completed in December 1977. At the end, the project had total capital invested of NT$36.9 billion, of which 42 percent was equity and 58 percent was a loan. The equity collected from the private sector was only NT$682 million, so China Steel formally became a public enterprise.[33]

Production began in 1978. After one year, China Steel started to show

---

TABLE 2-9

Steel Production, Demand, and Trade, 1967–1977 (1,000 tons)

Year	Production	Demand	Import	Export
1967	650	866	336	120
1968	761	1,025	351	87
1969	953	1,208	413	158
1970	1,065	1,266	519	318
1971	1,220	1,532	638	326
1972	1,497	1,702	661	456
1973	1,444	2,028	820	236
1974	1,178	2,359	1,335	154
1975	1,246	1,776	746	216
1976	1,726	2,458	987	255
1977	2,404	3,350	1,199	253

Source: Adapted from *The Assessment of the Ten Major Development Projects* (1979).

a financial profit, although it is unlikely that it made an economic profit after taking into account the cost of the various forms of government subsidy. Because China Steel could provide better-quality and lower-cost materials to the downstream users, many domestic mini steel mills were forced to close down or upgrade their products.

China Steel had the reputation of being a model for public enterprises due to its good management and handsome financial profits. The Taiwan government did, however, provide it with a substantial level of protection up until the mid-1980s. First, to avoid domestic competition, no private steel mill was allowed to set up or expand between March 1978 and October 1983. Second, to avoid foreign competition, government gave China Steel the authority up to 1987 to review and to reject or to grant approval to all steel import applications.

Although the purpose of establishing a large-scale steel mill was for import substitution, at the beginning of its operation, the domestic market could not absorb all the output of China Steel. More than 50 percent of its products then were exported in 1978 and 1979. Downstream users accused China Steel of charging higher prices in the domestic market to subsidize its exports. Gradually, the situation changed. Under government promotion, China Steel and the downstream firms formed a central–satellite relationship, where China Steel played the role of central firm and actively provided technical assistance to the satellite firms.

In the 1980s, China Steel expanded its production capacity twice. The production volume of crude steel in 1994 was the 24th in the world. In the mid-1980s, the steel industry was fully liberalized. By the mid-1990s, around 80 percent of China Steel's products were sold domestically, making for a domestic market share of about 45 percent.

Shipbuilding

In the 1960s and 1970s, with exports expanding rapidly, the demand for shipping was also increasing. Taiwan's government saw this as an opportunity to acquire both a cargo fleet flying the national flag and a shipbuilding capacity that could build the cargo ships for this fleet. At the time the decision was made to go ahead, shipbuilding also appeared to be a sound investment. Profits in ocean shipping in general were high and profits in the oil tanker business were particularly high. With the low oil prices then prevailing, the world's existing tanker construction capacity could not fill all of the orders coming in.

The largest shipbuilding facility in Taiwan in the late 1960s, which was owned by Taiwan Shipbuilding Co., a public enterprise, could handle only ships of 100,000 tons. In 1970, the plan to build a new shipyard was drawn up by the government. Instead of expanding the existing facility of Taiwan Shipbuilding Co., government decided to start a new enterprise, the China Shipbuilding Corporation. Several world-famous shipyards showed their interest in investing and in transferring the required technology.

The new enterprise was incorporated formally in July of 1973. Government invested a 45 percent share, Oswego Corporation of the United States invested 25 percent, and other domestic and foreign investors invested the rest. Oswego also ordered four 445,000-ton oil tankers. The new facility was to be a one-million-ton dry dock, which could build very large cargo carriers (VLCCs). The shipyard started construction in January 1974, and was completed in July 1976.

With the first oil crisis of 1973, however, the shipbuilding market slumped. Oswego canceled two of its four orders. For compensation, it gave up its shares in the company. Later, other investors also withdrew and in 1977, government became the sole owner of China Shipbuilding.

From its completion on, China Shipbuilding was unable to get enough orders to fill its huge capacity. Government tried several ways to save China Shipbuilding that included encouraging ships flying the national flag to be built by domestic shipbuilders. Government also arranged for China Shipbuilding to build cargo ships for other public enterprises such as Taiwan Power, China Petroleum, and China Steel, and directed loans to China Shipbuilding at below-market interest rates. Because domestic orders were insufficient to keep China Shipbuilding in operation at a scale large enough to make profits, and because the firm was not competitive enough to get many foreign orders, the company continued to run at a loss despite government subsidies.

In the 1990s China Shipbuilding was put on the list to be privatized. Because it was not a sound business financially, however, privatization was likely to be difficult. Government plans called for the firm to be fully privatized in the year 2000, but privatization in Taiwan generally has lagged behind the plan.[34]

Automobiles

The government also played an active role in Taiwan's automobile industry, but its effort was never as systematic as its effort in petrochemicals or steel, and well into the 1980s, there wasn't much to show for those efforts.

Yue-loong Automobile Manufacturing Corporation produced its first passenger car in 1960. In the 1966 to 1976 decade, another five automobile manufacturers were established. This initial development was much similar to that found in the early stages of development elsewhere in Asia. Tariff protection on finished passenger cars, at a nominal rate of 60 to 65 percent, was extremely high, and there were other restrictions on imports as well. Given the limited demand for automobiles, and particularly given the high government-imposed prices, no single producer manufactured more than a few thousand vehicles a year, far below the level needed to achieve economies of scale. All of these firms had licensing and technology assistance agreements with foreign automobile manufacturers, but only Ford-Liu Ho Motors had any significant foreign investment. These enterprises would have been nothing but CKD (complete knockdown kits) assembly operations if it the government had not imposed a 60 percent local content requirement on the industry in 1965. This local content requirement was a boost to the local automobile parts industry, but it did little to help the industry become competitive. Not only was the industry not close to being competitive internationally, it also had difficulty competing in price and quality with high-priced imports (priced high because of tarrifs).[35]

Believing that the problem was the small scale of existing automobile plants, the government in 1979 announced plans to build an automobile plant with the capacity of 200,000 vehicles a year. China Steel was expected to form a joint venture with a foreign manufacturer, but the foreign manufacturer was not to have more than 45 percent of the equity in the new venture. Toyota was chosen from among several firms that had expressed interest as the joint venture partner. But, when negotiations started in 1982, the government insisted that 50 percent of the output should be exported, and it later added a 90 percent content requirement. Toyota at that point withdrew and in 1984 the whole project was canceled.[36]

The joint venture between the Taiwan Machinery Corporation, a public enterprise, and General Motors to build heavy trucks was another failure of the government in this industry. The joint venture was approved in 1980. The new company, named Hua-Tung Car Manufacturing, started production in 1981, but later the government felt the price of their truck was too high and decided to lower the promised protection. General Motors withdrew in 1982. The Japanese Hino Company later took over all the assets of Hua-Tung and formed another company. [37]

It was not until 1985, when government policies had shifted clearly toward liberalization, that a new Automobile Industry Development Plan was announced. With lowered tariffs, lowered domestic content requirements, and removal of other import restrictions, Nissan, Mitsubishi, and Toyota all formed joint ventures with local private companies (Yue-loong, China Motors, and Ho-Tai Motors respectively). In addition, by the 1980s the automobile parts industry had become a major exporter, and the efficiency of the parts industry made local content targets much easier to achieve.

Other Heavy Industries

Most other sectors normally classified as heavy industries either relied mainly on imports or left production to the private sector and joint ventures. Machinery is a clear case in point. Most machinery firms were small in scale and run by "black hand" entrepreneurs who had come out of the blue-collar ranks. Needless to say, most of these black hand entrepreneurs were also Taiwanese, not mainlanders. Import duties on machinery were kept low, and so the rapidly rising demand was accompanied by a decline in the share of demand provided by domestic producers, going from 45 percent in 1965 to 1970 to 23 percent by 1981. [38] Despite the lack of subsidies, however, machinery's share of both GDP and exports rose slightly. By the end of the 1970s, Taiwan was an important exporter of sewing machines, machine tools, hand tools, and bicycles.

Electronics was another nominally heavy industry sector where fast growth was generated mainly by private-sector activity. Most of these were joint ventures with U.S. or Japanese firms in the early stages. The first investment by an American electronics firm was by General Instruments in 1964. Twenty-four other U.S. firms followed in the next two years, primarily setting up assembly operations for black-and-white or color television sets destined for foreign markets. Japanese joint ventures, in contrast, produced refrigerators, washing machines, air conditioners, and stereos mainly for the highly protected Taiwan market.

The government did fund the Electronic Research and Service Organization (ERSO) under the Industrial Technology Research Institute (ITRI) beginning in 1974. In 1977, it set up a model plant for design and fabrication of integrated circuits based on a technology contract signed with RCA in 1976. In 1979, a joint government-private enterprise, United Microelectronics, was set up to commercialize the technology being developed by the model plant.[39] These efforts to promote high-technology industries were to have increasing significance in the 1980s, but were not a major component of either GDP or exports in the 1970s.

CONCLUSION

By the end of the 1970s, after nearly three decades of growth, Taiwan's industry had come a long way from the sugar mills and refugee textile mills of the 1950s. The structural changes in the economy that occurred in this and later periods will be analyzed at greater length in Chapter 6. The central issue of this chapter has been the role of government in bringing about these structural changes in the decades prior to the 1980s. This review of the history of this earlier period tells us several things about the contribution of the state to the process.

The first point to make is that the role of the state in the industrial economy of the 1950s through the 1970s was large. Government restrictions on imports for the purpose of promoting domestic industries were pervasive throughout these three decades. Tariffs were high, domestic content requirements for joint ventures were common, and government gave certain firms outright monopolies of the domestic market. In the case of several important heavy industries, the government turned the development task over to state-owned enterprises and supported them with government-controlled funds.

To say that government was heavily involved in the industrial economy, however, is not to say that the government was primarily responsible for the industrial boom that indisputably did occur. Government policy clearly made possible a considerable amount of import substituting industrialization, and in some sectors firms in these industries did move down the learning curve to become internationally competitive. In other cases they remained as high-cost producers behind high walls of protection. Several of the state-owned heavy industrial firms, notably in petrochemicals and steel, were successful in the sense that they eventually achieved a positive rate of return at international prices. Other state efforts to create new heavy industries, notably shipbuilding and automobiles, were clear failures.

The way in which government intervened in the economy, as argued above, also had much to do with why Taiwan's industrial organization structure was so different from that of South Korea. This difference existed despite the fact that the two economies were at similar stages of development and both faced a similar and far-from-friendly external environment. It was in the interests of the political elite of South Korea, however, to foster large conglomerates that in turn would support the governing party. The mainlander elite that dominated the Taiwan government, in contrast, had no comparable political interest in building up an economically powerful group of Taiwanese-owned firms.

Could the private sector have achieved import substituting industrialization and the establishment of new heavy industries without so much government help? Perhaps, but that is one of those counterfactual questions that cannot be authoritatively answered. Given that the private sector did later build large-scale petrochemical and steel plants, there is little doubt that the private sector eventually could have built plants that required large-scale financing and complex management structures. But could Taiwan's small-scale enterprise dominated private industry have done this in the early 1970s?

The one unquestioned fact about Taiwan's industrialization in the 1950s through the 1970s is that the leading sectors after 1960 were all major exporters and virtually all of the major manufacturing firms exporting firms were privately owned. These firms were not the beneficiaries of high tariff walls or domestic monopolies. They benefited from a devalued exchange rate and easy access to imports of intermediate inputs. They also required land on which to build plants and licenses allowing them to operate. All of these things they obtained because of government policy changes from 1960 on. Government policy thus played a critical role in the boom in export of manufactures, but it was a liberalizing role even if liberalism applied only to exporters. The main achievement of government reforms in the 1960s and 1970s was to cut away the barriers to open economy development that had been erected by earlier government policies.

Notes

1   Hsu (1994a, pp. 32–313).

2   Chou (1963, pp. 34–35).

3   Yeh (1983).

4   Council for Economic Planning and Development, *Taiwan Statistical Data Book, 1974* (1974, p. 199).

5   Hsu (1987). See Chapter 2, "The Nationalist Economy Policy Transition on the Chinese Mainland Prior to 1949."

6   Hsu (1994b).

7   Hsu (1994b, p. 13).

8   The "restriction of capital" (*chieh-chih tsu-pen*), or, in a more perfect form, the "restriction of private capital and promotion of state capital" (*chieh-chih sz-jen tsu-pen, fa-ta kuo-chia tsu-pen*) as well as the "equalization of land property rights" (*ping-chu ti ch'uan*) had long been raised by ideologists as the fundamental Sun guidelines. These two policy slogans reflected a strong socialist ideology. Throughout the policy debates in the 1940s, and especially after moving to Taiwan, the top political leaders avoided mentioning these two slogans. Instead, President Chiang advocated "equity and wealth" (*chun fu*) as the essence of the Doctrine of Livelihood or the *Min-Xheng* principle. In linguistic tone and semantic meaning, the Chinese word *chieh-chih tsu-pen* includes an interesting ambiguity. In the original text, it was usually understood as the "restriction of capital." In response to economist T.Y. Wang's (*Wang Tso-Lung*) liberal view, Chiang expressed his own opinions by saying that *chieh-chih* should be interpreted as *tiao-chieh kuan-chih*, or regulation, rather than *hsieh-chih*, or restriction.

9   This discussion is based on Kuo, Ranis, and Fei (1981, pp. 66–68).

10   This discussion is based on Hsu (1987, pp. 267–270). The original material is from Shen (1972).

11   Hsu (1987, pp. 262–264).

12   Hsu (1987, pp. 270–277).

13   Chen and Mo (1995, Chapter 7).

14   Much of this paragraph is based on interviews with Yeh Wan-an, a senior economics official and a veteran of much of the period being discussed.

15   For Tsiang and Liu's participation, see *The Reminiscences of Dr. S. C. Tsiang*, Oral History Series No. 43, published by the Institute of Modern History Academic Sinica, 1992, pp. 79–99.

16   For policy debates between various parties, see Wang (1993, pp. 123–127).

17   Chen and Mo (1995).

18   Wang (1993, pp. 138–144).

19   Wang (1993, p. 141).

20   The content of the Nineteen Points is found in Shen (1972, pp. 510–514).

21   *Tzu-chi tzu-tsu* (self-sufficiency) was a policy slogan frequently used by political and economic leaders in the 1950s and early 1960s. This policy meant different things to different people in different periods, however. From referring to an effort to maintain independence from external economic and monetary disturbances in the period of import-substitution, it turned to an emphasis on self-sufficiency and independence from US AID in the early 1960s.

22   Lin (1973, Chapter 5).

23 *Yearbook of Financial Statistics of the R.O.C.*, Department of Statistics, Ministry of Finance, various years.

24 Foreign direct investment was most important in Taiwan's overall investment picture during 1967 to 1973 when the total reached 6 to 9 percent of total gross domestic investment.

25 Li 's oral history, pp. 144–148.

26 *Yearbook of Financial Statistics of the R.O.C.*, Department of Statistics, Ministry of Finance, various years.

27 The impact of these measures on exports is analyzed at length in another volume in this series of studies that is forthcoming.

28 Hsu and Chuang (1991).

29 These two naptha crackers were part of the Ten Major Development Projects.

30 The fourth naptha cracking plant was completed in 1984.

31 See Appendix B of this volume for a complete history of petrochemical industry development.

32 According to *The Assessment of the Ten Major Development Projects* (published by the Council for Economic Planning and Development, Executive Yuan, 1979), firms or individuals who submitted to the government feasibility studies for establishing a steel industy included: Aetna of the United States in 1956, Kaiser of the United States in 1962, Kloeckner of West Germany in 1965, and Kloiber, an expert consultant to the planning agency.

33 Under the privatization policy, government gradually sold off its shares in the 1990s. In April 1995, the government share finally fell below 50 percent.

34 *Yearbook of Public Enterprises Supervising Committee*, Ministry of Economic Affairs, 1995.

35 *Industrial Development Yearbook of the R.O.C.*, Industrial Development Bureau, Ministry of Economic Affairs, various years.

36 The details of the negotiation process between China Steel and Toyota can be found in "The Event of the Big Auto Plant" in *The Strategic Productivity Magazine*, May, June, and July, 1991 (in Chinese).

37 See *Industrial Development Yearbook of the R.O.C.*, Industrial Development Bureau, Ministry of Economic Affairs, 1982.

38 See *The Development Plan for the Machinery Industry*, 1982–1989, Council for Economic Planning and Development, 1983.

39 See Appendix C of this volume for a complete history of the development of the Electronics Industry.

3 Policies in the Context of Rapid Structural Change: 1979 to 1996

When economic change is rapid, policy makers who stand still are soon overwhelmed by events. Taiwan's policy makers from about 1958 through the 1970s had developed a policy framework that proved highly effective in launching Taiwan on a sustained period of rapid growth in GDP and labor-intensive manufactured exports. That framework, presented in the previous chapter and often described as "mercantilist," combined powerful export incentives with a vigorous policy of import substitution. Import substitution was fostered by tight controls on competitive imports combined with direct state promotion of heavy industries through the creation of new state-owned enterprises. There had been two external economic shocks to this system in the form of the Organization of Petroleum Exporting Countries (OPEC)-generated increases in the import price of energy in 1973 and 1979, but Taiwan had ridden through these crises easily. Vigorous but conventional fiscal and monetary policies had quickly brought inflation under control at the price, in each instance, of two years of slowed, but still positive, economic growth.

The Magnitude of Change

These policies, which had generated so much successful development, continued on into the early 1980s, but with results that soon forced fundamental changes in both the economy and the policies. Changes of the magnitude that was required in Taiwan in the 1980s and 1990s are not easily managed. Even in countries where growth and structural change occur more slowly, changes in policy can lag far behind the requirements of the situation. It can take years, or even decades, before the leaders of a society recognize intellectually that circumstances have changed and that policies and systems should change as well. Even when the new situation is understood at the intellectual level, vested interests within the government bureaucracy and the society at large can block badly needed reform.

It is testimony to the resilience of Taiwan's economic system that major adjustments have occurred despite the presence of many forces resisting needed change. These adjustments occurred in part because of effective national leadership, and in part because Taiwan's economic system had changed without the need for much leadership.

The major forces at work in the 1980s and 1990s can be broken down into macroeconomic changes, the changing nature of popular and interest group pressures on national policy, external pressures for policy change, and changing intellectual currents within Taiwan's policy-making establishments.

Macroeconomic Changes

The macroeconomic changes of principal relevance here were of two types:

1. By 1980, per capita GNP in real terms had risen fourfold over the level of 1960, at an average rate of 7.2 percent per year. Real wages, which lagged behind per capita GNP growth in the early years of export led industrial growth, took off after 1968. Prior to 1969, the average growth rate in real wages was 4.2 percent per year; from 1969 through 1978 it was 10.8 percent per year.[1] Prior to 1969, industry was mainly absorbing low-productivity agricultural workers. After that, the absolute number of workers in agriculture began to decline and real wages in agriculture also took off, growing at 7.9 percent per year. By 1980, therefore, real wages in industry were nearly four times their level in 1960. Taiwan was rapidly ceasing to be a low-wage economy. The fourfold rise in real income per capita was from an original base in the 1950s that was already double or more the per capita income of such potential competitors as Indonesia or Thailand. In the twenty years since the 1950s, Taiwan's real wages had risen to levels that industrial development in Western Europe and North America had taken seven or eight decades to accomplish.

2. In the 1980s, Taiwan began running large trade surpluses together with large surpluses of savings over domestic investment. These

macro imbalances are central to understanding the economic changes that occurred in the 1980s and 1990s; a formal analysis of the forces that brought about change is presented in Chapter 5. Here only the principal economic outcomes need to be noted.

The most obvious impact of the foreign trade surpluses was the large accumulation of reserves of foreign exchange at the Central Bank. These large reserves brought pressures to revalue the NT dollar, and the revaluation of the NT dollar radically changed the competitive position of Taiwan's manufactured exports. The weakened position of labor-intensive manufactured exports led many businesses to look abroad for more favorable places to build new factories. The existence of large foreign exchange reserves meant that the government no longer was so worried about capital flight, and so permission to invest abroad was granted.

The excess of savings over domestic investment also meant the rapid buildup of bank deposits that were not matched by an equally rapid increase in lending to industrial and infrastructure investors. Sitting on large reserves of domestic funds, investors looked around for alternative places to put their money, triggering a boom in both real estate prices and the stock market.

In Taiwan, however, unlike Japan, the savings/investment and export/import imbalances did not last. By the 1990s these savings and export surpluses were on the decline. The real estate and stock market bubbles had also burst, and yet real growth of GNP continued at a lower but still rapid pace.

Industrial Interest Group Pressures

In the 1950s and 1960s, industrial interest groups were too small and weak to have any influence on policy. Government technocrats were relatively free to do whatever they thought was best for the economy, or for their fellow bureaucrats, as long as they had the support of the president or other top political leaders in what was still a highly authoritarian system of governance. By the 1980s, industrial entrepreneurs and workers were large in number and organized into associations of various kinds. Even in an authoritarian system they had the capacity to bring pressure on the political leadership. In the 1970s, for example, the Taiwan Association of Machinery Industries pressured government to have its sector included in the sectors receiving government incentives. There were well over a hundred such organizations, and their leaders met often with high government officials to press their case.[2]

Of even greater importance, even in purely economic terms, was the fact that the authoritarian system was itself giving way to democratic forces. There were competitive local elections going back as far as 1959, and there was some competition in national elections beginning after 1972. Popular voices were sometimes heard loudly enough to influence economic policy. The most important changes, however, occurred in 1986 and 1987, with the formation of the Democratic Progressive Party (DPP), a genuine opposition party, and the lifting of martial law. A series of competitive elections for seats in the Legislative Yuan, the National Assembly, and for mayoralties of cities followed in rapid succession, culminating in the direct election of the President in 1996. Economic policy was no longer the exclusive territory of a few technocrats and senior politicians.

External Pressures for Change

Not all of the political pressures came from domestic forces. Taiwan's trade surpluses, together with the weakened trading position of the United States, brought Taiwan to the attention of negotiators for the U.S. Trade Representative's Office. The United States was no longer willing to look the other way at the restrictive trade practices of her major Asian trading partners, and the pressures to liberalize trade became steadily stronger.

More important than these external trade pressures was the gradual erosion of Taiwan's international position culminating in the transfer of U.S. diplomatic recognition from Taipei to Beijing. By the late 1980s and early 1990s, direct contacts between Taiwan and the Chinese mainland were themselves expanding rapidly, but the most fundamental questions about the nature of the relationship between Taiwan and the Chinese mainland remained unresolved. Fear of the consequences of Taiwan's democratization for the international position of the island culminated in large military maneuvers in the Taiwan Straits in early 1996 and again in 1999.

On balance, the issues connected with Taiwan–mainland political security relationships have had a conservative influence on economic policy. Taiwan, at least through the late 1980s, could not afford a poorly conceived and executed economic development program. Populist economic policies and personal rent seeking by government bureaucrats and politicians were possible only as long as the overall thrust of economic decision making was not much affected. Economic decision making, therefore, was still to a large degree the responsibility of technocrats. Which technocrats would most influence the decisions made, however—economists or engineers or career government officials who were neither economists nor engineers—was still an issue.

Changing Intellectual Currents

Economic shocks and political interest groups influence decisions about economic institutions and policies, but those decisions still require a rationale, an intellectual foundation. Ideas do matter, but individuals with different kinds of training often hold quite different views about what a particular situation requires. In much of Asia, not only in Taiwan, the basic battle over industrialization strategies has been between individuals trained as engineers and those trained as economists. A third element in many of these decisions has been government bureaucrats and politicians trained in other fields such as law, public administration, or medicine. The lines between those with different kinds of training are not rigidly drawn, and individuals with enough intellectual curiosity do study the views of those outside their profession as K. Y. Yin studied economics in the late 1950s (see the previous chapter). But the world views of engineers and economists are quite different and, in the context of an activist government industrial policy, must somehow be reconciled.

One way of resolving this conflict is to accept laissez-faire economic principles, in which case government no longer directly intervenes in the allocation of goods and services. In that context, the ideas of government officials, however they were trained, no longer matter that much. The laissez-faire ideal, however, is itself a construct of economists and has limited appeal to individuals who were not trained as economists and who themselves have never lived for any length of time in an economy governed mainly by market forces. Much of Taiwan's leadership in economic policy was in the hands of people who were not economists and who had spent much of their careers designing and operating a highly interventionist industrial policy.

All of these various forces, from macroeconomic and political pressures to ideas, played a role in the economic decisions made in the 1980s and 1990s. The remainder of this chapter is devoted to sorting out the history of how and why economic decisions were made during this period. Subsequent chapters will analyze the impact of those decisions in a more formal manner.

New Situation, Old and New Policies: 1979 to 1984

In certain respects, the macro trends that dominated the 1980s were already apparent in the 1970s, but one had to be a very astute analyst to see them. The two OPEC-generated increases in petroleum prices obscured the trends. In the early 1970s, Taiwan had already begun to run small balance of trade surpluses that, as in the 1980s, were driven by a modest excess of savings over investment. The huge oil price jumps temporarily wiped out these surpluses. In 1973 to 1974 and 1979 to 1980, however, only someone with profound understanding of commodity cartels and their limitations could see that the OPEC-generated crises were truly temporary phenomena. The more common view was that oil prices were on a steady climb upward, a major problem for any country, such as Taiwan, that was completely dependent on imports to meet its energy requirements.

The 1974 to 1981 period for Taiwan, therefore, was much like a roller coaster ride. The first OPEC price increase led to a large jump in domestic wholesale and retail prices, which in turn caused a large revaluation of the real exchange rate. Strong anti-inflationary policies brought price increases down to the low single digits by 1975, whereas much of the rest of the industrial world did less well in controlling prices. Taiwan's real exchange rate thus was steadily devalued through 1978, until the 1979 oil price increase started the general price level and the real exchange rate to rise once again. The cycle then repeated itself, with the government, through tight fiscal and monetary policies, driving price increases down. The nominal exchange rate was also devalued modestly in 1981 and 1982 (by 12 percent) and the real rate also steadily devalued through 1986, although not as sharply as in the 1975 to 1978 period.

The dominant macro influence of the early 1980s was the steep recession in a number of industrial countries, notably the United States. President Reagan and his economic advisors were determined to wring double-digit inflation rates out of the U.S. economy, and they sent the economy into a nosedive in order to do so. In the early 1980s, more than a third of all of Taiwan's exports were still sold in the U.S. market. Despite the industrial country recession, however, Taiwan's exports held up surprisingly well. Taiwan's imports, however, fell sharply as a percentage of GNP and large trade surpluses began to appear. The fall in import shares reflected the fact that Taiwan's anti-inflationary policies had slowed growth to what for Taiwan was the slow annual rate of 5.7

percent (1980–1982). Again, most analysts saw these circumstances as a cyclical phenomenon requiring adjustments essentially temporary in nature. It was some time before Taiwan policy makers were aware that they were facing a fundamental structural change in their economy whose effects would not disappear once the OPEC price increases had been absorbed and the U.S. recession ended.

If many of the macro forces at work appeared to be cyclical in nature and hence essentially temporary, the rise in petroleum prices seemed to be anything but temporary. For Taiwan, dependent as it was on energy imports, that belief had clear implications for the island's industrial policy. First subtly, and then more explicitly, the emphasis in industrial policy began to shift away from heavy or "high class" industry toward technology intensive industry. Some of the heavy industries, after all, were major consumers of energy inputs and hence made Taiwan even more dependent on foreign oil. The issue became one of how to upgrade Taiwan's industry so that it would remain internationally competitive, but to do so without becoming increasingly dependent on high-priced foreign oil. The diagnosis of the problem, of course, was wrong. Foreign oil did not remain high priced for long. By the mid-1980s, petroleum prices had fallen sharply and prices remained low for the next decade. Incorrect diagnoses, however, sometimes lead to appropriate policy outcomes, and that appears to have been the case in Taiwan in the late 1970s and early 1980s.

In the case of the technology upgrading policy, the central figure was Li Kuo-t'ing (K. T. Li). K. T. Li was still Minister of Finance during the first half of the 1970s, but, as pointed out in the previous chapter, he had had serious conflicts with Premier Chiang Ching-kuo over implementation of the Ten Major Development Projects. In 1976, Premier Chiang succeeded in getting Li removed from the Finance Ministry, but he respected Li's scientific background enough not to want him out of the government altogether. In addition, the premier needed someone skilled in international economic relations and Li had proved adept in that area as well. K. T. Li was made a Cabinet Minister without Portfolio, but, in many ways what was of greater importance, he was also made chairman of the Coordinating Committee for the Application of Science and Technology to National Objectives.[3] In the past, science and technology affairs had been handled by the National Science Council under the Executive Yuan and by Academia Sinica under the Presidency. These two organizations had usually emphasized basic academic scientific research and did not deal with applied science concerned with national industrial developmental objectives. Thus, the establishment of this new ministerial committee itself was a new direction for science and technology policy.

The other important changes in personnel in this period were when Chiang Ching-kuo assumed the Presidency on May 20, 1978, and in doing so promoted Sun Yun-hsuan, the former Minister of Economic Affairs, to be the Premier. Sun had a typical technocratic career under Kuomintang rule. He earned his degree in electrical engineering at Harbin Industrial University and was sent to the United States to receive professional training by the Council of Resources late in World War II. Moreover, Sun was one of the first groups of engineers arriving in Taiwan in 1945, working as a junior engineer in the Taiwan Power Company. He was promoted to the position of chief engineer and then to the presidency of the company. From 1967 on, Sun had been the Minister of Communications and the Minister of Economic Affairs under the Yen and Chiang Administration. In 1969 and 1970, Sun visited South Korea and was impressed by Korean science and technology development efforts. Inspired by the South Korean experience, Sun created the Industrial Technology Research Institute (ITRI) and began the process that led to the establishment of the Hsinchu Science-based Industrial Park.[4] As he assumed the premiership in 1978, Sun had hoped to invite K. T. Li, his former colleague and superior, to become Minister of Economic Affairs, but Li declined, preferring to stay in his positions as Minister without Portfolio and Chairman of the Science and Technology Coordinating Committee. President Chiang had retained an interest in the promotion of traditional heavy industries such as steel, but the attention of K. T. Li by the late 1970s was focused elsewhere and he persuaded Premier Sun to support him.[5]

The relevance of technology-intensive industries to Taiwan's future had been percolating up through the government bureaucracy for several years prior to 1978. The Investment Review Council of the Ministry of Economy, for example, was responsible for reviewing and approving foreign and overseas Chinese investments in Taiwan. In 1976, this council declared that it would give priority to technology-intensive investments.[6] In February 1978, the Ministry of Finance allocated NT$200 million to a program designed to encourage foreign and domestic technical experts to create technology-intensive industries in Taiwan.[7] The Taiwan Development Trust was made responsible for implementing the program by reviewing applications and arranging loans for the purchase of land, buildings, and equipment.[8] More im-

portantly, the Statute for Encouraging Investment, the central industrial policy legislation discussed in the previous chapter, was revised
and the revision passed by the Executive Yuan Conference in July 1980.
The revision gave priority to capital-intensive and technology-intensive industries when it came to government decisions to award tax
holidays to new firms and investments.[9] The slogan used to describe
government industrial policy, which had stressed the importance of
the "transition from light to heavy and 'high-class industry,'" was replaced with a slogan stressing "industrial upgrading from labor-intensive to capital- and technology-intensive industry."[10]

Pressures were also arising from the business sector itself, much of
it from machinery and electronics manufacturers. In meetings with Yu
Kuo-hua, then the chairman of the Council on Economic Planning
and Development, and with others, these business sectors pushed for
government help in testing and research, tasks seen as too complex
and expensive for any single small enterprise to undertake. They also
asked for help in marketing and related activities that would help them
expand their exporting capacity.[11]

One milestone in the development of a technology policy was the
First National Conference for Science and Technology promoted by K.
T. Li with the explicit support of Premier Sun and President Chiang.
The conference was held in July 1978, and the conclusions drawn by
the conference provided the foundation for Li's draft of a Science and
Technology Development Program. The Council of the Executive Yuan
formally approved this program on May 18, 1979.[12]

The Program had three broad objectives: (1) to strengthen the defense industry by developing new weapons and building a self-sufficient defense system; (2) to develop the economy by promoting technology-intensive industries, furthering agricultural modernization, and
making more efficient use of natural resources; and (3) to improve
human welfare by strengthening medical research, improving nutri-
tion, protecting the environment, and strengthening the capacity to
predict and forecast natural disasters.[13] To achieve these broad objectives, each relevant government department was expected to develop a
Science and Technology Plan, including a budget. These plans and budgets were to be collected and coordinated by the National Science Council for eventual approval by the Executive Yuan.

The first science and technology research plan covered the years
1979 to 1981. The nine broad categories in this plan dealt with everything from strengthening science and technology education to making

sure that research was fully integrated with production in the various sectors. The approach was a holistic one covering a wide range of technologies and the support infrastructure required by a broad-based science and technology development effort. This was not a program to pick a handful of new technologies and then try to make Taiwan a leader in these special fields. Technology targeting was practiced, but it was not characteristic of this very broad based program. As required, the program was amended and new, related programs initiated. One central effort, started in 1983, was the Program for Strengthening the Education, Training, and Recruitment of High-level Science and Technology Personnel. All of these efforts were under the leadership and guidance of the Coordinating Committee for the Application of Science and Technology to National Objectives.[14]

In 1976, the Electronic Research and Service Organization (ERSO) under the Industrial Technology Research Institute (ITRI) did set up a prototype plant for wafer fabrication and signed a technology transfer contract with the U.S. firm RCA. Based on this technology and in order to commercialize this effort, the United Microelectronics Corporation (UMC) was founded in 1979 with 40 percent of its equity capital from the government and the remainder from private firms. UMC became the center for developing and diffusing integrated circuit technology in the 1980s for telephones, timers, and much else. A cluster of downstream user firms arose as a result, and Taiwan began exporting a variety of new products.[15]

Taiwan, however, still did not have the capacity to develop very large scale integrated circuits, a lack that led in 1987 to the government creating Taiwan Semiconductor. Except for UMC and Taiwan Semiconductor, however, most of the efforts of the government under the rubric of science and technology development did not involve government targeting of individual firms for special support.

The industrial targeting that was practiced under the rubric of science and technology development was more broad based than that practiced under the heavy industry effort. Government efforts were directed at paving the way for small- and medium-sized firms. K. T. Li, for example, had a particular interest in the information industry, and all three Ministers of Economic Affairs who served during this time were engineers, who had both an interest in this sector and an understanding of its requirements.[16] The information industry was also made up mainly of small- and medium-sized firms that fit Taiwan's industrial organization structure well. In December 1979, the government promoted a computer exhibition, called Information Month, to educate the public about computers, an exhibition that became an annual event.

In 1979, the Institution for Information Industry (III) was established as a nonprofit organization, with funding donated by the Ministry of Economic Affairs and private enterprises. The mission of III was to promote the development of the information industry, especially software development. It educated the government and the private sector on how to use the computer. A program was also set up to train people to work in this industry. While these training efforts were taking place, between 1978 and 1984, government offices were being computerized in a serious way, thus creating a demand for computer services together with increasing knowledge of their potential role.[17]

Of particular importance in this process was the decision by the National Science Council in December 1980 to create the Hsinchu Science-based Industrial Park. The original idea behind the creation of the Hsinchu Park was a high-technology version of an export processing zone. The park would attract foreign companies, particularly in computers and integrated circuits, to set up factories in Taiwan and employ local labor. Foreign companies did come to the park, but under the leadership of Hsu Hsin-hsiu, chairman of the National Science Council and an overseas Chinese scholar who taught at Purdue University before the Hsinchu Park was established, the park began to play a very different role. The people being attracted to the park were not mainly foreign companies but individuals or groups from Taiwan who had gone abroad for training, mainly to the United States, and had stayed on in that country to work, many in such places as Silicon Valley.

From the 1950s through the 1970s, large numbers of students trained through the undergraduate level in Taiwan's universities went to the United States, and to a lesser degree Europe, to pursue graduate work. Exact figures are not available, but 90 percent or more of these students prior to the 1980s did not return, creating a substantial brain drain among Taiwan's educated elite. By the 1980s, however, this flow began to reverse itself.[18] There were many motivations behind this reversal. Taiwan's higher standard of living and higher wages after two decades of rapid development made jobs in Taiwan more competitive with those in the United States. Taiwan's society was also becoming more open and cosmopolitan, and the island's future, despite the loss of diplomatic recognition and United Nations membership, appeared much less fragile than had been the case earlier. Much the same phenomenon was occurring in South Korea and for many of the same reasons.[19]

The establishment of Hsinchu Park did not create this brain drain reversal, but it substantially reinforced this trend, particularly among engineers and scientists in the information and other high-technology fields. It set up a National Experimental High School in 1983, complete with bilingual education for those returnees (and foreigners) whose children had not been educated in Chinese. Residential and recreational areas were up to standards found in the industrialized countries. Most of all, there were good jobs for those with strong technical backgrounds. In 1981, the park had only seventeen companies with paid-in capital of US$18 million. By 1994, those numbers had risen to 155 companies with paid in capital of US$2.56 billion. Integrated circuits, computers, and peripherals accounted for 79 percent of the paid-in capital and 88 percent of total sales in 1994. Domestic investors provided 81 percent of the paid-in capital.[20]

One clear case of government industrial targeting in the high-technology field was the establishment of Taiwan Semiconductor Manufacturing Company (TSMC), founded in 1987 to manufacture very large scale integrated (VLSI) circuits. Integrated circuit design and assembly did not require large amounts of capital, but a manufacturing facility required anywhere from NT$3 to 10 billion, well beyond the financial capacity of most private Taiwan firms. Most foreign semiconductor companies were fully integrated and were not interested in another manufacturing facility based in Taiwan. The exception was Philips, which, in the end, put up 25 percent of the initial capital of NT$5.5 billion. The government put up 48 percent and twisted the arms of several large domestic companies to put up the remaining 28 percent.[21]

Chang Chung-mou (Morris Chang), a mainland China–born Chinese recruited by K. T. Li from the United States, was responsible for the task of establishing TSMC and remained the chairman of the company for many years after its establishment. Chang was the leading figure of the semiconductor department of Texas Instruments (TI) for many years prior to his return to Taiwan, and TI had long been active in Taiwan. The head of TI was a regular visitor to Taiwan, and K. T. Li was in turn a regular visitor to TI headquarters in the United States. K. T. Li became acquainted with Chang and tried to invite him back to Taiwan starting in the early 1980s. Chang left TI in 1984 for another job for a short period of time, before finally returning to Taiwan to take the position as the president of Industrial Technology Research Institute (ITRI) in 1985. By the mid-1990s, of the 800 engineers at Taiwan Semiconductor, 100 had degrees from U.S. Universities and another 10 had worked from ten to fifteen years in the United States before returning.[22]

Taiwan Semiconductor became profitable in financial terms after only a year of operation, although the full extent of start-up capital costs may not have adequately been taken into account in this profit calculation. As a result of this perceived favorable performance, many other companies soon entered the field. Where in 1987 there had been only one fabricating company and seven design houses, by 1994 there were eleven fabricating companies and sixty design houses. The new firms were private, and Taiwan Semiconductor was also run as a private company, albeit one with government as a majority shareholder. All of these semiconductor firms were located in the Hsinchu Science-based Industrial Park.

Although TSMC was one of the few individual industries and firms to be targeted by government for development, the government continued to give special treatment to sectors and firms that it favored for one reason or another. There was a wide range of criteria used in determining which sectors should receive tax breaks and other forms of help. Export industries and small- and medium-scale firms continued to receive special treatment. Altogether there were eleven categories of firms eligible for tax breaks or low-cost loans, and many of the categories were overlapping. The category most relevant to the discussion here and to targeting industrial policies in general was strategic industries.

The term *strategic industries* officially first appears in the 1978 revision of the six-year plan. In the early 1980s, it was in active use at national economic conferences sponsored by the government. Strategic industries eventually became defined by six criteria, which were referred to as the "two bigs, two highs, and two lows": (1) big linkage effects to other sectors, (2) large market potential, (3) high-technology intensity, (4) high valued added, (5) low energy intensity, and (6) low pollution intensity.

Because strategic industries received more special favors from the government than industries not so classified, a lively debate ensued among industrialists as to just who should be classified as strategic.[23] Not surprisingly, the new high-technology industries favored criteria confined to industries breaking into businesses that were new to Taiwan and hence faced special risks. Older, more-established sectors such as plastics and garments argued that the size of the current contribution to exports or the economy should define strategic, or alternatively that all heavy industries should be considered strategic. Some, such as Wang Yung-ch'ing, the head of the giant Formosa Plastics, argued against the designation of any particular industry as strategic.

The debate over the criteria for strategic industries demonstrated that industrial policy choices could no longer be made by government technocrats and then readily accepted by the business community or the general public. Even before democratization and contested elections began to play an important role, businessmen had found their voice, and they represented powerful economic interests of the business community. Active government intervention in favor of one sector or another inevitably generated powerful resistance from the others.

Generalized efforts to promote technology, however, were not controversial. Investment in research and development (R and D), over half of which was provided by the government, expanded from 0.89 percent of GNP in 1982 to 1.74 percent in 1992 (see Tables 3-1 and 3-2). In nominal terms, this represented nearly a sixfold rise in R and D spending in a single decade; in real terms, the rise was perhaps four-

TABLE   3 - 1

Research and Development Expenditure in Taiwan

	Total R and D Expenditures		Government R and D Expenditures	R and D Researchers (persons)	
Year	Million NT$	as % of GNP	as % of Total R and D	Total	with Doctorates
1980	10,562	0.71	NA	NA	NA
1982	16,864	0.89	58.2	18,386	1,733
1984	22,444	0.95	683.3	22,354	2,887
1986	28,702	0.98	60.1	27,747	3,146
1988	43,839	1.21	56.5	35,437	4,163
1990	71,548	1.62	45.8	46,071	5,939
1992	94,828	1.74	52.2	48,356	10,039
1994	114,682	1.78	48.5	55,405	NA

Sources: *Taiwan Statistical Data Book*, 1995 (1995: pp.107, 109); and *Monthly Bulletin of Statistics* (April 1996, p. 14).

NA = not available.

fold.[24] Research and development manpower was rising equally rapidly. Doctor's degree holders rose more than sixfold between 1981 and 1992; Master's degree holders in R and D expanded nearly four times.

The distribution of R and D expenditures and personnel across sectors was, of course, very uneven. The highest levels, as a percentage of sales, were in electronics and plastics. The lowest levels were in industries that were in decline by the late 1980s, such as wearing apparel, leather goods, and wood products (see Table 3-3).

The government still had an important role to play in the development of high-technology industries, but the nature of that role had changed fundamentally by the late 1980s and early 1990s. Industry- and firm-specific targeting, an important element in government industrial policy in the 1970s and early 1980s, was on the way out. New private firms in a wide range of new high-technology industries from telecommunications to opto-electronics and precision machinery were starting up in increasing numbers, sometimes relying on the work of government-supported research, but not directly initiated or heavily subsidized by government. The subsidies that did continue to exist were available to all that met certain general criteria.

Taiwan's industrial economy, as the debate over the definition of strategic industries demonstrated, had become too large and complex and had too many conflicting interests for government to play an active sector-by-sector leadership role. The increasing complexity of the industrial economy and the rising assertiveness of the various indus-

TABLE 3-2

International Comparisons of Research and Development Expenditures (as a percent of GDP/GNP)

	1980	1985	1990	1993
Taiwan	0.71	1.01	1.62	1.74
South Korea	0.58	1.56	1.88	2.09[a]
United States	2.3	2.8	2.7	2.6
Japan	2.35	3.19	3.35[b]	2.91

Sources: *Monthly Bulletin of Statistics* (April 1996: 14); *Major Statistics of Korean Economy*, 1995.2 (1995:284); *Statistical Abstract of the United States*, 1994 (1994:607); *Japan: An International Comparison* (1981, 1991, and 1996 issues) (Tokyo: Keizan Koho Center, 1980, 1990, and 1995: 23, 26, and 35).

[a] 1992

[b] 1988

TABLE 3-3
Research and Development Expenditure as a Percentage of Total Sales Amount of the Manufacturing Industries

Industries	Year									Annual Average Rate	
	1982	1984	1986	1987	1988	1989	1990	1991	1992	1982–86	1987–92
Total for Manufacturing	0.56	0.79	0.47	0.64	0.52	0.73	0.92	0.94	0.92	0.59	0.78
Food	0.30	0.41	0.48	0.44	0.69	0.50	0.53	0.43	0.38	0.33	0.50
Beverages & Tobacco	0.03	0.04	0.23	0.12	0.07	0.08	0.28	0.13	0.10	0.13	0.13
Textiles	0.21	0.29	0.16	0.34	0.24	0.13	0.52	0.55	0.40	0.25	0.36
Wearing Apparel	0.24	0.52	0.12	0.35	0.12	0.07	0.24	0.24	0.08	0.34	0.18
Leather	0.40	0.86	0.24	0.20	0.03	0.34	0.06	0.45	0.26	0.35	0.22
Lumber & Furniture	0.84	0.31	0.11	0.26	0.06	0.08	0.04	0.03	0.10	0.31	0.10
Paper & Printing	0.19	0.61	0.16	0.42	0.14	0.19	0.20	0.21	0.10	0.27	0.21
Chemical Materials	0.38	0.81	1.07	0.46	0.40	0.53	0.88	0.84	1.08	0.65	0.70
Chemical Products	1.53	0.81	0.80	1.10	1.06	0.78	0.86	0.89	1.24	0.98	0.99
Petroleum & Coal Products	0.08	1.13	0.41	0.39	0.77	0.48	0.73	0.86	1.13	0.37	0.73
Rubber Products	0.51	0.00	0.51	0.92	0.30	0.96	0.27	0.52	0.75	0.55	0.62
Plastic Products	0.57	0.56	0.72	0.68	0.11	0.55	0.39	1.12	1.57	0.60	0.74
Nonmetallic Mineral Products	0.23	0.84	0.27	1.00	0.62	1.15	0.21	0.11	0.15	0.46	0.54
Basic Metals	0.21	0.29	0.29	0.47	0.32	0.27	0.33	0.32	0.37	0.31	0.35
Metal Products	1.10	1.55	0.36	0.44	0.30	0.32	0.29	0.25	0.30	0.79	0.32
Machinery	2.08	1.88	0.86	1.56	0.75	0.66	0.44	0.55	0.60	1.50	1.26
Electrical Machinery & Appliances	1.14	1.46	0.65	1.00	1.04	1.59	2.53	2.41	2.05	1.03	1.77
Transport Equipment	0.54	0.75	0.48	1.17	0.62	1.18	0.99	1.01	0.93	0.66	0.98
Precision Instruments	0.50	2.38	0.48	2.09	0.91	0.43	0.39	0.68	1.27	1.14	0.96
Miscellaneous	0.38	1.17	0.74	0.31	0.33	0.86	0.82	0.35	0.53	0.75	0.53

Source: *Indicators of Science and Technology, ROC* (various years).

trial groups, however, comprised only one aspect of the pressures on the government to begin to liberalize economic policy systematically. External pressures were also present and, most importantly, there was an active intellectual debate over the appropriate role for government intervention that was changing the way the government's economic leadership thought about the way it should intervene in industrial development.

ECONOMIC LIBERALIZATION IN THE MID-1980S

From the 1950s into the 1970s, individuals who were trained as engineers and other government officials who thought of themselves as planners dominated the intellectual framework shaping industrial policy. As pointed out in the previous chapter, economists' views were heard and taken into account on occasion, but these views only moderated the highly interventionist policies of the day, they did not change their basic interventionist orientation. This orientation began to come under increased attack beginning in the mid-1970s.

The push toward economic liberalization was initiated, to a large degree, by a paper written as a policy recommendation entitled "A Discussion of Future Economic and Financial Policy in Taiwan" put out in 1974 and submitted to the government.[25] Although the paper itself dealt mainly with macroeconomic issues such as repressed interest rates, its influence on thinking about the appropriate role of market forces versus government intervention was much broader. The authors of the paper were six prestigious economists, most of whom were simultaneously members of Academia Sinica and professors at major American research universities. The six were Liu Ta-chung (T.C. Liu, Cornell); Hsing Mo-huan (Chinese University, Hong Kong), Fei Ching-han (John Fei, Yale); Chiang Shih-chieh (S.C. Tsiang, Rochester and Cornell); Ku Ying-chang (Anthony Koo, Michigan State) and Tsou Chih-chuang (Gregory Chow, Princeton). All were liberal neoclassical economists whose views, in the American context, were closer to those of the University of Chicago than they were to the more activist Keynesian views that were most influential at many other American research universities.

This paper was written immediately after the first oil price crisis and in the first stages of the economic recession that followed. The paper praised the vigorous efforts of Premier Chiang Ching-kuo to rein in the inflationary consequences of the oil price rise, but then launched into a broad analytical discussion of the way economic policy should be carried out. At the most general level, they argued that economic policy should be consistent with the supply-and-demand forces on the market. In the terminology of the 1990s, government interventions, if needed at all, should be market conforming. Certainly the objective should be having supply and demand in equilibrium so that government intervention would be unnecessary. If the government wanted to control prices, it should worry mainly about changes in the overall level of prices, not what was happening to the prices of particular commodities.

Much of the paper, given the economic situation of the time, focused on monetary policy issues when it came to making policy-relevant recommendations, but the underlying purpose of the paper was to change much more than just monetary policy. Monetary policy was the vehicle for introducing liberal economic principles into the making of economic policy. The price level, the paper argued, should be controlled by managing the quantity of money in circulation, not by the government controlling individual prices. To keep the growth in the money supply in line with the growth in the economy, the six economists advocated the creation of a money market. They also advocated establishing a foreign exchange market and a forward foreign exchange market together with a policy of flexible exchange rates.

To create a money market, they advocated abolishing the existing system in which government treasury bills could be purchased only by government monetary agencies at fixed, government-set, interest rates. This system would be replaced with a market open to the public where bills were sold at market-determined rates of interest. The paper attacked the notion that the government should set interest rates at all. If interest rates were set too low, demand for credit would exceed its supply and credit rationing would be the result. When credit rationing was practiced, allocation of credit was bound to be subjective and inefficient. In the Taiwan context, small- and medium-scale enterprises were the most likely to lose out, as had been the case throughout the 1960s and early 1970s.[26]

The paper triggered a debate both inside and outside of government. The six authors realistically did not expect to persuade many senior economic decision makers, but they did hope to influence two key individuals central to any changes in the sphere of monetary policy: Yu Kuo-hua, the head of the Central Bank, and Chiang Ching-kuo, the Premier. Some changes did in fact begin to take place in response to the recommendations in the paper. In 1976, for example, Yu Kuo-hua took steps to establish a money market by creating three companies authorized to deal in commercial paper. Interest rates, it was stated, were to be determined by market forces, but in reality they were still set by government through a more indirect process.

On July 11, 1978, the government announced that it was abandoning its fixed exchange rate policy and replacing it with a flexible exchange rate system.[27] The NT dollar did in fact appreciate in 1978, by 5.2 percent, but the move to flexibility was not as much of a change in practice as had been advocated. The Central Bank did create a foreign exchange market on February 1, 1979, and it authorized five (state-owned) commercial banks to buy and sell foreign exchange, but the Central Bank continued to give direction to these commercial banks when it came to setting the exchange rate.[28] By March 1980, however, the Central Bank had withdrawn from direct interference in the setting of the exchange rate and abolished the upper and lower limits on the movement of the rate. From then on the Central Bank intervened in setting the exchange rate mainly by buying or selling foreign exchange on the market.

The government, not market forces, however, was still the driving force in setting the exchange rate. In August 1981, for example, exporters were exerting increasing pressure on the government to depreciate the rate. Up through early 1981, the exchange rate had appreciated for three straight years as a result of the impact of oil price rises on the general domestic price level. Exporters wanted relief even though exports were growing in real terms, and Taiwan had a substantial balance of trade surplus in all years except 1980, when high oil prices led to a small deficit. A debate ensued within the cabinet with the Minister of Economic Affairs siding with the exporters and the Minister of Finance opposing depreciation because of its impact on inflation. Ultimately President Chiang sided with the exporters, and the NT dollar was depreciated by 4.9 percent in nominal terms.[29]

Public debates over the direction of economic policy continued in the press. One prominent debate, which began in early 1981 and lasted for more than a year, was between S. C. Tsiang and Wang Tso-yung, the so-called Tsiang-Wang debate. Once again the main issue was how to control inflation while maintaining a high rate of economic growth. Chiang once again took the liberal market-oriented view that inflation should be controlled by regulating the money supply and that loans at below market rates of interest were a major source of excessive expansion in the supply of money. Wang Tso-yung basically argued for a version of the government's existing policies of selective intervention.[30]

These debates occurred against a background of fundamental structural changes in Taiwan's economy. The most obvious manifestation of these changes was Taiwan's growing balance of trade surplus and accumulating foreign exchange reserves. These surpluses, as already pointed out, had begun to appear in the latter half of the 1970s but disappeared temporarily in 1980 after the 1979 oil price increase. The surpluses reappeared in 1981 and then rose sharply from 2.9 percent of GDP in 1981 to 14.8 percent of GDP in 1984 and 22 percent in 1986. Taiwan's foreign exchange reserves skyrocketed and were rapidly becoming one of the largest reserves in the world. All of this was happening during what, for most of the industrial world and for Taiwan as well, was a major economic recession.

The underlying cause of these foreign exchange surpluses was a radical shift in investment behavior. Taiwan's savings rate had risen to high levels by the late 1970s, as had the investment rate. The savings rate remained high in the 1980s, but the investment rate fell sharply from 1981 on, resulting in a large excess of domestic savings over domestic investment. This savings investment gap was in turn directly related to the trade surplus. In 1981 or 1982 it was reasonable to assume that this surplus was a temporary phenomenon caused by the world recession and Taiwan investors' response to that recession. By 1983 and 1984, when both Taiwan's economy and the world economy had resumed growth, however, the view that the problem was cyclical was no longer tenable.

Much of this trade surplus manifested itself as a large bilateral trade surplus with the United States. Because large Japanese trade surpluses with the United States had already become a political issue there, U.S. politicians quickly saw the rising surplus of Taiwan as a growing problem. This view was increasingly prevalent in the U.S. Congress, which contained powerful protectionist elements. President Reagan and his economic advisors, in contrast, were committed free traders who did not see bilateral trade deficits as of much economic significance. The Reagan Administration in the first half of the 1980s, therefore, chose to bring pressure on Taiwan, not over the surplus per se, but over Taiwan's highly restrictive import barriers. Pressure from the United States, therefore, was clearly on the side of pushing Taiwan toward a liberal market-oriented trade regime. That pressure was to become much stronger by 1986, but it was already present by 1983 to 1984.

By the mid-1980s, therefore, there were a variety of both internal and external forces pushing the government toward a change in its approach to economic development. On the intellectual front, liberal market-oriented ideas were increasingly being heard and understood. President Chiang Ching-kuo was directly involved in discussions of these issues, as was Yu Kuo-hua, who was appointed as Premier in 1984.

After debate within the government, it was President Chiang's practice to promulgate new policy directions and instructions at Financial and Economic Symposia or Colloquia that were held every few weeks during the 1978 to 1984 period. President Chiang's first statement endorsing a more liberal approach to economic policy was presented to the sixth Financial and Economic Heads Colloquium in 1983.[31] Like other instructions issued at these meetings, this one received wide publicity and was taken by government officials as a guide for future policy formulation and implementation. The 1983 instruction dealt mainly with opening up the economy to imports as a way to reduce the trade surplus.

Of even greater importance were President Chiang's instructions at the ninth Financial and Economic Heads Colloquium of April 10, 1984.[32] Part of these concerned the decision to end many special measures designed to deal with Taiwan's economic recession, a recession that by then had been over with for nearly two years. Several longer-term themes for the future, however, were also presented. Among these were two directly related to the question of liberalizing the economy. President Chiang instructed government agencies to construct an economic environment that promoted sufficient competition and one that took full cognizance of those areas where Taiwan's economy enjoyed a comparative advantage. The phrases *sufficient competition* and *comparative advantage* provided common themes in the newspaper articles and public commentary that followed, and were seen as an attempt to move economic policy in a more liberal direction.[33]

Yu Kuo-hua, previously the head of the Central Bank, became Premier on May 20, 1984, and immediately made "economic liberalization, internationalization, and institutionalization" the three basic policy guidelines of his premiership. By *liberalization* he meant that government should respect market forces and minimize interference in industry and other economic activities. *Internationalization* involved reducing the barriers to the international flow not only of goods and services but also cultural and scientific exchanges. *Institutionalization* referred to the need to establish transparent rules to govern the economy and society in place of the complex, nontransparent, and often discretionary decisions of government officials.[34]

Four economists were asked by the Council on Economic Planning and Development (CEPD) to research how to liberalize the economy. Liu Tai-ying worked on trade liberalization, Hou Chia-chu on investment liberalization, Pan Chih-ch'i on financial liberalization, and Liang Kuo-shu on foreign exchange liberalization.[35] By July 1984, the CEPD had drawn up a plan to implement many of their recommendations, including the recommendations to reduce import duties and to appreciate the exchange rate. Import duties, to be sure, had been reduced earlier, and there had also been a shift away from the use of import quotas to a primary reliance on import tariffs. These earlier moves did represent partial moves toward trade liberalization, but the basic mercantilist orientation of trade policy in those years remained very much intact. Certainly in these earlier periods there was no real willingness on the part of policy makers to allow in those imports that competed in a major way with domestic industries that the government was trying to support.

There was opposition to some of the new proposals, notably from the Ministry of Economic Affairs and the Agricultural Council, presumably reflecting the interests of their business and farmer constituencies.[36] Nevertheless, the broad proposals went forward to President Chiang who endorsed them, and his instructions to the Financial and Economic Heads Colloquium of November 6, 1984, called for, among other things, the development of a social and individual capacity for meeting the challenges of liberalization, institutionalization, and internationalization.[37]

November 1984, however, was the last time President Chiang was able to preside at a meeting of the main economic officials. Illness largely removed him from the economic decision-making process for the remainder of his time in office until his death in 1988. A statement of principles had been enunciated, but the implementing rules and legislation had yet to be worked out. In the absence of President Chiang, major changes in policy required a consensus of the various ministers responsible for economic affairs, and that was difficult to achieve.[38] The financial crisis of the Tenth Credit Cooperative in 1985 preoccupied major economic officers, distracting them from more important long-term goals.[39] In addition, Chiang Nan's murder in the United States,[40] which involved an alleged conspiracy of the secret intelligence agency of the Kuomintang government, was also a major political scandal in the mid-1980s, which further weakened the ability of the government to deal with the liberalization of the economy.

By 1986, however, the momentum behind change had built to a point where action was again possible. Pressure from the United States was becoming stronger. The U.S. House of Representatives, for example, passed a bill that, if signed into law, would have required trade surplus countries—Japan and Taiwan were the two the U.S. lawmakers had in mind—to reduce those surpluses by 10 percent per year. American trade negotiators, under pressure from the Congress itself, began pressing more vigorously for an appreciation of the NT dollar, the opening of Taiwan's market through a decline in tariffs and nontariff barriers, and the opening of Taiwan's service sectors to foreign investment.

In September 1986, five prominent Taiwan economists presented a concrete set of proposals to the government in what became known as the "Five Economists' Paper." The five included S. C. Tsiang; Wang Tso-yung, who had converted to the liberalization view; John Fei; Anthony Koo; and Yu Tsong-hsien. These economists attacked the neomercantilist views held by many in Taiwan head on, including those who wanted to use special tax breaks and low interest rates to promote high-technology industries.[41] Taiwan's success, they argued, was not based on an export-oriented industrial policy backed up by all kinds of trade restrictions. It was all right for government to support scientific education and research and to recruit high-level engineers and scientists from abroad. From then on, however, it was up to the private sector to invest wherever it thought it could do well without the benefit of subsidies and in accordance with Taiwan's comparative advantage.

Taiwan's business community was also becoming less solid in its backing of protection measures. Wang Yung-ch'ing, the head Formosa Plastics, for example, had actively supported protection measures in the early 1970s. By 1986 he was a supporter of trade liberalization in part because he recognized that, if Taiwan were to continue to have access to the U.S. market, Americans were going to insist on access to the Taiwan market.[42] It was also the case, as pointed out in the discussion of the promotion of new technology-intensive industries, that established industries were coming to realize that targeted subsidies for industries on new frontiers weren't necessarily going to help them, and might actually even work against their interests.

By 1986, therefore, powerful interests were behind the liberalization move, although there were still many advocates of protectionism. The increasing dominance of the more liberal-minded exporting sectors and the economists who helped articulate a liberalization strategy combined with external pressures, mainly from the United States, to bring about significant changes in the conduct of Taiwan's industrial policy.

It was no coincidence that many of the kinds of pressures were act-ing to change South Korea's interventionist industrial policies at much the same time. Internal and external influences were combining to push South Korea in the direction of economic liberalization. The actors and the issues were not identical to those in Taiwan. In South Korea, small- and medium-scale producers, and their increasingly vocal po-litical representatives, particularly resented the favors done for the large *chaebol* conglomerates in the name of industrial policy. South Korea also was not running a chronic balance-of-trade surplus, although that fact does not appear to have reduced U.S. liberalizing pressures on that country by much. In South Korea, as in Taiwan, key U.S.-trained econo-mists played a key role in articulating the new policy direction, although the South Korean economists did this mainly from inside the govern-ment, whereas Taiwan's economists mainly worked from outside the government.[43]

ECONOMIC LIBERALIZATION MEASURES

As part of the liberalization effort, there is no question that by the latter half of the 1980s Taiwan's government had begun to eliminate many of the restrictions on imports and foreign direct investment that had been important components of the country's interventionist industrial policy.

TABLE 3 - 4

International Comparisons of Distribution of Tariffs on Industrial Products (in percentages)

Tariff Rate	Taiwan (1988)	USA[a]	EEC[a]	Japan[a]
Free	8.7	31.1	37.9	56.3
0.5–5.0	20.6	44.1	19.0	25.2
5.1–10.0	33.0	17.1	32.5	14.6
10.1–15.0	22.7	1.9	9.1	2.9
15.1–20.0	9.6	2.2	1.3	0.8
20.1–25.0	3.8	0.8	0.2	0.1
Over 25.0	1.6	2.8	0.0	0.1

Sources: The original data are from studies by B. Balassa and C. Balassa and by Chaw-hsia Tu and Wen-thuen Wang as reported and compiled by James Riedel in *Taiwan: From Developing to Mature Economy*, (1992, p. 296).

[a] These figures are for the early 1980s.

Tariff rates were still higher than those in the United States, Europe, and Japan (see Table 3-4), but the average tariff rate had fallen to around 6 percent by the late 1980s and under 5 percent by the early 1990s.

Of equal or greater importance, the remaining nontariff barriers were gradually dismantled. Import procedures for steel products were simplified, for example, and local content requirements for VCRs and color televisions were eliminated.[44]

Toward a Service Economy

From the latter half of the 1980s into the first half of the 1990s, as the previous discussion makes clear, Taiwan's industrial sector successfully made the transition from a sector based on low-wage products to one based on increasingly high level technology and knowledge. Exports, which were mostly manufactures, also made the transition to reliance on capital and technology-intensive products, and overall exports continued to grow in real terms despite the revaluation of the NT dollar. The pace of export growth in real terms, however, was significantly slower in the 1991 through 1998 period than it had been over the previous decade (the quantum index of exports grew by 5.6 percent per year from 1991 through 1998 as compared with 10.6 percent per year in the 1981 through 1990 decade).

What became apparent only gradually to observers in and out of Taiwan was that Taiwan was not only making the transition to technology- and capital-intensive industries, but Taiwan was also making a transition away from an industry-based economy to an economy increasingly based on services. From 1985, when the service sector accounted for 47.6 percent of GDP to 1998, the share of the service sector rose steadily, reaching 63.1 percent in 1998. The share of industry in general and manufacturing in particular, as a share of GDP, declined by an equivalent percentage. Put differently, GDP in the eight years beginning in 1988 averaged a still quite rapid rate of growth of 6.8 percent per year. Manufacturing during this same period, however, grew by only 4.0 percent annually, although this rate of growth picked up slightly in 1996 and 1997 before slowing again in 1998 with the impact of the Asian financial crisis. Manufacturing was no longer the engine of growth pulling the rest of the economy along. Agriculture, of course, had long since ceased to play a leading role and grew at only 0.8 percent annually over the ten years beginning in 1988. It was the service sector that was carrying the economy, and within services it was finance and business services plus commerce that led the way. These latter two sectors grew over the 1988 through 1995 period at 12.0 percent a year, substantially faster than GDP as a whole.

At one level there is nothing particularly remarkable about the rising role of the service sector in Taiwan. Taiwan was simply following along the same path of structural transformation blazed by numerous European and North American countries in previous decades. By the early 1990s, the share of services in the GDP of these already industrialized countries was generally above 60 percent. The one G7 industrialized country whose service sector was still below 60 percent was Japan. The major difference between Taiwan and the already-industrialized world was that Taiwan was making this transition at a lower per capita income than had occurred elsewhere.

There is more to the shift toward a service-based economy, however, than simply the rising quantitative share of services in GDP. There is also a question of quality—the kind of service sector that was being created. In the context of the debates in Taiwan discussed in this chapter, a fundamental question is whether Taiwan's business and financial services at the end of the millenium were developing along protected mercantilist lines, as was the case with manufacturing prior to the late 1980s, or developing in the context of an open economy freely facing the forces of international competition, as was the case with Taiwan manufacturing in the 1990s.

The choices facing the Taiwan modern service sector in the 1980s and 1990s can be better understood if the situation with respect to these Taiwan sectors is compared with the two quite different models existing elsewhere in East Asia of how a service sector might evolve. One model is that of Hong Kong and Singapore. Both of these economies, but particularly Hong Kong, have become primarily service based. The service sector of Hong Kong by 1993 already accounted for 79 percent of the territory's GDP (the figure for Singapore was 63 percent in the same year). More importantly, Hong Kong and Singapore had established themselves as the commercial and financial centers for the entire East and Southeast Asian region except for Japan and Korea. Even Taiwan itself was dependent on Hong Kong for many commercial and financial transactions, notably those involving the Chinese mainland. There is no mystery as to how Hong Kong and Singapore rose to this central position in the region. Both had built up a considerable commercial and port infrastructure under British colonial administration both before and immediately after the Second World War. Beginning in the 1950s and accelerating in the 1960s and thereafter, the dominant force behind this development became the local Chinese community with its network of ties throughout the Asian region. Early on, both the British colonial government and the independent Singapore government made a decision that their economies would remain open to all comers not only for trade and manufacturing, but for all manner of services as well. Increasingly these two island economies became the corporate headquarters for multinationals from all over the world. Resident visas were easily obtained. Land could be freely bought or leased. Communications of all kinds were fully developed and efficient. Most imports came in duty free. There were no requirements about the number of local people who must be hired or how much of the content of whatever was produced had to come from domestic sources. Money in whatever form was moved in and out by pushing a few electronic buttons, whatever the amount or whatever the purpose. The banks that survived in this environment did so because they were good managers of their resources, not because they could count on government to bail them out if they got into trouble. One could go on in this vein, but the point is a simple one. Hong Kong and Singapore became major regional commercial and financial centers because they started with a strong foundation and then built on that foundation by relying on free and open competition from whoever wanted to participate.

The alternative model was that of Japan, although Japan itself was moving slowly away from this model by the late 1990s. Japan's international trading firms were formidable competitors, but for much of the post-war era, Japanese commerce was for Japanese only. The domestic commercial sector in particular was almost completely closed to foreign competition until the 1990s. More importantly, that sector was extremely inefficient, with very high markups on consumer products by the time they actually reached the consumer. Japanese banks were among the largest banks in the world with huge assets, but many had trouble in the 1990s meeting the minimum capital requirements needed to be considered safely solvent. Until the late 1990s, it had always been understood implicitly that the government would never let a major bank go under. Japanese banks and financial institutions in general seldom faced much foreign competition on their home field. Numerous other restrictions inhibited foreigners from setting up service businesses such as law firms, buying land, or bringing in large numbers of foreign employees. Japan was by any standard a formidable manufacturing giant, and the world also turned to Japan as a major source of capital. Few foreigners, however, turned to Japanese institutions for other banking and financial services, for commercial and legal services, for computer software, for higher education, or for much else in the service sector. Japan's service sector was largely run by and for Japanese, but, unlike the manufacturing sector, the service sector didn't always serve its Japanese constituents very well either.

Where did Taiwan's 1980s and 1990s modern service sector stand in comparison with these two models? On the positive side, there were some parts of Taiwan's service sector that could clearly compete internationally. Taiwan, for example, was no longer just a supplier of components to be marketed by others under their brand names. Brands such as Acer or Datung were becoming increasingly well known around the world. More importantly, as Taiwan lost its labor-intensive manufactured products to the Chinese mainland and Southeast Asia, Taiwan retained the high value added marketing and design service components of those products. Taiwan was also becoming a competitive center for high-technology software. The software component of Taiwan's information technology sector was still small relative to the hardware component (US$2 billion in 1996 versus US$25 billion for hardware if offshore manufacturing is included), but the software component was growing at over 20 percent per year.[45]

To find the negative side, one does not have to look much further than Taiwan's banking, insurance, and other financial sectors.[46] The continued dominance of state-owned banks went together with continued government controls restricting the use of many financial instruments that were commonplace in the advanced industrial countries of the world and in Hong Kong. Right through into the 1980s, Taiwan's banking system was dominated by procedures not unlike those one might expect from a government bureaucracy. Interest rates were controlled, although they were kept at positive levels unlike the controlled interest rates in many other countries. Loans were made on the basis of collateral, and government directed loans to favored sectors—state-owned enterprises and exporters in particular. Other firms, particularly the newer and smaller firms, had to go to the informal credit market to obtain the capital that they needed. Taiwan's financial sector may have been less repressed than that of South Korea, but it was behind even Japan in this respect, let alone Hong Kong. The change in the banking law in 1989 was a major step away from this repressed system, and by 1992, sixteen new banks had been created, most associated with large business groups. These new banks had the potential to bring formidable competitive pressures to bear on the older banks. Taiwan's central bank, however, remained cautious about revisions in prudential regulations, so liberalization did not proceed as fast as it might have. Whether this caution also prevented the kinds of excesses sometimes found elsewhere in the course of rapid financial deregulation is a question that will have to await further analysis.[47] Taiwan did avoid the financial meltdown experienced by a number of other Asian economies in 1997 through 1998, but this had more to do with Taiwan's huge foreign exchange reserves and its large current account surplus than it did to any inherent strength of its financial system.

The controls over the banking sector were not the only evidence of limits on the development of Taiwan's financial sector. The insurance industry was even less developed. The law allowing foreign insurance companies in general to operate in Taiwan was not passed until 1994.[48] U.S. insurance firms, under great pressure from the U.S. government, were let in a few years earlier. The bond market was also underdeveloped, with government and corporate bonds accounting for only 7 percent of the total loans and discounts of financial institutions. The stock market was underdeveloped as well. As late as 1989, there were only 167 companies listed on the Taiwan Stock Exchange. Through the 1980s and into the early 1990s it is more appropriate to say that Taiwan's industrial sector grew in spite of the underdeveloped financial sector rather than because of it.[49]

Part of the motivation behind the increasingly rapid liberalization of the service sector was Taiwan's desire to become a member of the General Agreement on Tariffs and Trade (GATT) and then the World Trade Organization (WTO). Much new legislation was passed designed to ease the restrictions on foreign participation in Taiwan's economy, although these changes fell short of full national treatment for foreigners. Foreigners were allowed to invest in existing banks and in foreign exchange brokerage firms. Foreign credit cards circulated worldwide could be issued in Taiwan. The guidelines that restricted foreign securities firms from establishing branches in Taiwan were abolished, and numerous other guidelines or laws of this sort were either revised in a liberalizing direction or eliminated.

In a system with a substantial degree of discretion in the hands of the government bureaucracy, however, changes in laws and guidelines are not always as liberalizing as they appear to be on the surface. Even when the intent of the legislation is clear, the government bureaucracy is often in a position to thwart change and frequently has the incentive to do precisely that. Most of the relevant legislation has been passed in the 1990s, and in many areas it is simply too early to tell how large an impact the changes will have.

By the end of the 1990s, therefore, Taiwan's service sector was going through a process not unlike the process the manufacturing sector went through in the 1980s. The sector was being opened up to foreign competition in part because of external pressure, but this was occurring not just because that was the only way to avoid foreign sanctions but also because leaders of the economy on Taiwan recognized that a liberal market economy was something Taiwan needed for its own sake. Although the overall direction was clear, however, there were still barriers to the realization of a fully open system. One such barrier was the presence of vested interests on Taiwan, and these could point to the Asian financial crisis of 1997 to 1998 as evidence that full liberalization or "globalization" was fraught with danger.

Another barrier was the continued existence of tense political relations with the Chinese mainland. Political difficulties with the Chinese mainland were important because many of the benefits of full liberalization of Taiwan's economic system, particularly its service sector, depended in part on Taiwan becoming a major center of high value added service activities. These service activities, however, depended on being able to maintain close ties with related manufacturing activities, many of which were on the Chinese mainland as well as in Southeast Asia. This effort to turn Taiwan into a service center for the rest of Asia has even acquired a name—its advocates speak of Taiwan becoming a "Regional Operations Center" for all of Asia. Whether or not such a concept will become a reality will depend in large part on whether Taiwan can complete the opening of the service sector and establish the international competitiveness of that sector. With respect to manufacturing, this process at the beginning of the new millennium was largely completed. With respect to the service sector, the process was still in the beginning stages.

Notes

1   Kuo, Ranis, and Fei (1981, pp. 20–21).

2   Hsu (1995).

3   Wang (1993, pp. 219).

4   Li (1976, pp. 125–141).

5 Li (1976, p. 219–221).

6 *Economic Daily News,* November 29, 1976.

7 *Economic Daily News,* February 23, 1978.

8 Ibid.

9 *Industrial and Commercial Times* (Kung-shang shih-pao), June 14, 1980.

10 This slogan began to appear with increasing regularity, but it did not come from a specific document or source.

11 *Economic Daily News,* March 18, 1978.

12 Li (1976, p. 222).

13 These objectives were stated when the Science and Technology Development Program was promulgated.

14 K. T. Li, Oral History, p. 227.

15 Interview.

16 Interview.

17 Interview.

18 The government does report figures on the number of students studying abroad and those who have returned, but these figures are incomplete, particularly after July 1989 when only those on government scholarship, a tiny fraction of the total, were included in the totals.

19 Song Ha-joong, 1991, "Who Stays? Who Returns? The Choices of Korean Scientists and Engineers," Cambridge: unpublished doctoral dissertation, Harvard University.

20 Science-based Industrial Park, *Statistics Quarterly,* June 1994.

21 Interview.

22 Interview.

23 See, for example, the lively debate between the head of Formosa Plastics, the president of ACER, and the general secretary of the textile association reported in the *Industrial and Commercial Times,* April 24, 1982.

24 To deflate R and D expenditures, one would need a price index made up of the changes in wages and salaries of research personnel plus a price index for research materials and equipment. Neither is available. The real increase referred to here assumes that R and D salaries and other R and D–related prices rose at a rate similar to the rise in the general wage index.

25 Chiang (1985, pp. 262–283).

26 Chiang (1985, pp. 263–267).

27 *Economic Daily News,* July 11, 1978.

28 *Economic Daily News,* March 4, 1980.

29 *Economic Daily News,* August 14, 1981.

30 The debate was headline news and widely reported by the newspapers at the time. A transcription of the debate and a number of related works were later collected and published by the Industrial and Commercial Times (Kung-shang shih-pao, editor), *Ts'ai-ching cheng-ts'e ta byan lun: Taiwan ching-chi wen-t'i yü tui ts'e t'ao-lun-hui shih-lu* (*The Great Debate on Financial and Economic Policy: A Record of the Discussion Meeting on Taiwan Economic Issues and Policies*) (Taipei: Times Publishers, 1982).

31 Economic Research Department of the Economic Construction Council (1984, pp. 69–70), and *Economic Daily News,* August 9, 1983.

32 Economic Research and Development of the Economic Construction Council (1984, pp. 73–75), and *Economic Daily News,* April 11, 1984.

33 See, for example, the remarks of Dr. Yu Tsong-hsien at a symposium held by the *Economic Daily News* on April 5, 1984.

34 "Economic Policy and Economic Growth: Yu Kuo-hua's Response to News Reporters' Interviews," *Economic Daily News,* May 26, 1984.

35 Interview.

36 For example, the *China Times,* on December 12, 1984, in an editorial entitled "Liberalization should not be paper work," accused the Agricultural Council of continuing efforts to limit imports of agricultural goods.

37 *United News,* November 7, 1984.

38 Interview.

39 This case started in February, 1985, and lasted for a year, until the completion of the government bailout in January, 1986. During this period, the Economic Minister and Finance Minister were forced to step down.

40 Chiang Nan was a Chinese American who was the author of the unauthorized biography of Chiang Ching-kuo. He was murdered in October 1984.

41 For the reaction to this paper, see, for example, the editorial, "We Support the Five Scholars' Policy Suggestion of Carrying Out Thoroughly Liberalization," *Industrial and Commercial Times,* September 14, 1986.

42 Wang Yung-ch'ing, "How Should We Go Our Own Way?" *Industrial and Commercial Times,* September 1 and 2, 1986.

43 Stern, Kim, Perkins, and Yoo (1995).

44 Riedel (1992, p. 296)

45 These figures are from The Institute for Information Industry, "An Overview of the IT Industry in Taiwan," (unpublished tables).

46 A revision in the banking law in 1989 was followed in 1991 with the establishment of sixteen new private banks that brought considerable competitive pressure to bear on the established banks. Hsueh, Tu, and Wang (1995, p. 147).

47 For a discussion of these issues, see Shieh (1966, p. 9).

48 Technically Taiwan allowed U.S. insurance companies to operate in Taiwan beginning in 1981, but they were allowed only to service the insurance needs of Americans on the island. In 1986 and 1987, under considerable pressure from the United States, these U.S. companies were allowed to broaden out into more general insurance activities. See Hsueh , Tu, and Wang (1995, pp. 153–156).

49 This discussion of the financial sector is based on Shea and Yang (1994, pp. 193–230); Yang (1994, pp. 288–324); and Patrick (1994, pp. 325–371).

4 THE ORGANIZATION OF PRIVATE AND PUBLIC ENTERPRISES

How did industrial firms, private and public, respond to the government policy changes and to the macroeconomic environment described in the previous two chapters? Some evidence of the nature of this response has already been presented, but a clearer portrait of the way Taiwan's modern economic sectors were organized is needed.

As in most developing countries, in Taiwan there were structural features of the economy that inhibited the free flow of goods and services between firms and between sectors. It was not just government policy that departed from some laissez-faire ideal. The firms that produced the goods and services also fell well short of the perfect market model. These imperfections had an important impact on how firms behaved in the face of various incentives and shocks. Some of these structures have eroded over time, but none have completely disappeared.

In its early development, there was a clear dual structure to the modern sectors of Taiwan's economy. Elements of that duality lasted, although in steadily weakening form, into the 1990s. There were several dimensions to this duality. To start with, there was the division between private and public enterprises. Taiwan's public sector enterprises dominated the economy in the 1950s, but the private sector dominated the economic growth story thereafter. The role of public enterprises remained an important one even in the 1990s, however. Although the decision was made to privatize most of these public enterprises in the 1990s, the actual process of privatization even at that late date was a slow one.

The duality between private and public enterprises also largely coincided with the division between large-scale import-substituting heavy industry and smaller-scale export-oriented light industry. The export industries were completely dominated by the private sector. Public ownership, however, dominated much of heavy industry, particularly in the early years, but to some degree into the 1990s as well. State-owned firms dominated steel, shipbuilding, petroleum, and petrochemicals. These sectors were mostly oriented toward import substitution, that is, toward replacing imports of key inputs with domestic sources of supply. It would not be much of an overstatement to say that, prior to the 1980s, any sector that enjoyed substantial economies of scale was in public hands.

Much smaller firms, in contrast, dominated the private modern enterprise sector, and a large number of these firms were export-oriented. Although not all private firms were export oriented, by the 1970s and 1980s the great majority of all exports came from the private sector. Most commercial wholesale and retail establishments were also in private hands.

The financial system, in contrast, was underdeveloped and largely in public hands. Commercial banks were by far the main holders of deposits and dispensers of loans, and of the sixteen locally incorporated banks prior to the 1990s, thirteen were either wholly owned or majority owned by the government. There were no independent savings banks, the insurance sector was weak, and the access of local branches of foreign banks to local currency deposits and loans was severely limited. The postal savings system, although the holder of large individual deposits, was not allowed to make loans.[1] The public sector had considerably easier access to this organized financial system than did the private sector. Private firms regularly had to resort to the informal credit market characterized by inter-firm loans, often in the form of postdated checks.

The final duality was that leadership of the private sector enterprises was mainly in the hands of individuals born in Taiwan when Taiwan was under Japanese colonial rule. In contrast, it was mainly Chinese mainlanders, many of whom also played leading roles in the government, who led public sector industrial firms. In Chinese societies, where personal relationships often count for much more in business than legal contractual arrangements, distinctions such as this matter. In the decades immediately after 1949, relations between those born on the mainland and those born on Taiwan were not close.

For many countries, these kinds of duality have often stifled the economy. The public sector, dominated by a privileged minority, has often exploited the system for personal gain. The private sector, in this situation, is seen as a source of funds to be milked through high prices for services provided by public enterprise. That has not, however, been Taiwan's experience. Despite the various kinds of duality that clearly existed, and although some sectors fared better than others, Taiwan's modern economy functioned well.

The Rise of Private Industry

The real story of Taiwan's industrialization, as the previous two chapters made clear, lies with the export of manufactures, and the firms that did the exporting were overwhelmingly private except during the 1950s when exports were dominated by sugar and rice. After 1960, exports were made up first of light consumer manufactures such as textiles and shoes, and later increasingly of consumer electronic products. By the 1990s, high-technology electronic products, many produced in the Hsinchu Science-based Industrial Park, were playing a larger and larger role. These exporting sectors had virtually no state-owned firms at all. State-owned firms largely stuck to import substitution.

This modern private sector started from modest origins in the early 1950s. In 1951 there were only 1,035 incorporated firms in Taiwan, of which 257 were in manufacturing (see Table 4-1). Most were in commerce and transport, and all were extremely small. The average registered capital per firm was NT$1.2 million, or about US$80,000 at the then prevailing exchange rate (see Table 4-2). Total registered capital of all incorporated firms taken together was, therefore, under US$100 million. By 1961, the total had risen to only US$300 million and the total number of firms to 5,760, of which 2,213 were in manufacturing. The average paid-up capital per firm, however, actually declined to US$50,000 (NT$2.15 million).[2]

Among these small numbers, a few are worth special mention. The four groups of firms described in Chapter 2 that were taken over from the Japanese by the state after 1945 and then privatized to Taiwan's former landlords formed one foundation on which large enterprises were later built. Although Taiwan Cement was the only one of the four groups to become a large conglomerate, components of the other three helped a number of former landlords to get started in business.

Another important group of enterprises was in the textile sector. Shanghai had developed a large textile sector by the 1930s. After 1949, many of these firms packed up their machinery and their key workers and moved to Hong Kong or Taiwan. The ten firms that came from

TABLE 4-1
The Number of Registered Incorporated Firms

Year	Total[a]	Agriculture, Forestry, Fishing, & Animal Husbandry	Mining & Quarrying	Manufacturing	Electricity, Gas, & Water	Construction	Commerce	Transport & Storage	Financing, Insurance, Real Estate, & Business Services	Personal Service & Others
1951	1,035	120	25	257	NA[b]	NA[b]	411	164	NA[b]	58
1956	2,249 (16.8)	126	51	971	6	74	549	304	28	140
1961	5,760 (20.7)	281	145	2,231	3	253	1,934	493	117	321
1966	18,696 (26.6)	744	312	7,569	44	938	6,245	1,411	267	1,166
1971	59,909 (26.2)	1,816	744	20,991	6,479	2,783	19,996	3,208	430	3,462
1976	143,776 (19.1)	2,874	1,510	52,008	5,394	6,819	61,140	4,868	2,557	6,534
1981	270,878 (13.5)	3,875	2,176	90,534	7,039	13,226	127,488	7,259	3,283	15,998
1986	280,692 (0.7)	2,831	1,726	105,870	195	16,141	125,162	9,509	13,805	5,453
1991	394,512 (7.0)	3,187	1,922	146,063	199	24,891	168,946	12,269	29,266	7,769
1992	426,538 (4.0)	3,103	2,014	152,487	246	28,270	181,654	12,585	37,836	8,343

Source: *Economic Statistics Annual Taiwan Area, the Republic of China*, Department of Statistics, Ministry of Economic Affairs, various years.

Note: The growth rate drastically dropped in 1986 because licenses of those companies without an operation record were revoked during a company registration updating survey held in 1986.

[a] Numbers in parentheses indicate five-year average growth rates (%).

[b] NA indicates data not available.

TABLE 4-2
Total Registered Capital of Incorporated Firms (million NT$)

Year	Total[a]	Agriculture, Forestry, Fishing, & Animal Husbandry	Mining & Quarrying	Manufact- uring	Electricity, Gas, & Water	Con- struction	Commerce	Transport & Storage	Financing, Insurance, Real Estate, & Business Services	Personal Service & Others
1951	1,277	672	101	168	NA[b]	NA[b]	304	67	NA[b]	9
1956	6,353 (37.8)	101	347	5,040	293	23	168	322	9	51
1961	12,370 (14.3)	513	528	7,582	2,005	90	945	400	173	133
1966	30,738 (20.0)	1,393	1,057	18,541	2,027	617	3,973	1,769	316	1,045
1971	106,576 (28.2)	3,987	2,794	60,721	3,855	3,276	16,133	9,260	603	5,946
1976	369,634 (28.2)	10,113	6,934	197,995	9,161	24,844	71,917	23,111	8,984	16,575
1981	804,753 (16.8)	15,768	9,595	360,645	18,574	73,311	212,122	43,748	21,044	49,946
1986	1,660,644 (15.6)	25,081	35,143	796,301	123,748	82,631	306,279	86,707	183,282	21,472
1991	4,240,188 (20.6)	51,807	44,065	1,804,024	207,569	182,578	806,501	184,022	891,387	68,235
1992	4,921,945 (7.7)	55,101	56,677	1,945,748	208,221	220,701	824,967	202,274	1,232,532	75,724

Source: Economic Statistics Annual Taiwan Area, The Republic of China, Department of Statistics, Ministry of Economic Affairs, various years.

[a] Numbers in parentheses indicate five-year average growth rates.

[b] NA indicates data not available.

Shanghai to Taiwan formed the basis for most of the textile industry development in the 1950s, a development based primarily on Taiwan's domestic market.[3] Several of these firms went on to become major exporters, and in a few cases—notably the Far Eastern Group, the Tun Tex Group, and Tainan Spinning—to become large diversified conglomerates.

The Taiwan government and the USAID program also played a role in helping new industries to develop and old firms to expand. The government most of all provided tariff protection for a wide range of consumer industries. USAID provided significant amounts of capital to about 400 firms in the 1952 to 1958 period, accounting on average for 23.7 percent of all the capital these firms received.[4] Most of Taiwan's larger, but still mainly small firms, benefited from this program at a time when domestic sources of capital were extremely tight. Most of the private firms, however, were small Taiwanese-owned trading firms and cottage industries. By the mid-1950s, there were approximately 200,000 employees in all of private industry and the average number of employees per firm, including more than 10,000 unincorporated firms, was around ten.[5] By the latter half of the 1950s, this number was no longer growing, as incentives encouraged enterprises to import labor-saving machinery and equipment.

The changes in policy in the 1958 to 1960 period that led to the export orientation and rapid growth of Taiwan's industry were described at length in Chapter 2. By 1986, there were 280,692 registered incorporated firms, of which 105,870 were in manufacturing. By 1992, these figures had increased to 426,538 and 152,487 firms respectively. These firms were still quite small, however. In U.S. dollar terms, their registered capital averaged only US$170 thousand per firm in 1986 and US$450 thousand per firm in 1992. When inflation is taken into account, these per-firm figures are little if any larger than the per-firm figures of the 1950s. In aggregate terms, of course, the registered capital of Taiwan's incorporated enterprises was hundreds of times larger than in the 1950s even if the figures are deflated by an appropriate price index.

The small size of Taiwan's incorporated firms in general and manufacturing enterprises in particular has been noted by many authors. It is accepted as one of the most distinguishing features of Taiwan's industrial organization structure and is often seen as the source of Taiwan's industrial strength, but it is also a potential source of future weakness.

The small size of Taiwan's firms would seem to imply that Taiwan's industry was less concentrated and hence more competitive than industry elsewhere. One major study of industrial concentration in Taiwan, however, suggests that the degree of concentration sector by sector in Taiwan in 1976 was very similar to that found in the United States, although less concentrated than in France or Britain.[6] Comparisons between Taiwan, a relatively small developing country, and several large, fully industrialized nations, however, can be misleading. Small countries in the early stages of industrial development are likely to have higher concentration ratios, particularly in sectors where there are substantial economies of scale. A single steel plant, for example, will be able to produce enough to supply easily the entire domestic market in a country at the level of the requirements of Taiwan or South Korea of the 1970s. Using similar reasoning, a very large developing country will tend to have a lower level of industrial concentration than a small developing country.

Information on concentration ratios in developing countries is regrettably scarce, so systematic comparisons between Taiwan and these other developing countries would require a lengthy separate study. We do know that in South Korea in 1975, the five largest conglomerates (*chaebol*) accounted for 15 percent of all manufacturing, and the forty-six largest *chaebol* accounted for 37 percent.[7] We do not have comparable value-added figures for Taiwan businesses, but we do have total sales or operating revenues. In 1980, the five largest Taiwanese manufacturing firms had sales of US$68.5 billion, which was roughly 3 percent of all operating revenues in manufacturing in that year. The top forty-six firms accounted for 10 percent of all revenues. In 1992, the percentage of total sales accounted for by the largest five and the largest forty-six firms were 3.5 percent and 13 percent respectively.[8] These figures would appear to confirm the view that Taiwan manufacturing was markedly less concentrated than that in South Korea. The shares in manufacturing of the largest firms in India and Pakistan were even larger than those shares in Korea.[9]

Individual industry studies further back up the small-scale nature of Taiwan's industry. In footwear in the 1980s, for example, both Taiwan and South Korea had footwear exports of US$1.5 to 2.0 billion per year, but these exports were produced by 83 firms in Korea and 1,140 firms in Taiwan.[10]

THE STRUCTURE OF SMALL AND MEDIUM ENTERPRISES

Although there is no real question, therefore, that Taiwan's industrial organization was based on small firms and low levels of industrial concentration, Taiwan firms did not entirely fit the textbook definition of firms in an atomized competitive market. The textbook ideal of a firm is an independent unit that buys inputs from an impersonal market and sells its output on an equally impersonal market. Most of what a firm's management knows about the world outside of its own factory, and all it really needs to know, is what is happening to the prices of its inputs and outputs. Imperfect competition modifies this picture somewhat even in the textbooks, and managers, in addition to knowing output prices, require advertising and other marketing devices to sell their product to the mass of consumers. If an industry has only a few firms, managers also have to be concerned about how their immediate competitors would respond to particular moves on their part or vice versa. Collusion between the management of firms could alter this decision-making process, but anti-monopoly laws exist to prevent such collusion. Even in an oligopolistic industry, therefore, firms are quite independent of each other and their behavior reflects that independence.

Taiwan's firms do not fit easily into this model of impersonal competition in response to market forces. Taiwan's society, like that of Chinese societies elsewhere, is based first and foremost on a network of personal relationships. The family provides the closest and most important relationships, but family can be defined to include distant cousins. Relationships with school classmates and with people who come from the same part of the country can also take on some of the characteristics of family ties.

There are many reasons why personal relationships (*kuan-hsi*) play such a large role in Chinese societies, but one of these reasons is economic. The rule of law has never played a very important role in Chinese societies either in the political or the economic sphere. If you had good rulers, the saying went, you didn't really need good laws. But Chinese societies, like many others, often were not governed by good rulers. People, including businessmen, often needed protection against the ruler. Equally important, they needed a secure environment in which promises to deliver goods at a particular price or to repay loans would be kept. Personal ties based on long-standing relationships were what provided the necessary foundations of trust required by any economic system that has risen above the level of subsistence agriculture. Throughout Chinese history, courts of law have seldom provided a practical alternative to this need for trust. Ending up in court was most often seen as a situation where the politically powerful would use the manipulation of the rudimentary legal system to ruin their opponents.

As Taiwan has developed, a system based more and more on formal laws and published procedures has gradually evolved, but even in the 1990s that system bore only a vague relationship to the court- and lawyer-based rule-of-law systems of North America or Western Europe. In a wide variety of economic situations, a strong set of personal relationships still counted for more than a strong legal system and formal contracts.

The relevance of this point about personal relationships is that Taiwan's industrial enterprises were not really fully independent firms in the textbook sense. Nor were they simply bureaus or departments of some large corporation. They were enterprises in a complex set of relationships with other enterprises in the same industry.

Taiwan's industrial organization structure, particularly with respect to the hundreds of thousands of small- and medium-scale firms, can be seen as a kind of pyramid. At the base of the pyramid were a large number of family firms employing fewer than ten people. Typically they were involved in one step of the production process and utilized relatively simple technologies. Management consisted of the firm's owner with occasional help from one or another member of the family. The next step up the pyramid consisted of firms employing ten to thirty people. These firms might produce more than a single component of a larger product and typically had a management structure that consisted of more than simply the owner.

Small and medium firms with thirty to one hundred employees often could produce final products, they had more complex management structures, and they could be passively but directly involved in exporting channels.

Finally, at the top of the pyramid were medium- to large-scale firms, employing more than one hundred people. These firms could produce final products, and had financial as well as production management capacity. Most importantly, they had the capacity to deal directly with foreign buyers.

The small family firms could not survive by themselves. They existed within a network of subcontracting relationships woven between the different sizes of firms. Medium- to large-scale firms played the central role in this net. They got the orders from foreign buyers, and subcontracted these jobs down through the pyramid. These central firms could be either a manufacturing firm, or a trading firm. In the former case, subcontractors usually performed a single step of processing or produced individual parts, and the parent company assembled them into a final product. The relationship between firms in this case was a vertical one. In the latter case, trading firms specialized in getting orders and subcontractors specialized in production. Each parent company might have hundreds of small family firms working for it.

According to extensive interviews carried out in small firms in several industries by Chen Chieh-hsuan and his colleagues, subcontracting within these networks in Taiwan was of two types: internal subcontracting and external subcontracting.[11] In internal subcontracting, the parent company provided space in the plant, and also provided materials and supplies; subcontractors provided machines and workers. The subcontractor was like an independent boss of a production line within a factory. By subcontracting, the parent company could reduce some fixed costs, avoid the threat of labor shortage, and better control deadlines and the quality of the product relative to external subcontracting. In the external subcontracting case, subcontractors had their own plant site. They were more independent than the internal subcontractors and they usually worked for several parent companies at the same time. The parent company sometimes did and sometimes did not provide materials for the external subcontractors. In prosperous times, subcontractors were often willing to assume more risks in order to gain more profits by providing the materials themselves. In periods of economic recession, materials provided by the parent companies was the more prevalent practice.

In addition, different sizes of firms could also cooperate horizontally. They might work together to produce a part or a product. They could also cooperate to fulfill a big order, and cooperation of this sort was seen quite often between small/medium- and medium-scale firms. When one company received an order that exceeded its capacity, it subcontracted part of that order to other firms in the same business. This subcontracting relationship could be reversed when the next order came to another firm in the group.

The advantage of this network system was that it could pool the limited resources of each firm to accomplish large production and export tasks. The individual firm might appear weak, but the whole network of small- and medium-scale firms was stable. It was also dynamic. The combination of firms could be changed quickly in response to external demands. Profit motives and personal relationships both played important roles in maintaining the network. The successful central firm needed to be able to get export orders continuously, however. As long as there were enough orders to ensure the profits of subcontractors, subcontractors were willing to do their best—that is, to work overtime, to learn new techniques, to improve quality, and to meet urgent deadlines of the parent company. Into the early 1980s, this need for continuous orders did not present a problem in the light-industry sectors where these practices prevailed because export orders grew rapidly. After 1987, however, exports and production in many of these sectors began to decline.

Besides maintaining and expanding export channels, the central firm also played a role of coordination, quality control, and dissemination of new information and technology. The subcontractors in their turn willingly cooperated and, as surveys have shown, worked extremely hard for very long hours. Most of the heads of these subcontracting firms were former blue-collar technical workers in other factories, the "black-hand bosses." They started up their businesses using the technology they had learned and one or two machines that they purchased. Often they were subcontractors of the firms they originally worked for.[12]

Taiwan Li-Wei Machinery Corporation provides a good example of the networking relationship between firms. Li-Wei was established in 1980, with seven employees and US$8 million in capital. By 1995, after fifteen years of hard work, it had 600 employees, US$524 million in capital, and US$2.3 billion in revenue.

Li-Wei originated as a trading company. When it began, it specialized in designing and assembling final products, and contracted out the production of parts and components of its machines to twenty to thirty satellite firms. In this way, Li-Wei minimized the use of its own resources and achieved a large volume of business. When Li-Wei grew, the number of satellite firms increased to around 150, and some of these satellite firms also grew substantially in size along with Li-Wei. Their relationship was maintained and strengthened through business ties as well as through personal friendship. Except in special cases that required strict specifications or delivery date, no formal contracts were necessary.

Li-Wei and fifty or so major contractors held weekly meetings to discuss issues such as the production schedule, quality control, and so on. Their interactions in the technical field were very close, and equipment could be shared among contractors. Financially, however, each firm was independent. Usually, contractors had to pay the cost of materials and wages with their own funds, and they collected money from Li-Wei six months after they delivered their products. Li-Wei rewarded good satellite firms by giving them bigger orders and a shorter turn-around period for payment.

As Li-Wei's sales volume grew, in order to control better and to upgrade its production, the company gradually increased its own production capability. For those parts requiring higher technology, strict delivery dates, and so on, Li-Wei decreased the portion contracted out. In contrast to the 100 percent outside contracting in the early 1980s, by the 1990s Li-Wei contracted out only around 25 percent of its production to satellite firms.[13]

"Relationship" Enterprises

The central firms cooperated not only with their subcontractors, but they also often cooperated actively with each other. This latter kind of cooperation could take two quite different forms.

One form of cooperation was the industrial association. Each of the major exporting sectors had its own association, and most central firms in the industry were members. As in the case of industrial associations elsewhere in the world, one function of these associations was to lobby the government for support of one kind or another. These associations also carried out functions that in other countries have been managed by the government or by individual private firms (especially large firms) on their own. The Taiwan Textile Federation established in 1975, for example, was initially concerned mainly with managing textile export quotas, negotiating price agreements between upstream and downstream producers, and fending off foreign accusations of dumping by the industry. As emphasis within the textile industry shifted toward upgrading the quality of the industry's product, however, the federation, together with the government, helped promote research and fabric design that would then be shared industry wide.[14]

Another good example is provided by the Taiwan Electrical Appliances Manufacturer's Association (TEAMA). It is the sole representative of the industry and served as an instrument of government–industry collaboration. The government delegated to TEAMA the power to issue export licenses and to control imports of certain products. The government also cooperated with TEAMA in foreign marketing, standardization, quality control, technological upgrading, product design, and investment financing.

TEAMA successfully performed the duty of intra-industry cooperation. It regularly coordinated production and sales, disciplined free-riders, provided business and legal services to members, and advised the government on revisions in the trade regime. It also supplied several kinds of collective goods to its members, such as help in the collective purchasing of materials.[15]

The other form of cooperation was the business group, or *kuan-hsi* (relationship) enterprises as they are called in Chinese. By the 1990s, these loosely organized conglomerates in some cases had become large multinational corporations with international name recognition. Groups such as Formosa Plastics, Tatung, and Evergreen had more in common with the Korean *chaebol* by the 1990s than they did with Taiwan's small- and medium-scale industrial origins. These conglomerates did not start out large, however, nor were close ties to government investment programs the critical ingredients in their success. In a very real sense these large business groups were simply the most successful of the leading medium-scale enterprises.

As these large business groups rose in importance, they increasingly became the focus of attention. The largest 100 of them are now surveyed annually by the China Credit Information Service Corporation. Data from two of these surveys, from the 1974 and 1994 editions of *Business Groups in Taiwan*, are presented in Table 4-3. The first thing to note about these 100 largest business groups is that as recently as 1974, most of them were still quite small. The average capital per group was only NT$336 million, or US$8.4 million, at the exchange rate then prevailing. They were also quite labor intensive, with the average amount of capital per worker being only NT$137 thousand (US$3.4 thousand). Each business group contained an average of seven separate firms, so each firm had only around 350 employees. In short, even these largest of Taiwan's businesses were really only expanded versions of the typical small- and medium-scale firm network.

By 1994 such a statement was far less true. Average capital per business group had risen to NT$32.3 billion (US$1.2 billion), and capital per employee came to NT$7.5 million (US$285 thousand). Production was no longer carried out by a large number of employees working with a few simple and inexpensive machines. Another notable feature of the largest 100 business groups in 1994 was that 72 of them were not in the top 100 firms in 1974. That is, 72 large groups, if they existed at all in 1974, had at most less than NT$200 million (US$5 million) in capital, the lowest amount of any business group on the list at that time. By 1994, the capital of these groups had risen well over 100 times. Many of those that succeeded in achieving this kind of rapid expansion were in

TABLE 4-3

Comparison of Big Business Groups in Taiwan Between 1974 and 1994

		1974		1994	
(1)	Number of groups	111		101	
(2)	29 groups appeared in both years (%)	26.1		28.7	
(3)	Established year	*Number of Groups*	*Share (%)*	*Number of Groups*	*Share (%)*
	1910s	2	1.8	2	2.0
	1920s	1	0.9	1	1.0
	1930s	0	0.0	2	2.0
	1940s	14	12.6	8	7.9
	1950s	61	55.0	35	34.7
	1960s	32	28.8	36	35.6
	1970s	1	0.9	14	13.9
	1980s	0	0.0	3	3.0
(4)	Total number of firms in the groups	768		918	
(5)	Average number of firms per groups [(4)/(1)]	7		9	
(6)	Groups total capital (million NT$)	37,284.65		3,265,540	
(7)	Average capital per group [(6)/(1)]	335.9		32,332.10	
(8)	Group's total employees	271,247		435,969	
(9)	Average employees per group [(8)/(1)]	2,444		4,317	
(10)	Number of groups invested in foreign countries	11		57	
(11)	Percent of total groups invested in foreign countries [(10)/(11)]	9.9		56.4	

new industries such as electronics, or were part of the rise of large trading and business services companies. Others, however, grew out of the early light industry exporters of the 1960s and 1970s.

Case histories of individual firms give a more complete picture of how these business conglomerates grew. One such group with origins that date back to the 1920s on Taiwan was the Tainanbang or Tainan

Spinning group.[16] The Hou and Wu families that dominated this group began as owners and managers of clothing stores in Tainan city. Both families were from the same county on Taiwan, and the Wu family actually got started working in the Hou family store. Although they left to found their own store, they retained close ties with the Hou family and the latter provided part of the capital for the new Wu family store.

In 1953, the Kuomintang government announced that it would issue licenses for two new 100,000-spindle spinning mills and the Wu family, in partnership with the Hou family, went after one of those licenses. Success was achieved by recruiting a prominent politician who was also named Wu and who was from the same village (they had common ancestors several generations back). The other license went to a firm in which the Kuomintang Party had a substantial investment.

In the years that followed, additional textile firms were established by the Hou and Wu families, and in 1967 the group supported the creation of a new food company, the President Enterprise Corporation, to be run by Kao Ch'ing-yuan, a former trusted employee in Tainan Spinning. By the 1990s there were some twenty-seven differently named entities in the Tainanbang. The President Enterprise Corporation became the largest food products manufacturer in Taiwan. These twenty-seven entities were, in legal terms, independent firms and to some degree were run as such. But the different firms were all owned by varying combinations of the same families. In some cases there was no formal corporate tie between the firms other than the common ownership. In other cases one firm was owned by a parent firm, which was in turn owned by the families.

Oversight of these firms was in the hands of a board of directors that typically included key family members, many of whom sat on many different boards. Only day-to-day management was entrusted to people outside the family circles. It is the overlap of board members who have worked closely together on a variety of enterprises that makes the separate firms into a group. In more recent years, a number of formal holding companies have been formed to clarify the nature of the inter-firm group relationship. One motive for these new holding companies is connected to keeping the group together as a new generation of family members takes over. Generation transitions have always been difficult for family-based Chinese firms, in part because the son (or, increasingly, a daughter) may not be as able as the father. It is also the case that, where more than one family is involved, as in the case of the Tainanbang, the next generation may not enjoy the same close relations as the first. Chinese inheritance practices that divide the inheritance equally among the sons further complicate the situation, something the holding company form can be used to ameliorate.

Somewhat differently from the Tainanbang, the Tatung conglomerate evolved into an integrated modern conglomerate. Tatung, however, had close links to a network of over 1,000 supplier companies that were formally independent, and many did in fact produce some output for other large firms, but the ties to Tatung were close. Tatung also illustrates another aspect of the rise of Taiwan's conglomerates: the speed of this rise. Although the company was founded in 1918, in 1942 it still had only 100 workers producing electric fans and rice cookers for the domestic market. When Tatung finally began to export domestic appliances in 1966 it had 2,000 employees. By 1994 the number of employees had risen to 30,000, and it had major subsidiaries in the United States, Canada, Japan, Singapore, Indonesia, and elsewhere.[17]

Returning to the more general picture, just what kind of people were these who ran these large conglomerates? Some relevant figures are presented in Table 4-4. That a large percentage of the key corporate figures had close family ties to the founder or current leader goes without saying. The increase in numbers of key figures without family ties suggests some movement toward professionalism and depersonalizing management, but even many of those without familial ties had long personal connections of some other kind. To use the terminology of the sociologist Talcot Parsons, Taiwan business was still governed by particularistic values rather than universalistic values where objective measures of merit govern selection to key posts.

A second feature of this business leadership group was that the great majority of these leaders were born on Taiwan when Taiwan was under Japanese colonial rule. It was not inevitable that Taiwanese, simply because of their greater numbers, dominated these large business groups. Given the central activist role played by the government and the fact that the mainland-born had closer ties to government, it would not have been surprising if mainlanders had played the leading role in these large firms. The fact that the Taiwan-born did dominate suggests that private sector development was just that, the product mainly of private sector initiative, albeit in a favorable policy environment.

Finally, and perhaps most surprising, is the relatively low level of formal education of the central leaders of these large business groups. In a society that had several thousand university graduates a year in the 1950s and over 100,000 per year in the 1990s, half of the leaders of

TABLE 4-4

Comparison of Central Figures of Big Business Groups Between
1974 and 1994

	1974		1994	
	Persons	Share (%)	Persons	Share (%)
Place of Birth				
China	26	23.4	19	18.8
Taiwan	85	76.6	80	76.2
Foreigner & overseas Chinese	0	0.0	3	3.0
Decade of Birth				
1890s	5	4.5	0	0.0
1900s	26	23.4	2	2.0
1910s	40	36.0	16	15.8
1920s	27	24.3	28	27.7
1930s	13	11.7	19	18.8
1940s	0	0.0	28	27.7
1950s	0	0.0	6	5.9
1960s	0	0.0	1	1.0
Education				
College & graduate school	18	16.2	48	47.5
Junior college	10	9.0	27	26.7
High school	59	53.2	15	14.9
Primary school	21	18.9	11	10.9
None	2	1.8	0	0.0
Relation Between Central and Other Important Figures				
Father & children	30	18.1	44	16.2
Husband & wife	3	1.8	6	2.2
Brother or sister	47	28.3	54	19.9
Relatives	19	11.4	25	9.2
Others	67	40.4	143	52.6
Total	166	100.0	272	100.0

these groups even in 1994 had not gotten beyond high school or junior
college. In 1974, over 80 percent did not get beyond high school or junior college. If one looks at a broad sample of business leaders in firms
of all sizes, the number with college or university education drops to 10
percent of the total in the 1990s as well as the 1970s.[18] University graduates, or at least the great majority of them, were not headed toward
careers as business entrepreneurs. In 1979, 48 percent of them went
into government, and by 1992 that number had fallen only to 40.7 percent, still an extraordinarily high figure. Comparable figures for the
United States are not available, but the number of university graduates

going into government would be well under 10 percent of the total number of graduates.

Family-run firms where nepotism was critical to getting ahead, therefore, dominated Taiwan's businesses. Most of the business leaders had only a modest level of education. The well educated, in contrast, went into government or the professions. In addition, the government, as already pointed out, was dominated by those born on the Chinese mainland, and there was considerable enmity between the two groups, at least in the early years after Chinese rule was reestablished on Taiwan. This combination of factors would not appear to be an ideal set for business success, but it was.

THE ROLE OF PUBLIC ENTERPRISES

Although the private sector played the leading role in many Taiwan industries, particularly those that were export oriented, public or state-owned firms often played a leading role in industries whose primary orientation was toward the domestic market.

When the Kuomintang government moved its capital to Taipei in 1949, as pointed out in Chapter 2, public sector firms dominated Taiwan's industry. Most of the existing industry on Taiwan had been owned and controlled by Japanese. Some three quarters of paid-up capital in registered firms was held by the Japanese, and these included the large sugar refining sector, the railroads, and major public utilities such as electric power. Private industry in Taiwanese hands was largely confined to small-scale food processing enterprises. For the most part, the formerly Japanese-owned assets were simply taken over by the Kuomintang government and incorporated into the public sector. Several of these firms remained in public hands into the 1990s.

Prior to the late 1980s and 1990s, there was only one serious effort at privatization of industry, and that privatization was driven by concerns having little to do with the growth or efficiency requirements of the industrial sector itself. Taiwan's land reform, like most land reforms, was carried out for political reasons: to create a stable rural polity so as to avoid the rural instability that had been so effectively exploited by the Communists on the Chinese mainland. Neither the Kuomintang government nor its U.S. advisors, however, wanted simply to confiscate the land from the landlords and hand it over to the tenants. On the other hand, government revenues, even with U.S. aid included, were only a bit over 20 percent of GNP, not nearly enough to compensate landlords fully or partially while maintaining large military expenditures.[19]

The solution decided upon was to turn over four firms, or, more accurately, four groups of firms, to the former landlords as partial compensation for their land. This solution was carried out in the years 1952 to 1954. The four privatized groups of firms were Taiwan Cement, Taiwan Paper, Taiwan Minerals and Industries (*Kong-Kuang*), and Taiwan Agriculture and Forestry (*Nong-Lin*). Taiwan Minerals and Industries was comprised of 163 small- and medium-sized firms in businesses ranging from coal mines and machine shops to textiles and glass making. Similarly, Taiwan Agriculture and Forestry comprised 45 firms concerned with pineapple canning to fish and animal products.

Two-thirds of the shares in these four groups, with a face value of NT$659 million (US$42 million at the exchange rate of the early 1950s) were distributed to Taiwanese landlords as compensation for the loss of their agricultural land. The remaining shares were either sold to the public or retained by the government (18.6 percent of the total). Most landlords then sold their shares almost immediately, with the result that share prices initially were driven down to less than half of their face value. A few large landlords and merchants bought most shares, and share prices did rise above their face value in 1955 before falling again in 1956 and 1957. Although all four of these groups were still listed on the Taiwan stock market as of the mid-1990s, three were little more than landholding companies. Only Taiwan Cement, whose shares had been bought by four of the island's wealthiest families, went on to become a giant conglomerate.[20] In aggregate terms, however, about 5 percent of the value-added in manufacturing as of 1952 was changed from public to private hands, and, as a result, public ownership of manufacturing fell below 50 percent, although just barely.

The basic data on public ownership in the economy as a whole and in the manufacturing sector in particular are presented in Tables 4-5 and 4-6. In the 1950s and 1960s, the share of the public enterprises in the output of all nonagricultural enterprises was about one-quarter; that share did not begin to decline until the 1970s, and then did so only slowly. The share of public enterprises in manufacturing, in contrast, although starting at half or more of all manufacturing, declined steadily. The difference between these trends is accounted for by the fact that such major sectors as utilities and much of transport remained firmly in government hands.

The importance of public sector enterprises in Taiwan can be seen most clearly when Taiwan's experience is compared with that of other

TABLE 4-5

The Public-Private Share of Gross Domestic Product (as Percent of Total)

Year	Total Gross Domestic Product	Government Services	Public Enterprises	Private Nonregulated Enterprises	Agriculture
1951	100.0	10.9	17.4	NA	NA
1956	100.0	10.7	15.0	48.8	25.5
1961	100.0	11.3	16.7	46.5	25.5
1966	100.0	11.0	16.1	50.4	22.5
1971	100.0	11.5	16.8	58.7	13.1
1976	100.0	9.8	16.8	62.0	11.4
1981	100.0	10.4	16.0	66.3	7.3
1986	100.0	9.4	14.3	70.7	5.5
1991	100.0	11.4	13.4	71.4	3.9
1994	100.0	10.6	NA	NA	3.6

Source: Statistic of National Income in the Taiwan Area, Directorate General of Budget, Accounting and Statistics, Executive Yuan, R.O.C., various years.

NA indicates data not available.

developing and industrialized countries. The share of these enterprises is, of course, far below that found on the Chinese mainland in the 1950s through the 1970s, or in other countries that patterned their system after that of the Soviet Union. In those countries, even where agriculture was not collectivized, state enterprises accounted for well over half the GNP, and if government administrative services and the military were added in, the share would climb to 60 or 70 percent of the GNP. On the Chinese mainland in the 1990s, by way of contrast, state-owned enterprises accounted for around 30 percent of the GNP, a bit over 40 percent if government services in general are added in.[21]

A more meaningful comparison is with countries that did not adopt a Soviet-type command economy. Figures from a number of developing and industrialized nations are presented in Table 4-7. When Taiwan is compared with these mixed public/private but market-oriented economies, it is clear that public enterprises played a larger role in Taiwan than they did in most other developing countries and a far bigger role than the one played in most industrialized countries. Taiwan is similar to India or Indonesia, two countries where state-owned enterprises played a central role in industrial development. The percentage share for South Korea is significantly lower than it is for Taiwan. Fig-

TABLE 4-6
The Public and Private Shares in Gross Domestic Product by Industry (as Percent of Total)

Year	Total Public Share	Total Private Share	Agriculture, Forestry, Fishing, & Animal Husbandry Public Share	Private Share	Mining & Quarrying Public Share	Private Share	Manufacturing Public Share	Private Share	Electricity, Gas, & Water Public Share	Private Share	Construction Public Share	Private Share	Commerce Public Share	Private Share	Transport & Storage Public Share	Private Share	Financing, Insurance, Real Estate, & Business Services Public Share	Private Share	Personal Service & Others Public Share	Private Share
1951	18.7	81.3	3.6	96.4	32.9	67.1	49.3	50.7	NA	NA	3.3	96.7	9.5	90.5	67.2	32.8	16.1	83.9	NA	NA
1956	16.7	83.3	3.5	96.5	23.7	76.3	36.7	63.3	NA	NA	4.5	95.5	6.1	93.9	54.6	45.4	22.2	77.8	NA	NA
1961	18.6	81.4	3.3	96.7	23.2	76.8	35.2	64.8	NA	NA	2.7	97.3	6.7	93.3	54.4	45.6	24.4	75.6	NA	NA
1966	17.8	82.2	3.7	96.3	17.8	82.2	29.5	70.5	99.4	0.6	3.8	96.2	4.0	96.0	43.3	56.7	23.3	76.7	1.3	98.7
1971	19.5	80.5	6.2	93.8	20.0	80.0	23.0	77.0	98.8	1.2	10.8	89.2	2.3	97.7	44.9	55.1	25.9	74.1	2.6	97.4
1976	20.3	79.7	6.0	94.0	21.6	78.4	19.8	80.2	97.8	2.2	29.1	70.9	1.2	98.8	46.4	53.6	29.1	70.9	3.6	96.4
1981	20.8	79.2	6.5	93.5	14.1	85.9	17.5	82.5	98.0	2.0	16.7	83.3	0.6	99.4	47.1	52.9	33.3	66.7	3.9	96.1
1986	19.1	80.9	3.9	96.1	18.4	81.6	15.8	84.2	97.7	2.3	17.8	82.2	0.4	99.6	44.5	55.5	27.8	72.2	3.3	96.7
1991	18.3	81.7	2.3	97.7	19.6	80.4	16.6	83.4	98.0	2.0	14.4	85.6	0.3	99.7	44.7	55.3	23.5	76.5	7.1	92.9
1996	17.3	82.7	2.3	97.7	13.0	87.0	15.3	84.7	98.1	1.9	11.4	88.6	0.2	99.8	47.4	52.6	20.9	79.1	7.1	92.9

Source: Statistic of National Income in the Taiwan Area, Directorate General of Budget, Accounting and Statistics, Executive Yuan, R.O.C., various years.

NA indicates data not available.

TABLE 4-7

Share of State-Owned Enterprises in Nonagricultural Gross Domestic Product

	1978–1971 (unweighted averages in percent)
18 Latin American and Caribbean Economies	11.6
14 African Economies	17.1
8 Asian Economies	10.9
8 Industrial Economies	8.3
India	17.4
Indonesia	19.9
Republic of Korea	11.3
Taiwan (1950s–1960s)	21
Taiwan (1980s–1990s)	14–17

Sources: The Taiwan data are derived from Table 4-5. The other figures are from The World Bank, *Bureaucrats in Business: The Economics and Politics of Government Ownership* (1995: Table A.2, pp. 272–275). This World Bank table gives a figure for Taiwan of 7.8 percent of nonagricultural GDP in 1978–1991, but it is difficult to see how such a low figure could have been obtained and the source does not explain it in sufficient detail.

ures from earlier years, before South Korea began actively privatizing, were considerably higher at around 12 to 13 percent of nonagricultural GNP in the 1970s,[22] but still considerably below the share of Taiwan in either the earlier or later periods.

What accounts for this large continuing state-owned enterprise role in Taiwan? This reliance on public ownership did not result from an active debate among politicians and the public over the proper role for state enterprises in industrial development. It was more, as pointed out in Chapter 2, that many leading economic officials in the government came from an industrial and engineering background and several had worked for the China Petroleum Corporation, a government enterprise, prior to coming to Taiwan.[23] In certain industrial sectors, it was pretty much taken for granted that these officials and the government would take the lead. Private manufacturing, dominated by small Taiwanese firms, was assumed not to be in a position to play a role. Only later, when a number of these Taiwanese manufacturing firms had become very large, did they succeed in pushing their way into some of the government-dominated sectors.

The relatively large role of state enterprises probably also resulted from the already-mentioned division between a government run by mainlanders and a private business sector largely run by those born on Taiwan. Turning heavy industry over the private sector in Taiwan meant that the government lost a major lever of control over the economy, not to mention a source of high-level employment opportunities for its political allies in the mainlander community. In South Korea, where there was no division comparable to that between mainlanders and Taiwanese,[24] Korean government officials lost neither control nor employment opportunities by letting the private conglomerates actually build the new heavy industries. The South Korean conglomerates generally did what the government asked them to do.

The sectors dominated by state-owned enterprises, as pointed out above, included virtually all utilities, most of heavy industry, and certain large infrastructure projects, mainly related to transportation. These sectors were seen as being natural monopolies requiring government supervision, industries vital to defense, industries enjoying large-scale economies, or a combination of all three. The electric power sector, including the very active nuclear power program, was a government effort throughout. In the 1960s, the main activity in the manufacturing sector was the rapid development of light consumer industries that were almost all private, but in the 1970s the government began a major effort to build a modern heavy industry sector.

That both Taiwan and South Korea began their heavy industry drives in the early 1970s was not a coincidence. Both countries were at a similar stage in the growth process with similar levels of per capita income, although Taiwan was a bit ahead of Korea in this latter regard. Both had completed a decade of export-led growth based on consumer manufactures, and the demand for intermediate products was rising rapidly enough to provide import-substituting possibilities. Taiwan in fact had had trouble obtaining supplies of such inputs as scrap steel in the early 1970s, and this provided an added impetus for ensuring the availability of an adequate domestic supply. Finally, the early 1970s were a period when there was increasing questioning of the depth of the U.S. defense commitment to the region in the aftermath of America's involvement in Vietnam, reinforced in Taiwan's case by mainland China's entry into the United Nations. A national defense industry requires a heavy industrial core, or so it was believed at the time.

The broader program started in the early 1970s, of which the heavy industry effort was a part, was the Ten Major Development Projects program of Premier Chiang Ching-kuo discussed in Chapter 2. The three heavy industries involved were steel, shipbuilding, and petro-chemicals. Originally the private sector had been invited to participate in these projects, but the 1973-to-1974 energy crisis dampened the enthusiasm of the private sector. The decision was made to go ahead with state-owned enterprises.

There were both similarities and differences between the heavy industry drives of Taiwan and South Korea. Both emphasized the same sectors, but South Korea turned to the private sector to carry out much of the development, although there were notable exceptions, such as the case of steel. South Korea, however, dealt with private sector reluctance to proceed by introducing subsidies that made the projects attractive to the private sector, whereas Taiwan simply had the state run the effort directly. The scope of Taiwan's heavy industry drive was also more modest than that of South Korea. Where South Korea was willing to devote a large share of net investment in the 1970s to heavy industry, even to the point of fueling inflation and running up a large external debt, Taiwan was not willing to go that far. As pointed out previously, priority in Taiwan after the 1973 to 1974 oil and inflation crisis was to keep both prices and international debt under tight control. A Korean-style heavy industry program would have made Taiwan's stabilization goals unachievable.[25]

Taiwan, like Korea, however, knew from the start that heavy industry had to produce inputs that were priced to keep Taiwan's exports competitive. The China Petroleum Corporation, for example, was ordered to set its prices at the international price level even when the international price began to fall sharply in the 1980s. Downstream prices for steel were also priced at international levels.[26] Despite charging international prices for its products, China Steel, which had been expected to take six years to break even, did so in only three years. One of the reasons why state-owned enterprises continued to play such a large role in Taiwan is that firms, or some of them at least, became profitable early on and were not a major drain on the resources of the government or of downstream users of their products.

By the latter part of the 1970s and the 1980s, however, a number of these newer state-owned enterprises had run into difficulty. Taiwan Aluminum and Taiwan Metallic Minerals, for example, both chronic losers, were closed down in 1987. There was also increasing pressure from the private sector to move into heavy industries, and many domestic firms had grown to a size where the required large scale of investments no longer presented a problem.

Formosa Plastics, for example, moved upstream and became a major producer of petrochemicals. The larger scale end of the electronics sector was mainly private, as was much of the transport equipment sector, such as Yue-loong and Ford-Liu Ho Motors. Some of the largest investments by the private sector in the first half of the 1990s were in basic metals. As the center of gravity of Taiwan's industry shifted away from labor-intensive consumer goods, the private sector moved with it, and the large state-owned firms put up less and less resistance to this encroachment on their domain.

Finally, in the late 1980s and early 1990s, the government began to put together a privatization program for at least some of its state-owned firms. Privatization of state-owned firms came under active discussion from the mid-1980s on. In July 1989, a special task force of the Council on Economic Planning and Development was established to get the process of privatization underway. This task force drafted the Statute for the Privatization of Public Enterprises, which was then passed by the Legislative Yuan in June 1991. Altogether in the early 1990s there were 102 important state-owned enterprises, 52 of which were controlled by central government ministries, 35 by the Taiwan Provincial Government, and the remainder by city and county governments.

The Council task force initially selected twenty-two firms for the first wave of privatization, nine controlled by the central government and the remainder by the Taiwan Provincial Government. Many of these firms were chronic money losers and initially found few buyers for their shares. Strong resistance also came from provincial legislators and bureaucrats, for whom privatization meant a loss of power and perquisites that went with their supervision of these enterprises. These legislators and bureaucrats found active allies among the employees of these firms who feared their loss of job security.

By the end of 1995, only the four central government enterprises: China Steel, China Petrochemical, China Engineering and Construction, and China Property Insurance had been formally privatized. One uses the term "formally" because, although over 50 percent of the shares in these companies were in private hands, the government remained the largest single shareholder.[27]

Even with the privatization program, the government continued to set up new enterprises with a substantial level of state ownership when the private sector was unable to go ahead in a sector that government planners felt was critical for the long-term health of Taiwan's economy. The best example of this was Taiwan Semiconductor, which brought in the very large scale integrated (VLSI) circuit manufacturing technology. As pointed out in Chapter 3, it was started in 1986 as a joint venture with Philips, with the government putting up 49 percent of the funds and Philips another quarter of the money. These private firms in Taiwan had first tried to get into the VLSI semiconductor business, but had great difficulty in raising capital. As with many previous state efforts, Taiwan Semiconductor, far from being a failure and a drain on the government budget, was an almost immediate success. Expecting to break even in three years, the firm actually became profitable in financial terms within eighteen months.

The state-owned enterprise sector thus was a central part of Taiwan's industrialization effort for over four decades. Even by the early 1990s, few state firms had been privatized, and major new state-invested firms were started as recently as the late 1980s. It is interesting to speculate why state ownership continued to play such a central role in Taiwan's industrialization when elsewhere in Asia privatization proceeded with increasing speed. The variants of socialist ideology that once played an active role in Kuomintang thinking cannot be an explanation for a phenomenon of the 1980s and 1990s. A more likely explanation, as the first efforts at privatization demonstrated, is that the interests of the government bureaucracy, in alliance with senior politicians, is what kept this emphasis alive. These older state enterprises were a source of both power and jobs for those in government. Privatization, particularly privatization to one of the large Taiwanese-owned firms, would fundamentally change this situation. The more recent government investments in firms, it should be noted, involved mainly the provision of venture capital rather than outright government control over management. These more recent investments, therefore, did not involve the same level of benefit for the government bureaucracy as earlier state-owned effort had.

None of these political considerations would have carried much weight if these public enterprises had been poorly managed. Taiwan could not have afforded, either economically or politically, a large number of sick state enterprises that drained the country's resources. Taiwan's survival depended on having a heavy industry sector that was efficient enough not to undermine high rates of export-led growth. That pressure in turn forced Taiwan politicians to leave the management of the most important parts of the state-owned sector to competent technocrats and to keep politics and rent seeking out. Around the world, state-owned enterprises, when they are not weighed down by outright corruption and incompetence, still have to pursue multiple objectives dictated by the political interests of the government leadership. In that context economic efficiency is only one of several objectives, often not the most important one. In Taiwan, a technocratic government was able to ensure that economic efficiency was the main if not the only criteria for such key sectors as steel, petrochemicals, and semiconductors.

CONCLUSION

Throughout the half century that began with the restoration of Chinese rule over Taiwan after the Japanese occupation, certain features have been characteristic of the way industry on Taiwan was organized. As the description in this chapter has shown, Taiwan's industry had a dual structure in which a large public sector existed and prospered alongside a dynamic private sector. The public sector was characterized by large firms in markets with a high degree of industrial concentration, at least at the beginning. This sector was dominated by immigrants from the Chinese mainland who had risen through the government bureaucracy. The private sector was made up mostly of small, highly competitive firms. This sector was dominated by individuals born on Taiwan who were largely excluded from the higher levels of government, both under the Japanese colonial period and, until recently, under the Kuomintang-dominated government. Private sector firms, even the largest, were family enterprises.

There were some changes over the course of these four decades in the way industry on Taiwan was organized and run, but the changes did not fundamentally alter the system. Privatization in the 1990s began to dismantle the state's direct management of the large heavy industries, but bureaucratic resistance kept the state more actively involved than it was in many other rapidly industrializing economies. Private firms became steadily larger, but most remained small. Firm managers and owners were better educated than their predecessors, but family relationships still dominated most top-level ownership and control. The Taiwan-born/mainlander-born split was declining in the society at large, but the central role played by family ties ensured that most private industry remained in the hands of the Taiwan-born.

Did this structure rise and persist because it was peculiarly well suited to conditions on Taiwan? Brian Levy has argued that Taiwan, unlike many other developing countries, had an economy where low transaction costs connected with the entry of new businesses made it possible for so many small firms to get started.[28] The main idea is that there were few barriers to the entry of new firms because Taiwan's markets worked efficiently with respect to new entrants. There were also few barriers to Japanese firms establishing subcontracting relationships with Taiwan firms, or to Taiwan firms subcontracting with each other. This is in contrast with South Korea, where barriers to entry and to subcontracting raised the cost of startups and made it more efficient to rely on large enterprises and hierarchical relationships rather than market relationships.

That argument may explain why so many small firms arose in the first place, but it is less persuasive as to why this small-scale structure has persisted. Most Organization of Economic Cooperation and Development (OECD) nations have lower transaction costs than Taiwan with respect to new entrants and subcontracts, and yet they have higher concentration ratios than Taiwan in most sectors.

Do cultural values, notably the strength of the Chinese family system, explain the persistence of so many small firms? If family ties were the primary basis for trusting relationships, that fact could limit firm size. But the Korean *chaebol* were also family controlled, and the Southeast Asian landscape is dotted with multibillion dollar Chinese family conglomerates. Clearly Chinese family values do not prevent firms from becoming large, although they may make the process more difficult. Also Chinese family firms throughout Southeast Asia are known for having difficulty making the transition to the second and third generation.

The late twentieth century Western management model has large corporations run by professional managers selected on the basis of merit. The challenge is to design a system where the managers (the agents) work in the best interests of the owners (the principals). Chinese family firms on Taiwan did not really have this problem with controlling top management because owners and top managers were the same people.

In the West, the separation of ownership and management came about in part because large corporations needed to attract equity capital from far larger numbers of people than were available through family ties. There was also a need to ensure competent management that one could not count on the owner's descendants to provide. Because most firms on Taiwan were relatively young, these generation-change issues had only begun to come to the fore by the late 1990s. The comparative efficiency of modern capital markets also meant that a family firm had far greater access to capital than had been the case two or three generations ago. Taiwan's family-based industrial enterprises may, therefore, gradually give way to impersonal professionally managed firms, but the process is likely to be a slow one.

NOTES

1 Chiu (1992, pp. 125–132).

2 These figures were derived from the data in Tables 4-1 and 4-2.

3 Liu Chin-ch'ing, *Taiwan chan-kou ching-chi fen-hsi* (1992*)*, p. 207.

4 K.T. Li, "The Growth of Taiwan's Private Industry," in Tu (1976, p. 41).

5 K.T. Li, *The Experience of Dynamic Economic Growth on Taiwan* (1976), pp. 324–325.

6 Hsiao (1982, pp. 43–56). The article provides several different measures of concentration for Taiwan industries, but the international comparisons are based on the shares of the largest four firms in each four-digit industry.

7 Jones and Sakong (1980, pp. 260–267).

8 The firm sales data are from *China Credit Information Service, Business Groups, in Taiwan,* 1980 and 1992 editions (Taipei: China Credit Information Service, 1980 and 1992), and the operating revenue data for all of manufacturing are from the Report on the Industrial and Commercial Census Taiwan-Fukien area.

9 Leroy P. Jones and Il Sakong, *op. cit.,* p. 268.

10 Levy (1991, p. 151).

11 Chen (1991).

12 The discussion in this section is based on Chen (1991).

13 This discussion is based on Sun (1996, pp. 65–68).

14 Research and product development in the textile sector is discussed at greater length in Appendix A on the textile and apparel industry.

15 Kuo (1990, pp. 159–183).

16 This description is based on Numazaki (1993, pp. 485–510).

17 *An Introduction to Tatung Co.* (1993).

18 This figure was derived from data in the government's labor force survey of Taiwan.

19 Direct and indirect taxes plus revenues from government monopolies in the early 1950s came to only 14 to 16 percent of gross national product. Lundberg (1979, p. 303). U.S. aid was averaging about US$100 million per year in the early 1950s, which was about 8 percent of GNP at the then exchange rate. Council for Economic Planning and Development, *Tai-*

wan Statistical Data Book, 1974 (1974).

20 This discussion of the early privatization effort is based on Liu (1992), Chapters 1 and 3.

21 By the mid-1990s, virtually all of agriculture and a large share of services were no longer in state hands. In the case of industry, state-owned enterprises on the Chinese mainland accounted for less than half of all industry, although the other half, made up of joint ventures and township and village enterprises, was not formally privately owned.

22 The South Korean state enterprise value-added figures are from Song (1990, p. 118). The nonagricultural GNP figures were taken from National Statistical Office, *Major Statistics of Korean Economy*, various years.

23 Interviews.

24 South Korea did have divisions, notably those between the citizens of the Kyongsang Provinces and the citizens of the Cholla Provinces, but heavy industry was either in Seoul or in the Kyongsang Provinces, which were the political supporters of President Park and his immediate successors. The Cholla Provinces remained largely agricultural and regularly voted against the government prior to the election of President Kim Dae Jung in 1997. The lack of industry in the Cholla Provinces, therefore, was partly the result of a direct decision by the government to concentrate investments in provinces friendly to the Park and later governments.

25 The South Korean experience is described in Stern, Kim, Perkins, and Yoo (1995).

26 Interviews.

27 This discussion of privatization in based primarily on Lin and Chang (1995, pp. 40–51).

28 Levy (1991, pp. 151–178).

5 MACROECONOMIC POLICY

Michael Roemer and Chou Ji

Previous chapters have focused on the Taiwan government's industrial policies and how they influenced the changing structure of Taiwan manufacturing. As these preceding discussions have made clear, however, industrial policy was only one element shaping Taiwan's industrial development. Macroeconomic forces and policies often had a profound influence in determining which industries would thrive and which would decline. The objective of this chapter is to understand better the macroeconomic forces at work and how they influenced Taiwan's industrial development.

Macroeconomic policy was a major focus of Taiwan's government ever since that government moved from the Chinese mainland in 1949. Hyperinflation on the Chinese mainland and its impact on the political fortunes of the mainland Kuomintang government comprised one important reason for the emphasis on macroeconomic stability on Taiwan, an emphasis that continues. A strong desire to avoid the consequences of inflation, for example, had much to do with the vigorous response of Taiwan policy makers to the impact of the OPEC-generated increases in petroleum prices in 1973 and 1979, as pointed out in Chapter 2.

The stabilization policies of the 1950s, 1960s, and 1970s were an important foundation for Taiwan's industrial development in those decades, but it is the macroeconomic trends of the 1980s that profoundly altered Taiwan's industrial structure. The nature and impact of these macroeconomic trends are still not fully understood, and they are the focus of much of the analysis in this chapter. Only by understanding the trends of the 1980s and 1990s can one comprehend why Taiwan's industrial structure shifted so rapidly toward high-technology industries or why Taiwan's manufacturers shifted a significant portion of their investment abroad to the Chinese mainland and to Southeast Asia. These changes in industrial structure were achieved while the overall level of investment in Taiwan, as a percentage of gross national product, was falling sharply.

It is now commonplace to stress the importance of macroeconomic stability as being central to any successful development strategy. As the work of Stanley Fischer demonstrates, low inflation, low budget deficits, and low black market exchange rate premia are closely correlated with rapid economic growth; the causal direction appears to be from macroeconomic policies to rapid economic growth, rather than the other way around.[1] This emphasis on sound macroeconomic policy, however, was not commonplace among developing countries in the 1950s and 1960s. Taiwan was a leader in placing macroeconomic policies at the forefront of development strategy. By the 1980s, it appeared that policy makers might have overdone this emphasis on conservative macroeconomic policies. Domestic savings grew as a share of GNP as investment's share fell, exports exceeded imports by growing margins, and foreign reserves accumulated to the point of wasteful investment. A major question posed in this chapter is whether policy makers intended to overbalance the economy toward external surplus or whether this was a result of mismanagement.

ANTECEDENTS: MACROECONOMIC POLICY FROM 1950 TO 1980

Before getting to the 1980s and 1990s, it is useful to recount the pattern of macroeconomic policies established by Taiwan from the pioneering days of the 1950s through the oil shocks of the 1970s. Because this experience is considered at length in many other published works, the discussion here will be brief.

This discussion begins with land reform. It may seem strange to begin an analysis of macroeconomic policy with land reform, but land reform played an important role in Taiwan's macroeconomic management. In the 1940s and 1950s, Taiwan was an agricultural country whose main products were rice and sugar. Although land reform was carried out for other reasons, it had an important impact on price stabilization and, subsequently, on industrialization. Land reform created strong incentives for the former tenants and new farmer-owners to invest in their land. Farm productivity and output increased sufficiently to contribute to the eventual stabilization of food prices. Rising agricultural productivity also helped create a work force for the rapid industrialization that began in the 1960s, while growing rural incomes contributed to increased savings that financed Taiwan's rapid development. The reforms also played a major role in creating and maintaining one of the world's most equal income distributions throughout Taiwan's development, a factor that in turn made rapid change and macroeconomic austerity more acceptable to the population. Thus land reform was one of the pillars of Taiwan's development and helped make possible its characteristic approach to macroeconomic management.

Turning to macroeconomic policies proper, the government played an active role in this period in setting interest rates. In March 1950, the government created the Preferential Interest Rate Deposits Scheme (PIR), which at first paid a nominal 7 percent a month on one-month deposits. At the time, inflation was running at 10 percent a month (225 percent a year) after five years of even higher rates of inflation. Within a few months, PIR plus other savings and time deposits had risen from under 2 percent to 7 percent of the money supply, and inflation had fallen to 6 percent a month. By the middle of 1952, PIR deposits earned real interest rates of over 3 percent a month, interest-earning deposits accounted for over half the money supply, and prices were stable.[2]

A policy of high deposit rates was a break from the practice in developing countries at the time and for two or three decades thereafter. Although most economists urged then that interest rates be set at, or be freed to seek, market-clearing levels, most developing countries suppressed interest rates as a way of reducing the costs of borrowing and thus promoting investment. Taiwan's policy makers recognized early, however, that the interest rate is both a supply and a demand price and that suppressed rates would discourage savers from channeling their assets through the banking system, which would frustrate borrowers. They may also have believed that higher deposit rates would encourage households to save a higher share of their income, although later research on many countries has called this assumption into question.[3]

S. C. Tsiang, writing in 1984, implies that policy makers also used high interest rates on deposits as the main weapon against inflation.[4] Inflation was a preoccupation with the Kuomintang government as a result of its experience with hyperinflation on the Chinese mainland before 1949,[5] and so it is plausible to argue that interest rate policy, like other macroeconomic policies, was designed to fight increases in prices. Whatever the intent of government, inflation fell dramatically within a few months of the introduction of the PIR deposit scheme. Monetary policy was also restrained, however. By March 1952, when prices finally stabilized (and for a time began to fall), the real money supply (M2) was 20 percent below its level of two years earlier. High deposit rates tightened liquidity even more. Interest-bearing deposits had grown to 31 percent of the money supply by March 1952. It is arguable that, with real rates on deposits running at 25 to 40 percent a year, savings deposits were not highly substitutable for cash and checking deposits in consumers' minds, so that M1 rather than M2 was a better indicator of liquidity. Real M1 had fallen by more than 40 percent from March 1950 to March 1952.[6]

The resumption of United States aid after the outbreak of the Korean War also helped to staunch inflation. This was accomplished through the increased supply of imported goods and the sterilization of a substantial part of the proceeds from the sale of U.S. goods. U.S. counterpart funds were partly used to finance budget deficits that had previously been financed by central bank borrowing and partly impounded in counterpart accounts in the Bank of Taiwan. By July 1954, these sterilized funds amounted to 40 percent of the money supply, a strongly contractionary element in monetary policy at the time.

Thus, from the very beginning, Taiwan's policy makers established monetary and especially interest rate policy as a foundation for economic management and development strategy. Until 1980, real interest rates remained positive and high.[7] From 1955 to 1965, real rates on deposits ranged from 6 to 20 percent a year.[8] In the years after 1965, real deposit rates were positive in all but three years and ranged from 4 to 11 percent a year. Nonpreferential rates on secured loans were generally 2 to 8 points higher.

Taiwan did not leave the cost and allocation of loan finance entirely or even primarily to market forces, however. In July 1957, when banks were charging 20 percent a year on secured and 22 percent on unsecured loans, the Bank of Taiwan began offering loans at 12 percent to manufacturers who were attempting to penetrate export markets. This activity expanded during the 1960s and 1970s using a rediscount facility at the Central Bank.[9] Because three large government-controlled banks dominated the banking system in Taiwan, it was relatively easy for the authorities to control interest rates and to subsidize credit directed at export firms in this as well as other ways.[10]

Even in this notable use of directed subsidized credit, Taiwan distinguished itself from most other developing economies. First, as in Japan before and South Korea shortly after, directed credit contained a targeted subsidy for exporters rather than being offered indiscriminately to manufacturers in general and import substitutions industries in particular, as happened so often in other developing countries.

Because the bulk of Taiwan's exports came from small firms, however, it is unlikely that directed credit was a decisive factor in financing the growth of manufactured exports. A key distinguishing feature of Taiwan's credit market is that directed credit in the formal sector coexisted with a well-developed informal credit or *curb market*. Nominal interest rates in this market were nearly double those on unsecured loans from commercial banks.[11] Also the curb market was large. Loans by enterprises and households rose from 20 to 31 percent of domestic financial assets from 1965 through 1983. Over the same period, securities issued by enterprises, some of which may have been traded in the curb market as well, declined from 35 to 26 percent of total financial assets. It is thus possible that the curb market mobilized as much finance as the formal financial system. The government even supported curb market activity by making postdated checks, the most-often used instrument in that market, legally enforceable. Indeed, it was a criminal offense to bounce a postdated check.[12]

Thus Taiwan made its mark on financial market strategies in developing countries by pioneering high interest rates as an instrument of both stabilization and credit allocation, by directing credit toward (probably large-scale) exporters, and by encouraging the informal market to become a major financial intermediary. The strategy seems to have succeeded in all respects. Inflation was kept low from 1962 to 1973, when growth in the wholesale price index averaged less than 2 percent a year. Even during the 1970s, when prices rose by 10 percent a year, this was below the rates in the industrial countries.[13]

Not all observers applaud Taiwan's approach. Cheng Hang-sheng argues that interest rate policy was not stabilizing because bank loan rates were adjusted slowly relative to inflation and sometimes counter to it. He notes that Taiwan did run a partially repressed financial policy. Domestic savings were diverted into the largely unregulated, and therefore riskier, curb market; this presumably reduced investment below the optimal rate that could have been expected in a fully free market.[14] In December of 1975, the authorities did begin to develop a money market that traded in bills issued by the Ministry of Finance under market-determined rates. It was not until the late 1980s, however, that formal credit markets began to be fully deregulated, banks became more competitive, and loan rates became more flexible.[15]

Another distinguishing feature of Taiwan's macroeconomic policy in these years was its approach to exchange rate management. As pointed out in Chapter 2, during a relatively brief period of import-substituting industrialization, a dual exchange rate was maintained, with a basic rate for some importers and a higher (more depreciated rate) for other importers and exporters. By April of 1958, the rates had become overvalued and government then devalued the basic rate from 15.55 to 24.58 NT$/US$. Exporters were also permitted to earn exchange surrender certificates (ESCs) that could be sold to importers at market prices. In August of 1959, the rates were unified at NT$ 38.08 per US dollar, and then allowed to drift up to NT$40 in 1960 and pegged there until 1973.

The devaluation and unification of the NT dollar was a major incentive for exporters, as pointed out in Chapter 2, but two additional components were needed to realize Taiwan's potential for rapid export growth. First, the price stability of the 1960s, promoted by conservative monetary policies and high interest rates, kept the real exchange rate at rewarding levels for exporters. Second, a gradual relaxation of controls and tariff rates on imports of direct concern to exporters, combined with a duty rebate scheme and preferential loans to large exporters, helped cement the incentive system and set off the export boom. In 1971, it was estimated that exporters on average received incentives of NT$5.71 above the official exchange rate from interest subsidies and tax rebates.[16]

Taiwan's legacy in exchange rate management in these early years, therefore, was to adopt a unified nominal rate that gave incentive to actual and potential exporters of nontraditional products, to add tax rebates and credit incentives, and then to maintain a steady real rate through prudent monetary management that focused on maintaining high interest rates. In this approach, Taiwan differed from South Korea, which permitted much faster inflation during the 1960s and moved its nominal exchange rate substantially in order to maintain exporters' real incentives.

This approach to exchange rate management on Taiwan was not universally applauded. John Fei, for example, wrote that "persistent undervaluation to favor exporters (who) quickly became the dominant vested interest group in which 'everything for export' was sloganized to represent a social consensus".[17] The exchange rate, in Fei's view, was a political instrument in an essentially command economy, one that created windfall profits for an entrepreneurial class through political favoritism. If so, it can still be said that Taiwan's favored class of exporters produced more for their economy and its population than did the entrepreneurial classes favored in so many other countries where import substitution ruled until growth ground to a halt. The key point, one consistent with all observers' views of Taiwan's exchange rate strategy, was that the government always saw the exchange rate as an essential incentive to exporters. That attitude carried through the 1980s and 1990s as well.

MACRO-MANAGEMENT OF THE OIL SHOCKS OF 1973 TO 1980

The oil price shock of 1973 to 1974 was a major test of macroeconomic management for all economies, but particularly for those, like Taiwan, that imported oil and other raw materials and exported manufactures. In 1972, 63 percent of Taiwan's imports were raw materials, including petroleum, and 83 percent of exports were manufactures. The impact of oil shocks can be seen in the share of minerals in total imports, which went from 7.5 percent in 1972 to 11.6 percent in 1975 and 23.6 percent at the peak of oil prices in 1980. The balance of trade in goods and services, which had turned positive in 1970, as pointed out in previous chapters, went back into deficit, a deficit that reached 7.8 percent of the GNP in 1974. This first shock was particularly harsh as the trade balance worsened by 12 percent of the GNP from 1973 to 1974.

Although the abrupt shift in the external balance must have seemed threatening to the authorities, they did not take precipitate action. The money supply continued to increase by 10 to 12 percent of the GNP throughout the first crisis. A sharp fall in reserve accumulation was offset by greater increases in private domestic credit. Nominal interest rates changed very little, so real rates turned sharply negative in 1974, then recovered as inflation was brought under control. Government expenditure was cut severely in 1974, from almost 20 percent of the GNP to 16 percent, but expenditure was restored to 20 percent a year later. As the revenue share of GNP hardly changed, the budget was close to balance except in 1974, when it ran a surplus of 4 percent of the GNP. With the end of the Bretton Woods Agreement, the nominal exchange rate no longer had to be fixed; it actually appreciated by 5 percent from 1972 through 1974. The real exchange rate, calculated using consumer price indices (see discussion below), appreciated even more sharply, but the real rate, calculated using world prices of tradables, depreciated by 5 percent in the face of the world commodity price boom. Taken together, these measures suggest a government determined to control inflation, but in measured ways that avoided any suggestion of panic.

The economy did respond to this gentle medicine. In 1974, there was a spike in imports to almost 50 percent of GNP while the export share declined and the trade deficit, as previously mentioned, reached 7.8 percent of GNP. The import spike was deliberate as government encouraged manufacturers to stock up on imported raw materials by suppressing real interest rates and by keeping the exchange rate from depreciating. Inventory investment shot up to 10 percent of the GNP. By 1976, however, the trade balance had been restored, with exports reaching a new plateau of over 45 percent of the GNP. Wholesale prices, which rose 23 percent in 1973 and 41 percent in 1974, declined by 5 percent in 1975 and rose by about 3 percent a year for the next three years. The oil shock did interrupt the previously steady growth of savings and investment as shares of GNP. Investment spiked because of the inventory surge in 1975, and then fell to lower levels that were nevertheless above the pre-shock investment shares of GNP. Savings, especially private savings, fell sharply during the crisis but soon recovered to a high plateau between 30 and 35 percent of GNP. Thus the first oil price boom, however unsettling at the time, now appears as a sharp but short disruption in Taiwan's steady economic growth and macro-economic balance.

The second shock had a similar but somewhat muted impact. The trade balance did deteriorate by 7.6 percent of the GNP from 1978 through 1980, but was then still only in deficit by 1.2 percent of the GNP. This time the export share did not fall and, although imports once again shot up to 45 percent of the GNP in 1980, they then began a steady decline that is an important part of the story of the 1980s. Savings remained high and investment actually rose through the second shock. This time, however, monetary policy was relatively tight. Although net foreign assets once again stopped growing, this time the authorities did not sterilize changes in reserves but instead put a damper on private domestic credit. Monetary growth, as a result, fell from 15 percent of GNP in 1978 to only 5 percent in 1979 and 10 percent in 1980. Once again government expenditures were cut, and the budget went from deficit to surplus with a swing of about 3 percent of GNP. Although Taiwan continued to peg its exchange rate, the end of the Bretton Woods Agreement allowed Taiwan to appreciate the nominal exchange rate slightly during 1977 through 1979, contrary to the expectations of most observers. This managed float, begun in 1978, brought the rate by 1980 to NT$35.96.[18] Wholesale prices rose rapidly during 1979 to 1981, with inflation averaging 15 percent a year, but then prices fell during the early 1980s. As oil prices began to recede, the economy was under tight macroeconomic control and began generating the large external surpluses of the 1980s.

Taiwan's approach to the two oil shocks contrasts markedly with the policies of most other oil-importing developing countries, including South Korea. Government expenditures in South Korea during the first oil shock were cut sharply (as a percentage of GNP), and South Korea accepted very large current account deficits and borrowed abroad to cover these deficits. Domestic credit in South Korea, however, rose by an average of 35 percent per year from 1972 through 1980. The money supply (both M1 and M2) grew from 25 to nearly 40 percent per year throughout the 1970s, and wholesale prices jumped by 42 percent in 1974 and 26 percent in 1975 before falling back toward single digits. Wholesale prices rose again by 18.6 percent in 1979 and 39 percent in 1980 before the new South Korean government of Chun Doo Hwan made fighting inflation a high priority in South Korea for the first time since it had regained its independence from Japan. Many other oil-importing developing countries did not make much effort to cut back government expenditures or to rein in domestic credit. Instead, like South Korea, they borrowed heavily abroad, but, unlike South Korea, they did not steadily devalue their nominal exchange rates in order to keep their exports competitive. Taiwan came out of the 1970s unscathed; South Korea also suffered little long-term damage, since it remained internationally competitive although it did acquire a sizeable foreign debt. Many other developing countries, such as a number of those in Latin America, had acquired an unsustainable level of international debt that was to lead to the worldwide "debt crisis." These countries would experience a decade with little or no economic growth.

Macroeconomic policies in the 1960s and 1970s, therefore, were an essential component of Taiwan's export-oriented industrial development. In the absence of sound macroeconomic policies, the rapid growth of Taiwan manufacturing and manufactured exports would not have occurred.

GENERATING EXTERNAL SURPLUSES: 1980 TO 1987

As previous chapters have made clear, the 1980s were a period of profound change in Taiwan's economy and economic policy. There were major changes in the structure of industry and exports. The 1980s mark the beginning of large foreign direct investment by Taiwan firms in the Chinese mainland and in Southeast Asia. The whole approach to government's role in influencing industrial development undergoes a profound shift away from direct intervention and toward greater reliance on unfettered market forces. None of these changes can be understood without first understanding what was happening in the macroeconomic sphere. The direction of causation goes from macroeconomic change to changes in industrial policy, not the other way around. An important related issue is whether the macroeconomic changes occurring were the result of deliberate government policy, or the unintended consequences of macro trends that the government either did not fully understand or over which it had only limited control.

Although from the perspective of 1980 Taiwan's economy appeared to be in trouble, by 1983 the economy had recovered to grow by over 8 percent, and GNP growth throughout the latter part of the 1980s (1983 through 1989) averaged 9.5 percent a year. This high real growth rate was achieved despite a dramatic fall in the rate of investment from over 30 percent of the GNP throughout much of the latter half of the 1970s to a more modest 23.4 percent in 1983 and a low of 17.1 percent in 1986.[19] The rate of savings, in contrast, remained high, averaging above 30 percent of GNP throughout the decade. The surplus of savings over investment peaked at 19.5 percent in 1986 and averaged 13.5 percent during the 1983 through 1989 period. Exports of goods and services exceeded imports over the same period by an average of 12.4 percent of GNP. As early as 1986, foreign exchange reserves had risen to us$47 billion, equivalent to a year and a half of imports, and those reserves kept on rising. All of this was a new experience for Taiwan's policy makers. Prior to the 1980s, savings and investment and exports and imports were roughly in balance back to the 1950s, when investment exceeded savings and imports were larger than exports in both cases by a wide margin.

What accounts for this extraordinary change in macroeconomic structure and the continued high rates of growth despite the sharp fall off in investment? The erosion of oil prices helped: Taiwan's terms of trade improved steadily throughout the 1980s, rising by 22 percent from 1981 to 1986, a gain of about 8 percent of GNP. But policies played a central role, and it is important to try to understand the nature of that role. What follows, therefore, is an analysis of the components of national income and the indicators of macroeconomic policy change. The purpose of this analysis is to attempt to explain what happened to key macroeconomic variables and why it happened. What caused the marked fall in domestic investment and what led to the massive accumulation of international reserves in the first half of the 1980s? How did this accumulation of reserves, by precipitating new domestic and international problems, force the authorities to change their approach to macroeconomic policy and much else after 1986?

The framework for this analysis is the national income identity,[20]

$$Y = Cp + Cg + I + E - M,$$

which, with S defined as in Figure 5-1

$$S = Y - (Cp + Cg),$$

results in the identity between the savings-investment balance and the current account balance,

$$S - I = E - M.$$

A simple model would make savings and imports functions of income; savings and investment functions of real interest rates, r, (or monetary policy); and exports and imports functions of the real exchange rate, p:

$$S(Y, r) - I(r) = E(p) - M(Y, p)$$

$$+\ + \qquad - \qquad + \qquad +\ -$$

with the signs indicating the direction of change.[21]

In Taiwan before the mid-1980s, both the nominal exchange rate and the nominal interest rates were managed by the authorities rather than allowed to move freely in response to market forces. We can, therefore, treat these as exogenous or policy variables, at least in the short term. If these nominal rates were used to target the real exchange and interest rates, however, then the latter would be the independent or policy variables. The data on the real exchange rate for the period up to 1980 suggests such targeting. We also know that, from the early 1950s on, government policy makers were concerned to keep real interest rates positive. Thus we treat the real rather than the nominal exchange and interest rates as the exogenous or policy variables.

Taiwan's economic recovery in the early 1980s, with its generation of large external surpluses, required monetary (interest rate) and exchange rate policies that simultaneously increased the internal savings-investment and external trade balances. In the discussion that follows, we examine each of these two balances separately in order to attempt an answer to two questions. First, can economic policies explain the large savings and current account surpluses of the early 1980s—indeed, were policies even consistent with these outcomes—or were underlying long-term structural changes involved? Second, if policies were the deciding influence, did policy makers intend to generate such surpluses or did the policies adopted to generate a recovery in 1980 simply go too far?

We shall also speculate about a third question. Was it domestic savings and investment behavior, and the policies that influenced that behavior, that were the primary forces generating the trade surplus? Or were the trade surpluses and the trends in exports and imports that generated those surpluses the primary force driving the surplus of savings over investment?

The Determinants of the Excess of Savings over Investment

The basic savings and investment data for Taiwan are presented in Figure 5-1. This figure confirms the statement made above, that 1980 marked the end of a long period during which savings and investment were roughly in balance. From 1981, for over a decade, savings in Tai-

FIGURE 5-1
Savings and Investment

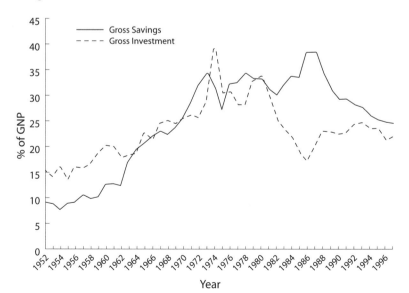

Year

wan exceeded investment often by a very wide margin. After 1991 or 1992, however, the gap falls to only 2 or 3 percent of the GNP, although it does not disappear altogether.

As Figure 5-1 indicates, two forces drove the large savings-investment surplus of the early 1980s. First was the sharp drop in the rate of gross investment (gross capital formation) as a share in the GNP. Second was the continued rise in the already high rate of gross savings. The data in Figure 5-2 provide a clear picture of the sources of the rise in gross national savings. Savings by government and public enterprises fluctuated as a share of the GNP in the 1980 to 1986 period, but taken together did not change much. The increase in private savings, both households and private enterprises, accounts for virtually the entire 7 or 8 percent rise in gross savings. Household savings in turn accounts for most of the rise in private savings. Between 1980 and 1986, household savings rose from 11 to 19 percent of the GNP and alone accounted for 61 percent of the rise in savings in that period. As fast as household savings rose in the early 1980s, it fell in the decade that followed. By the 1990s, household savings fell back to 12 or 13 percent of the GNP.

Any attempt to explain the rise and subsequent fall of Taiwan's savings behavior, therefore, must somehow account for the parallel rise

FIGURE 5-2
Components of Savings

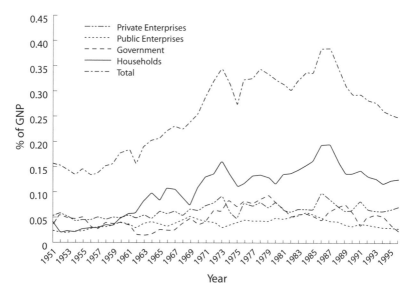

and fall of household savings. There is also the question of why Taiwan's household savings rate was so high relative to that found in so many other economies at comparable stages of development. High levels of private savings, it has often been noted, is a defining characteristic of a number of East Asian rapidly growing economies. Explanations for this high level point to the absence of formal pension mechanisms and to the importance in household budgets of privately financed education, among other things.[22] Changes in the rate of savings over time, however, in East Asia as elsewhere, are usually explained using some version of the "life cycle hypothesis." Savings, according to this hypothesis, are likely to be highest during the peak earning years of households when the children are grown and in the work force, and before one or more household members has retired.

It is in the spirit of this hypothesis that in the savings regressions in Appendix D, two variables for dependency ratios were included. The two variables used were the share of the population under the age of fifteen and the share of those over the age of sixty-five. In the log-linear form of the regression (only), the coefficients for both of these variables were negative and statistically significant. Taken together, however, the rise in the share of the population over sixty-five lowers the rate of savings by roughly the same amount as the fall in the share of the population under fifteen raises the savings rate. Furthermore, the share of the over-sixty-five group begins rising in the 1960s, and the rate of increase in the share is quite steady from the late 1970s through the 1990s. In a similar manner, the share of the under-fifteen population begins falling in the late 1960s and falls at between 0.4 and 0.7 percent a year in most of the years thereafter. The estimates of the regressions in this study may differ from those in other studies, and the coefficient for the over-sixty-five population is, in our opinion, implausibly large. It does not seem likely, however, that any plausible estimates for these dependency coefficients will explain the sharp rise and then fall of Taiwan household savings in the short span of a decade.

If the life cycle hypothesis does not explain this savings bulge in the 1980s, what does? Direct action by the government intended to raise public savings does not explain the rise because there is no rise in public savings in the early 1980s. The fall in public savings in the 1990s may account for some of the decline in gross savings in that period, however. Still, the main problem is to explain private household savings. If government was responsible for this bulge, high government-set interest rates might be the explanation. Interest rates in the early 1980s did move in the right direction. Although nominal interest rates on three-month deposits fell from 10 percent a year in 1980 to 4 percent in 1986, inflation also fell sharply from the double-digit levels of the second oil crisis. The net result was that the real interest rate on three-month deposits soared from negative 7 percent in 1980 to a high of 6.5 percent in 1984 and was still over 3 percent in 1986.

Short-term interest rates and other conventional macroeconomic policy instruments typically have a weak impact on private savings.[23] In the regressions in Appendix D, however, we found a statistically significant elasticity of the savings-GNP ratio with respect to the real deposit rate of +0.9. As explained in the appendix, if we allow for the gradual adjustment of the savings rate to higher values of the interest rate, for the six years from 1980 through 1986, the 5 percent rise in the interest rate could have been responsible for a rise in the savings rate of only 11 percent. The actual savings-GNP ratio, by way of comparison, rose 50 percent. Alternative estimates account for a rise of only 7 percent at most. It appears, therefore, that, although interest rate policy may have had some impact, it cannot explain much of the rise in savings rates in the 1980s. Nor does interest rate policy appear to account for much of the decline in savings rates after 1987, since real short-term deposit rates were generally positive in the 2 to 3 percent range in the 1990s.

A fourth explanatory variable for the savings-GNP ratio could be the high rate of growth of per capita income in the 1983 through 1987 period. GNP grew at an annual rate of 10.1 percent in that period. Given that GNP in the previous three years, during the second oil shock, grew at only 5.6 percent a year, it may be that households in Taiwan saw the rise in income in 1983 through 1987 as a short-term windfall rather than as a rise in their permanent income. Households generally save a large share of what they consider to be a windfall. This fourth explanation appears to us to be the most plausible explanation for the spike in the savings rate in the mid-1980s. Other longer-term influences, notably the relatively low and falling dependency ratios, probably account for the high average level of savings throughout the 1970s, 1980s, and 1990s.

The decline in the gross investment-GNP ratio in the mid-1980s appears to have been even more dramatic than the rise in the savings ratio and is equally hard to explain in any definitive way. Part of this decline, however, is more apparent than real. The spikes in investment in 1974 and 1979 to 1980, for example, are partly the result of abnormally high buildups in inventories in those years (10.7 percent of the

GNP in 1974). In the 1980s and 1990s in general, inventory growth averaged only 1.0 percent of the GNP a year, as contrasted with an average of 3.3 percent in the years 1970 through 1980 and 3.4 percent a year in the years 1960 through 1969. Large inventories of inputs are a characteristic of command economies and other economies with a high degree of government intervention.[24] The decline in inventory growth in the 1980s and 1990s, therefore, may mainly reflect the fact that in a more liberalized economy, firms could easily and quickly obtain needed inputs from home or abroad and hence did not need large inventories.

In a similar vein, the decline in the rate of fixed capital formation reflects the fact that, in the 1980s and 1990s, the prices of capital goods relative to other goods declined when compared with the prices of the 1960s and 1970s. This relative price change may also have been the result of liberalization policies, since many capital goods had to be imported, but further work would be required to establish that this was in fact the case. In real terms, the peak-to-trough fall in fixed capital formation between 1980 to 1981 and 1986 to 1987 was 7 percent of GNP as contrasted with the 13 percent decline in current prices. When the impact of changes in the growth rate of inventories is taken together with the change in relative prices, the peak-to-trough decline in the investment that really mattered for long-term growth was more like 8 percent of the GNP. This compares with the 17 percent decline in gross investment in current prices. Part of the decline in the rate of investment in Taiwan, therefore, may reflect the fact that investors could do as well as they had in the past with a smaller expenditure from their current income.

Still, for understanding the savings-investment gap, it is the current price investment figures that matter, and these fell sharply. What are some other explanations for this drop? One clear explanation is that, although government investment held up, investment in public enterprises plummeted from 12 to just over 3 percent of GNP (see Figure 5-3). The decline of public enterprise investment in the early 1980s mainly reflects the delay or suspension of several large industrial projects in the face of new environmental concerns. The failure of public enterprise investment to recover in the decade after the mid-1980s reflects the government's decision to move away from reliance on public enterprises and to begin privatizing those that already existed.

The tightness of domestic credit policy in the first half of the 1980s is another part of the story. Real interest rates rose enough to have caused half, and possibly more, of the marked fall in private invest-

FIGURE 5-3

Gross Capital Formation

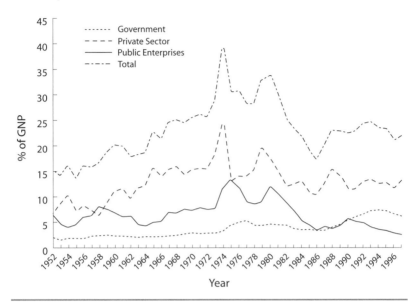

ment relative to GNP. If the government's aim had been to encourage private investment, then its monetary policy would have encouraged relatively low real interest rates. Although the nominal rate of interest fell, however, so did inflation, causing a net rise in the real rate. Nominal rates on secured loans fell from 15 percent in 1981 to 10.75 percent the following year and 9 percent in 1986. The sharp decline in inflation, however, allowed real rates to soar from slightly negative during the second oil crisis to a range of 8 to 10 percent in the five years from 1982 through 1986.

In the regressions reported in Appendix D, equations using the contemporaneous interest term yield negative and large short-term elasticity's (−3.1 in the log-linear form and −1.3 in the log-difference form). This result suggests a rather rapid response by investors to changes in interest rates. Allowing for gradual adjustment from one level of interest rates to another, the observed shift in rates using the higher elasticity estimate is able to explain considerably more than the observed fall in the investment rate. The more credible elasticity estimate of −1.3, however, explains only a drop of 18 percent compared with the observed decline in the investment-GNP ratio of 40 percent between 1980 and 1986.

The monetary policy behind these shifts in interest and inflation rates appears to have been lax. As the data in Figure 5-4 show, there was a steady rise of the increment in M2 as a share of GNP throughout the period from 1980 through 1987. The rise, however, was from a low base. Money supply in the late 1970s had grown relatively slowly, bringing annual increases in M2 down from 15 percent of GNP in 1977 to only 5 percent in 1978.[25] The steep rise in annual increments from 1978 through 1988 can be seen as a return (with some overshoot) to the previous trend of rising ratios of increments in M2 to GNP. A regression of the *stock* of M2 as a share of GNP on GNP per capita confirms this: the residuals for 1979 to 1984 are all negative.

Almost three-fourths of the rise in nominal money during the early 1980s was due to an increase in net foreign assets. Because government decreased its net debt to the banking system, there was still room for some nominal expansion of private credit, and the rise in private credit accounted for almost 40 percent of the rise in nominal M2. But increases in private credit fluctuated as a share of GNP, rising from 1980 to 1983, then falling precipitately until 1986, and then rising again even more steeply thereafter.

There is some evidence, therefore, that private domestic credit grew

---

FIGURE 5-4

Changes in Money Supply

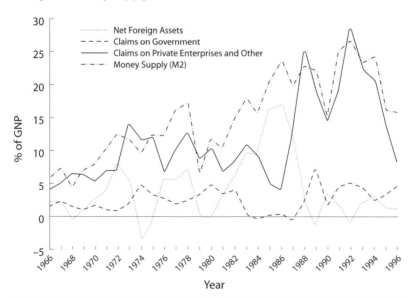

relatively slowly during the three-year period from 1984 through 1986 when increments in net foreign assets rose steeply as a share of GNP. Was this deliberate? In an interview with the authors, Central Bank officials stated that the bank did intend to sterilize 80 percent of the increase in reserves by expanding domestic credit at lower rates. They believed, however, that private liquidity was adequate during this period and was not a constraint on investment. Exporters who sold foreign exchange to the banking system, of course, owned the resulting local currency deposits and presumably had ample and growing liquidity. Other firms might have been squeezed if they depended mostly on the banks for credit, but, as pointed out repeatedly in this study, firms did not rely solely on the banks. It is likely that liquid export firms advanced credit to other companies either directly via trade credit or indirectly by lending through the informal curb market.

Bank officials cite the stock market boom as further support for their view that domestic credit was not a binding constraint on investment. Stock prices rose by 72 percent from 1981 to 1986, although this was only slightly more than nominal GNP. The real boom, an explosion of the index by a factor of nine in three years, began only in 1986 at the end of the period.

An attempt to raise international reserves through tight monetary policy would have to be backed up by tight fiscal policy. Reduced government consumption or increased revenues would contribute to increased savings, while budget surpluses could be used to reduce net government indebtedness to the banking system, thus curbing money growth. Government expenditure did indeed fall as a share of GNP (Figure 5-5) from 1980 through 1986, but tax revenue also fell. The net result was that the government balance as a share of GNP fluctuated between balance and a deficit equivalent to 2 percent of the GNP, with no trend until 1988–1989 (Figure 5-6). Fiscal policy, therefore, appears to have been approximately neutral; it does not seem to have been supporting a tight monetary policy. Thus domestic credit policy was tight enough during the first half of the 1980s, and real interest rates rose enough, to have caused half or possibly much more of the fall in private investment relative to GNP.

Were there structural factors in Taiwan that might have contributed to the sharp decline in investment in the first half of the 1980s despite the rise in savings? One possibility is that Taiwan's underlying comparative advantage was changed in the 1980s as wages rose relative to productivity in some sectors and the work force became better edu-

FIGURE 5-5

Government Revenue and Expenditure

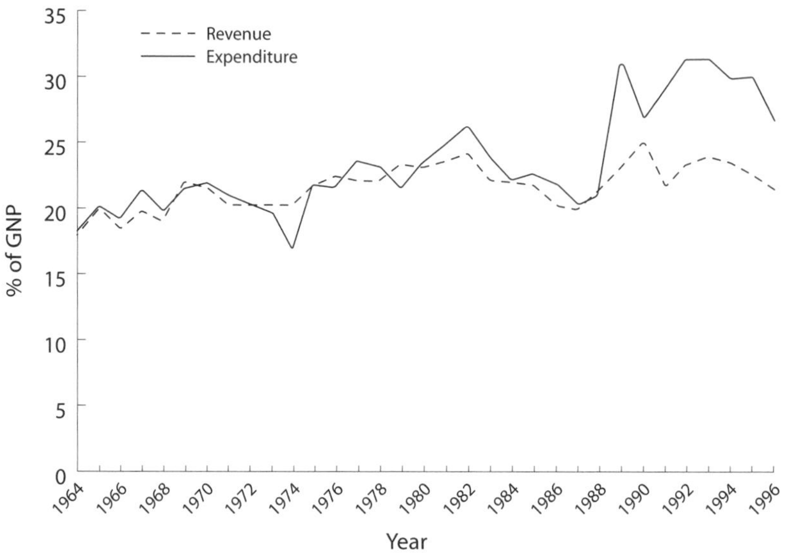

cated. As previous chapters have made clear, light industrial output focused on producing consumer products did peak in the mid-1980s and then began to fall absolutely as well as in terms of its share in total industrial output.

Taiwan's entrepreneurs could have responded to these influences in two ways. First, they could have continued investing in the same kinds of labor-intensive businesses, but outside of Taiwan in countries with abundant low-cost labor. These entrepreneurs did in fact do precisely that, but not until after 1986, so the outflow of direct investment to mainland China and Southeast Asia cannot explain the initial fall in gross domestic investment. Direct investment abroad may have had some influence on the level of domestic investment during the peak years of outflow in 1988 through 1990, but there was little if any overseas direct investment in the early 1980s.

Second, entrepreneurs could have begun to invest domestically in new industries that used human and physical capital more intensively. Shifting from one industrial sector to another would not have been easy for many of these entrepreneurs, and thus the shift could have occurred with a considerable lag. Taiwan small businesses, for example, knew their own particular business and little else. Limited access to bank credit

FIGURE 5-6
Budget Balance

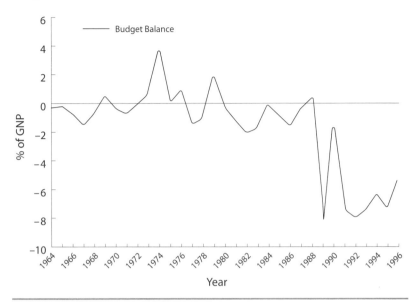

might also have hampered a rapid shift into new industries by these smaller firms. The resulting lags in new investments thus could account for part of the overall drop in gross investment. Some government economists believed this was the case,[26] but what is the evidence for it?

That Taiwan's comparative advantage was shifting away from labor-intensive industries in the 1980s cannot be doubted. The most dramatic shifts, however, occurred in the latter half of the 1980s, when the output of many of these sectors peaked and then began to fall. The shift in industrial structure in the latter half of the 1980s was clearly triggered in part by the revaluation of the NT dollar in that period, and this part of the story will be considered below in our discussion of the trade imbalance. The hesitation to invest in labor-intensive industries could have anticipated by several years that these industries were no longer going to be competitive.

The data on investment growth and efficiency wages in Table 5-1, however, provide only very limited support for the above hypothesis. The overall decline in investment is consistent with the hypothesis, but the sector composition of that investment presents a more mixed picture. Textiles and leather experienced rapid investment growth from 1978 through 1985, and these are commonly thought of as labor-inten-

TABLE 5-1

Growth (percent per annum) in Real Wages per Unit Output and
Investment at Constant Prices, 1978–1993

Industry	Real Wages Per Unit Output		Investment at Constant Prices[a]	
	1978–1985	1985–1993	1978–1985	1985–1993
Manufacturing	5.2	4.5	3.0	6.2
Food Products	8.8	7.4	6.0	3.9
Beverages & Tobacco	9.9	12.1	−14.5	−48.6
Textile Mill Products	11.1	4.7	15.2	−1.0
Apparel	4.3	9.5	0.4	−3.4
Leather Products	0.6	5.8	10.8	−6.4
Wood Products	5.5	6.2	0.4	−3.5
Pulp & Paper Products	2.3	2.9	2.8	8.2
Industrial Chemicals	0.8	5.5	−7.1	7.0
Chemical Products	−0.3	6.7	—	—
Rubber Products	5.1	3.8	1.0	7.6
Nonmetal Mineral Products	5.4	2.8	10.6	2.6
Basic Metals	7.3	4.4	1.6	10.6
Fabricated Metals	13.5	5.6	1.6	7.6
Nonelectrical Machinery	6.4	3.1	−2.4	8.3
Electrical Equipment	5.1	2.9	7.3	8.9
Transport Equipment	3.7	1.8	2.9	11.4
Precision Instruments	9.0	4.4	NA	0.5
Miscellaneous Manufactures	9.2	4.2	0.2	−7.0

[a] Based on three-year averages centered on 1978, 1985, and 1993.

"—" represents data combined with industrial chemical data.

sive sectors (although that is only partially true of textiles). Investment
in clearly labor-intensive sectors such as apparel and beverages and
tobacco is also low. Industrial chemicals are capital intensive, but chemical products, which in Taiwan in the early 1980s included all kinds of
consumer plastics, are often quite labor intensive. The growth rate of
investment in industrial chemicals and chemical products actually fell
in the early 1980s. The slow growth in investment in basic and fabri-
cated metals, nonelectrical machinery, and transport equipment would
be consistent with either the hypothesis that investment in these new

sectors was lagging behind opportunity or the hypothesis that comparative advantage had not yet shifted decisively toward these sectors.

Regressions of investment growth on efficiency wage growth show no significant correlation for the early 1980s, but give the anticipated strong negative correlation for the second period. It does not appear that the early-period changes in efficiency wages caused the investment pattern of the later period: the correlation of investment on the efficiency wage is not significant. If anything, causality runs the other way. A regression of the efficiency wage in the second period on investment in the first period yields a negative coefficient that just fails to be significant at 5 percent, so that faster growth of investment in period one may have led to slower growth of efficiency wages in period two. Thus the suggestion that a shift in comparative advantage caused a temporary slowdown in investment in the early 1980s finds some support in the data, but the results are not totally convincing.

Whatever the precise causes of the fall in the share of investment in the 1980s and the simultaneous rise in the level of savings, the most important point is that the savings-investment gap that opened up was temporary. By the early 1990s it had largely disappeared. Investment never recovered to the peak levels of the 1970s, but it was the peak levels of the 1970s, driven in part by a large inventory buildup, that was abnormal. In real terms, fixed capital investment by the 1990s comprised as large a share of the GDP as it ever had, with the exception of the single year 1975. The jump in the savings rate was also temporary. By 1990, the savings rate had fallen back to pre–oil crisis levels, and the rate continued to decline throughout the first half of the 1990s.

Government monetary policy probably played a role in this large but temporary gap between savings and investment, but forces that the government neither controlled nor fully understood probably played at least an equal role. The spike in savings, as pointed out above, may have been driven by the lag in consumption growth behind the very large increases in real income in the early 1980s. The fall in investment may have resulted to a significant degree from changes in company inventory policies and lags in the ability of investors to respond to the rapid pace of change in comparative advantage occurring in the 1980s. If government policy did create the large savings-investment gap, it is unlikely that that was the original intent of this policy. High real interest rates were a response first to the second oil crisis, and their continuation into the first half of the 1980s may reflect little more than the fact that this was a period when the president's poor health made it

difficult to achieve any major policy changes. After 1986, major changes
in policy once again became possible and the gap soon declined, although it did not disappear altogether.

The Causes of the Gap Between Exports and Imports

The role of policy in driving the gap of the 1980s between exports and
imports is much clearer than it is in the case of the savings-investment
gap. The basic story of what happened to the trade balance is well
known, and the relevant data are presented in Figure 5-7. In 1982, after
two decades, when exports and imports were generally in balance, a
surplus in exports over imports opened up and grew steadily wider
through 1986 to 1987. Taiwan's foreign exchange reserves (net foreign
assets in Figure 5-7) ballooned to 60 percent of the GNP in 1987. After
1987, the surplus of exports over imports disappeared almost as rapidly. By 1992, Taiwan's exports and imports of goods and services were
once again roughly in balance.

There are two principal government policy instruments that have
an influence on foreign trade and the external balance of payments.
The first is the real exchange rate. The second includes a wide range of
government tariffs and subsidies and nontariff barriers affecting im-

---

FIGURE 5-7
Foreign Trade and Reserves

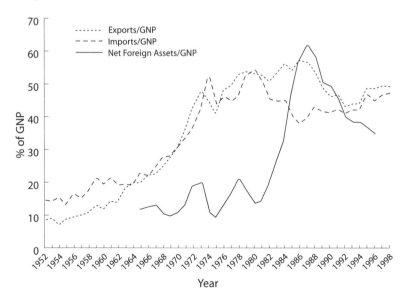

ports and exports. Tariffs and nontariff barriers, however, are not instruments that lend themselves easily to short-term policy requirements. One can lower these barriers in order to facilitate imports, but the international trading rules make it very difficult to turn around a few years later and raise them again. It is the real exchange rate, therefore, that is the preferred instrument for short-term policy purposes.

What happened to the nominal and real exchange rate in Taiwan in the period of concern here? The nominal rate is the easiest to follow. From 1972 through 1980, the nominal exchange rate against the US dollar was allowed to appreciate by 10 percent, from NT$40 to NT$36 per US dollar. From 1981 through 1983, however, this trend was reversed and there was a gradual devaluation back to NT$40, where the rate remained through 1985. After 1985, the rate once again appreciated to a low of NT$25 by December 1990. The nominal rate then remained at roughly this level (NT$26 or 27) until 1997, when the Asian financial crisis led the government to allow a nominal devaluation of nearly 20 percent (NT$32.8 in early 1998).

Although the nominal exchange rate is the policy instrument available to a government to alter relative prices between foreign and domestic goods and services, it is the real exchange rate—which government cannot control directly—that matters to producers and traders. The real exchange rate is conventionally defined as:

$$RER = eP^*/P,$$

where e is an index of the nominal exchange rate in local currency per unit of foreign currency, P^* is a measure of foreign prices, and P is a measure of domestic prices. As conventionally measured, P^* and P are consumer price indices of the foreign trade partner and the home country, respectively. Generally a weighted RER is calculated for the major trading partners, using either export or import weights.

For Taiwan, a weighted average of the RERs for the United States, Japan, and mainland China covers the major trading partners and a majority of the export trade, while data for only the United States and Japan are required to cover over half of the import flows. The data in Figure 5-8 show that, based on the conventional measures using consumer price indices, both the export and import RERs depreciated with the nominal rate after 1980, the export rate depreciating by 10 percent and the import rate by about 25 percent by 1986. In Figure 5-8, it should be noted, a rise in the index is a depreciation or devaluation. From 1986 onward, however, both real rates appreciated substantially, the

FIGURE 5-8

Nominal and Real Exchange Rates

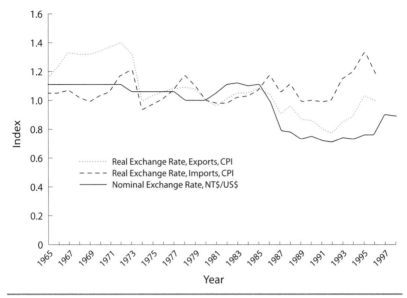

export rate by 39 percent and the import rate by 20 percent by 1991. Over the decade of the 1980s, the import rate remained much more depreciated than the export rate. The principal reason was that the yen, which was appreciating during the period relative to both the US and NT dollars, had a much greater weight in the import index (nearly 60 percent compared with only 20 percent).

The conventional measure of the RER using foreign consumer price indices, however, is a poor measure of the real exchange rate. Both trade and macroeconomic theory suggest that the proper measure of international competitiveness is a comparison between the prices of tradables and nontradables, or

$$RER = eP^*/P,$$

where P^* is a measure of tradable prices in foreign currency and P is a measure of nontradable prices.

The home country's Consumer Price Index (CPI) is not a bad measure of P, although it includes tradable goods, but the foreign CPI is a poor measure of tradable prices because nontradables have a heavy weight in most consumer goods baskets. The International Monetary Fund now gives price indices for exports and imports for the industrial countries. Using these instead of the CPI for Taiwan's trading partners gives a very different picture for the two RERs. As shown in Figure 5-9, the real export rate, which uses partners' import prices, appears to have been quite steady from 1968 to 1980, with some tendency to depreciate in the late 1970s, but then shows no sign of depreciation after 1980 despite the nominal depreciation of the NT dollar. The import rate, which uses partners' export prices, shows a general tendency to appreciate through the period from 1980 through 1992 and shows none of the sharp post-1980 depreciation of the CPI-indexed RER. A rise in the index in Figure 5-9, it should be noted once again, represents a depreciation of the exchange rate. Other measures of the real rate, using imputed domestic prices of tradables and nontradables from Taiwan's national accounts, are more erratic but show similar trends.[27]

Until recently, economists have used the CPI-indexed real rate because better measures were not generally available. Hence policy makers in Taiwan during the late 1970s would almost certainly have tracked the CPI-indexed version. Thus it is quite possible that policy makers did target the real rate, using nominal devaluation as their policy tool, and intended the kind of depreciation that the CPI-indexed rate showed.

FIGURE 5-9

Real Exchange Rates (Using Partners' Trade Prices)

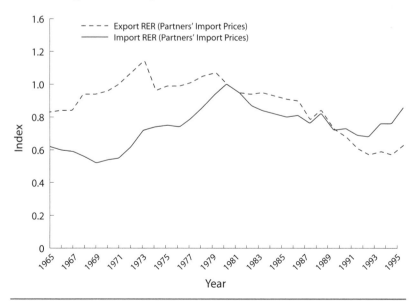

It is not clear, however, that the change in incentive was in fact being transmitted to Taiwan's producers. In the markets of these producers, on average the NT dollar was not depreciating at all.

Say, for the sake of argument, that producers were sensitive to the CPI-indexed real rate. Would the depreciation of the early 1980s have led to the observed surplus? The regressions reported in Appendix D give unstable and contradictory results. The most plausible estimate for exports shows a short-term elasticity with respect to the CPI-based real exchange rate of 0.5. This estimate implies that, allowing for gradual adjustment over six years from 1980 to 1986, the real devaluation could have explained an 18 percent rise in the ratio of exports to GNP, compared with the actual rise of 26 percent. The import equations in the appendix, however, do not give plausible results.

It may be that the explanation for the growing export share of GNP lies in a very different exchange rate story. The real exchange rate based on trade partners' import price indices was remarkably stable from the late 1960s to 1986, helping to establish a dependable environment favorable for investment in export industries. Following this incentive, investors established an efficient manufacturing structure that became increasingly competitive in world markets, so that Taiwan specialized to a growing extent in manufacturing for export. The steep appreciation of the real exchange rate after 1986 could have resulted both from larger and increasingly low-cost supplies of exportables from Taiwan and from policy decisions made feasible, or even necessary, as a consequence of past investments in exports. This story cannot be tested with our simple econometric model, because we would be trying to explain export growth with a variable that was stationary for a long period. Nor can the efficiency wage data (real wages per unit of output) in Table 5-1 be used to test this proposition. However, the finding that investment in the earlier period (1978–1985) is correlated with the lower efficiency wages in the later period (1985–1993) is consistent with this story.

Monetary policy appears to have supported reserve accumulation. We have already noted that monetary policy had been stringent during 1979 through 1981, so that the rapid money growth from 1982 through 1987 served only to bring the ratio of M2-GNP back to the trend established before 1979 (Figure 5-4). A possible interpretation is that the demand for liquid assets was growing faster than the money supply during the 1980s, so that rapidly growing foreign reserves did not lead to inflation. Rapid increases in the money supply did not begin to dampen reserve accumulation until 1988.

Whatever our revisionist view of the real exchange rate or our econometric results may prove, policy makers at the time were concerned about the impact of the exchange rate on exports. During interviews conducted in 1994, the authors learned that government officials at the time believed, and acted as if, the exchange rate were a crucial determinant of exporters' profitability and of export growth. As it became necessary to let the rate appreciate during the latter half of the 1980s, policy makers monitored export firms' profits to ensure that export growth would not be endangered.[28]

Participants in the economic policy debates of the 1980s offer different, but not necessarily contradictory, views of policy makers' intentions toward the growing external surplus. S. C. Tsiang, writing in 1987, argued that it was the trade surplus that drove savings and investment, rather than the reverse. But this surplus was not so much an objective of policy as a condition forced on Taiwan by the large U.S. budget deficit that, in turn, generated a large trade deficit. Tsiang notes that both Japan and Germany began to run larger surpluses with the United States from 1982 through 1986, once the U.S. budget deficit rose (from US$80 billion in 1981 to over US$200 billion from 1983 through 1986).[29] Tsiang was right that Taiwan's surplus was due largely to its bilateral trade with the United States. In 1985 and 1986, in contrast to its trade with the United States, Taiwan ran a large deficit with Japan, smaller surpluses with Hong Kong and mainland China, and had roughly balanced trade with Germany.

Taiwan's government, however, had two options available if it chose not to accept the burden of validating the U.S. trade deficit and financing the U.S. budget deficit (by accumulating U.S. Treasury Bills as part of Taiwan's growing reserves). First, Taiwan could have allowed the exchange rate to appreciate during the early 1980s rather than waiting until the late 1980s. Instead Taiwan allowed the real exchange rate to depreciate. Second, Taiwan could have reduced tariffs, liberalized imports, and removed currency controls. Tsiang in fact argued for precisely this course. From the perspective of 1982 to 1986, however, the U.S. trade and budget deficits seemed temporary to most observers in Taiwan, including Tsiang, and it appeared that more balanced trade with the United States would soon reassert itself without a change in the real exchange rate. This desire to wait before acting to reduce the trade surplus was further reinforced by the mercantilist tilt among many Taiwanese policy makers, who wished to protect both exporters from appreciation and import-competing firms from reduced protection.

Not all of the reluctance to appreciate the exchange rate and liberalize imports was the result of the deliberate efforts and desires of economic policy makers. As pointed out in Chapter 3, many of these policy makers perceived a need to do something about the growing external surplus as early as 1984. By then they felt that the devaluation and monetary restraint of the early 1980s, policies introduced in response to the second oil crisis, had gone too far. In 1983 and 1984, a series of failures in the financial industry diverted the attention of key economic decision-makers for a time. Later in 1984, however, there was a growing consensus among these key macroeconomic policy makers that exchange rate appreciation, import liberalization, and a relaxation of foreign exchange controls was necessary. But by mid-1984, President Chiang Ching-kuo was ill and inactive. Without the authority of the president to support the macroeconomic policy officials, a wide consensus among ministers was needed to implement so basic a policy shift. Strong mercantilist interests within the cabinet and among private interest groups were mobilized against these changes in macroeconomic policy. It was not until 1986, in the face of intensifying pressure from the United States, that proponents of change were able to implement the new policy regime.

APPRECIATION, LIBERALIZATION, AND THE END OF INTERNAL AND EXTERNAL SURPLUSES

The changes in policy and macroeconomic performance from 1986 to 1987 on were as dramatic as the changes that occurred in the first half of the 1980s. As fast as the internal and external surpluses of savings and exports appeared, they disappeared. As was the case during the early 1980s, the key policy instruments in the late 1980s and the 1990s were the exchange rate and the rate of increase in the money supply.

Exchange rate policy after 1986 was part of a package that included a wide range of trade liberalization measures. Appreciation of the exchange rate versus the US dollar began in 1986 as the NT dollar was allowed to float. The nominal exchange rate appreciated immediately, but the real rate did not begin to revalue until 1987, reversed itself in 1988, and then revalued again from 1989 through 1992. This pattern is observable in all of the measures of the real exchange rate (Figures 5-8 and 5-9). Exports as a share of GNP peaked in 1986 and 1987, and then the share fell steadily through 1992. Similarly, imports as a share of GNP bottomed out in 1985 to 1987, and then their share recovered slightly, more or less matching the export GNP share by 1992.

After 1992 through 1997, exports and imports moved together. As trade liberalization measures progressed, however, real exchange rates once again depreciated. Using the CPI-based real indices, the real exchange rates for both imports and exports devalued after 1992. Using partners' trade prices to deflate, however, only the import exchange rate depreciates while the export exchange rate index remains largely unchanged. It is testimony to the success of Taiwan's efforts to convert from labor-intensive to capital- and technology-intensive exports that, despite the revaluation of the exchange rate, exports in real terms grew at a rate of 6.1 percent a year in the decade after 1987. This real export growth rate actually accelerated to 8.3 percent a year during the five-year period 1993 through 1997. Given this export performance, Taiwan's decision to allow a nearly 20 percent nominal devaluation of the NT dollar in response to the Asian financial crisis of 1997 to 1998 is difficult to understand. Did this devaluation reflect panic in the face of attacks on Asian currencies in general or a mercantilist desire to take advantage of the international crisis atmosphere to make sure that Taiwan's exporters did not suffer?

Although Taiwan itself experienced a sharply declining share of labor-intensive exports in total trade, Taiwan's firms remained very active in sectors such as textiles, garments, and footwear. Capital market liberalization, however, allowed these firms to carry on the manufacturing part of their business abroad. Beginning in a small way in 1987 and accelerating rapidly in 1988, Taiwan manufacturers began large-scale foreign direct investment in Southeast Asia and the Chinese mainland. Taiwan's foreign direct investment peaked at US$6.95 billion in 1987 but continued at levels ranging from US$2 to 4 billion in the decade that followed. Taiwan in this period was second to only Hong Kong in investments in the Chinese mainland and was one of the top two or three foreign direct investors in Malaysia, Vietnam, and Indonesia.

Despite the outflows of foreign direct investment and the rough balance between exports and imports, Taiwan's foreign exchange reserves (net foreign assets) continued to rise through 1994 and then declined significantly in 1995 through 1997 before rising back to the 1995 level in 1998. Net foreign assets as a share of the GNP, however, declined sharply throughout this decade. Where the increase in net foreign assets was the major reason for the rapid increase in the money supply through 1987, it played only a minor role through the first half of the 1990s and no role in the latter part of the 1990s.

Monetary policy makers after 1987, therefore, faced a very different situation from the one that existed during the first half of the decade. They responded by allowing increases in private credit as a share of the GNP to rise dramatically from levels often below 10 percent of the GNP to levels ranging from 15 to nearly 30 percent of the GNP in the years 1988 through 1994. With private credit as the driving force, the money supply (M2) as a share of the GNP rose by between 15 and 25 percent a year throughout the 1988 to 1994 period (Figure 5-4). The monetary ease that these movements reflected were reflected in declining real interest rates, which had exceeded 7.5 percent a year on secured loans from 1982 through 1988, but fell steadily to 3.6 percent by the end of 1992.

One side effect of this rapid increase in the money supply may have been the stock market that began in 1986 and topped out in 1989 before falling back in the next two years. When the rollercoaster ride was over, the stock market was still at four times higher than it had been in 1986. The phasing of the stock market rise with money creation and private savings behavior is presented in Figure 5-10. The peak in private savings occurred in 1986, just as the stock market boom was getting started, and the savings rate fell steadily thereafter. It was the rise in net private domestic credit that appears to foreshadow the rise of the stock mar-

---

FIGURE 5-10

Sources of the Stock Market Bubble

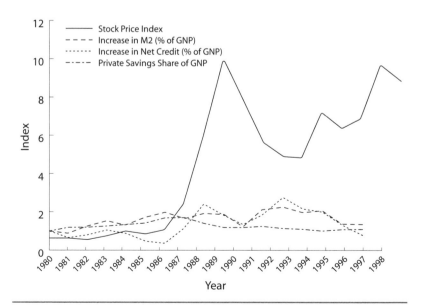

ket. Private domestic credit peaked a year before the stock index and then fell precipitately as a share of the GNP, declining about a year ahead of stock prices.[30]

The expansive posture of credit policy was reinforced by fiscal policy. Government expenditure soared during 1989, rising from 20 to over 30 percent of the GNP in one year, and remained high through 1995, declining slightly in 1996 (Figure 5-5). The deficit that opened up, since revenues did not rise significantly, averaged 6 percent of the GNP, in contrast to earlier years when there was hardly any deficit at all. Although all components of government expenditure expanded as a fraction of the GNP after 1988, those categorized as "economic development" expanded most rapidly. Except for the spike in economic development expenditure in 1989, which was due to the purchase of private land to be reserved for government's future use, however, the rise in government and public enterprise investment was gradual. It is likely, therefore, that this gradual rise reflects major increases in recurrent expenditures. Much of the post-1988 government deficit appears to have been monetized. Changes in net domestic credit to the government shifted from negative territory before 1989 to a range of from 2 to 5 percent of the GNP thereafter.

Government fiscal policy, together with the easing of monetary policy, account for at least a part of the closing of the savings-investment gap. The rise in investment consisted first of a spike in private investment in 1988 through 1990, followed by the above-mentioned rise in government investment with public enterprise investment rising as well but only through 1991. On the savings side, private enterprise savings began to fall in 1987, household savings followed a year later, and government savings was falling by 1990. Although low real interest rates may have something to do with the decline in household savings, much of the fall in that rate may have reflected the decline in GNP growth to an average of 6.3 percent a year from 1990 through 1996. Households probably saw increases at this rate as reflecting a rise in permanent income rather than a temporary windfall.

CONCLUSION

For Taiwan, therefore, the 1980s were a critical decade of change triggered to a substantial degree by rapid shifts in the external balance between exports and imports. The external and internal imbalances that appeared and then disappeared in the 1980s were partly the result of international trends over which Taiwan had little control, notably the large and growing U.S. trade deficit. Policy makers in Taiwan, however, were also slow to respond to these external influences, and so macroeconomic policies overshot their goals, particularly during the first half of the decade.

Policy makers were slow, to be sure, only in the sense that they did not respond fast enough to prevent Taiwan from running large external and internal imbalances for a little over a decade. Given the magnitude and scope of the policy changes required, Taiwan's macroeconomic policy makers could be plausibly said to have moved very rapidly. At the beginning of the 1980s, policy makers were following policies that had been in place since at least the early 1960s, mercantilist-style export promotion on the one hand combined with strong anti-inflationary measures on the other hand. By the latter half of the 1980s, Taiwan had begun a broad program of trade liberalization and had eased up substantially in the monetary and fiscal policy realms.

Some of these changes were in response to external pressures, but many were not. It can be argued that Taiwan's macroeconomic policy makers deliberately set out to create large balance of payments surpluses and then were forced to change when the United States objected. But the above discussion of macroeconomic policy, together with the political economic analysis in Chapter 3, fits better the view that policy change lagged behind the externally changing situation and that the large surpluses were the mainly accidental result.

The macroeconomic story of the 1990s is one of external and internal balances rather than imbalances. The large stock of foreign exchange reserves continued to exist, but grew only slowly and then stopped growing altogether. Liberalization of the economy proceeded, and the exchange rate together with domestic monetary policy adjusted to maintain balance. Mercantilism in Taiwan was not totally dead. Allowing the NT dollar depreciate in 1997 to 1998 by a nominal 20 percent, when Taiwan still had very large reserves and a sizeable current account surplus, could be seen as a mercantilist-style reaction to the Asian financial crisis. Certainly Taiwan's move did little to help stabilize the situation, although later offers by Taiwan of financial support did help, as did the subsequent appreciation in the nominal exchange rate in 1999. Competitive devaluation and other export promoting measures were not the dominant characteristics of Taiwan in the 1990s. During most of that decade, Taiwan was managed more and more like an open industrial economy.

NOTES

1 Fischer (1993, pp. 485–512).

2 Tsiang (1984, pp. 314 and 324).

3 Fry (1995, pp. 162–169). Our own regressions on Taiwan, reported below, find significant but small the coefficients (elasticities) on real interest rates, but these do not cover the early 1950s.

4 Tsiang (1984, p. 318).

5 Ranis and Mahmood (1992, p. 119).

6 These figures are approximations based on incomplete data supplied by Tsiang (1984, p. 324).

7 Ranis and Mahmood (1992, p. 120).

8 Kuo (1983, p. 17).

9 Myers (1990, pp. 35–36).

10 Cheng (1986, p. 154); and Emery (1991, p. 243).

11 Myers (1990, p. 35).

12 Cheng (1986, pp. 146 and 149).

13 Myers (1990, p. 43).

14 Cheng (1986, pp. 152–153).

15 Emery (1991, p. 269); and Kuo (1993, p. 5).

16 Schive (1987, pp. 320–321).

17 Fei (1992, pp. 3–24).

18 Myers (1990, p. 51).

19 These are the figures for gross capital formation as a percentage of GNP all in current prices. As discussion later will point out, the fall in real terms was not quite so large, but there was still a substantial fall.

20 The symbols have the usual meanings: Y = gross national income, C = consumption of private agents (p) or government (g); I = gross investment, E = exports of goods and services, M = imports of goods and services, and S = gross national savings.

21 A more realistic model would allow for the influence of monetary policy on the trade balance and possibly for the impact of exchange rate changes on investment. Although we experimented with these more complete specifications, the results were either statistically insignificant or gave counterintuitive signs. Thus, in what follows, the simpler structure is emphasized.

22 Scitovsky (1990, pp. 127–182); and McGinn et al (1980, pp, 70–71).

23 Fry (1995, pp. 162–169).

24 The relationship between command economies and input inventories was first noticed by Janos Kornai; the ratio of output to input inventories is known as the *Kornai index.*

25 The second rise in oil prices contributed to a drop in the accumulation of foreign reserves, while the growth of domestic credit also slowed. As real interest rates were not especially high during these years, the reduction in net domestic credit can probably be attributed to a fall in demand for credit rather than in tight monetary policies.

26 Interview.

27 The shortcomings of the conventionally measured RER, and the misleading behavior of the Japanese CPI in particular, have been pointed out by Radelet, who urges use of some trade-based price index instead. See Radelet (1996).

28 Interview.

29 Tsiang (1987).

30 Quarterly data would have been better suited for this analysis, but the annual data are roughly indicative of the trends.

6 PRODUCTIVITY AND STRUCTURAL CHANGE

Dwight H. Perkins and Lora Sabin

Describing what the government on Taiwan did to change economic policy and reform its economic system, as was done in Chapters 2 and 3, is straightforward. Analyzing the impact of those policies and reforms on economic performance is more difficult. Determining whether those policies and reforms performed better than some alternative set of policies and reforms that might have been carried out is virtually impossible. The focus of this chapter is on the former of these two questions: the relationship between policies and performance. The measures of performance that are used are the rate of productivity growth in Taiwan's various economic sectors and the structural change that occurred within and between sectors.

Economic growth, whether in industry or the economy as a whole, can be "explained" or accounted for by the increase in capital and labor needed to produce output growth and by the increase in the amount of output obtained from a given amount of capital and labor. The latter is generally referred to as an increase in *total factor productivity*. Economic growth through productivity increases is in some sense superior to growth achieved primarily through increases in the quantity of capital and labor, in part because the former does not require the sacrifices of current consumption and leisure that is required by the latter. Productivity growth may be embodied in improved capital and labor, or it may be unrelated to the increases in these factors of production.

Measuring the contribution of capital, labor, and productivity increases to the growth of the various sectors of Taiwan's economy is a straightforward, although data-intensive and time-consuming, process. There are a number of existing studies of the sources of growth of the Taiwan economy and, in many ways, the results presented in this chapter are consistent with the results in some of those earlier studies, notably the work of Alwyn Young.[1] What differentiates the estimates reported in this chapter from those studies is that a conscious effort is made to relate the results of the accounting exercise to the policies and reforms described in earlier chapters. There are also some differences in methodology from the earlier efforts that are seemingly small, but that have an important impact on how the estimates should be interpreted. These methodological issues will be dealt with later.

SOURCES OF GROWTH: ESTIMATES

Estimates for the sources of growth for Taiwan's economy as a whole and for the industry, agriculture, and services sectors individually are presented in Tables 6-1 and 6-2. To relate these results to the historical analysis in the previous chapters, one needs to look at the estimates period by period.

The initial period for which data are available covers the import-substitution years 1952 through 1960. The data used in these growth-accounting exercises are weaker for the 1950s than they are for later years mainly because the estimates of the growth rate of the capital stock are particularly sensitive to the assumptions made about the size of the initial capital stock. The growth rate of GDP during the first three years of the 1950s is a high 9 percent per year but falls to 6.7 per-

TABLE 6-1

The Sources of Growth of Gross Domestic Product in Taiwan

	Growth Rates (%)			
Period	GDP	Labor Input	Capital Input	Total Factor Productivity
1952–1955	9.00	3.51	5.70	4.83
1956–1960	6.70	4.87	6.04	1.47
1961–1965	9.50	4.75	7.78	3.84
1966–1970	9.37	10.43	12.76	−1.77
1971–1979	9.55	5.57	13.48	1.95
1980–1985	6.59	2.43	9.31	2.36
1986–1990	8.74	2.74	7.91	4.62
1991–1994	6.57	2.22	8.87	2.68

Source: See Appendix E for a description of how these figures were estimated.

cent per year over the next five years. This same basic pattern is observed in the manufacturing sector and in other services, including business and financial services. Only agricultural value added experiences a rise in its growth rate during the latter half of the decade. The main cause of the decline in the rate of output growth in the three sectors that experienced a decline was the sharp fall in total factor productivity growth. The growth rate of the workforce, which includes improvements in the quality of labor, does not decline. The rate of gross capital formation as a share of GDP actually rises slightly during the latter half of the 1950s, although this higher rate of investment still translates into a marginally slower growth rate of the capital stock because of the decline in the GDP growth rate.

The decline in productivity growth in the latter half of the 1950s probably reflects the end of the period of recovery from the war with Japan and the disruptive impact of the move of so many Chinese mainlanders to Taiwan. It may also reflect the fact that the possibilities for import-substituting industrialization were quickly exhausted. Agriculture's deviation from the pattern found in the other sectors presumably reflects the impact of land reform and the many other mea-

TABLE 6-2

Total Factor Productivity by Sector

Sector	1952– 1955	1956– 1960	1961– 1965	1966– 1970	1971– 1979	1980– 1985	1986– 1990	1991– 1994
Total Economy	4.83	1.47	3.84	−1.77	1.95	2.36	4.62	2.68
Agriculture	3.54	3.99	0.36	−1.76	2.52	1.10	2.33	1.30
Nonagriculture	5.96	0.71	5.67	−1.71	1.67	2.36	4.40	2.51
Industry	8.64	2.17	7.60	−0.23	1.83	2.58	3.16	3.07
Mining	0.88	5.19	11.01	0.89	8.39	3.15	6.38	16.67
Manufacturing	10.81	2.73	9.04	−0.20	1.18	3.41	2.97	3.20
Utilities	−19.56	−2.65	1.74	0.20	0.27	−1.73	3.70	7.32
Construction	6.64	−0.10	−0.70	−5.37	4.89	0.19	1.09	0.20
Services	4.68	−0.43	4.95	−3.18	1.03	2.42	5.69	2.64
Commerce	3.38	0.33	5.98	−6.94	1.49	2.28	5.62	4.23
Transport	5.26	0.55	−2.05	−0.02	5.46	7.34	4.40	3.45
Other	6.46	−0.44	2.49	−1.51	0.81	1.78	5.90	2.41

Supporting data and methodology: See Appendix E.

sures undertaken at the time to promote that sector. If the policies of the 1950s in industry and services had continued into the 1960s, a plausible hypothesis is that total factor productivity growth would have fallen further, possibly into negative figures, and that GDP growth would have fallen with it. If the lower GDP growth rate had led to a lower savings rate and fewer investment opportunities that translated into a constant or declining rate of gross capital formation, then the annual rate of increase of GDP might have fallen even further.

The policies of the 1950s did not continue into the 1960s, however. As the historical overview in Chapter 2 made clear, there was a dramatic change in policy in 1960. Economic incentives in Taiwan were restructured to favor manufactures, particularly those that were oriented toward exporting. The impact on GDP growth was immediate. The GDP growth rate rose from 6.7 to 9.5 percent per year during the five-year period beginning in 1961 and ending in 1965. Capital formation as a share of GDP, in contrast, rose only marginally, from an annual average rate of 17.6 percent (1956–1960) to 19.6 percent (1961–1965). The growth rate of the workforce was virtually unchanged. The principal change that led to the higher rate of GDP growth was the doubling of productivity growth. This increase in productivity growth accounted for over half of the rise in the growth rate of GDP. If the speculation that, in the absence of policy changes, productivity in the early 1960s might have fallen to zero or even into negative numbers is correct, then the contribution of productivity growth to the GDP performance of the early 1960s was even larger. Because the question of whether there was or was not high productivity growth in Taiwan in the early 1960s is controversial, the issue will be discussed further in a later part of this chapter devoted to methodological issues.

If high productivity growth "explains" the jump in output growth in the early 1960s, the same is clearly not true of the next one-to-two decade period. The years 1966 through 1979 can be lumped together for the discussion here. The mercantilist policies of the early 1960s that promoted manufactured exports while maintaining high barriers to imports for the domestic market remained in place throughout the period. It is in this period, not the early 1960s, that gross domestic capital formation as a share of GDP soared, reaching an average of 25.2 percent in 1966 through 1970 and 30.1 percent in 1971 through 1979. The growth rate of the workforce also took off in the late 1960s when the improving quality of the workforce is taken into account.[2] The workforce rate of increase then slows down in the 1970s, but to a rate in the economy as a whole that is still nearly three percentage points higher than it was in the late 1950s and early 1960s. The rapid increase in the number of university graduates was one reason for this high workforce adjusted for quality growth rate. Total factor productivity, in contrast, becomes negative in the late 1960s and is positive only in the 1970s.

Taiwan's growth in GDP, and in the manufacturing sector in particular, over the two decades beginning with the reforms of 1960, therefore, begins with a burst in productivity that was presumably caused by the reforms. Causation is not proved, of course, because there is only a correlation between reform and the spurt in GDP and productivity growth, but the reforms are the most plausible explanation for these events. The boom in manufactures and manufactured exports creates expanding investment opportunities that contribute to the sharp rise in the rate of capital formation. All of this occurs as the population dependency ratio (the ratio of the nonworking population to total population), which had been rising, begins to fall. This facilitates increases in the rate of savings that also contributes to the rising rate of investment.[3] The expansion in the education system that generates the large numbers of graduates in this period also predates the reforms of 1960. Without the expansion in educated labor, however, the rapid growth in manufacturing would have been much more difficult to achieve. Conversely, in the absence of the reforms, the productivity of that educated labor would presumably have been lower. The sequence of events, therefore, was from reform to productivity growth leading to accelerated GDP increases. Those increases, together with demographic and educational trends underway prior to the reforms, then facilitates the rapid rise in factor inputs and the continuation of the high GDP growth rate. This is a significantly different tale from the one told by analysts who see this experience as being mainly a story about rising rates of investment, presumably generated by an increase in the rate of savings, including foreign savings in the form of international aid. Investment in our story follows the spurt in growth and is, to an important degree, made possible by that spurt.

It is useful to note here that Taiwan's growth-accounting experience in the 1960s and 1970s is very similar to that of South Korea over much the same period. The relevant data are presented in Table 6-3. The growth-accounting methodology used to construct this table is a simplified version of the methodology used to construct the data in Table 6-1. The limited South Korean data available for the 1950s preclude a calculation of the sources of growth for that period. The South

TABLE 6-3

Sources of Growth of Gross Domestic Product in the Republic of Korea

| Period | GDP | Growth Rates (%) | | |
		Labor Input	Capital Input	Total Factor Productivity
1961–1965	7.49	3.21	−1.65	6.50
1966–1970	9.80	3.71	5.62	5.40
1971–1979	9.37	3.78	14.26	2.40
1980–1985	6.57	1.61	11.27	2.02
1986–1990	10.22	3.80	11.85	4.01
1991–1993	6.41	2.11	13.06	1.02

Sources and Methodology: This table was calculated using the increase in the employed workforce unadjusted for increases in workforce quality. The capital stock growth rates were obtained by adding net fixed capital formation (cumulative) to an initial capital stock figure that was assumed to be 1.5 times the GDP in 1960 and depreciated by 8 percent per year. The GDP growth rates and capital figures were in constant 1985 prices. All data were taken from the various statistical handbooks of the Economic Planning Board of the Republic of Korea.

Korean economic reforms also occur a few years after those in Taiwan— they begin in 1962 and 1963 rather than 1960—but the content of the reforms in the two economies was similar. Both introduced a wide variety of incentives for manufactured exports while continuing to restrict imports for the domestic market.

In South Korea, as in Taiwan, high GDP growth, which in the Korean case began in 1963 when the rate of increase jumped from 3.1 to 8.8 percent, was mainly the result of a large jump in productivity growth. In South Korea gross domestic fixed capital formation as a share of GDP, for example, hardly rises at all in the 1963–1965 period when compared with 1961–1962. The average share for the 1963–1965 period is 13.4 percent of GDP while the share for 1961–1962 is 12.8 percent. Beginning in 1966, however, the Korean average rate of gross fixed capital formation jumps to 23.0 percent of GDP in the years 1966 through 1970 and to an average of 26.8 in the years 1971 to 1979. The rate of growth of the workforce in South Korea also rises in the late 1960s and stays high in the 1970s. If we had included improvements in the quality of the workforce, as was done for Taiwan, the growth rate of the workforce would have risen even more. The 1960s and 1970s were years in which the number of secondary school and university graduates per year was increasing rapidly.[4]

The first few years of high growth in South Korea, as in Taiwan, were thus driven mainly by a large increase in the rate of growth of total factor productivity. The particular estimate of total factor productivity growth in Table 6-3 is subject to a wide margin of error. This wide margin is caused by the sensitivity of the estimate to the size of the initial capital stock in 1960, a figure that had to be assumed given the absence of reliable capital formation rates for the 1950s. That productivity growth was high during the initial growth spurt in South Korea as in Taiwan is as clear a conclusion as these kinds of estimates allow. Similarly, there is little doubt that the rate of productivity growth falls in the late 1960s and then falls much further throughout the 1970s. If workforce quality improvements had been included in the South Korea estimates, it is likely that total factor productivity in the 1970s would have been shown to have not grown at all.

The conclusion that productivity growth was low after an initial spurt caused by reforms is not really surprising. The initial spurt can be seen as a large innovative reallocation of resources from a less productive (import substituting) to a more productive (manufactured exports) use. Growth after that was achieved in both South Korea and Taiwan mainly by expanding the amount of capital and the number of workers in the more efficient exporting sector. In addition, in both Taiwan and South Korea, the 1970s saw a major shift in resources back toward import substitution through the promotion of heavy industries such as steel and petrochemicals. The productivity increases that did occur in Taiwan and South Korea in the 1970s probably involved little more than the shift of labor out of low-productivity agriculture into higher-productivity industry. There was also a steady process of learning on the job by both management and labor, particularly in the export-oriented industries. Research and development expenditures, while rising, were still below 1 percent of the GDP even at the end of the 1970s in both Taiwan and South Korea.

As the historical overview in Chapter 3 indicates, the early 1980s were a period of transition in Taiwan in which change had begun, but the overall performance of the economy was dominated by what went before. The period began with a recession in Taiwan generated by the second OPEC-generated increase in petroleum prices and the recession in North America and Europe that followed. Through the first half of the decade, Taiwan's exports of labor-intensive products continued to grow but at a slower pace, except in the field of consumer electronic goods. The effort to promote high-technology products had begun, but had not yet had much impact on the aggregate performance of Taiwan's economy. Only modest changes in the exchange rate were allowed, and talk of liberalization of the economy remained mostly talk.

Sources of Growth: The 1980s and 1990s

In terms of growth accounting, the most significant event of the first half of the 1980s was the sharp drop in the rate of gross fixed capital formation, from 30.7 percent of the GDP in 1980 to 18.5 percent in 1985. Investment in established sectors slowed markedly, while that in the newer high-technology sectors had just begun. Total factor productivity growth was similar to the low levels of the 1970s. The growth rate of the quality-adjusted workforce also slowed significantly, in part because earlier declines in the birth rate were beginning to show up in the workforce growth rate. The drop in the workforce growth rate in manufacturing and services was even more marked because the shift of labor out of agriculture had slowed. The combined result of these trends was a sharp drop in the rate of growth of GDP. The rate fell from 10.0 percent per year in the 1970s to 6.8 percent in the years from 1980 through 1985.

The experience of South Korea in the early 1980s is very similar to that of Taiwan, with notable exceptions. Total factor productivity growth in South Korea was no higher than it had been in the 1970s, and the rate of growth of the workforce fell. But South Korea's rate of gross fixed capital formation, unlike that in Taiwan, did not fall much at all in the early 1980s. Despite the higher share of capital formation in GDP, South Korea's GDP growth rate fell from 9.4 percent per year in the 1970s to 6.6 percent in the years from 1980 through 1985, a drop almost as large as the one that occurred in Taiwan.

The latter half of the 1980s tell a very different story. As discussed in Chapter 3, the government of Taiwan in the middle of the decade made a clear commitment to economic liberalization. Market forces plus U.S. pressure also led to a major revaluation of the NT dollar, which ended export growth in Taiwan based on labor-intensive manufactures. Finally, Taiwan also benefited from what in South Korea were referred to as the "three lows": low oil prices, a low exchange rate relative to the Japanese yen, and low world interest rates. The sharp revaluation of the Japanese yen from ¥ 238 per US dollar in 1985 to a low of ¥ 128 in 1988 gave Taiwan, like South Korea, the opportunity to compete in many sectors that until then had been dominated by the Japanese.

The combined impact of these changes plus other changes that we may not yet fully understand was to restore Taiwan's GDP growth to

9.1 percent per year throughout the last half of the decade. In current prices, Taiwan's rate of gross fixed capital formation did not rise, but the current price data in this case are misleading. If instead of using current price data to measure the ratio of gross fixed capital formation to GDP, one uses fixed prices, the results are quite different. In fixed prices, the rate of gross fixed capital formation does fall in the first half of the 1980s, but not as far as the current price data would imply. By the end of the 1980s—this was even truer in the first half of the 1990s— the rate of gross fixed capital formation in fixed prices had recovered to the peak levels achieved in the mid-1970s. The growth rate of fixed capital in real terms was thus higher than one would have assumed, given the sharp drop in the rate of investment in current price terms. Investors, it would appear, benefited from a major improvement in their terms of trade vis-à-vis consumption goods. The presumed cause of this lowered relative cost of fixed capital was the revaluation of the NT dollar together with the trade liberalization measures that began in the latter half of the 1980s, but further analysis is required before one can have confidence in this explanation. Whatever the cause, investors in the late 1980s and 1990s were able to get the same real increase in their capital while saving a smaller share of their income.

The growth rate of the quality-adjusted workforce fell even further in the latter half of the 1980s than it did in the first half of the decade. The return to high growth, therefore, was accounted for in part by a marked rise in total factor productivity. But gross fixed capital measured in real terms also contributed significantly by continuing to grow at a fairly rapid rate, a rate higher than one would have expected given the still-low rate of investment in current price terms.

The growth-accounting story in the first half of the 1990s is similar to that of the late 1980s. When looking at the economy as a whole, the growth rate of the workforce falls further and the capital stock increases at a rate only slightly higher than they did in the 1980s. Unlike in the period after the reforms of 1960, however, the growth rate of total factor productivity in the early 1990s does not slow down. In the manufacturing and agriculture sectors, in fact, the total factor productivity growth rate actually rises. Overall, GDP growth slows from 9.1 to 6.8 percent per year from the late 1980s to the first half of the 1990s. With little or no increase in the quality-adjusted workforce, growth rates at the 9-to-10 percent annual level could not be sustained. Much of the GDP growth that did occur took place in the business services sector. The growth rate of the capital stock and of the workforce in business services stayed high or actually rose in the early 1990s, while the work-force in manufacturing and agriculture fell. The net flow of labor out of manufacturing and into business services may itself have pressured manufacturers to raise total factor productivity while, at the same time, it reduced pressure on the services sector to do so as well.

The South Korean experience in the late 1980s and early 1990s is very similar to that of Taiwan. The GDP growth rate first accelerated and then fell back to just over 6 percent per year, and there was a pronounced shift away from manufacturing toward business services. The main growth-accounting difference between South Korea and Taiwan is that the growth rate of the capital stock in South Korea was considerably higher than that in Taiwan, particularly in the early 1990s, and total factor productivity growth in South Korea was much lower. Why this difference existed is a question that requires further research.

Sources of Growth: Demand Side Story

The above analysis looked at the sources of Taiwan's growth from the supply side. The story on the demand side is simpler. The share of private consumption in GDP fell steadily throughout the 1960s and 1970s, from 68 percent of the GDP at the beginning of the period to around 50 percent at the end. There was also a modest decline in the share of government consumption. Growth of aggregate demand at nearly 10 percent per year was sustained by the rapid increase in the share of exports that rose from 11 percent of GDP in 1960 to over 50 percent by the end of the 1970s. The increasing shares of investment and imports in GDP were largely derived from the need of the export sector for capital and intermediate inputs. These figures simply confirm the well-known fact that the 1960s and 1970s were a period of export-led growth.

The pattern of the 1980s and 1990s on the demand side is quite different. The shares of private consumption and exports do not change much in the early 1980s, but after 1987, private consumption's share rises steadily from 47 percent to 59 percent by 1994 to 1995. Exports, in contrast, fall from 56 percent of the GDP in 1987 to 44 percent in 1994 before rising again to an average of 48 percent in 1995 to 1996 and 49 percent in 1997 to 1998, despite the Asian financial crisis. Export demand remained important, but it was the rising share of domestic private consumption that allowed the GDP growth rate to stay at a relatively high level. In real terms, exports grew at 7.6 percent per year while private consumption grew considerably faster at 8.7 percent between 1987 and 1998. This rising and central role for private consumption is presumably one of the main effects of the liberalization of the rules governing Taiwan's economy, but tracing the precise nature of the connection between liberalization and private consumption is beyond the scope of this study.

METHODOLOGICAL ISSUES

Although the results of the above analysis, particularly those that approach the sources of growth from the supply side, are similar in many respects to the findings of other studies, there are also significant differences. Given that these results are the principal means we have of appraising the impact of policy reform on economic performance in Taiwan, consideration needs to be given to whether the results reported here are sensitive to the choice of methodology and assumptions about initial conditions. The studies with which we shall compare our results are those of Alwyn Young, Lawrence Lau and his several collaborators, and an unpublished study by Dale Jorgenson and Liang Chi-Yuan.[5] The differences fall under five broad headings. First, there are the differences in the periods covered by the various studies. Young begins his analysis of the sources of growth of Taiwan with the year 1966, which is six years after the Taiwan export drive began. He thus misses what we have argued are the critical first years after reform, when productivity growth was high and investment rates and the growth rate of the capital stock were relatively low. Our study also ends the 1970s subperiod in 1979, but this is simply to avoid the distorting effects of the sharp recession that hit Taiwan in 1980.

A second difference is that our study explores the implications of different assumptions about the initial capital stock figure that is used to construct the increase in the capital stock from year to year by the perpetual inventory method. Young states that his results are insensitive to the assumed initial capital stock.[6] That is true if one is concerned only about the twenty-five–to–thirty-year period of rapid growth as a whole or only with the later years of that period. It is decidedly not true if one is interested in what happened in the early years of growth unless one has a good rate of capital formation series that predates the period in which one is interested by at least a decade or more. For Taiwan, Young avoids this problem by simply ignoring the 1950s and first half of the 1960s in his analysis, with consequences that limit the conclusions one can draw from his findings. For South Korea, where Young's calculations do go back at least to the beginning of reforms, the problem appears to be more serious. In the years 1961 through 1966, gross fixed capital formation in South Korea averaged 14.3 percent of GDP; Young estimates that this rate of capital formation produced a growth rate of the capital stock of 7 percent per annum. We did not have access to the underlying data that Young used to make these calculations. One could get a capital stock growth rate of this magnitude for South Korea, however, if one assumes either a very low initial capital stock level for the year 1960 or a very low rate of depreciation in the years 1961 through 1966. Young uses depreciation rates for the United States taken from a work of Dale Jorgenson, whereas we use the depreciation rates in the Taiwan national accounts, but that is not likely to be a major difference between the two studies. The probable difference results from a low estimate of the 1960 initial capital stock by Young, an estimate that would imply a capital output ratio for the nonagricultural sector of less than one. Although that is possible, to us it does not seem very likely.

A third difference between this study and that of Young is in the coverage of the economy. We look at the whole economy as well as its various component sectors, while Young looks only at the nonagricultural share of the economy. Young's focus is perfectly legitimate given that he is primarily interested in showing that modern sector growth can be explained by the increase in modern sector inputs, but the focus does leave one important source of productivity growth out of the story. At least since the work of Edward Dennison, it has been well known that simply shifting inputs, notably labor, from traditional sectors such as agriculture to modern industry and services raises GDP even if there is no net increase in these inputs.

The fourth significant difference, in this case between the work of both Young and this study, on the one hand, and the work of Lawrence Lau, on the other, is in the nature of the production function used and the way in which the parameters of that function are estimated. The production function used in both this and the Young study is a standard neoclassical production function in the tradition pioneered by Robert Solow. The parameter estimates are the shares of labor and capital income in national income, also following Solow. The Lau estimates, in contrast, use what he labels a "meta" production function in which the parameters are estimated econometrically. A meta function assumes that the underlying production function is the same for all countries in the sample, and therefore that the capital stock and workforce data for all of these countries can be pooled. Because the parameters are not derived from the national accounts, there is no need for Lau to assume constant returns to scale. In fact, Lau discovers that his method indicates that there were substantial economies of scale for the East Asian countries in his sample and, by implication, for all low-income countries, but no economies of scale for high-income countries. Lau and his collaborators conclude from these estimates that there was no total factor productivity growth in East Asia. All growth can be explained by increases in capital stock and the quality-adjusted workforce. It is just that in the early stages of growth, countries get more from these inputs because of the presence of economies of scale.

The problem with the Lau approach is that we do not know much more about what economies of scale mean at the aggregate production function level than we do about what drives productivity growth. A plausible hypothesis is that the two are really different names for much the same thing. At the aggregate level, economies of scale could be produced by the kinds of externalities that one typically finds as economies grow larger. The greater the number of educated people you have, for example, the more they can learn from each other and hence don't depend just on what they learn in school. Such externalities, however, can equally be used to account plausibly for why one gets periods of high productivity growth in a neoclassical production function without economies of scale. The Lau approach, therefore, does not really conflict with any of the arguments made in this study of Taiwan. In one sense, however, there is a conflict. Lau, in order to estimate a meta production function, assumes that economies of scale in his production function are a function of per capita income. Total factor productivity, as that term is used in this study—which would include economies of scale[7]—is not just or even primarily a function of income. In the Taiwan case at least, it appears to be more closely related to the timing of major policy reform efforts than to income, among other things.

The fifth methodological difference applies only to the Jorgenson and Liang study. They include intermediate inputs in their sector production functions, whereas the other studies—including this one—do not. The more one disaggregates one's analysis of the sources of growth, the more important it becomes to take into account the contribution of intermediate inputs to the sources of sector growth. When we analyze the sources of growth sector by sector within manufacturing, we shall use the Jorgenson and Liang estimates rather than calculate estimates of our own. Elsewhere, when analyzing sector sources of growth, we shall present both our results and those of Jorgenson and

Liang. The main advantage of our estimates is that they include the whole period covered by this book. In addition, our periodization is more closely related to the timing of the major shifts in national economic policy than is the periodization used by Jorgenson and Liang.

For all the differences in methodology, the growth-accounting results from the three studies that followed the Solow methodology are similar. The total factor productivity estimates by sector in these three studies are presented and compared in Table 6-4. The differences in periodization make precise comparison difficult, but the only results that stand out as different are the Young total factor productivity estimates for the 1966 through 1970 period.

In concluding this discussion of methodology, it is worth noting that growth accounting remains an imprecise art. The data underlying our calculations as well as those of others are subject to a number of potential biases, and the theoretical foundation of the aggregate pro-

---

TABLE 6-4

Alternative Estimates of Total Factor Productivity in Manufacturing and Services

Study	Period							
This Study	1952– 1955	1956– 1960	1961– 1965	1966– 1970	1971– 1979	1980– 1985	1986– 1990	1991– 1994
Nonagriculture	5.96	0.71	5.67	−1.71	1.67	2.36	4.40	2.51
Industry	8.64	2.17	7.60	−0.23	1.83	2.58	3.16	3.07
Manufacturing	10.81	2.73	9.04	−0.20	1.18	3.41	2.97	3.20
Services	4.68	−0.43	4.95	−3.18	1.03	2.42	5.69	2.64
Agriculture	3.54	3.99	0.36	−1.76	2.52	1.10	2.33	1.30
Jorgenson/Liang Study	1961–1973		1974–1982		1983–1987		1988–1993	
Manufacturing	3.69		0.84		5.41		1.76	
Services	2.14		0.19		4.73		4.13	
Agriculture	0.19		0.24		3.08		0.32	
Young Study	1966–1970		1971–1980			1981–1990		
Nonagriculture	3.4		1.5			3.3		
Manufacturing	3.1		0.1			2.8		
Services	4.0		2.9			3.9		

Sources: For this study's estimates, see Appendix E. Jorgenson-Liang estimates are from Jorgenson and Liang (unpublished paper submitted to the Chiang Ching-Kuo Foundation for International Scholarly Exchange). The Young estimates are from Young (1995: 110(3), p. 661).

duction function is itself weak. Growth accounting is useful because it allows us to make some quantitative judgments, however imprecise, about what it is that makes it possible for nations to grow rapidly.

STRUCTURAL CHANGES IN GDP AND INDUSTRY

The analysis to this point has focused on the sources of growth as seen from the perspective of the economy as a whole. We now consider what happens when we disaggregate this analysis first to the major components of GDP (manufacturing, agriculture, services, etc.) and then disaggregate further to the industrial sectors within manufacturing.

The basic growth-accounting data disaggregated to the major components of GDP are presented in Table 6-2 (the estimates of this study) and Table 6-5 (the Jorgenson-Liang estimates). The periodization of these two sets of estimates differs, but the basic findings of the two studies are similar. The principal finding is that sectoral changes in total factor productivity mostly mirror the patterns seen when the economy was looked at as a whole. The early 1960s, following the reforms of 1960, are a period of high productivity growth in most sectors. Similarly, most sectors slow down in the late 1960s and throughout the 1970s, but then productivity picks up again sometime in the mid-1980s and continues into the 1990s. There are exceptions to this

TABLE 6-5

Total Factor Productivity by Sector (Jorgenson-Liang Estimates)

Sector	Period			
	1961–1973	1974–1982	1983–1987	1988–1993
Agriculture	0.19	0.24	3.08	0.32
Mining	4.39	−0.86	6.75	6.63
Manufacturing	3.69	0.84	5.41	1.76
Electricity, Gas, & Water	4.75	−4.54	12.91	7.90
Construction	2.96	0.22	2.21	4.95
Transportation & Communications	2.04	6.03	7.11	3.38
Services	2.14	0.19	4.73	4.13
Whole Economy	0.47	−0.14	4.31	2.74

Source: Jorgenson and Liang (unpublished paper submitted to the Chiang Ching-Kuo Foundation for Scholarly Exchange). The estimates are for the growth of real value added total factor productivity.

consistency in productivity performance across sectors. There is no spurt in agricultural productivity in the early 1960s, but that is not surprising because the reforms in that period were not directed at agriculture. In both the Jorgenson-Liang estimates and the estimates of this study for the 1970s, transport is another exception to the general very low level of productivity growth in that period. Overall, however, both studies indicate that the forces driving the growth of total factor productivity were not confined to one or two sectors in any given period. What appears to have been at work were economy-wide forces that led to across-the-board accelerations and slowdowns in productivity.

What happens when one disaggregates further to sectors within manufacturing? Given that Taiwan's government pursued an active industrial policy, one could hypothesize that the government influenced productivity performance by pushing one industrial sector over another. This influence could be either positive or negative depending on whether the government promoted sectors with high productivity growth or did just the opposite.

Before looking at total factor productivity estimates industry by industry, it is first useful to consider whether there was anything unusual about the way manufacturing in Taiwan developed. Were certain industries promoted over others in ways that made Taiwan's manufacturing structure unique? Regression lines showing the changing structure of Taiwan manufacturing are presented in Figures 6-1 through 6-7. The comparison is with eight other industrializing nations in East and Southeast Asia and with Japan and South Korea individually.[8] The patterns may surprise those who think of Taiwan as mainly a platform for the export of manufactured consumer goods. To begin with, those sectors dominated by consumer manufactures were a sharply declining share of total manufacturing, while those sectors dominated by producer goods experienced a rising share.[9] The declining role of sectors dominated by consumer manufactures is even more pronounced in Taiwan than it is in Japan or South Korea.

The share of major exporting consumer goods sectors such as textiles, footwear, and apparel did grow very rapidly during the early decades of Taiwan's growth, but that share plummeted below the average Asian pattern as GDP per capita rose above US$7,000. Food, beverages, and tobacco plus wood products were consistently below the Asia-wide average at all levels of per capita GDP. The contrast is with petroleum products and industrial chemicals plus metal and metal products, where

FIGURE 6-1

Japan, Korea & Taiwan vs. East Asia

June 26, 1997. Dependent Variable: group 1[*]; Explanatory Variables: ln gdp[**], ln gpd[2***]

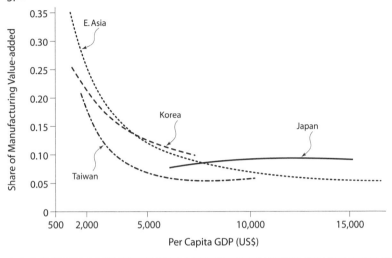

[*] Group 1: sum of shares of manufacturing VA of food, beverages, and tobacco
[**] log per capita gdp
[***] log per capita gdp squared

Notes:

1. East Asia includes China, Hong Kong, Japan, Korea, Malaysia, The Philippines, Singapore, Taiwan, and Thailand.
2. Manufacturing Value Added includes petroleum refineries and petroleum/coal products.

Taiwan rose above the Asia-wide average share as per capita GDP passed US$5,000 and kept on rising. Taiwan's petroleum product and industrial chemical share was even larger than that of Japan and South Korea when they were at the same level of per capita GDP. Machinery, electrical machinery, and transport equipment are the one group of sectors that exactly track the Asia-wide patterns.

Given that several of these producer goods–dominated sectors, at least in the early decades, were dominated by state-owned firms, one might expect to see this emphasis on producer goods accounting for the slowdown in productivity growth on a manufacturing-wide basis. As the estimates of Jorgenson and Liang presented in Table 6-6 indicate, however, such was not the case. Productivity growth in the early consumer goods–exporting sectors such as textiles and shoes was high during the boom years of the 1960s and 1970s but slows to a crawl in

TABLE 6-6

Total Factor Productivity in Manufacturing by Sector

Sector	Period			
	1961–1973	1974–1982	1983–1987	1988–1993
Food	0.70	9.59	7.03	−0.16
Beverages & Tobacco	3.32	3.57	2.72	6.20
Textiles	8.04	5.36	5.30	0.84
Clothing & Apparel	2.03	12.45	0.25	−1.19
Leather & Products	8.88	1.39	0.77	−0.98
Wood & Furniture	3.67	−7.35	8.44	−5.80
Paper & Printing	3.15	2.33	2.54	−0.45
Chemicals & Plastics	9.06	2.15	12.28	2.63
Basic Metals	1.65	−8.26	11.72	6.04
Metal Products	10.84	−1.40	4.34	−0.82
Machinery	2.25	1.33	8.24	1.85
Electrical Machinery	15.78	−0.02	6.65	2.75
Transport Equipment	12.19	5.18	1.84	3.35
Miscellaneous	11.42	9.11	3.06	−0.17
All Manufacturing	3.69	0.84	5.41	1.76

Source: Jorgenson and Liang (unpublished paper submitted to the Chiang Ching-Kuo Foundation for Scholarly Exchange). The estimates are for the growth of real value added total factor productivity.

the 1980s and 1990s, and in most consumer sectors it becomes negative. Total factor productivity in the producer goods–dominated sectors is high in the 1960s when these sectors were small, but falls to negligible levels in the 1970s just as in the consumer goods sectors and the economy as a whole. Unlike consumer manufactures, however, productivity in the producer goods sector picks up dramatically in the 1980s and then begins to slow down again in the late 1980s and early 1990s.

Private investors and industrial policy makers, it would appear, generally knew what they were doing. They targeted sectors where large productivity gains were possible and withdrew from sectors where this was not the case. Total factor productivity growth, of course, is not the same thing as private profits. It is not even equivalent to the social rate of return on investment where the *social rate of return* refers to the rate of return on investment when benefits and costs are measured in world prices (rather than domestic prices distorted by trade restrictions and other distortions). Total factor productivity is a measure of the "sur-

FIGURE 6-2

Japan, Korea & Taiwan vs. East Asia

June 26, 1997. Dependent Variable: group 2[*]; Explanatory Variables: ln gdp[**], ln gdp[2***]

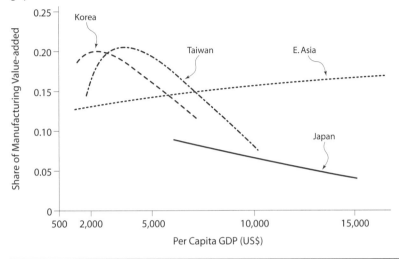

[*]   Group 2: sum of shares of manufacturing VA of footwear, textiles, leather, and wearing apparel
[**] log per capita gdp
[***] log per capita gdp squared

Notes:
1. East Asia includes China, Hong Kong, Japan, Korea, Malaysia, The Philippines, Singapore, Taiwan, and Thailand.
2. Manufacturing Value Added includes petroleum refineries and petroleum/coal products.

plus" gains from all inputs, gains over and above what would have been earned if the increase in output had been simply equal to the total payments to labor, capital, and intermediate inputs valued at world prices. The fact that Taiwan's industrial decision makers consistently shifted emphasis toward high-productivity sectors and away from low-productivity sectors, therefore, is a good indication that they were making decisions that were correct from the standpoint of achieving high growth.

This statement about Taiwan's industrial policy decision-making capacity, of course, does not apply to every one of the decisions made even when looked at on this aggregate level. The sharp productivity decline in basic metals and metal products in the 1970s, for example, may reflect poor decisions connected with the establishment of state-owned enterprises in those sectors at that time. Still, it is hard to find major flaws in the way Taiwan's manufacturing structure evolved. At

FIGURE 6-3

Japan, Korea & Taiwan vs. East Asia

June 26, 1997. Dependent Variable: group 3[*]; Explanatory Variables: ln gdp[**], ln gdp^{2}[***]

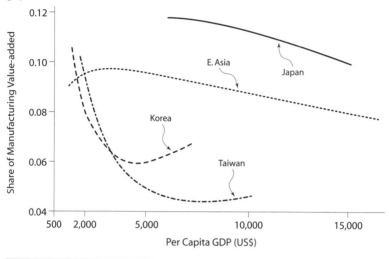

Per Capita GDP (US$)

---

[*]   Group 3: sum of shares of manufacturing VA of wood, furniture, paper, and printing
[**]   log per capita gdp
[***]   log per capita gdp squared

Notes:

1. East Asia includes China, Hong Kong, Japan, Korea, Malaysia, The Philippines, Singapore, Taiwan, and Thailand.
2. Manufacturing Value Added includes petroleum refineries and petroleum/coal products.

---

the firm level, myriad mistakes were made, but mistakes are part of any development process. The issue is whether the mistakes made were of sufficient magnitude to slow growth to a rate below growth a well-managed economy could have achieved. Shifting emphasis in industrial policy to those sectors with little or no productivity growth could have been a mistake of this kind. In Taiwan manufacturing, however, the shift was toward high-productivity sectors, not away from them.

Conclusion

The principal finding of the analysis in this chapter, therefore, is that an analysis of the data on inputs and outputs supports the view that Taiwan's government and private decision makers followed a development strategy that got the most out of those inputs. Policy reforms did lead to spurts in productivity, and these spurts in productivity created

FIGURE 6-4

Japan, Korea & Taiwan vs. East Asia

June 26, 1997. Dependent Variable: group 4*; Explanatory Variables: ln gdp**, ln gdp²***

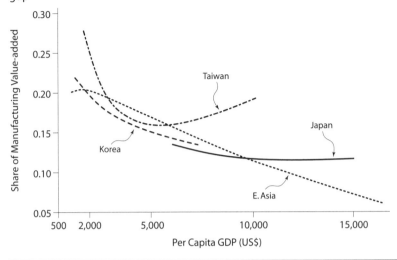

---

*   Group 4: sum of shares of manufacturing VA of industrial chemicals and other chemical products, petroleum refineries, petroleum and coal products, and rubber.

** log per capita gdp

*** log per capita gdp squared

Notes:

1. East Asia includes China, Hong Kong, Japan, Korea, Malaysia, The Philippines, Singapore, Taiwan, and Thailand.

2. Manufacturing Value Added includes petroleum refineries and petroleum/coal products.

---

investment opportunities with high rates of return. High rates of return were an important reason that investment and hence capital formation rates were high throughout the four decades. Inputs were used efficiently, on average, in the economy as a whole. Entrepreneurs shifted resources from one industry to another as new opportunities for increases in productivity arose. Taiwan's growth story, therefore, is not primarily a tale of draconian efforts to hold back consumption in order to accumulate more and more capital. It is a story of well thought out government policies and the eager and efficient response of private businesses to the favorable climate for investment created by those policies. High rates of capital formation were one end product of these policies and the private response to these policies, but not the only or even the most important end product. The most important outcome was a high rate of growth of national product.

FIGURE 6-5

Japan, Korea & Taiwan vs. East Asia

June 26, 1997. Dependent Variable: group 5[*]; Explanatory Variables: ln gdp[**], ln gdp^2[***]

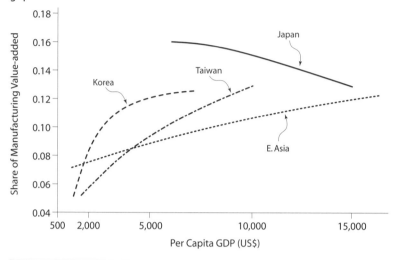

---

[*] Group 5: sum of shares of manufacturing VA of iron and steel, nonferrous metals, and metal products

[**] log per capita gdp

[***] log per capita gdp squared

Notes:

1. East Asia includes China, Hong Kong, Japan, Korea, Malaysia, The Philippines, Singapore, Taiwan, and Thailand.

2. Manufacturing Value Added includes petroleum refineries and petroleum/coal products.

NOTES

1 Young (1995, pp. 641–680).

2 There was a very large increase in the number of graduates of secondary schools and universities in this period, which explains in part the very rapid increase in the quality-adjusted workforce in the late 1960s. Growth accounting assumes that the wages received at the time of graduation reflect the productivity of those graduates. If, instead, there is a lag of several years before these graduates truly earn their marginal product, then the impact of this expansion in education should be spread out over a longer period than is done in this growth-accounting exercise.

3 Higgins and Williamson (1997, pp. 261–293). This article argues that the decline in the population dependency ratio not only facilitates a rise in domestic savings in Asia, but also is a stimulus to investment. This is likely to be the case, but the implication of the analysis in this chapter is that the

FIGURE 6-6

Japan, Korea & Taiwan vs. East Asia

June 26, 1997. Dependent Variable: group 6[*]; Explanatory Variables: ln gdp[**], ln gdp²[***]

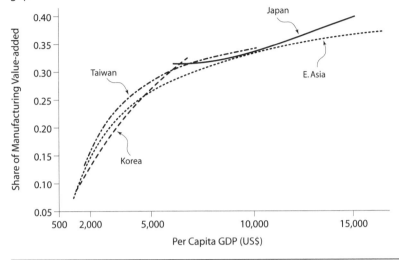

---

[*]   Group 6: sum of shares of manufacturing VA of machinery, electrical machinery, and
     transport equipment
[**] log per capita gdp
[***] log per capita gdp squared

Notes:

1. East Asia includes China, Hong Kong, Japan, Korea, Malaysia, The Share of Manufactur-
   ingShare of ManufacturingPhilippines, Singapore, Taiwan, and Thailand.
2. Manufacturing Value Added includes petroleum refineries and petroleum/coal products.

---

primary stimulus to investment on the demand side lay elsewhere. Specifically, there was an accumulation of potential investment opportunities in the 1950s in both Korea and Taiwan, but it took the policy reforms
of the early 1960s to make that potential a reality.

4   Labor quality changes were not included in the estimates in Table 6-2
    because the effort involved is large and was not necessary for the limited
    use to which the South Korean data are put in this study. For workforce
    growth rates that do include quality changes, see Alwyn Young (1995, p.
    660). The Young figures, which are for the nonagricultural workforce only,
    show an increase in the workforce growth rate from 7.2 percent in the
    years 1961 through 1966 to 10.3 percent in 1967 through 1970 before falling
    back to 5.4 percent in the 1970s.

5   Young (1995); Kim and Lau (1994, pp. 235–271); Jorgenson and Liang (un-
    published).

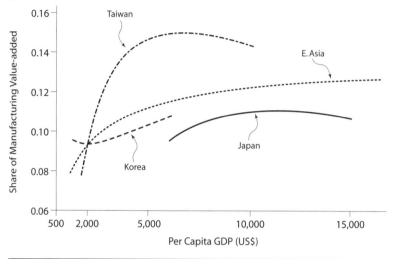

FIGURE   6-7

Japan, Korea & Taiwan vs. East Asia

June 26, 1997. Dependent Variable: group 7[*]; Explanatory Variables: ln gdp[**], ln gdp[2***]

---

[*]   Group 7: sum of shares of manufacturing VA of plastic, pottery, glass, nonmetal products, professional goods, and other industries

[**] log per capita gdp

[***] log per capita gdp squared

Notes:

1. East Asia includes China, Hong Kong, Japan, Korea, Malaysia, The Philippines, Singapore, Taiwan, and Thailand.

2. Manufacturing Value Added includes petroleum refineries and petroleum/coal products.

---

6   Young (1995, p. 652).

7   Edward Dennison usually included economies of scale as one of the explanations for the residual in his analysis of the sources of growth.

8   The other eight economies are China, Hong Kong, Japan, South Korea, Malaysia, Singapore, the Philippines, and Thailand.

9   The sectors presented in the graphs could not be rigorously divided into consumer and producer goods because each of the standard manufacturing sectors includes both types of goods. It is for that reason that we refer to sectors being "dominated" by one type of good or the other.

7   Conclusion

Different times call for different solutions. Never is this truer than when it comes to managing an economy during a period of high growth and rapid structural change. Taiwan has experienced nearly a half-century of rapid economic growth and has been transformed from a largely agricultural island into one of the premier producers of high-technology electronic products. Along the way, Taiwan passed through a stage in which it was one of the world's largest manufacturers and exporters of labor-intensive textile products and shoes, and then a major producer of petrochemicals and other heavy industry products. As the shift in emphasis from one industry to another occurred, so did the role of government in the process. What worked well in the 1960s was no longer viable by the 1980s, and changes in economic structure in the 1990s called for further major changes in economic policy and the role of government.

Not everything changed from decade to decade as Taiwan's economy was transformed, however. There were certain fundamental premises, which underlay the government's approach to economic development, that did not change. In one sense, the very flexibility of the government in its approach to a constantly changing economic environment was itself a fundamental premise. Policies and rules were driven by what worked in the specific situation. In some areas, however, such as parts of macroeconomic policy, change was neither required nor desirable. In these areas, with some exceptions, Taiwan policy makers stuck with policies that worked throughout the nearly five decades. The simplest way to sort out which economic policies and institutions changed and which stayed the same is to review briefly Taiwan's economic transformation period by period since 1949.

TRANSFORMATION: TAIWAN IN THE 1950S

There were two major strands to the government's approach to the Taiwan economy in the 1950s. One involved stabilization and was both financial and political. The other, inherited in part from the Kuomintang's experience on the Chinese mainland, called for an active state role in building industries that would produce mainly for the domestic market. The first task of financial stabilization was to bring an end to hyperinflation, a task that was accomplished by 1951. The end of hyperinflation was important to political stabilization because spiraling prices had helped undermine the Kuomintang's authority on Taiwan as well as on the Chinese mainland. Land reform, in which most landlord-owned land was turned over to the former tenants, was also central to political stability, but land reform contributed to beginning the transformation of the Taiwan economy as well. Former landlords were more or less forced to find other sources of income; some of them turned to business, in part with the help of the property turned over to them in partial compensation for their land.

Direct state ownership of much of industry and pervasive state control of enterprises that were formally private dominated the government's industrial policy in the 1950s. The goal was to build a manufacturing sector that could supply the needs of Taiwan's domestic market of eight million people. This goal was to be achieved by high protective barriers around domestic industries and state allocation of foreign exchange, including foreign exchange received through U.S. foreign aid. Eligible textile firms, for example, received quotas for their share of cotton imports from the government. The need for tight import controls was reinforced throughout this period by the government's decision to maintain an overvalued NT dollar. Government-owned firms, which accounted for over half of all industry in the first part of the 1950s, were simply ordered to do what the government wanted.

Economic growth in the 1950s was more than respectable. GDP growth rates in the early 1950s averaged 9 percent a year, spurred on by rapid total-factor-productivity (TFP) growth that mainly reflected recovery from wartime conditions and the early difficulties of resettling over a million migrants from the Chinese mainland. Even in the latter half of the 1950s, however, the GDP growth rate was 6.7 percent a year, a far higher rate than that achieved in most developing countries at that time.

By the late 1950s, however, problems with the economy were coming to the attention of the government. Much of the growth, for example, perhaps as much as half depended on the continued large flow of U.S. aid. As the estimates in Chapter 6 indicate, total factor productivity was also slowing markedly, although the government was only indirectly aware that this was happening. One reason for the lower productivity growth was that the small domestic market for many industrial products was quickly saturated, and production growth in those sectors began to slow down. Developing countries around the world, however, faced far worse conditions and yet kept on pursuing import-substituting industrialization through state intervention for one or two more decades or sometimes longer. Taiwan's leadership was made up of people many of whom shared the view that reliance on foreign trade for development was dangerous. They also shared the view of many of their developing country contemporaries that government had to use all the levers at its disposal to coax or force firms to do what was required for development.

TRANSFORMATION: TAIWAN IN THE 1960S AND 1970S

Despite this background, Taiwan's leaders did not stay on the import-substituting path. In a series of decisions that in retrospect were dramatic, the government in 1960 and thereafter tied its future to the international market. Taiwan's economic decision makers, however, did not follow the path to growth and integration with the international market advocated by institutions such as the World Bank, whose views were dominated by the neoclassical economist's or free trader's view of the world. Taiwan did not free up imports and prices in general and then step back and let the market do its work. Import restrictions remained tight. Imports of most consumer manufactures, for example, were virtually prohibited and could be found only on the black market. What Taiwan did instead was to put the government solidly behind the promotion of exports. Unification and devaluation of the exchange rate was one of the most important changes. It was also the main policy change that was consistent with the free market or liberalization approach to development. All of the other measures were designed either to create a simulated free market for exporters only or to go beyond the free market and subsidize exporters. The former category of measures included export processing zones, duty drawbacks, and price policies for intermediate inputs such as petrochemicals that ensured that exporters would not have to pay prices above those of their international competitors. The latter kinds of promotion efforts involved below-market rates of interest for certain exporters.

This policy of restricting imports, although promoting exports, has often been labeled "mercantilist," a label that fits the Taiwan situation of the 1970s and even the late 1960s well. In the early 1960s, Taiwan faced a large current account deficit that was filled by equally large inflows of foreign aid. As foreign aid phased out, it would have taken even a liberally oriented government time to adjust, and import restrictions would have been retained while that adjustment was taking place. As it was, the Taiwan government policy makers were anything but liberalizing free traders. Yin Chung-long was the major force behind the currency devaluation, but even he did not push for across-the-board reliance on market forces.

It is the experience of Taiwan in the 1960s that has drawn the most attention from scholars and countries interested in learning from and possibly emulating the success of Taiwan's transition from import substitution to export orientation based on manufactured exports. One lesson that can be safely drawn from this experience is that export promotion efforts work best when they are made available to virtually anyone with the will and the talent to produce for export. This was particularly important in the case of Taiwan, where most of the early exporters were small firms that had neither the political clout or the financial resources needed to negotiate special favors from the government. Studies of South Korea that compare the across-the-board subsidies to South Korean exporters of the 1960s with the effort of the 1970s that targeted particular industries and firms also conclude that the nondiscriminatory policies of the 1960s produced better economic results.

It is less clear that there is anything useful for other countries to learn from the import restriction side of Taiwan's experience. The danger of high and varied walls of protection against imports is that those receiving this protection form interest groups that become more powerful over time. If there are no countervailing forces, these interest groups can lock a country into a slow-growth import-substituting strategy for decades. In Taiwan, this did not happen for two reasons. First, Taiwan's policy makers knew that survival depended on achieving sustained economic growth, and they worked for a government that understood that fact. The authoritarian nature of that government and the fact that its power rested on a mainlander-dominated party and army also meant that government had the strength to turn decisions concerning economic policy over to a group of very able technocrats. Businessmen, who were mostly operators of small firms and were natives of Taiwan, had little political influence in the 1960s.

The 1970s in many respects were simply a continuation of the mercantilist policies of the 1960s. GDP growth continued at over 9 percent per annum throughout the decade. The spurt in total factor productivity that had led to high GDP growth rates in the early 1960s, however, had come to an end by the latter half of the 1960s and rose at only a modest rate throughout the 1970s. High growth rates after 1965 were driven instead by steadily rising rates of investment in both physical and human capital. Exports continued to boom, and imports, other than inputs for exporters, continued to face major barriers.

In two respects, however, the 1970s were different. First, there were the two OPEC-generated increases in oil prices in 1973 and 1979. Many developing countries, including South Korea, dealt with the resulting current account deficits by borrowing heavily abroad. Even some of the major oil exporters, believing that oil prices would continue to climb, also borrowed against what they believed would be higher export earnings in the future. The result was the debt crisis of the 1980s and stagnation in those heavily debted countries that had failed to promote exports. Taiwan, in contrast, moved decisively on the macroeconomic front to restore price stability and to bring the current account back into balance. The option of borrowing abroad was eschewed. Taiwan, like Germany, learned from the hard lessons of its own past. Low inflation and macroeconomic stability in general are an essential ingredient both for sustained development and political survival. Macro stability has been one constant that holds for Taiwan throughout the half century since 1949.

The second respect in which the 1970s were different from the 1960s was that the 1970s marked the beginning of Taiwan's push to develop heavy industry. Taiwan's heavy industry effort was in many ways very similar to the much better known and studied South Korean heavy and chemical industry drive that took place at the same time. Taiwan's heavy industry drive, like that in South Korea, marked the high point of state intervention in the economy.

The core of the heavy industry drive on Taiwan was carried out directly by the state through state-owned enterprises. The private sector, after all, was made up mostly of very small firms who had neither the managerial experience nor the access to financing that was required by a sector characterized by large economies of scale, or at least so many in the government believed. Certainly Taiwan's large conservative state-owned banks were not ready to lend large sums to huge new private ventures without government backing. In any case, the state-owned China Petroleum Corporation already had a monopoly of the petroleum and upstream petrochemicals market, and it had the formidable political strength to maintain that monopoly at least in the 1970s. Lacking anything comparable to the large South Korean *chaebol* business conglomerates, Taiwan's government turned to those it did have confidence in, its own senior officials and the experienced managers of the existing state enterprises.

It is this portrait of an economy dominated by mercantilist trade policies, large state-owned heavy industry firms, and large state banks that some put forward as the Taiwan model of economic development, a model whose success could be emulated by others. It was also an economy where much of the energy of even private producers was devoted to lobbying government for special favors. As a portrait of Taiwan's economy in the 1970s, it is as accurate as modeling exercises of this sort get. Whether it is a model that others should emulate is another matter. Certainly governments determined to hold onto state ownership of large-scale heavy industries could learn something from Taiwan's experience. Unlike the case in so many other countries, many of these Taiwan state enterprises were profitable and certainly were not a major drag on the economy. It is likely, however, that the presence of these state-owned heavy industries was one of the reasons why the growth of total factor productivity was relatively low in the 1970s. Taiwan's economic policy makers themselves, it should be noted, concluded that these enterprises were more of a burden than a help and began an effort to privatize them a decade later.

TRANSFORMATION: TAIWAN IN THE 1980S AND 1990S

It was not just the large state-owned enterprise feature of the 1970s Taiwan model that the government began to move away from. Almost as soon as this state approach to development was in place, economic policy makers began efforts to dismantle it. The early 1980s were a period of transition. Macroeconomic forces played an important role in Taiwan's move away from a state-directed mercantilist policy, and these forces were already present by 1981. Taiwan's large current account surpluses and rising foreign exchange reserves may have been caused in part by the large trade deficits being run by Taiwan's major trading partner, the United States. Taiwan's own macroeconomic policies and trends, however, also played a role. Continued high rates of personal savings may have reflected individual behavior rather than national policy. The bulge in savings in the mid-1980s, in particular, appears to have been mainly the response of consumers to what was accurately perceived to be a windfall increase in income that would soon dissipate. The sharp drop in the share of investment in GDP in the early 1980s, in contrast, was at least partly the result the government's policy of maintaining high real rates of interest on loans.

Whatever the cause, the large excess of savings over investment and the closely related excess of exports over imports put pressure on the government to change its policies. The slower but still quite high growth rate of GDP may also have had an effect. Some of the pressure for change came from abroad, notably from U.S. concern about Asia's large surpluses with the United States. Other pressures, however, came from within Taiwan. The emerging new economic situation provided liberal economists with ammunition in their long-running argument against a state interventionist approach to development. High government officials were also beginning to come around to a more liberal economic view, although concrete action was delayed by the illness of President Chiang Ching-kuo.

Government policy interventions to promote industry were not completely on the way out, but the nature of these interventions was changing in a direction more consistent with an economy driven mainly by market forces. High prices of petroleum and the increasing strength of environmental concerns had called into question some of the earlier efforts to promote particular heavy industries. It was in the late 1970s and early 1980s, as a result, that Taiwan policy makers began to shift their emphasis toward high-technology industries. A few firms were set up with government help, but the main effort in the promotion of high technology was through the vehicle of education and research. University curricula were overhauled, and the government itself was computerized so that more people would be familiar with the new technologies. Funds also poured into the government industrial research units. Engineers and scientists trained in the United States were encouraged to return home, and the Hsinchu Science-based Industrial Park was created in part for this purpose. The handful of large high-technology firms that did receive direct government support received mainly capital. Management of these firms was independent from government interference, and they were expected to behave like any other private firm.

The real break in the approach to industrial development came in the latter half of the 1980s. The buildup of foreign exchange reserves finally forced a revaluation of the NT dollar. That revaluation, together with two decades of rapidly rising real wages, marked the end of the era in which Taiwan relied mainly on the export of products that depended on cheap labor to be competitive. The rising reserves also facilitated the government's decision to allow Taiwan firms to invest abroad. Instead of abandoning their labor-intensive factories, therefore, they moved them abroad. High value added elements such as design and marketing were retained in Taiwan, while production facilities were moved to the Chinese mainland and to Southeast Asia.

The government's abandonment of direct intervention industrial policies happened gradually, not with one dramatic move toward liberalization. Tax rebates for favored industries were cut back, as were special loans to exporters. Tariff rates were brought down further to an average nominal rate of 6 percent in the late 1980s and 5 percent in the early 1990s. Of equal or greater importance, most nontariff barriers to trade were gradually abandoned. The monopoly of the China Petroleum Corporation over upstream petrochemical activities was eliminated, as were the government-directed production and distribution agreements with midstream and downstream producers, agreements that depended on tight restrictions on imports. The elimination of most import controls over petrochemicals, therefore, effectively ended the government's role in this area as in so many others.

Cumulatively, these liberalization measures probably account for the big jump in total factor productivity that occurred in Taiwan in the latter half of the 1980s. Total factor productivity was particularly pronounced in the service sectors that began to be liberalized in this period, but TFP also rose markedly in manufacturing. Taiwan's annual GDP growth rate, which had been slowing down in the early 1980s, as a result, rose by more than two percentage points, almost back to the near double-digit rates of the 1970s.

Taiwan also joined the worldwide movement to privatize state-owned industrial enterprises, although it did so slowly. Resistance from the enterprises themselves was a major obstacle to privatization, and the movement did not really begin to gather much momentum until the late 1990s. Where Taiwan's government did participate in the development of new enterprises, that participation mainly involved the provision of capital and help in getting the firm organized and little more.

By the late 1980s and early 1990s, there was increasing recognition that Taiwan's economy was too large and complex to be run by a small number of government bureaucrats. Industrialists themselves, at least many of them, had come to realize that government restrictions and subsidies were not an unmixed blessing. Government's support for new industries often meant higher costs for older industries. Restrictions on imports into Taiwan made it more difficult for industrialists to avoid barriers to their exports in foreign markets.

This process of economic liberalization continued throughout the 1990s. Taiwan's goal of admission to the World Trade Organization (previously the General Agreement on Tariffs and Trade) led to a steady effort not only to lower trade barriers. A major effort was initiated to rewrite all manner of laws that made Taiwan's practices inconsistent with those of the advanced industrial economies of North America and Europe. Not all of the old trade promotion practices were completely abandoned, to be sure. The NT dollar was devalued significantly during the early phases of the Asian financial crisis of 1997 to 1998, despite the fact that Taiwan continued to enjoy current account surpluses and large foreign exchange reserves. The move certainly helped protect exporters from some of the impact of the crisis, but it did nothing to foster stability in the region as a whole. By 1999, however, the nominal exchange rate for the NT dollar once again began to revalue, although Taiwan's foreign exchange surpluses, which had actually fallen in 1996 and 1997, continued to rise throughout 1998 and into 1999.

The real challenge of the late 1990s and beyond, however, was not how to stay on the cutting edge of industrial technologies. Taiwan's industrialists were at least as skilled in that area as their major competitors in the rest of the developing world. The main challenge that began in the late 1990s was how to raise the competitiveness of Taiwan's service sector, particularly business and financial services, to an internationally competitive level. Like Japan, Taiwan built up a formidable industrial export economy, but Taiwan's financial system lagged far behind. Reforms in financial and business services, including a much larger role for foreign competition, were being put in place in the late 1990s, but there was still a long way to go.

Service sector reform is also a central component in achieving another of the government's goals for the future—turning Taiwan into a regional operations center for all of East and Southeast Asia. Taiwan's relations with the Chinese mainland, of course, complicate that goal. It is difficult to see how Taiwan can become the major service center for the region unless it can establish open and stable economic ties with the cities and provinces on the mainland. Stable ties with the Chinese mainland, however, are not determined by Taiwan's actions alone. Strengthening and liberalizing Taiwan's financial and business service sectors, on the other hand, are largely in the hands of Taiwan itself. Continuing government restrictions on the financial sector may have been of some help in avoiding most of the impact of the Asian financial crisis of 1997 to 1998, although the current account surplus and large foreign exchange reserves were of much greater importance. Over the long run, however, Taiwan needs to be able to weather such crises because its financial sector is too strong and well managed to be brought down by a financial panic of the kind that occurred in 1997. The alternative—of relying on state controls—could well lead Taiwan into a situation not unlike that experienced by Japan throughout the 1990s.

Transformation: Lessons To Be Learned from Taiwan

What then are the lessons that other countries should draw from Taiwan's modern sector development experience? One lesson is that certain economic fundamental premises do matter. Foremost among these economic fundamental premises is the consistency of Taiwan's policy of maintaining macroeconomic stability and avoiding an overvalued exchange rate. The government in Taiwan had to learn this lesson the hard way from its experience with hyperinflation on the Chinese mainland, but, once learned, it was not forgotten.

The second general lesson that can be learned from Taiwan's experience is that flexibility in policy making and in economic institutions is essential. Flexibility is particularly important in an economy that is undergoing rapid structural change, something that is inevitably the case when GDP growth averages over 9 percent a year. Different situations require different policies. Taiwan in the 1960s was able to prosper through active government intervention in industry despite a weak financial system. Taiwan in the 1990s cannot afford either an interventionist government bureaucracy or a weak financial system.

Flexibility was partly forced on Taiwan by macro forces beyond its control and by pressure from a United States worried about its trade deficit. But flexibility was also possible because, at least in the economic sphere, there was an active debate over the proper course for policy.

The engineer technocrats who did so much to make possible the early industrial and export successes were never given the chance to turn their approach into unchallenged orthodoxy. Prominent liberal economists challenged their interventionist approach from the beginning, and, when conditions changed, that liberal view increasingly became the new orthodoxy.

Flexibility, of course, is desirable only if it leads from one appropriate set of policies to another. Did Taiwan's economic policy makers always choose the right policies, and is what was right for Taiwan also appropriate for other economies at comparable stages of development? These questions are not easy to answer.

There is ample evidence that the policies worked well for Taiwan itself. The high GDP growth rates that prevailed throughout the three decades are one measure of the success achieved. The spurts in total factor productivity that occurred first after the reforms of 1960 and then again during the liberalization efforts of the 1980s are direct evidence that it was policy reform, not just good luck or favorable external conditions, that explained the high GDP growth rate.

The most controversial issue is whether the policies that have been described in this study as mercantilist would work equally well in numerous other settings. Would state intervention through special tax breaks, subsidized loans, and limited access to foreign exchange have accomplished the same results elsewhere? Similar policies did work in South Korea and, in an earlier period, in Japan. But would they have worked equally well in Latin America or Africa? There are grounds for skepticism.

A related question is whether Taiwan could have done equally well or even better if it had simply moved to a fully open market economy in the first place. The counterfactual question of whether Taiwan itself could have done better in the 1960s and 1970s with a liberal set of policies can never really be answered. It is also completely unrealistic to think that Taiwan's government would ever have considered such a policy as early as the 1960s and 1970s. The political support and the intellectual foundation for such approaches were completely absent from Taiwan at that time. What the island had in the 1950s was a highly interventionist ideology and set of policies that could easily have led to slow growth or economic stagnation. To their credit, the economic policy makers of the time recognized this danger and began systematically to intervene in a very different direction. They intervened successfully in part because they were talented and well educated, but in even larger part because they knew that failure would be disastrous for them and for all of Taiwan.

Could other country's economic policy makers do as well? If the survival of their country depended on it, they might. If they were largely insulated from local politics and personal rent seeking, they might also have done as well. But most economic policy makers, unlike those on Taiwan in the 1960s and 1970s, do not work in countries whose very survival depends on them making the right decisions. Nor is most economic policy around the world as insulated from politics and rent seeking, as was the case in Taiwan during the first phases of its industrial development.

For most countries, the relevant lessons from Taiwan lie more in the industrial policies of the 1980s and 1990s than in those of earlier periods. The efforts to develop a capacity in the high-technology sectors, beginning in the late 1970s and continuing to the present, are particularly noteworthy. With a few exceptions, these efforts avoided industrial targeting, or picking winners, and instead attempted to create conditions conducive to private entrepreneurial activity.

These efforts at engineering education reform and at attracting Taiwanese engineers back from Silicon Valley were described above and at greater length in Chapter 3 and will not be repeated here. They differed from the interventions of earlier years in that government acted mainly when it was clear that the private sector was not going to be able to do the job on its own. Education, and some kinds of research in particular, are areas where market failure in the form of large externalities makes private efforts less profitable than they should be. These externalities are likely to be particularly large if most firms are small, as was the case in Taiwan.

By any reasonable standard, Taiwan's approach to industrial development was a great success and, if the same skill and effort is put into reforming business and financial services, those sectors should become internationally competitive as well. No country's achievements, however, can be simply duplicated elsewhere with equal success. Conditions across countries differ too much for copying another to be an effective development strategy. In Taiwan's case, conditions differed markedly not only from other countries but from one decade to the next. The strength of Taiwan's policy making and economic institutions was that they could adapt to these different and changing circumstances.

A

THE TEXTILE AND APPAREL INDUSTRIES

Ying-yi Tu

1. THE PERIOD OF RELIANCE UPON IMPORTS (BEFORE 1948)

Taiwan, during the Japanese occupation, came within the scope of Japan's "rice and sugar policy." Emphasis, as a result, was placed on the development of agriculture. The textile industry, by contrast, was already very well developed in Japan. Japan initially established in Taiwan only a number of textile factories manufacturing gunnysacks out of hemp used for packaging rice and sugar. It was not until 1941, in response to the needs of the Japanese imperial army's southward strategy, that cotton and wool factories were set up in Taiwan. During most of the colonial period, more than 80 percent of textile products in Taiwan were imported from Japan, and a further 10 percent were imported from elsewhere. According to estimates for 1921 to 1942, Taiwan's textile industry, measured in terms of value of output, accounted for only between 1.0 percent and 2.6 percent of total manufacturing output, and was ranked at the bottom of the list of industries.[1]

In 1945, when Taiwan was returned to China, there remained only two cotton textile, one woolen textile, and two hemp factories that had been set up under the Japanese and had been Japanese owned. These factories became part of the Taiwan Textile Company and were subsequently merged with the operations of the provincial-level Taiwan Mining Company. Because of devastation caused by the war, however, the facilities of these operations were dilapidated. Taiwan still needed to rely on imports of textile products, but now they came from mainland China rather than Japan. Much clothing was also imported, and the remainder of the apparel "industry," if it can be called that, was made up of families who made their own clothes or had them made in small family shops.

2. THE PERIOD OF IMPORT SUBSTITUTION (1948–1954)

From 1948 onward, as the situation on the mainland became increasingly unstable, a number of textile businesses moved their operations from mainland China to Taiwan. Between 1948 and 1953, eleven cotton factories, including Hwa Nan and Ta Chin; four wool factories, including Chung Pen and Chin Yi; and a number of towel-making and other factories relocated to Taiwan. Therefore, beginning in 1948, as a result of this influx of funding, equipment, and personnel, the production capacity and volume of output of the Taiwan textile industry significantly increased. As can be seen in Table A-1, the number of electrically powered weaving looms in the cotton industry increased twelve-fold between 1945 and 1951, while production during the same period increased fifty-fold. Because a large number of the textile factories that relocated from the mainland had originated in either Shanghai or Shantung, reference was made to the "Shanghai gang" or the "Shantung gang."

Inflation gradually subsided following the currency reforms of 1949, but the prices of textile products significantly increased during the second half of 1950, as the demand for these goods outstripped supply. In order to guard against a general price increase, the government lowered tariff rates on textiles as a temporary measure. Strong government support for the industry soon returned, however, based on the view that (1) textile products were necessities, (2) foreign exchange needed to be conserved, and (3) the prices of textile products and of goods in general needed to be stabilized. The government actively assisted the industry by implementing an import-substitution policy. Although K. Y. Yin spoke in support of developing the textile industry, saying that "importing fabric is not as good as importing yarn, which in turn is not as good as importing cotton," there were some who were opposed to government help to this sector. These people were of the opinion that, since Taiwan did not produce cotton, it was not suited to developing a textile industry. K. Y. Yin, however, pointed out that neither England nor Japan produced cotton, yet their textile industries were already very advanced, and had spurred on the development of other industries.[2] This appeased those opposed to government support in this sector, and the textile industry became the main focus of attention in the government's First Four-Year Economic Plan (1953–1956).

Government external policies implemented to develop the textile industry included a temporary stoppage of imports of cotton fabrics

TABLE A-1
Major Pieces of Equipment and Number of Employees in Taiwan's Textile Industry, 1945–1954

| Year | Cotton Textile Industry | | | | Woolen Textile Industry | | | Hemp Textile Industry | Textile Industry |
	Cotton Spinning Equip. (spindles)	Electrically powered Weaving Looms (no.)	Output of Cotton Yarn (metric tons)	Output of Cotton Fabric (kms)	Woolen Spinning Equip. (spindles)	Output of Woolen Thread (metric tons)	Woolen Textile Products (kms)	Number of Gunny-bags Produced (1,000s)	Number of Employees
1945	8,268	428	150	1,016	NA	NA	NA	NA	NA
1946	10,664	794	410	2,493	NA	NA	NA	1,301	NA
1947	14,564	1,087	411	6,001	NA	NA	NA	1,197	NA
1948	18,108	1,791	730	12,455	NA	NA	NA	2,737	NA
1949	23,787	2,557	1,805	19,051	638	NA	NA	4,263	110,747
1950	56,020	3,326	3,115	39,730	1,922	82	NA	5,077	338,738
1951	97,636	5,207	7,454	56,543	4,402	69	NA	5,318	444,512
1952	130,906	9,467	13,576	87,639	NA	86	482	6,593	443,225
1953	168,940	11,138	19,546	133,618	NA	144	1,588	8,497	449,502
1954	168,940	11,138	23,614	166,648	NA	166	1,469	9,044	449,785

Sources:
1. Huang Tung-Chi, "Taiwan's Textile Industry," *Taiwan's Textile Industry*, Economic Research Division, Bank of Taiwan, Taiwan Research Periodical, No. 41, pp. 9–12, 1956.
2. *Industry of Free China*, Vol. 15, No. 4, 1961.

and cotton yarn (1951, 1953), and a raising of tariffs (1954, 1959). Internal policies with the same purpose included restrictions on textile product prices, together with controls over production and sales, and restrictions on setting up and expanding factory capacity. In addition, the government adopted a multiple exchange rate system, assigning relatively favorable rates with respect to imports of raw materials and equipment by the textile industry. As indicated by the data in Table A-2, from 1950 to 1954, these measures contributed to an annual average rate of increase in the textile industry of 63 percent. The share of textile industry output value in total industrial output also rapidly increased, reaching 21.4 percent in 1954.

TABLE A - 2

The Structure of Output Value in the Textile Industry, 1921–1958

	Textile Industry				As a Proportion of Total Industrial Output (%)	As a Proportion of Total Manufacturing Output (%)
	Output Value	Growth Rate (%)	Public (%)	Private (%)		
	(million yuan)					
1921	1.8	NA	NA	NA	1.3	NA
1942	11.7	9.4	NA	NA	1.7	NA
	(million NT$)					
1949	71.8	NA	NA	NA	4.7	NA
1950	290.7	30.5	NA	NA	14.3	NA
1951	NA	NA	NA	NA	NA	17.0
1952	1,001	NA	27.3	72.7	16.9	19.2
1953	1,642	64.0	19.7	80.3	20.0	22.5
1954	2,048	24.7	15.1	84.9	21.4	23.9
1955	2,361	15.3	4.8	95.2	20.9	23.4
1956	2,579	9.2	3.8	96.2	18.6	21.0
1957	2,760	7.0	3.7	96.3	16.2	18.5
1958	2,782	0.8	4.2	95.8	15.2	17.7

Source: *Industry of Free China*, Vol. 11, No. 4, 1959.

Note: The textile industry shown here includes the apparel industry.

Of the different government support measures adopted, the most important one was the implementation of the Textile Subcontracting Measures. Because the private sector lacked funds as well as goods and materials, there was a low willingness to invest. In order to induce private investment, government promulgated the Textile Subcontracting Measures in order to guarantee profits. As a result, the U.S. Economic Cooperation Administration between 1951 and May 1952 provided wages or the right to exchange cotton for wages to those private yarn manufacturers who were commissioned to produce yarn. Between June and September 1952, this policy was changed to a policy where U.S. aid was used to purchase cotton that yarn manufacturers were asked to turn into yarn. The yarn thus produced was received by the Cotton Textiles Association and then sold, at restricted prices, to the weaving factories, and then in turn sold at set prices to the Central Trust of China. From September 1952 to June 1953, the policy was changed again to one where both yarn and fabric were either allocated or auctioned among recipients.[3] Thus the government completely controlled both the quantity of textiles produced as well as the prices at which they were sold. The role played by the industry associations was that of assisting the government in matching the quantities of cotton and filament supplied with what was demanded.

As the government implemented policies designed to protect the industry and guarantee profits, a large number of new textile manufacturers were encouraged to enter the industry while others expanded existing facilities. Many companies that were marginal in terms of efficiency and profitability continued to exist. In response to this inefficient production, the government in 1952 and 1953 gradually relaxed its restrictions, and instead adopted policies that auctioned as well as allocated yarn and fabric. In addition, the government allowed textile products to be freely and competitively bought and sold within price limits prescribed by the government. In 1954, the government went a step further and completely abolished the Textile Subcontracting Measures, while still maintaining controls over prices. These changes resulted in the gradual restoration of the market mechanism, and, in 1953 and 1954, the most inefficient producers ceased to operate. As stated in a research report by Lin Pang-yun:

> According to a survey conducted by the Taiwan Cotton Textile Industries Association on December 19, 1953, of the 87 textile fabric factories in Taipei at the end of 1953, only 20 managed to operate normally;

17 factories had ceased production altogether, and the other 50 had partially halted their operations. For the whole of Taiwan, a total of 40 factories ceased to operate, and 128 were partially closed. For this reason, Mr. K. Y. Yin had no choice but to cry out that he could no longer tolerate the great mess that the industry was in. If the rotten meat was not taken out, new muscle would not develop. Mr. Yin was not afraid of seeing the small and inefficient factories with insufficient scale of operation eliminated through competition, but only feared that the efficient factories would not be able to expand their operations.[4]

The presence of excess capacity in the textile industry also led the government to announce in 1954 a series of measures designed to encourage exports of textile products. These measures included guaranteeing exporters a portion of the foreign exchange earned, providing export subsidies, providing tax rebates on imports of raw materials used in the manufacture of goods for export, and low-interest loans. The year 1954, as a result, was the first year that Taiwan successfully exported cotton fabric, although the amount exported was only NT$ 1.84 million. Excess capacity, however, also led the government to adopt in 1954 a "planned economy" approach, whereby it restricted the setting up of new plants or the expansion of existing facilities. It was only in 1958 that this restriction was lifted.

Thus the textile industry, during its early stages of development, benefited from funds, equipment, technology, and personnel from the mainland, support from U.S. aid, and all kinds of protection and preferential measures that served to stimulate its development.

Both private enterprises and the government organizations had important roles to play in this process. Of particular importance within the government system was the technocratic bureaucracy represented by men such as K. Y. Yin. In addition, the Textile Committee of the Council for U.S. Aid, the Textile Committee of the Taiwan Production Board, the Council for U.S. Aid, and the Central Trust of China each had very important parts to play in allocating resources. U.S. aid in particular had an extremely important role to play in this process. As can be seen from Table A-3, the proportion of Taiwan's imports of raw cotton that relied on U.S. aid–related foreign exchange ranged from 81 percent to 99 percent over the 1951 through 1954 period, and still remained above 60 percent in 1960.

Public enterprises after 1952 played a declining role in the development of the textile industry. As is shown in Table A-2, the public sector accounted for 27.3 percent of the textile industry in 1952. This share

TABLE A-3

The Structure of Foreign Exchange Used to Purchase Imports of Raw Cotton, 1951–1967

Year	Foreign Exchange Provided by the Government Amount (US$000s)	Share (%)	Foreign Exchange Provided by U.S. Aid Amount (US$000s)	Share (%)	Other Sources of Foreign Exchange Amount (US$000s)	Share (%)	Total Amount (US$000s)
1951	118	1.19	9,799	98.81	NA	NA	9,917
1952	1,844	13.97	11,353	86.00	NA	NA	13,197
1953	2,337	13.26	14,338	81.34	952	5.40	17,627
1954	1,047	5.04	19,718	94.91	11	0.05	20,776
1955	849	4.17	19,513	95.82	2	1.00	20,364
1956	2,897	14.65	15,537	77.73	1,502	7.61	19,756
1957	1,343	6.75	18,353	92.28	192	0.07	19,888
1958	823	4.40	17,119	91.56	755	4.04	18,697
1959	4,808	25.16	13,598	71.16	702	3.68	19,108
1960	7,097	35.05	12,991	64.17	158	0.78	20,246
1961	16,496	55.43	12,030	40.43	1,232	4.14	29,758
1962	18,220	51.82	16,335	46.46	608	1.72	35,163
1963	13,664	51.56	12,819	48.37	21	0.07	26,504
1964	24,298	73.15	8,916	26.84	5	0.01	33,219
1965	23,760	60.28	15,649	39.70	8	0.02	39,417
1966	27,036	75.47	8,760	24.45	28	0.08	35,824
1967	32,238	64.99	8,427	16.99	8,939	18.02	49,604

Source: Import and Export Foreign Exchange Settlement Statistics, Bank of Taiwan. Obtained from Lin Pang-yun, "A Study on the Development of Taiwan's Cotton Textile Industry," *Collection of Presses of Taiwan's Industrial Development*, Lien-ching Publishing company, 1976, p. 445.

steadily declined, with the decline becoming particularly marked from 1955 onward, after which the public share was maintained at around 5 percent.

During this period, the apparel industry also gradually developed, although its growth was on a somewhat smaller scale. As data in Table A-4 indicate, during the 1951–1954 period, the share of the textile industry in total manufacturing was between five and eight times that of the apparel industry. The textile industry accounted for between 15 and 21 percent of manufacturing, while the apparel industry accounted for only between 2 and 3 percent.

TABLE A-4

The Respective Shares of the Textile and Apparel Industries in GDP

	Textile Industry		Apparel Industry		
Year	GDP (million NT$)	As a Share of Manufacturing Industry GDP (%)	GDP (million NT$)	As a Share of Manufacturing Industry GDP (%)	Manufac- turing Industry (million NT$)
1951	277	15.16	34	1.86	1,827
1952	347	15.62	59	2.66	2,221
1953	530	18.28	72	2.48	2,900
1954	803	20.18	95	2.39	3,979
1955	899	19.19	117	2.50	4,685
1956	851	14.88	132	2.31	5,721
1957	898	12.83	147	2.10	7,001
1958	865	11.47	159	2.11	7,541
1959	1,275	12.69	258	2.57	10,045
1960	1,422	11.92	323	2.71	11,925
1961	1,472	11.13	377	2.85	13,228
1962	1,630	10.59	390	2.53	15,393
1963	2,099	10.95	575	3.00	19,177
1964	2,712	11.61	1,032	4.42	23,364
1965	3,046	12.14	726	2.89	25,095
1966	3,314	11.67	696	2.45	28,403
1967	3,846	10.57	851	2.34	36,371
1968	4,130	9.17	1,091	2.26	45,041
1969	6,050	10.56	1,732	3.02	57,296
1970	7,593	11.48	2,899	4.38	66,168
1971	9,820	11.83	5,047	6.08	82,979
1972	12,961	11.96	6,338	5.85	108,388
1973	19,309	12.78	8,243	5.46	151,065
1974	16,359	9.08	10,057	5.58	180,129
1975	18,997	10.44	8,284	4.55	182,012
1976	26,451	11.07	11,985	5.02	238,965
1977	29,320	10.34	15,281	5.39	283,621
1978	36,394	10.30	18,500	5.24	353,265
1979	39,040	9.09	21,942	5.11	429,320
1980	49,876	9.29	29,335	5.46	537,089
1981	59,503	9.42	8,628	6.11	631,812

continued

TABLE A-4 *(CONTINUED)*

The Respective Shares of the Textile and Apparel Industries in GDP

	Textile Industry		Apparel Industry		
Year	Textile Industry GDP (million NT$)	As a Share of Manufacturing Industry GDP (%)	Apparel Industry GDP (million NT$)	As a Share of Manufacturing Industry GDP (%)	Manufacturing Industry (million NT$)
1982	59,577	8.90	50,654	7.57	669,528
1983	60,560	8.02	51,985	6.88	755,336
1984	73,185	8.32	59,685	6.78	880,124
1985	79,497	8.55	58,973	6.34	929,778
1986	94,959	8.38	66,721	5.89	1,133,358
1987	105,070	8.26	64,633	5.08	1,272,324
1988	95,385	7.22	57,290	4.33	1,321,705
1989	97,462	7.06	56,865	4.12	1,380,199
1990	100,629	6.94	59,880	4.13	1,450,447
1991	115,292	7.12	54,957	3.39	1,618,844
1992	123,968	7.26	52,579	3.08	1,707,918

Source: *National Income, Taiwan Area, the Republic of China*, DGBAS, Executive Yuan, 1994.

3. THE PERIOD OF ADJUSTMENT FROM IMPORT SUBSTITUTION TO EXPORT EXPANSION (1955–1958)

By 1954, Taiwan was already self-sufficient in the production of cotton fabrics. From 1956 onward, it no longer imported cotton yarn. In 1954 and 1955, Taiwan's textile industry, in response to the saturated domestic market and the attractions posed by the government's incentives, directed its attention toward export markets. In 1957, the Ministry of Economic Affairs established the Textile Exports Committee, and, in the following year, representatives of the weaving industry made plans to organize a Dyeing and Weaving Trading Limited Company, to further manage and promote the textile trade.

With the export door opened, the controls over the establishment of new factories were no longer seen as necessary. The government in 1958, therefore, abolished the restrictions with regard to the setting up of new factories. In addition, the regulations that had been in place since 1951 regarding the matching of sales of cotton, yarn, and fabric no longer tallied with current needs, and further resulted in the black market impeding the operation of the legal market. For this reason, the government in 1959 abolished the *Regulations Governing the Management of Cotton Textile Products*, allowing free trade to take place instead. The removal of these two sets of controls constituted the first step in the process of liberalizing the textile industry. These liberalization measures resulted in significant growth. As can be seen from Table A-4, the textile industry, measured in terms of value added, grew by 47.4 percent in 1959 alone, with the apparel industry growing by as much as 62.3 percent in that year. As the data in Table A-5 indicate, exports of textiles and apparel increased sevenfold, with the result that the share of such exports in total exports increased from 1.6 percent in 1958 to 8.8 percent in 1959.

4. THE PERIOD OF EXPORT EXPANSION (1959–1971)

A. Expansion of Exports in the Textile and Apparel Industries

The year 1959 may be regarded as the year in which there was a clear transition from import substitution to export expansion.

At that time, not only did the products sold by the textile manufacturers within the domestic market benefit from government protection in the form of import controls, but goods exported were eligible for low-interest rate loans and export subsidies, making it possible for handsome profits to be reaped. The lifting of the restrictions on the establishment of new facilities thus led to a large influx of new investment. The rapid increase in supply, however, finally resulted in cutthroat competition, and profits fell significantly, even to the extent that losses were incurred. This, added to the overall slackness of the world textile market in 1960, caused textile industrialists to switch from competing against each other to uniting. In 1961, the Cotton Textiles Industries Export Promotion Committee was set up and a cooperation agreement was signed. This agreement stipulated that (1) output should be temporarily reduced by 25 percent; (2) 20 percent of cotton imports should be set aside as cooperation funds, to be refunded when goods were exported and deposited in an export mutual assistance fund (with there being no refund in respect of the portion of goods sold in the local market); and (3) individual manufacturers were each responsible for ensuring that a certain percentage of their goods were exported. Because the domestic market continued to benefit from government protection, the cooperation agreement drawn up by the manufacturers had the effect of a cartel. The reduced output as well as the responsibility to export a certain percentage of goods produced served to guarantee the profitability of the goods sold in the domestic market, and these profits also served to subsidize goods produced for export. The contents of the agreement were modified on several occasions, with the percentage of required exports (as a share of output) ranging between 60 and 80 percent. Toward the end of the 1960s, the agreement still formed the basis of the joint production and sales behavior of the cotton textile industrialists.[5]

Taiwan's export-oriented apparel industry also flourished in this period. As shown in Table A-4, the apparel industry grew by on average 28 percent in each year between 1959 and 1971, and exports of apparel also grew significantly. Between 1961 and 1971, the value of exports of apparel and accessories increased by an average of 54 percent each year (Table A-5). Exports of apparel paralleled those of textiles throughout the period, and in 1970 apparel exports exceeded exports of yarn and fabric, accounting for 51.7 percent of the total value of textiles and apparel and becoming the major export item. However, as Table A-4 indicates, apparel value added was only about half that of textiles. Thus the degree of export dependence in the case of apparel was significantly larger than in the case of textiles.

B. The Development of the Manmade Fiber Industry

During the 1960s, there were two additional developments that affected the growth of the textile and apparel industry. One of these was the development of manmade fibers, resulting in their gradually replacing natural fibers and becoming the most important upstream activity in the textile industry. The other was that the industrialized countries, in order to protect their slowly declining textile industries, began to impose quota restrictions on imports of textile products.

The development of Taiwan's manmade fiber industry came about as a result of the strong demand for these fibers as the textile industry flourished. In 1954, the first manmade fiber company—the China Manmade Fibre Co.—was established. After bringing in technology used in the production of rayon filament, it commenced production in 1957. At first the scale of operations was very small, and production and sales did not progress smoothly. However, in view of the increasing demand for imports of manmade fibers among local textile manufacturers, the China Man-made Fibre Co. continued to expand its operations, and its range of products was gradually increased to include rayon staple and nylon filament. Because the prospects for the manmade fiber industry appeared bright, the Formosa Plastics Corporation entered the

TABLE A-5
The Value of Taiwan's Exports of Textiles and Apparel

Year	Manmade Fibers Value (US$000s)	%	Yarn, Thread, Textile Products, Knitted Textile Products Value (US$000s)	%	Fabric Value (US$000s)	%	Other Textile Products Value (US$000s)	%	Total Total (US$000s)	As a Share of Total Net Export Value (%)
1952	778	97.3	12	1.5	0.0	0.0	10	1.2	800	0.6
1953	354	93.3	24	6.4	0.0	0.0	1	0.3	379	0.3
1954	106	27.6	177	46.4	98	25.6	2	0.4	383	0.5
1955	149	18.7	643	80.6	1	0.2	5	0.6	798	1.0
1956	170	5.0	1,749	51.6	1,465	43.3	5	0.1	3,389	2.9
1957	92	3.2	310	10.7	2,302	79.6	187	6.5	2,891	1.9
1958	116	6.6	542	31.0	900	51.5	191	10.9	1,748	1.6
1959	630	4.6	2,704	19.6	9,188	66.5	1,287	9.3	13,809	8.8
1960	1,229	5.4	5,528	24.3	12,713	55.9	3,280	14.4	22,750	13.9

Year	Manmade Fibers Value (US$000s)	%	Yarn, Fabric Value (US$000s)	%	Apparel & Accessories Value (US$000s)	%	Total Total (US$000s)	As a Share of Total Net Export Value (%)
1961	336	1.2	24,669	81.8	5,070	16.8	30,105	15.4
1962	490	1.1	32,978	75.2	10,366	23.7	43,834	20.1
1963	1,182	2.4	38,654	77.3	10,200	20.4	50,036	15.1
1964	979	1.6	43,612	70.8	17,046	27.7	61,637	14.2
1965	1,545	2.3	46,124	68.6	19,588	29.1	67,527	15.0
1966	2,705	3.0	61,077	68.2	25,755	28.8	89,537	16.7
1967	1,569	1.2	83,365	63.6	46,169	35.2	131,103	20.5

Year								
1968	2,260	1.3	95,426	52.8	83,065	46.0	180,751	23.0
1969	5,842	2.2	134,633	50.4	126,808	47.4	267,283	25.5
1970	3,171	0.8	194,617	47.5	211,606	51.7	409,394	27.6
1971	5,801	0.9	228,283	37.0	383,690	62.1	617,774	30.0
1972	2,028	0.3	352,259	43.2	461,647	56.6	815,934	27.3
1973	7,192	0.7	570,897	54.8	462,854	44.5	1,040,943	23.2
1974	11,691	0.8	626,206	40.9	892,028	58.3	1,529,925	27.1
1975	17,073	1.1	648,025	41.7	889,035	57.2	1,554,133	29.3
1976	30,419	1.3	975,881	42.8	1,319,616	55.9	2,325,917	28.5
1977	33,229	1.5	920,454	40.5	1,320,858	58.1	2,274,541	24.3
1978	58,388	2.0	1,162,862	39.2	1,748,334	58.9	2,969,584	23.4
1979	85,704	2.4	1,562,720	43.1	1,982,017	54.6	3,630,441	22.0
1980	109,487	2.5	1,790,727	41.4	2,426,583	56.1	4,326,797	21.8
1981	134,089	2.7	2,038,407	40.6	2,848,735	56.7	5,021,231	22.2
1982	159,876	3.3	1,767,843	36.7	2,890,757	60.0	4,818,476	21.7
1983	175,697	3.5	1,828,213	36.7	2,983,308	59.8	4,987,218	19.9
1984	191,480	3.1	2,192,924	35.7	3,761,006	61.2	6,145,410	20.2
1985	229,225	3.7	2,518,503	40.2	3,512,515	56.1	6,260,243	20.4
1986	277,648	3.6	3,097,991	40.6	4,259,005	55.8	7,634,644	19.2
1987	329,478	3.5	4,152,112	43.8	4,995,879	52.7	9,477,469	17.7
1988	448,150	4.6	4,638,266	47.4	4,703,836	48.1	9,790,252	16.2
1989	615,370	6.0	5,215,783	50.5	4,497,659	43.6	10,328,812	15.6
1990	602,558	5.9	5,912,350	57.5	3,771,844	36.7	10,286,752	15.3
1991	653,789	5.5	7,029,573	58.6	4,306,573	35.9	11,989,935	15.7
1992	700,399	5.9	7,245,131	61.2	3,892,544	32.9	11,838,074	14.5
1993	664,577	5.5	7,872,559	65.4	3,507,453	29.1	12,044,589	14.2

Sources: 1. *Monthly Statistics of Trade, the Republic of China*, Statistical Dept., Inspectorate General of Customs, R.O.C., 1952–1969.
2. *Statistic on Taiwan Textile and Apparel Industries*, Taiwan Textile Federation, 1979–1993.

fray and in 1965 made preparations to construct a polyacrylonitrile staple factory, completing it in 1967. However, because of problems with the production process, product quality was not good, and it was only after two years of improvements that product quality was raised. The early stages of Taiwan's manmade fiber industry, therefore, did not proceed without a hitch. Investing in manmade fiber production technology required huge sums of money. In addition, although there was a strong demand for manmade fibers on the part of the textile industry, imports were readily available at competitive prices, which furthered the reluctance of domestic firms to invest in the industry. To become competitive, therefore, China Man-made Fibre Co. and the Formosa Plastics Corporation, in the subsequent construction of their production facilities, depended on the government's support for their completion. These efforts to develop the manmade fiber industry are described at greater length in Appendix B on the petrochemical industry.

By the second half of the 1960s, global economic conditions led the prices of intermediate raw materials to rise, and the profitability of the manmade fiber industry greatly increased. Furthermore, government policies toward the end of the 1960s placed greater emphasis on developing the heavy and chemical industries. Several new manmade fiber factories were established toward the end of the 1960s, with the result that by the end of 1970s there was a total of 217 such plants. As can be seen in Table A-6, output of manmade fibers in Taiwan increased by more than 45 percent per annum between 1967 and 1971. These manmade fiber factories were established mainly to supply the domestic textile industry, and there were very few exports of manmade fibers (Table A-5).

C. Imposition of Quotas

Quota restrictions on imports of textile products first began to be imposed by advanced industrialized countries in 1961. As the U.S. imported increased quantities of cotton textile products from newly industrializing countries, its own cotton textile industries were affected. Furthermore, during the Geneva round of GATT negotiations, a meeting on international cotton textile products was convened, resulting in the drawing up of a Short-term Arrangement (STA, 1961) and a Long-term Arrangement (LTA, 1962), whereby additional imports of cotton textile products were restricted.[6] Within the spirit of this multilateral agreement, the advanced industrialized countries from this time on successively signed bilateral agreements restricting trade in textile products with newly industrializing countries. For example, Canada (1964),

TABLE A-6
Production of Manmade Fibers in Taiwan, 1957–1981 (metric tons)

Year	Rayon Staple	Rayon Filament	Nylon Filament	Polyester Staple	Polyester Filament	Polyacrylonitrile Staple	Total	Growth Rate (%)
1957	—	759	—	—	—	—	759	—
1958	608	1,502	—	—	—	—	2,110	178
1959	1,195	1,740	—	—	—	—	2,935	39
1960	1,809	1,762	—	—	—	—	3,571	22
1961	2,130	1,888	—	—	—	—	4,018	13
1962	2,427	1,888	—	—	—	—	4,315	7
1963	2,881	1,857	—	—	—	—	4,738	10
1964	2,890	2,074	53	12	—	—	5,029	6
1965	2,805	1,989	668	595	—	—	6,057	20
1966	3,802	1,918	1,748	920	—	—	8,388	38
1967	7,622	2,630	2,231	1,895	—	200	14,578	74
1968	17,519	2,859	7,174	2,042	30	2,967	32,591	124
1969	18,986	3,050	12,860	5,246	1,960	3,100	47,202	45
1970	22,881	4,060	22,741	7,916	5,050	6,100	68,748	46
1971	29,684	3,326	31,884	14,590	9,383	20,616	110,483	61
1972	34,657	5,639	40,309	23,799	22,372	18,307	145,083	31
1973	46,955	3,350	40,807	28,692	29,174	30,007	178,985	23
1974	44,775	3,106	42,176	29,640	42,256	26,003	187,956	5
1975	46,326	2,664	63,834	50,922	79,699	34,997	278,442	48
1976	65,433	3,129	72,276	68,594	86,047	45,787	342,266	23
1977	66,418	2,990	77,577	114,679	98,620	63,190	423,474	24
1978	69,856	3,063	90,184	158,003	133,310	82,690	537,106	27
1979	69,962	2,978	102,198	172,509	154,598	91,974	594,219	11
1980	75,306	2,952	109,077	193,907	155,323	99,323	636,097	7
1981	96,686	2,975	115,912	199,114	182,339	89,652	686,678	8

Source: Man-made Fibers Manufacturing Industry Association. Obtained from Yang Hui-yi, Huang Ming-tsung, etc., *A Study on the R.O.C.'s Man-made Fiber Industry*, Specialized Research Bulletin No.7, 1981, First Commercial Bank.

the U.S. (1968), and the European Community (1971) all signed textile product agreements with Taiwan.

The impact that these cotton textile trade agreements had on Taiwan's textile and apparel industry did not immediately appear to check the growth of either output or exports. According to the data in Table A-5, between 1960 and 1970, the annual average growth rate of textile and apparel exports continued at the high level of 33.5 percent per year. The rapidly growing exports of Taiwan's manmade fiber textile products took the place of exports of cotton textile products. Manmade fiber textile products were not subject to the restrictions that the agreements imposed on cotton textile products and could be freely exported. Table A-7 lists exports of manmade fibers and products for the period from 1961 through 1970. Apart from the year 1965, the export growth rate of manmade fiber textiles ranged between 45 and 83 percent, and in 1968 surpassed the total value of natural fiber textile products, including both cotton and wool. This free trade loophole, however, was very quickly plugged in the early 1970s and manmade fibers were brought within the control of the Multi-Fibre Agreement.

The quota restrictions of the 1960s also caused the textile manufacturers to join forces. For instance, those in the weaving industry in 1963

TABLE A-7

An Overview of the Manmade Fibers, Synthetic Fiber, and their Production, 1961–1970

Year	Value of Export (NT$000s)	Growth Rate (%)	As a Share of the Total Value of Textile and Apparel Exports (%)	As a Share of Total Exports (%)
1961	184,467	NA	15.32	2.36
1962	290,460	57.46	16.57	3.33
1963	423,360	45.76	21.13	3.19
1964	726,267	71.55	29.44	4.18
1965	760,472	4.71	28.20	4.23
1966	1,151,433	51.41	32.16	5.37
1967	2,108,442	83.11	40.15	8.23
1968	3,681,580	74.11	50.70	11.66
1969	6,385,189	73.44	59.65	15.21
1970	10,565,639	65.47	66.99	18.49

Source: *Industry of Free China*, Vol. 36, No. 3, 1971.

agreed to reduce their output for the domestic market by 30 percent in order to avert a crisis that would result if sales of their products significantly dropped. Woolen textile manufacturers adopted a uniform pricing policy, and manufacturers of cotton textiles continued to sign cooperation agreements. In addition, the Apparel Industry Association joined forces with the Textile Manufacturers' Association to set up an export subcommittee.[7] Relations between the industry associations and the manufacturers were very close. The relationship between these associations and the government also gradually deepened. For example, during this period, each industry association not only assisted the government in handling rebates connected with exports, but also stepped up their efforts to assist in the allocation of export quotas and to reach agreement among manufacturers with regard to the sales prices of goods produced. For these reasons, the role of the industry associations in serving as a bridge between manufacturers and the government became increasingly important.

5. THE PERIOD OF MATURITY (1972–1979)

During the 1970s, the focus of government policy shifted from export expansion to a second period of import substitution.

Although exports of textiles continued to grow, the period was marked by a series of adverse factors on the international level that served to weaken performance. The chief of these was the first global energy crisis, which took place in 1973, followed by the effective implementation of the Multi-Fibre Agreement in 1974, and the second global energy crisis which occurred in 1979. Furthermore, toward the end of the 1970s, other newly industrializing countries became increasingly competitive in world textile markets. Although these adverse factors were insufficient in themselves to stop the growth of Taiwan's exports of textile products, the textile industry began to be regarded as a sunset industry.

Prior to the occurrence of the first energy crisis in 1973, the world economy was very prosperous, with the result that demand for intermediate raw materials was very strong, and great upward pressure was exerted on prices. During this period, international textile markets flourished, raw cotton prices gradually increased, and the supply of manmade fibers could not keep up with demand. Consequently there were sizeable profits to be made. For these reasons, local manufacturers of manmade fibers expanded their facilities and new factories were rapidly added. When the first major energy crisis unexpectedly occurred, the government adopted a low energy pricing policy in order to protect the heavy and chemical industries. The demand for manmade fibers declined, however, because the downstream textile and apparel industries were affected by the downturn in the world economy, resulting in an excess of production by local manmade fiber manufacturers. Many manufacturers subsequently ceased operating, while some manufacturers had to rely on government support to weather the crisis.

With regard to the apparel industry, the impact of the first major energy crisis may be observed from the growth rate data in Table A-8.

TABLE A-8

Textile and Apparel Industries' Output Link Indices, 1972–1993

Year	Manufacturing Industry	Manmade Fiber Industry	Textile Industry	Apparel and Accessories Industry
1972	22.7	39.1	20.7	5.7
1973	17.7	29.1	8.7	9.3
1974	−6.0	3.7	−2.8	−7.2
1975	8.0	46.1	23.1	−1.1
1976	25.6	20.9	12.9	57.7
1977	12.9	27.7	5.0	5.7
1978	26.3	25.1	11.4	24.8
1979	7.8	9.3	0.3	6.8
1980	6.2	6.5	11.8	22.5
1981	3.7	8.1	0.5	16.5
1982	1.3	4.1	−1.2	−0.4
1983	15.4	13.2	3.2	−1.0
1984	12.8	15.9	12.1	12.6
1985	1.2	7.4	3.4	−5.9
1986	16.1	26.3	9.1	6.3
1987	11.2	9.7	4.7	2.7
1988	3.8	3.4	−10.2	−16.6
1989	3.4	11.7	3.7	−2.2
1990	−1.7	12.6	−5.6	−9.7
1991	7.3	20.9	7.3	−0.9
1992	3.1	5.4	−2.2	−12.7
1993	2.2	6.8	−7.3	−11.1

Source: *Statistics on Taiwan Textile and Apparel Industries, Taiwan Textile Federation, 1979–1993.*

For example, in 1974, production of textiles declined by 3.2 percent, and production of apparel continued to decrease through 1975. The impact of this first major energy crisis on the textile and apparel industry, however, was short term and transitory. The Multi-Fibre Arrangement, in contrast, had a long-term effect.

The Multi-Fibre Arrangement originated in the early 1970s, with the United States being the main country among the importers of textile products to note the gradual increase in imports of non-cotton textiles. As the Cotton Textile Products Agreement of the 1960s was unable to control this situation, in 1973 an international textile products agreement, referred to as the Multi-Fibre Arrangement (MFA), became effective in 1974. This agreement took into account all kinds of fiber products. Each major textile trading country within the spirit of this Multi-Fibre Arrangement therefore signed bilateral agreements with Taiwan. Agreement with Europe, the United States, and Canada, the major markets for textile products, continued in existence into the 1990s.

It was also during the 1970s that the Republic of China suffered a series of diplomatic setbacks, beginning with its withdrawal from the United Nations in 1971 and followed by a rapid reduction in the number of countries that maintained diplomatic relations with Taiwan. The textile agreements that had been signed with these countries were thus no longer honored. For example, in July 1975, the European Community unilaterally announced the imposition of restrictions on imports of textile products from the Republic of China. Since Taiwan was no longer a member of the GATT nor a signatory to the Multi-Fibre Arrangement, it was unable to enter into negotiations with the European Community and was subjected to discriminatory treatment. Therefore, the ROC government appointed Min-chi Chang, Chiu-hsueh Liu, Mu-tsai Wang, Hsu-tung Hsu, and others to go to Europe to negotiate on behalf of the Taiwan Textile Federation. For political reasons, however, they were able to negotiate only on an informal level. After the delegation returned to Taiwan, the government encouraged the textile industry associations and the textile manufacturers together to establish the Taiwan Textile Federation (hereafter referred to as TTF). This federation, with its status as a nongovernmental association, thus could represent Taiwan in negotiations with the European Community with respect to trade in textile products. Later, in 1977, the federation entered into negotiations with both Canada and the United States.[8]

Although the TTF was a private organization, it was supervised and empowered by the government, and for this reason had an official flavor although it was not a recipient of government funding. Its role gradually expanded, and it became the major entity that represented the Republic of China in textile trade negotiations with other countries. With powers conferred upon it by the government, it also officiated in matters such as managing quotas and promoting exports of textile products.

By the late 1970s, many developing countries had begun promoting exports of textiles to bring about economic development. These countries included mainland China, Indonesia, India, the Philippines, Pakistan, and Thailand. They all used their abundant supply of cheap labor to compete against Taiwan's exports of textile products. During the very short four-year period extending from 1975 to 1979, average individual monthly wages in Taiwan's manmade fiber, textile, and apparel industries increased on average each year by 13.7 percent, 18.5 percent, and 19.6 percent, respectively. These rapid increases in wages resulted in Taiwan's gradual loss of competitiveness. As can be observed in Table A-9, there was a high degree of concentration of firms with fewer than thirty employees, and 40 to 50 percent of enterprises had ten or fewer employees. In addition to rising wages, therefore, the small scale of operations of the firms in the textile and apparel industries resulted in poor quality control and a lack of R and D and product design ability, which seriously impeded the development of the competitive strength of these industries. With the outbreak of the second oil crisis in 1979, and faced with another world economic recession as well as other unfavorable factors, the government in 1979 put forward the Guidelines to Speed up the Reform of the Textile Industry. These guidelines encouraged industrialists to develop their activities by merging their operations, replace their worn-out equipment, strengthen their R and D, raise product quality, diversify their export markets, and establish a Joint Export Promotion Group.[9]

In terms of value added, between 1972 and 1979, the average annual growth rates of the textile and apparel industries were 17.1 percent and 19.4 percent, respectively. The total of the contributions of these two industries to manufactured GDP during that period fluctuated between 11 percent and 18.5 percent of manufactured GDP for the economy as a whole. During the 1972 through 1979 period, textile and apparel industry exports increased on average by 23 percent, but exports in this industry as a share of total exports also fluctuated widely. In 1975, textile and apparel exports accounted for 29.3 percent of total exports, but this share gradually declined to 22.0 percent by 1979.

TABLE A-9
The Scale of Operations in the Textile and Apparel Industries, Based on the Number of Employees

Year	1–9 Employees		10–29 Employees		30–99 Employees		Over 100 Employees		Total	
	Number of Factories	Share (%)	Number of Factories	Share (%)	Number of Factories	Share (%)	Number of Factories	Share (%)	Number of Factories	Share (%)
Textile Industry										
1976	1,983	42.22	1,245	26.51	765	16.29	704	14.99	4,697	100.00
1981	3,061	50.82	1,486	24.67	916	15.21	560	9.30	6,023	100.00
1986	3,863	49.70	2,088	26.87	1,228	15.80	593	7.63	7,772	100.00
1991	4,479	56.98	2,087	26.55	946	12.04	348	4.89	7,860	100.00
Apparel Industry										
1976	1,031	50.29	457	22.29	303	14.78	259	10.63	2,050	100.00
1981	1,423	48.73	684	23.42	508	17.40	305	10.46	2,920	100.00
1986	1,298	39.32	961	29.11	688	20.84	354	10.72	3,301	100.00
1991	1,767	47.89	1,113	30.16	613	16.61	197	5.34	3,690	100.00

Source: *The Report on Industrial and Commercial Census Taiwan-Fukien Area, The Republic of China*, DGBAS, Executive Yuan, 1976, 1981, 1986, 1991.

6. The Period of Adjustment (1980–1993)

A. The First Stage of Adjustment

The outbreak of the second major energy crisis resulted in a global recession that hit bottom in 1982. For this reason, 1982 was an extremely difficult year for the textile and apparel industries. The output indices for the year 1982 in the case of the textile industry, and for the years 1982 and 1983 in the case of the apparel industry, markedly declined, and factory closures and work stoppages occurred frequently. This in turn led to many efforts aimed at self-preservation, most notably the appearance of several forms of collective behavior, such as joint purchases of cotton, joint decisions to reduce production, and a united voice when making proposals to the government. Furthermore, each of the textile and apparel industry associations had a very important role to play in the process, since they constituted the heart of all collective behavior.

The difficulties encountered in the market led the textile and apparel manufacturers to face up to the fact that the era of increasing quantity had already passed, and that in the future emphasis would have to be placed on raising quality. In 1982, the government also proposed the Guidelines for Reforming the Textile Industry. The main points of the guidelines were: (1) new textile yarn and fabrics plants were not allowed to be established and existing facilities were not allowed to expand; (2) those establishing new facilities to manufacture apparel would not be accorded any incentives, and would not be allowed to apply for quotas for exporting to those countries with import restrictions; (3) preferential loans would be extended to replace existing equipment with fully or semiautomated equipment, providing that the old equipment was discarded at the same time; (4) the setting up of dyeing and finishing plants would be encouraged to increase the value added of exports, provided that a certain scale of operations was achieved (an annual output of 15,000 meters), and provided that the plants were also equipped with facilities to prevent pollution; and (5) individual firms would be encouraged to merge their operations with those of others.[10] These guidelines were an extension of the Guidelines to Speed up the Reform of the Textile Industry put forward in 1979.

As a result of the self-preservation efforts on the part of the manufacturers and the stimulus provided by the government's incentives, dyeing and finishing factories were gradually set up and a considerable amount of worn-out equipment was replaced with highly efficient machinery brought in from abroad. As shown in Table A-10, in 1983 almost all equipment in the textile and apparel industries was significantly upgraded or replaced. From 1984 through 1986, one of the greatest changes was the increase in ring-frames in the cotton textile industry. The shuttleless loom also gradually replaced the shuttle loom, and yarn-dyeing equipment and equipment used during the dyeing process experienced significant increases. As for equipment used in the manufacture of apparel, lockstitch sewing machines, overlock sewing machines, and special sewing machines all increased in number.

Manufacturers thus relied on machinery in an attempt to retrieve the situation. The government's attempts to provide incentives to encourage mergers among firms did not make much headway. The structure of production remained predominantly small- and medium-firm based. Management skills continued to lag behind, the scale of operations was excessively small, and there was a lack of R and D and information regarding business conditions. In 1983, the U.S. economy experienced a recovery, which suddenly meant that local textile manufacturers no longer had to concern themselves with the need for industrial upgrading brought about by the recession, and production subsequently returned to former levels. Thus Taiwan's textile and apparel industries wavered between traditional and sunset status throughout the 1980s.

B. A Surge in Investment in the Chemical Fiber Industry

When the U.S. economy experienced a powerful recovery in 1983, the local textile and apparel industries suddenly had a new lease of life, and some apparel factory owners invested in Central America (Panama) in order to get around quota restrictions. In 1984, the shortage of workers and raw materials in the textile and apparel industries became increasingly serious, which led to an increase in the incidence of textile companies luring employees away from each other, and to a rapid escalation in the prices of manmade fibers. In order to stabilize the supplies and prices of raw materials, the textile industry associations and the Man-made Fibre Industry Association in 1984 reached agreement with regard to prices on several occasions.[11] Finally, five-year contracts were drawn up between both upstream and downstream companies. This experience, however, encouraged textile manufacturers to resolve to vertically integrate their activities. One by one they combined their efforts to invest jointly in upstream chemical fiber factories (especially ones engaged in the manufacture of polyester fiber) in order to gain full control of a stable supply of raw materials and arrive at reasonable prices.

It is estimated that NT$3 billion was invested in facilities to manu-

TABLE   A-10

The Results of a Survey on Production Equipment Used in the Textile and Apparel Industries, 1982–1992

Production	Equipment	Annual Unit of Measure	1982	1983	1984
Regenerated	Factories Surveyed	Factories	2	2	2
Fibers	Spinning M/C	Lines	52	48	52
	Fiber-Line Process M/C	Lines	9	9	9
Synthetic	Factories Surveyed	Factories	23	23	21
Fibers	Polymerization M/C	Lines	145	145	149
	Spinning M/C	Lines	233	233	197
	Fiber-Line Process M/C	Lines	46	46	46
Cotton	Factories Surveyed	Factories	146	146	173
Spinning	Ring-Frame M/C	Spindles	3,345,187	3,551,888	3,812,093
Sector	Open-End M/C	Lines	91,572	108,988	108,448
Wool	Factories Surveyed	Factories	64	65	82
Spinning	Manmade fiber	Spindles	321,412	261,216	258,760
Sector	Worsted Ring Frame	Spindles	88,220	88,444	109,400
	Worsted Spinning Frame	Spindles	57,922	59,820	69,240
Man-made	Factories Surveyed	Factories	54	61	62
Textured	Frictional False Twist M/C	Spindles	44,312	53,872	52,512
Sector	Pin-Spindle False Twist M/C	Spindles	248,466	271,086	271,274
	Air-Texturing M/C	Spindles	884	668	866
	Gear-Type Processor	Spindles	—	—	—
Weaving	Factories Surveyed	Factories	295	722	740
Sector	Shuttle Weaving Loom	Machines	50,345	62,986	61,963
	Shuttleless Weaving Loom	Machines	9,251	13,621	16,365
Knitted	Factories Surveyed	Factories	463	467	647
Sector	Warp Knitting M/C	Machines	641	809	831
	Circular Knitting M/C	Machines	6,437	6,571	7,438
Dyeing	Factories Surveyed	Factories	188	191	288
&	Yarn Dyed Equipment	Machines	843	917	1,169
Finishing	Dyeing Equipment	Machines	1,633	1,666	2,565
Sector	Printing Equipment	Machines	312	319	304
	Finishing Equipment	Machines	1,168	1,215	1,198
Apparel	Factories Surveyed	Factories	843	966	1,094
Sector	Lockstitch-Sewing M/C	Machines	70,677	80,034	88,793
	Overlock-Sewing M/C	Machines	17,451	19,806	21,408
	Special Sewing M/C	Machines	12,943	14,545	16,671
Sweater	Factories Surveyed	Factories	—	—	—
Sector	Flat Knitting M/C	Machines	—	—	—

Source: *Statistics on Taiwan Textile and Apparel Industries, Taiwan Textile Federation, 1979–1993.*

Note: "—" indicates data not available.

1985	1986	1987	1988	1989	1990	1991	1992
2	2	2	—	—	2	2	2
52	52	52	—	—	52	52	47
9	9	9	—	—	9	12	9
21	21	23	—	—	23	24	25
158	160	162	—	—	162	178	148
216	232	334	—	—	334	470	400
54	54	63	—	—	63	89	72
169	172	178	—	—	139	139	139
3,841,245	3,826,867	3,955,473	—	—	3,677,980	3,674,796	3,674,796
95,944	105,096	121,637	—	—	150,944	155,568	155,568
81	85	81	—	—	81	81	59
250,368	255,008	235,368	—	—	235,448	255,800	153,196
108,236	108,236	109,146	—	—	115,218	153,678	142,132
67,896	74,139	67,616	—	—	67,651	81,769	43,824
61	60	53	—	—	53	53	48
54,144	52,632	78,552	—	—	79,272	137,332	129,676
260,942	262,510	204,700	—	—	203,296	211,040	113,308
866	866	812	—	—	812	—	—
—	—	35,148	—	—	35,148	35,820	672
737	811	807	—	—	572	572	575
57,641	50,785	47,032	—	—	20,019	19,916	19,916
19,158	22,406	26,733	—	—	28,990	29,161	29,161
324	329	325	—	—	325	325	352
853	836	868	—	—	868	686	927
6,725	6,768	6,991	—	—	6,991	6,991	5,599
288	287	285	—	—	286	286	240
1,174	1,180	1,232	—	—	1,234	1,515	869
2,638	2,669	2,776	—	—	2,799	3,508	2,447
286	281	234	—	—	225	312	196
1,212	1,194	1,335	—	—	1,358	1,733	1,128
1,140	1,161	1,143	—	—	1,220	1,220	786
86,617	87,122	85,070	—	—	74,510	74,747	39,430
23,647	23,913	23,493	—	—	23,181	23,340	13,718
22,781	22,965	22,659	—	—	23,413	23,427	13,736
386	395	383	—	—	350	350	211
20,583	20,767	19,954	—	—	15,504	15,241	3,706

facture polyester staple as a result. This caught the government's attention and, in order to avoid what it considered to be excessive (or blind)
investment, the Ministry of Economic Affairs' Industrial Development
Bureau (IDB) convened a meeting to coordinate the capacity-expan-
sion plans with respect to the manufacture of polyester fiber. The IDB
also announced that, if it was unable to check such needless expansion,
it would request that the financial authorities refuse to support the
investment expansion plans of such manufacturers. In spite of these
measures, however, the IDB was still unable to curb such investment
by textile manufacturers. In 1984, investors in manmade fiber factories
included Far Eastern Textile Ltd., Chung Shing Textile Co., Shinkong
Spinning Co., Tun Yun Textile Co., and Tainan Spinning Co. Manmade
fiber equipment (especially equipment related to polyester) increased
from 1985 through 1987, and output of manmade fibers increased in
1986 by 26.3 percent.

The increase in manmade fiber production capacity resulted in Taiwan in 1990 becoming the world's third largest producer of manmade
fiber, being surpassed by only the United States and Japan. At the same
time, the way in which the manmade fiber industry marketed its output gradually changed. Formerly, the output of local manmade fiber
producers had almost always supplied the domestic market (in 1985
this proportion still exceeded 80 percent), while only that part not
needed locally was exported. As the NT dollar sharply appreciated from
1986 onward, however, orders for downstream textile and apparel industry products were redirected toward mainland China and Southeast Asia. In addition, textile and apparel factories one by one moved
offshore, resulting in a reduction in local demand for manmade fibers
while demand for them overseas increased. The quantities of textile
and apparel products and accessories all exhibited a decline. In order
to respond to these changes, manmade fibers gradually began to be
exported. Manmade fibers exports, as a proportion of total textile exports, increased from 3.6 percent in 1986 to more than 5.5 percent in
1993, resulting in Taiwan becoming an important provider of textile
raw materials in the Asian region.

C. Disputes and Reforms Regarding the Handling of Quotas

The problems associated with textile product quotas[12] constituted the
focal point of wide-ranging disputes between 1981 and 1985. In 1981,
the Economic Committee of the Control Yuan asked the Ministry of
Economic Affairs to explain why the textile product quotas at that time

were being manipulated by the large firms and were being illegally traded, resulting in an export bottleneck. This case led to the joint signing of a statement on the part of seventeen related textile and apparel industry associations that declared that the large firms had not been engaged in malpractice. Because the years 1981 and 1982 happened to be years when the textile and apparel industries were in a recession, such disputes did not disappear as time passed. In order to break through the difficulties facing the textile and apparel industries, the government decided to revise relevant regulations and completely overhaul the system of quotas. The result was that the government and the different vested interest groups (these vested interest groups tended to be composed of the leading representatives of textile companies or industry associations) became antagonistic toward each other. For example, the Ministry of Economic Affairs in April 1982 passed Regulations Governing the Handling of Textile Product Export Quotas, which substantially changed the way quotas were allocated. In July, freely allocated quotas were replaced with a system where quotas were auctioned off. These measures resulted in an escalation of disputes between the government and industrialists. In particular, in the Draft Guidelines for Reforming the Textile Industry drafted by the Industrial Development Bureau in August 1982, the goal was to attempt to nationalize all textile product quotas within ten years. The conflicts between the government and the industrialists came to a head and led to a war regarding rights over quotas. The industrialists who stood to benefit considered that the quotas were a form of private property they earned, as they had spent money to purchase equipment. The Ministry of Economic Affairs argued that the quotas constituted a public legal right. The Ministry went on to say that what the industrialists possessed was a conditional right of usage. The dispute between the two sides became very heated. The industrialists lobbied legislators to support their position. The inequities in the quota system as it then existed, however, had become readily apparent to both the technocratic policy makers and the general public. The government finally won the support of the Legislative Yuan, and thereby resolved the impasse between the government and the industry. This resulted in the Ministry of Economic Affairs in 1985 promulgating the Regulations Governing the Allocation and Implementation of Planned Quotas, in which the goal was to reallocate quotas in order to promote market diversification, to create own-brand names, to promote research and development, and to promote the replacement of worn-out machinery and profits. Industrialists were thus compelled to upgrade their operations, and disputes related to quotas gradually began to subside.

D. Investing Offshore and Industrial Upgrading

Beginning in the mid-1980s, the government's liberalization policies and the appreciation of the NT dollar had a very large impact on industries in the manufacturing sector, with the textile and apparel industries being affected the most. The appreciation of the NT dollar had a particularly profound effect on the export-oriented apparel industry. At the same time, however, the international economy was experiencing an upswing and the Japanese yen and the European currencies were also appreciating, and therefore exports of apparel still continued to increase, although with a considerable reduction in profits. As shown in Table A-11, the pretax profit rate in the apparel and accessories industry declined from 3.97 percent of sales in 1986 to 0.63

TABLE A-11

Pretax Profit Rates for the Textile and Apparel Industries, 1981–1992

Year	Manufacturing Industry	Textile Products	Apparel and Accessories
1981	2.81	2.21	4.19
1982	4.00	2.70	4.19
1983	6.02	0.32	4.31
1984	5.95	−0.44	4.01
1985	5.83	3.43	2.81
1986	6.67	6.45	3.97
1987	7.87	6.58	0.63
1988	8.38	5.24	0.62
1989	7.54	2.85	0.66
1990	5.37	3.88	1.94
1991	5.69	6.63	5.42
1992	5.49	3.32	4.58

Note: Pretax Profit Rate = Profit Before Tax / Sales x 100%

Sources: 1. *Report on Survey of R.O.C. Industry,* Statistics Division, Ministry of Economic Affairs, 1976–1982; *Report on a Sample Survey of Industrial Enterprises in Taiwan, R.O.C.,* Statistics Division, Ministry of Economic Affairs, 1983–1985; *Report on a Survey of Conditions Regarding Industrial Enterprises in Taiwan, R.O.C.,* Statistics Division, Ministry of Economic Affairs, 1987–1990.

percent in 1987. The textile industry was also affected by the appreciation of the NT dollar. In addition, it suffered from a shortage of labor and the resulting rapid rise in real wages. For these reasons, textile industrialists in both 1986 and 1987 continued actively to expand and replace their existing facilities, and many of the larger factories installed automated equipment. The years 1986 through 1987 differ from 1982 through 1985 in that, during the later period, most cotton textile machines were replaced with open-end machines, and shuttleless looms gradually exceeded shuttle looms in number. From 1980 onward, textile manufacturing equipment was constantly replaced and upgraded, in response to the difficulties brought about by a labor force that was increasingly short in supply and ever more expensive.

In addition to the appreciation of the NT dollar and the shortage of labor, rising U.S. protectionist sentiment added to the trade barriers that Taiwan was facing. These barriers became more apparent following the Textile and Apparel Trade Enforcement Act of 1985, sponsored by U.S. Congressman Jenkins and Senator Thurmond and the U.S.-ROC textile trade negotiations that took place in 1986. In addition, competition from newly industrializing countries became increasingly fierce. As these difficulties at home and abroad overlapped, from the second half of 1987 onward, the apparel industry first responded to its loss of competitiveness by sinking into a recession. Not long afterward, the unfavorable conditions in the downstream industries gradually moved upstream, affecting the weaving and textile yarn industries, and lasted until 1990, when the whole world economy was in recession. Due to the vibrancy of the textile industries in mainland China and Southeast Asia, however, the manmade fiber industry's exports were unimpeded.

As the textile and apparel industries were confronted with the above-mentioned influences, companies one by one adjusted their operations through diversification, internationalization, and industrial upgrading. With regard to the first of these, the most common approach adopted was to diversify by investing in different industries, especially in service businesses. With regard to internationalization, this chiefly consisted of investing overseas, at first on the part of the apparel manufacturers, but they were later gradually followed by textile manufacturers. Even some producers of manmade fibers engaged in overseas investment. These investments took place at first in Southeast Asia, but very quickly mainland China became the key area. The outcome of this internationalization became apparent in the early 1990s. As shown in Table A-8, output of apparel gradually declined from 1988 onward, while outward investment became concentrated in mainland China and Southeast Asia. This also caused Taiwan's exports of upstream raw materials (i.e., yarn and fabric) to mainland China via Hong Kong to increase rapidly. According to the export figures contained in Table A-12, from 1991 onward, exports of textile products to Hong Kong exceeded exports of

TABLE A.12

Major Export Markets of Taiwan's Textile Products

Year	Total Value of Exports (million NT$)	Structure of Export Markets and Major Products Exported		
		Country	Share (%)	Major Export Products
1989	10,328,810	U.S.	28.76	Apparel
		Hong Kong	19.77	Fabric
		Japan	11.77	Apparel
		Singapore	4.02	Fabric
		Germany	2.94	Apparel
		Others	32.74	
1990	10,286,752	U.S.	25.96	Apparel
		Hong Kong	25.25	Fabric
		Japan	7.66	Apparel
		Singapore	3.88	Fabric
		Philippines	3.04	Fabric
		Others	34.21	
1991	11,989,935	Hong Kong	29.70	Fabric
		U.S.	24.63	Apparel
		Japan	6.44	Apparel
		Germany	3.32	Apparel
		Singapore	3.27	Fabric
		Others	32.64	
1992	11,838,074	Hong Kong	31.39	Fabric
		U.S.	23.80	Apparel
		Japan	6.04	Apparel
		Philippines	3.18	Fabric
		Singapore	3.16	Fabric
		Others	32.46	
1993	12,044,589	Hong Kong	34.48	Fabric
		U.S.	22.69	Apparel
		Japan	4.36	Apparel, Yarn
		Philippines	3.09	Fabric
		Singapore	2.68	Fabric
		Others	32.70	Fabric

Source: *Statistics on Taiwan Textile and Apparel Industries, Taiwan Textile Federation, 1979–1993.*

such products to the United States, previously Taiwan's largest market.

Furthermore, in terms of the changes in the structure of exports, it can be seen from Table A-13 that in 1989 the respective proportions of exports of apparel and fabrics were about the same, with apparel accounting for 38.7 percent of textile exports and fabrics accounting for 36.7 percent. By 1993, however, the share of exports of apparel had declined to 22.97 percent, whereas that of fabrics had increased to 51.64 percent. Exports of the high value added finished fabrics gradually replaced exports of gray fabrics as the leading kind of fabric exported.

The measures taken by the government to promote liberalization caused tariff rates with respect to the textile and apparel industries to fall significantly, by more than 50 percent in both 1987 and 1988. The impact of this policy on the textile and apparel industries was very small, however. As the figures in Table A-14 indicate, from 1987 textile and apparel industry imports grew at a relatively faster rate only in 1987 and 1991. In the remaining years (i.e., 1988, 1989, and 1990), the changes were not significant, and the share of textile and apparel industry imports in total imports declined by 1.37 percentage points between 1987 and 1990. The reason that the impact was not larger was that the upstream manmade fiber industry had formerly already relied considerably upon imports. In addition, in order to reduce costs, a low-tariff policy had already been in place for years. Furthermore, a system of cooperation between the midstream and downstream textile and apparel manufacturers had been established early on and, with emphasis being placed on exports, the industry was already able to compete internationally. For this reason, lowering import tariffs did not have a marked impact on the industry, but instead altered the struc-

---

TABLE A.13

The Structure of Exports of Textile Products

Year	Manmade Fiber (%)	Yarn (%)	Fabric (%)	Apparel (%)	Accessories (%)	Total (%)
1989	5.96	13.80	36.70	38.07	5.48	100
1990	5.86	15.07	42.40	31.04	5.63	100
1991	5.45	14.54	44.09	29.32	6.60	100
1992	5.92	14.39	46.81	26.41	6.47	100
1993	5.52	13.72	51.64	22.97	6.15	100

Note: For the total value of exports, please refer to Table A.12.

Source: *Statistics on Taiwan Textile and Apparel Industries, Taiwan Textile Federation, 1979–1993.*

TABLE A.14
The Structure of Taiwan's Imports of Textile Products

Year	Total Value of Imports of Textile Products (US$000s)	Rate of Change (%)	Imports of Textile Products as a Proportion of Total Imports (%)	Total (%)	Manmade Fiber (%)	Structure of Imports			
						Yarn (%)	Fabric (%)	Apparel (%)	Accessories (%)
1986	12,070	21.50	5.00	100	50.84	48.24		0.92	
1987	17,090	41.00	4.89	100	52.64	44.93		2.43	
1988	18,720	8.00	3.77	100	43.88	49.16		6.94	
1989	19,550	4.40	3.74	100	45.34	15.48	28.35	8.39	2.44
1990	19,270	−1.40	3.52	100	36.32	17.46	30.79	12.05	3.38
1991	26,040	35.10	4.14	100	37.29	20.96	28.87	9.68	2.7
1992	27,310	4.90	3.79	100	29.15	22.14	32.72	12.29	3.7
1993	27,620	1.10	3.58	100	24.95	19.91	33.17	17.51	4.46

Source: *Statistics on Taiwan Textile and Apparel Industries, Taiwan Textile Federation, 1979–1993.*

ture of imports. Imports of textile raw materials declined while the share of imports of finished and semi-finished textile products increased.

E. The Assistance Provided by the Government and Government Departments

Because of the significant changes that took place in the industrial environment, it was not just the textile and apparel industries that were subjected to this pressure to upgrade their operations, but the whole of the manufacturing sector. For this reason, the government made every effort to promote industrial upgrading as a policy objective. In order to promote industrial upgrading in the 1990s, the government gradually increased its role in the development of the textile and apparel industries.

Apart from encouragement of a functional approach provided by the Statute for Promoting Industrial Upgrading, the Industrial Development Bureau of the Ministry of Economic Affairs also commissioned various projects to research institutes and the various industry associations aiming at assisting the textile and apparel industries to upgrade their operations. These programs are listed in Table A-15. This table also shows that, during this period, the functions of the various organizations situated in between the manufacturers and the government were also upgraded. For example, although the Textile Research Center was established in 1959, its function in the past was not very evident, and the amount of money spent on research was extremely small. It was only during this period, when the textile industry felt it was necessary to upgrade its operations, that the research center began to play a more significant role. Furthermore, during the 1980s, the main functions of the Taiwan Textile Federation and the other associations remained at the level of managing the quotas, resisting accusations from abroad concerning dumping, and negotiating price agreements between upstream and downstream suppliers. Later, however, these associations had an additional role to play: to promote the upgrading of the textile and apparel industries.

The results of this industrial upgrading in the textile and apparel industries since the late 1980s and early 1990s may be seen from Table A-16. The numbers of research personnel and expenditures on research in the textile and apparel industries were higher in 1990 and 1991 than in previous years. In addition, labor productivity in real terms also rapidly increased. Furthermore, the degree of capital intensity in the textile industry also increased significantly in 1990, whereas that in the

TABLE A.15
Textile and Apparel Industry Special Projects, Industrial Development Bureau, Ministry of Economic Affairs

Year	Title of Plan	Appointed Organization	Contracted Amount
1990	Project to Demonstrate and Offer Guidance in the Use of Comber Maintenance Technology	Textile Research Center	804
	Demonstrating and Offering Guidance Regarding the Use of Weaving Preparation Sizing Technology	Textile Research Center	1,092
	Offering Guidance with Regard to the Rationalization of Production and Supervision in the Finished (Woolen) Apparel Sector	Taiwan Textile Federation	1,000
	Training Research Personnel in the Development of High-level Textile Product Clothing Designs	Fu Jen Catholic University	3,057
	Project to Offer Guidance in Upgrading the Technical Capability of Dyeing and Finishing Factories	Textile Research Center	2,340
	Project to Promote the Computerized Testing of Raw Cotton in Line with the Development of Cotton Technology	Cotton Textile Industry Association	1,540
1992	Project to Offer Guidance in Upgrading Textile Industry Technical Capability	Textile Research Center	21,590
	An Analysis of Present Conditions and Future Trends in the Textile Industry	Taiwan Textile Federation	2,710
	Project to Promote the Computerized Testing of Raw Cotton in Line with the Development of Cotton Technology	Cotton Textile Industry Association	1,200
	Project to Initiate a Computerized Dyeing and Finishing System	Department of Chemical Engineering, ITRI	4,255
	Three-year Project to Offer Guidance in Upgrading Technology in the Apparel Industry	Hub-Satellite Development Center	13,200

(continued)

(continued)

Year	Project	Organization	Amount
	Project to Upgrade Design Capability in the Textile Industry	Taiwan Textile Federation	17,266
	Project to Train Research Personnel in the Development of Clothing Designs Involving Textile Products	Fu Jen Catholic University	4,350
	Project to Train Textile Industry Personnel over a Period of Five Years	Textile Research Center	3,000
	Project to Train Textile Industry Personnel in Design Capability	Taiwan Textile Federation	4,500
1993	Project to Offer Guidance in Upgrading Textile Industry Technical Capability	China Textile Industrial Research Center	17,000
	Project to Offer Guidance in the Technological Development of High-tech Textile Projects	Department of Chemical Engineering, ITRI	17,000
	Project to Analyze Present Conditions and Future Trends in the Textile Industry	Taiwan Textile Federation	5,000
	Three-year Project to Offer Guidance in Upgrading Technology in the Apparel Industry	Hub-Satellite Development Center	12,500
	Upgrading the Textile Industry's Design Capability	Taiwan Textile Federation	44,770
	Project to Train Textile Industry Design Personnel	Taiwan Textile Federation	6,000

Source: *Industry Information.* Industry Dept, Ministry of Economic Affairs, 1991,1993,1994.

TABLE A.16
Textile and Apparel Industries' Indicators of Upgrading

Item		1985	1986	1987	1988	1989	1990	1991
					Year			
Research and Development	R&D Expenditure (Million US$)							
	Manufacturing Industry	9,852	16,514	19,873	20,826	30,510	38,933	40,602
	Textile Industry	577	616	1,092	768	405	1,675	1,799
	Apparel and Accessories Industry	38	109	241	101	58	185	NA
	R&D/Sales (in %)							
	Manufacturing Industry	0.54	0.47	0.64	0.52	0.73	0.92	0.94
	Textile Industry	0.20	0.16	0.34	0.24	0.13	0.52	0.55
	Apparel and Accessories Industry	0.08	0.12	0.35	0.12	0.07	0.24	0.24
	Numbers of Research Personnel							
	Manufacturing Industry	9,021	10,767	14,670	17,538	21,807	23,827	23,247
	Textile Industry	437	494	1,013	460	631	1,636	1,252
	Apparel and Accessories Industry	24	70	132	286	171	235	134
Real Labor Productivity	Real GDP/Number of Employees (Thousand NT$/Number of People)							
	Manufacturing Industry	397	441	487	513	560	606	686
	Textile Industry	261	316	344	331	376	426	485
	Apparel and Accessories Industry	399	434	493	461	531	583	618
Fixed Capital Intensity	Net Fixed Capital/ Number of Employees (Thousand NT$/ Number of People)							
	Manufacturing Industry	505	505	505	551	596	680	739
	Textile Industry	668	694	764	784	936	1,098	1,166
	Apparel and Accessories Industry	145	144	139	145	140	141	139

Sources: *Indicators of Science and Technology*, R.O.C, National Science Council, 1988–1992; *Yearbook of Earnings and Productivity Statistics*, Taiwan Area, R.O.C, DGBAS, Executive Yuan, 1986–1992.

case of the apparel industry declined. This decline with regard to the apparel industry may be attributed to the increased division of labor between the two sides of the Taiwan Strait and the fact that much of the industry's equipment was moved offshore. Although industrialists began to upgrade their equipment during the 1980s, it was only as they entered the 1990s and were able to move together with the government and the industry associations in the same direction that the effectiveness of industrial upgrading became noticeable.

Over time, therefore, a significant transformation took place in terms of the relationship between the manufacturing sector and the government. From 1984 onward, the government was unable to stop industrialists from integrating their operations with those related to the manufacture of manmade fibers. Furthermore, if one considers the period from 1981 to 1985 when there was a conflict related to quota allocation, the later developments show that the government's ability to intervene in the textile industry had substantially diminished. As the textile and apparel industries became increasingly strong economically, the funds that they accumulated as well as their technological capability greatly increased, with the result that they became increasingly able to control their own destinies.

The development of this kind of industrial self-determination and emancipation from government control was most marked in the 1980s. For instance, in order to increase their bargaining chips in trade negotiations, the textile manufacturers in 1987 took the initiative to request that the government lower tariffs on imports of textiles. They also diversified and moved operations offshore in the late 1980s. In the early stages the apparel manufacturers invested in the Chinese mainland to such an extent that they went beyond the government's regulatory restrictions. In the end, it was government policies that instead had to respond to industrial developments. This phenomenon, whereby the industrial sector guided the development of government policies, differed significantly from what had characterized the earlier period of import substitution.

Government's influence on the textile sector, therefore, had declined markedly by the 1990s. The major exception to this trend was in areas that involved large externalities. Research, design, and manpower training continued to receive considerable support from the government and from such government-aided institutions as universities, research institutes, and industry associations.

NOTES

1 See Huang (1956, pp. 1–18

2 See Yin (1973, pp. 67–68).

3 See Lin (1976, p. 466).

4 See Lin (1976, p. 466).

5 See Lin (1976, p. 475).

6 See *The ROC's Textile Annual Yearbook* (1985, p. 345).

7 See Historical Data Compilation Committee (1990, p. 94).

8 See *The ROC's Textile Annual Yearbook* (1985, pp. 403–404).

9 See *Taiwan's Textile Industry* (1981, pp. 41–42).

10 See *Economic Daily News* (20 August 1982, p. 3).

11 This kind of coordination of prices between upstream and downstream manufacturers already existed prior to 1984.

12 Quotas consisted of the following two kinds: *planned* or *basic quotas*, and *free quotas*. In the case of basic quotas, the government, when drawing up a trade agreement, allocates the overall quota among the various manufacturers in accordance with their actual volume of exports. With regard to free quotas, newly established factories and traders, or else manufacturers that needed more quotas above basic quotas, are given the opportunity to apply. Basic quotas were allowed to be freely traded in 1979. Free quotas are allocated either on a first-come first-served basis (in the cases of nonpriority products) and on a basis of price comparison (in the case of "hot" or top-priority products). This has resulted in (1) exporters seeking to collude with overseas importers in order to offer a higher price, and therefore obtain the free quotas; (2) some of the manufacturers offering a high price in order to secure the bid, and then sell the quota, (the quota "scalpers"); and (3) since high profits may be realized by selling the quotas, this has led manufacturers who owned basic quotas not to produce, but instead to sell quotas for profit. Manufacturers even went further, seeking free quotas just for reselling, The purpose in having a price comparison rests in there being a fixed quantity of exports, allowing high value added products to be exported. Although this later degenerated into manufacturers not wanting to produce goods but rather generate profits by reselling the quotas, it was difficult to outlaw such profiteering, and those who stood to gain adamantly resisted any changes. See *The ROC s Textile Annual Yearbook* (1985, pp. 400–401).

B THE PETROCHEMICAL INDUSTRY

Ying-yi Tu

Taiwan's petrochemical industry developed through a process of backward integration. It was only when the downstream petrochemical industry had developed that the midstream and upstream segments got started in a major way. Moreover, it was during this process of backward integration that the government saw the petrochemical industry as an emerging one and began to support it. With strong support provided by the government, the private sector component of the industry grew rapidly, and its ability to influence government policy steadily increased. The second major oil crisis, however, was a major blow to its development. The very close relationship that had existed between the government, the publicly owned China Petroleum Corporation, and the private-sector petrochemical industry underwent a significant change. As pointed out in Chapter 3, from the middle of the 1980s onward, accompanied by the drive toward increased liberalization, the government gradually reduced its role in the development of the petrochemical industry.

1. DEFINING THE BOUNDARIES OF THE PETROCHEMICAL INDUSTRY

The *petrochemical industry* refers to the manufacture of all chemical products involving petroleum or natural gas. This includes the manufacture of upstream basic petrochemical feedstock; the production of the midstream petrochemical raw materials (mainly plastics, rubber and compound fiber raw materials); and the manufacture of downstream petrochemical products. The main products, as well as the relationships between upstream and downstream raw materials, are shown in Figure B-1. The downstream petrochemical industry, broadly defined, includes the manufacture of textiles, paints, and drugs. The analysis in this section, however, focuses on a narrower definition of the petrochemical industry, namely the upstream and midstream segments of the industry. These were the two stages where government involvement was most prominent.

2. The Relationship Between the Government and the Private Sector

During the years 1953 through 1956, a great number of private enterprises sprang up, and many of these engaged in downstream petrochemical industrial activities. Textiles, plastics, and dyeing and finishing started to flourish during this period, together with the publicly owned fertilizer industry. The rapid growth of these downstream products brought about an increase in the demand for midstream petrochemical raw materials and created an emerging opportunity for the development of the petrochemical industry in Taiwan.

During the Second and Third Four-Year Economic Plans (1957–1960 and 1961–1964), value added in the textile and rubber industries grew on average by around 15 percent in each year, while the chemical raw materials and chemical products industries grew on average by more than 20 percent in each year. It was the growth of the textile industry in particular that spurred on the early growth of the manmade fiber industry. In 1957 and 1967, respectively, the China Man-made Fibre Corporation and the Hualon Corporation were established, and in 1968 the first naphtha cracker was constructed.

The rapid development of the downstream petrochemical industry led to the government's decision to emphasize the development of upstream activities. The government in 1957 supported the establishment of the private Formosa Plastics Corporation, making use of an older and smaller scale carbide method that produced 1,200 tons of PVC annually. In 1959, the China Petroleum Corporation (CPC) commenced production of aromatics at its Chiayi plant by recombinated gasoline in order to supply downstream fertilizer and solvents manufacturers. In 1961, the CPC, by means of a joint venture with two U.S. companies, established the Mu Hwa Corporation (later acquired by the Taiwan Fertilizer Corporation and renamed Taiwan Fertilizer Corporation, Miaoli Plant), which made use of Miaoli's natural gas to produce liquid ammonia and urea. At the same time, the Taiwan Fertilizer Corpo-

F I G U R E   B – 1

The Relationships Among the Products of the Upstream, Midstream, and Downstream Petrochemical Industries

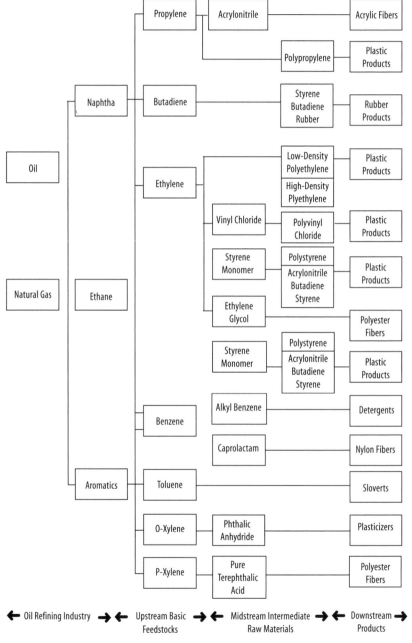

Source: R.O.C. *Chemical Industry Yearbook* 1991. Industrial Technology Research Institute and Taiwan Institute of Economic Research.

TABLE B-1
The Shares of Petrochemical-Related Industries in GDP (%)

Industry	Year									
	1951	1956	1961	1966	1971	1976	1981	1986	1991	1993
Chemical Raw Materials							5.8	6.8 (16.1)	6.7 (7.2)	5.2 (−2.9)
Chemical Products	13.4	6.2 (7.6)	7.8 (23.9)	10.1 (22.7)	10.1 (23.8)	11.6 (27.1)	12.4 (23.2) 1.3	15.4 (17.3) 1.7 (19.3)	15.1 (6.9) 2.2 (12.6)	2.6 (16.5)
Plastic Products							5.4	7.0 (18.1)	6.2 (4.9)	6.0 (3.5)
Petroleum and Coal Products Industries	3.2	3.6 (28.4)	5.2 (27.3)	9.8 (32.2)	10.5 (25.8)	6.8 (13.2)	6.8 (21.6)	7.1 (13.4)	8.6 (11.4)	7.4 (0.7)
Textile Industry	15.2	14.9 (25.2)	11.1 (11.6)	11.7 (17.6)	11.8 (24.3)	11.1 (21.9)	9.4 (17.6)	8.4 (9.8)	7.1 (4.0)	6.6 (4.1)
Rubber Industry	1.5	1.0 (16.1)	1.0 (18.5)	1.0 (15.8)	1.1 (27.3)	1.4 (28.9)	1.4 (21.4)	1.3 (10.9)	1.4 (8.7)	1.4 (8.3)
Total	33.3	25.7	25.1	32.6	33.6	30.8	30.1	32.2	32.2	29.2

Source: *National Income of Taiwan*, The Republic of China, DGBAS, Executive Yuan.

Note: Figures in parentheses represent average five-year growth rates of GDP for each industry. In the case of 1993, however, the figures in parentheses are the average growth rates for 1991–1993.

ration made use of its liquid ammonia to produce ammonium sulfate fertilizer, and in 1965 Changchun Corporation also made use of Miaoli's natural gas to manufacture methanol. In the same year, the Taiwan Fertilizer Corporation used liquid ammonia to produce urea.

The early growth and development of the petroleum industry, as pointed out in Chapters 2 and 3, was brought about by publicly owned enterprises. The government lumped the upstream part of the petrochemical industry (e.g., aromatics, ethylene, etc.) together with petroleum refining, and petroleum refining was a monopoly of the publicly owned China Petroleum Corporation. Although the government during this period did support the private Formosa Plastics Corporation, it felt that the petrochemical intermediate raw materials industry would be difficult for the private sector because it was capital-intensive and faced problems associated with the acquisition of technology. The government also saw the sector as a generator of sizeable profits for the government. The sector thus, by and large, was turned over to the public China Petroleum Corporation and the Taiwan Fertilizer Corporation.

There were four ways in which the government influenced the petrochemical industry during this early period:

1. Only the China Petroleum Corporation was permitted to handle the upstream portion of the petrochemical industry. As shown in Table B-2, until 1967, the main upstream petrochemical products, apart from a small proportion of benzene that was manufactured by privately owned enterprises, were all produced by publicly owned companies.

2. The government also fostered the establishment of the industry's private sector. Although the Formosa Plastics Corporation was a private company, the government assisted and participated in the planning and establishment of its plants, in its acquisition of technology, in its application for U.S. aid, and was even involved in the completion of its plants and first trial runs.[1]

3. Several enterprises that were classified as private firms actually received a large share of their investment from public enterprises. The public enterprises involved were the China Petroleum Corporation and the Taiwan Fertilizer Corporation. The nominally private firms included the Mu Hwa Corporation, which was a joint venture between two U.S. firms, and the CPC. Mu Hwa was later sold to the Taiwan Fertilizer Corporation.

4. The government continued to implement its policy of export expansion, thus providing the petrochemical industry with a steady increase in demand for its output. As shown in Table B-2, from 1961 to 1967, plastic products and compound fibers both experienced rapid growth. Plastics were largely for export and had a production growth rate of around 24 percent per annum. Production of plastic products reached 110,000 tons in 1967, 9.6 times the level of 1961. Synthetic fibers, on the other hand, were mainly used as substitutes for imports purchased by the export-oriented textile industry. Annual output of synthetic fibers in 1967 was close to 20,000 tons, 5.4 times that recorded in 1961.

The petrochemical industry continued to develop but remained in an embryonic state until after the completion of the China Petroleum Corporation's first naphtha cracker in 1968. As shown in Table B-3, the first naphtha cracker involved an investment in excess of NT$300 million. The plant's annual production of ethylene of 54,500 metric tons by and large provided Taiwan VCM Corporation with all of the ethylene it required to produce vinyl chloride monomer. In addition, because all of the demand for ethylene by the not-so-efficient Taiwan VCM Corporation was met, the surplus ethylene was used to supply the USI Far East Corporation (1975) in its production of low-density polyethylene (LDPE). The VCM and LDPE thus produced were in turn used to supply downstream producers of plastic products. For this reason, the first naphtha cracker led to midstream, and downstream investment programs amounting to NT$1.1 billion, and to increasing integration of upstream, midstream, and downstream production.

In the period 1969 to 1972, petrochemical complexes were established in both the northern and southern parts of the island of Taiwan. In the south, the naphtha cracking facilities at the oil refinery in Kaohsiung were expanded, and, in the north, natural gas was used to extract ethane, which in turn was used to produce ethylene. In 1973, the China Petroleum Corporation built an ethane cracker at Toufen, investing nearly NT$450 million in this Toufen petrochemical complex in the northern half of the island. The ethane produced by this cracker was used to supply the newly established public China Petrochemical Development Corporation with the raw material required to manufacture ethylene. The ethylene was then supplied to both the Taiwan VCM Corporation and the USI Far East Corporation in order to produce VCM and HDPE (high-density polyethylene). These midstream

TABLE B-2

Annual Production of Major Petrochemical Industry-Related Products, 1961–1973

I. Major Upstream Petrochemical Products

Year	Toluene (kiloliters) Public Sector	Xylene (kiloliters) Total	Xylene (kiloliters) Public Sector	Xylene (kiloliters) Private Sector	Ethane (kiloliters) Public Sector	Ethylene (metric tons) Public Sector	Benzene (kiloliters) Total	Benzene (kiloliters) Public Sector	Benzene (kiloliters) Private Sector
1961	1,305	322	322	—	310	—	946	946	—
1962	973	381	381	—	285	—	685	455	230
1963	2,619	1,179	1,179	—	1,109	—	1,357	1,032	325
1964	1,720	342	342	—	1,570	—	1,366	978	388
1965	3,081	1,010	1,010	—	2,015	—	2,087	1,535	552
1966	6,285	3,951	3,951	—	4,604	—	2,997	2,245	752
1967	7,149	5,465	5,465	—	1,445	—	2,869	2,393	476
1968	7,662	5,768	5,751	17	2,554	14,544	2,844	2,315	529
1969	9,043	7,860	7,186	674	4,178	34,433	3,797	2,881	916
1970	12,795	9,335	8,397	918	4,578	35,333	4,678	3,608	1,070
1971	17,049	14,319	12,777	1,542	5,009	45,609	4,815	3,664	1,151
1972	25,507	24,921	23,229	1,692	6,980	54,528	7,698	6,355	1,343
1973	38,680	38,034	35,578	2,456	8,317	56,861	19,697	18,291	1,406

TABLE B-2 (CONTINUED)

II. Major Midstream Petrochemical Products

Year	Vinyl Chloride Monomer (metric tons) Private Sector	Terephthalic Acid (metric tons) Public Sector	Methanol (metric tons) Private Sector	Formaldehyde (metric tons) Private Sector	Polystyrene (metric tons) Private Sector	Polyethylene (metric tons) Private Sector	Plastic Powder (metric tons) Private Sector
1961	—	—	—	2,739	—	—	7,260
1962	—	—	—	3,316	—	—	11,428
1963	—	—	—	6,772	—	—	16,751
1964	—	—	—	10,210	—	—	23,198
1965	—	—	—	18,133	195	—	25,305
1966	—	—	10,590	21,851	1,454	—	46,477
1967	—	—	19,083	24,920	1,739	18,579	67,676
1969	—	—	19,055	41,089	1,982	35,670	68,095
1970	—	—	32,341	51,047	2,693	35,917	106,624
1971	12,051	—	53,519	65,359	9,368	39,597	133,780
1972	24,045	—	60,605	58,791	12,740	41,632	171,781
1973	28,180	6,660	88,840	110,312	18,399	36,177	162,399

III. Major Downstream Petrochemical Products

Year	Plastic Products (metric tons) Private Sector	Compound Fibers (metric tons) Private Sector
1961	11,715	3,695
1962	22,817	3,979
1963	29,557	4,379
1964	44,425	4,629
1965	55,233	5,496
1966	84,307	11,894
1967	113,237	19,913
1968	160,707	42,269
1969	297,829	60,479
1970	258,407	87,646
1971	346,156	127,384
1972	439,140	172,740
1973	480,323	261,566

Source: *Monthly Statistics of Industrial Production, Taiwan, R.O.C.*, Department of Statistics, Ministry of Economic Affairs, 1977.

Note: — indicates data not available or production in sector not yet started.

TABLE B-3
Capacity and Investment of Naphtha Crackers in Taiwan

Cracker	Location	Date Plant Constructed	Annual Ethylene Production Capacity (metric tons)	Investor	Investment in Upstream Facilities (billion NT$)	Induced Investment in Midstream Facilities (billion NT$)	Total Investment (billion NT$)
1st Naphtha Cracker	Kaoshiung	1968 June	54,500	CPC	0.336	1.074	1.410
Ethane Cracker	Toufen	1973	54,000	CPC	0.449	0.863	1.312
2nd Naphtha Cracker	Kaoshiung	1975 Sept.	230,000	CPC	1.647	10.421	12.068
3rd Naphtha Cracker	Linyuan	1978 March	230,000	CPC	3.791	11.306	15.097
4th Naphtha Cracker	Linyuan	1984 April	385,000	CPC	7.600	35.411	43.011
5th Naphtha Cracker	Kaoshiung	1990	400,000	CPC	1.650	35.000	51.500
6th Naphtha Cracker[a]	Mailiao, Yunlin	1995	450,000	Formosa Plastics Group	35.300	NA	90–100
7th Naphtha Cracker[b]	Chiku, Tainan	1994	900,000	Tuntex Group		150	150
8th Naphtha Cracker[b]	Yunlin	1997	900,000	CPC and 18 Petro-chemical Manufacturers		150–200	150–200

Source: *Taiwan Industrial Yearbook*; *The Petrochemical Industry*, China Credit Information Service Limited, 1992; results of this study.
[a] Under construction
[b] At planning stage

and downstream investments amounted to some NT$1.3 billion, as can be seen from Table B-3.

Although the midstream petrochemical industry was opened up to the private sector, there were significant barriers to the entry of new producers. The first barrier was that the costs associated with setting up plants were huge. The second barrier was created by the restrictions in the production and sales contracts between the upstream and midstream and downstream manufacturers. At around the time that it built the first naphtha cracker, the China Petroleum Corporation first determined the quantities of basic feedstock that the midstream producers wished to purchase, and then drew up purchase and sales contracts. The prices set in those contracts, in addition to reflecting costs, also could not exceed prices charged by Japan, with the result that the China Petroleum Corporation did not experience any problem in selling its products. Furthermore, the midstream producers procured their basic raw materials at relatively low prices, so that they in turn were able to supply downstream manufacturers with intermediate raw materials at prices that were no higher than those which would have been imported (taking import duties into account). This production and distribution system enabled each of the upstream, midstream, and downstream manufacturers to benefit and to become increasingly operationally integrated. This increased integration in turn created entry barriers to potential new market entrants. Even though new manufacturers later gradually entered the market as the petrochemical industry developed, the midstream petrochemical industry in 1995 was still characterized by an oligopolistic market structure. As shown in Table B-4, there were approximately thirty midstream petrochemical manufacturers, all of which depended on the China Petroleum Corporation for their supplies of raw materials. These petrochemical firms were large in scale relative to the size of average firms in Taiwan. Protected by the high industrial barriers to entry, many of these midstream producers gradually developed themselves into groups of firms whose primary focus was on petrochemicals, such as the Formosa Plastics Group, the Chi Mei Group, the Changchun Group, the China Chemical Group, and the CGPC Group. Other business groups also started to invest in the petrochemical industry, such as the Oriental Union Chemical Corporation (the Far East Group), the President Fine Chemical Industry Corporation (the Tainan Spinning Group), the China Synthetic Rubber Corporation (the Koo's Group), and the China Man-made Fiber Company (the HuaLon Group).

TABLE B-4

CPC's Downstream Producers and Their Products

Series	Product	Manufacturer
Ethylene	Low-Density Polyethylene (LDPE)	USI Far East Corp. Asia Polymer Corp.
	Linear Low Density Polyethylene (LLDPE)	USI Far East Corp.
	High-Density Polyethylene (HDPE)	Formosa Plastics Corp. USI Far East Corp.
	Vinyl Chloride Monomer (VCM)	Taiwan VCM Corp. Formosa Plastics Corp. China General Plastic Corp.
	Ethylene Glycol (EG)	China Man-made Fibre Corp. Oriental Union Chemical Corp.
	Styrene Monomer (SM)	Taiwan Styrene Monomer Corp. Grand Pacific Petrochemical Corp.
	Ethylene Oxide (EO)	China Man-made Fibre Corp.
	Vinyl Acetate Monomer (VAM)	Dairen Chemical Corp.
	Acetaldehyde	Lee Chang Yung Chemical Industry Corp.
Propylene	Acrylonitrile (AN)	China Petrochemical Development Corp. (CPDC)
	Pure Acetonitrile	Ta Nun Corp.
	Methyl Methacrylate (MMA)	Kaohsiung Monomer Co. Ltd.
	Polypropylene (PP)	Taiwan Polypropylene Co. Ltd. Yung Chia Chemical Industries Corp.
	Propylene Oxide	Chiunglong Petrochemical Co. Ltd.
	Isopropanol, Acetone, Methyl isobutyl ketone	Lee Chang Yung Chemical Industry Corp.
	Acrylic Ester (AE)	Formosa Plastics Corp.
	Phenol/Acetone	Taiwan Prosperity Chemical Corp.
Butadiene	Styrene Butadiene Rubber (SBR)	Taiwan Synthetic Rubber Corp. (TSRC)
	Polybutadiene	Taiwan Synthetic Rubber Corp. (TSRC)

continued

TABLE B-4 (CONTINUED)

CPC's Downstream Producers and Their Products

Series	Product	Manufacturer
Butadiene	Acrylonitrile Butadiene Styrene (ABS) Resin	Grand Pacific Petrochemical Corp. Chi Mei Industrial Co. Ltd. Taita Chemical Co. Ltd.
	Latex	Jeou Lien Corp. President Fine Chemical Industry Corp. Shin Foong Corp.
	Methyl Tert-Butyl Ether (MTBE)	Taiwan Synthetic Petrochemical Corp.
	Methyl Ethyl Ketone (MEK)	Taiwan Synthetic Petrochemical Corp.
	Thermoplastic Rubber	Taiwan Synthetic Rubber Corp. (TSRC)
Aromatics	Pure Terephthalic Acid (PTA)	China American Petrochemical Co. Ltd. (CAPCO)
	Phthalic Anhydride (PA)	Union Petrochemical Corp.
	Plasticizer	Union Petrochemical Corp.
	Caprolactam (CPL)	China Petrochemical Development Corp. (CPDC)
	Polyethylene	Taiwan Styrene Monomer Corp.
	Styrene Monomer (SM)	Grand Pacific Petrochemical Corp.
	Alkyl Benzene	Formosan Union Chemical Corp.
	Bottom Oil	
	Carbon Black (CB)	China Synthetic Rubber Corp.

Source: *R.O.C. Chemical Industry Yearbook 1991,* Taiwan Institute of Economic Research and Union Chemical Labs, Industrial Technology Research Institute, 1992.

The government, with the objective of avoiding monopolistic behavior on the part of the large business groups, did not allow the petrochemical industry to develop into an integrated operation. Instead, the operations of upstream and midstream manufacturers were separated from each other. Midstream operations were in turn segregated into a series of manufacturing processes, with a corresponding increase in the number of manufacturers. This resulted in products at various stages of completion changing hands more frequently, and overall production costs increased. Furthermore, each manufacturer produced only one petrochemical intermediate raw material, resulting in relatively high operating risk. Since the world energy crisis had not yet taken place, however, oil prices remained stable and downstream producers were still very competitive in the world market. These problems did not become apparent during the late 1960s and the first years of the 1970s.

This initial stage in the development of the petrochemical industry was to a large extent brought about by capital investment undertaken by public enterprises. For example, if one considers the China Petroleum Corporation as a public enterprise, the China Petrochemical Development Corporation (CPDC) may be regarded as its investment, and the Taiwan VCM Corporation may in turn be viewed as an investment arising out of CPDC. The funds injected by the public sector caused local private enterprises to invest, and also resulted in foreign funds being attracted to the petrochemical industry. For example, both the Mu Hua Corporation and the Taiwan Polymer Corporation were invested in by U.S. companies, and, in the downstream petrochemical products industry, foreign investment was widespread. As shown in Table B-5, between 1952 and 1956 and between 1957 and 1967, foreign and overseas Chinese investment in the chemical products industry (including chemical materials) accounted for 14.89 percent and 13.30 percent, respectively, of total foreign and overseas Chinese investment in terms of the total number of cases. In terms of the total amount invested, the industry accounted for 35.82 percent and 22.80 percent respectively, the largest amount of foreign and overseas Chinese investment in any industry. Despite Taiwan's lack of crude oil deposits, the petrochemical industry was attractive to investors because of (1) an oligopolistic market structure with high entry barriers, (2) a production and distribution system that could be rigorously controlled under the government's policy of import substitution, and (3) a downstream sector that was well able to absorb petrochemical raw materials and products. During its initial phase, therefore, the petrochemical industry was still mostly guided by the public sector, with the private sector playing only a subsidiary role and exerting little impact on government policies. As the downstream petrochemical industry developed and exports flourished, however, it was the private sector that gradually began to play a leading role in the economy. Although the downstream petrochemical industry was mostly made up of small- and medium-sized export-processing firms that individually exerted little influence over government policy, their combined economic strength

TABLE B-5
Approved Inward Overseas Chinese and Foreign Investment and Outward Foreign Investment in the Chemical Products Industry,[a] 1952–1994

Period	Number of Cases		Total Investment		Average Size of Investment (US$000s)		Average Number of Cases per Year		Average Annual Investment (US$000s)	
	I[b]	O[c]	I[b]	O[c]	I[b]	O[c]	I[b]	O[c]	I[b]	O[c]
Emerging Opportunity in the Industry's Development, 1952–1956	7 (14.9%)[d]	0 (0.0%)	5,400 (35.8%)	0 (0.0%)	771	0	1.4	0.0	1,080	0
Embryonic Stage, 1957–1967	75 (13.3%)	0 (0.0%)	46,989 (22.8%)	0 (0.0%)	627	0	6.8	0.0	4,272	0
Initial Stage, 1968–1973	73 (5.5%)	1 (2.0%)	73,212 (8.4%)	100 (0.9%)	1,003	100	12.2	0.2	12,202	17
Rapid Development Stage, 1974–1979	71 (10.2%)	7 (11.9%)	127,680 (11.0%)	14,413 (33.8%)	1,798	2,059	11.8	1.2	21,280	2,402
Transition Stage, 1980–1982	42 (12.1%)	2 (6.45%)	136,234 (11.0%)	24,443 (37.9%)	3,244	12,222	14.0	0.7	45,411	8,148
Adjustment Toward Liberalization Stage, 1983–1986	83 (10.6%)	3 (3.7%)	523,596 (21.5%)	4,733 (3.2%)	6,308	1,578	20.8	0.8	130,899	118
Transformation Stage, 1987–1994	156 (4.1%)	71 (3.7%)	1,907,265 (14.2%)	1,003,185 (11.4%)	12,226	14,129	19.5	8.9	238,408	125,398

Source: *Annual Statistical Yearbook on Investment by Overseas Chinese and Foreigners in the R.O.C.*, Technical Cooperation, Outward Technical Cooperation, and Indirect Investment in Mainland China, Investment Commission, Ministry of Economic Affairs, 1994.

a The chemical products industry includes the petrochemical industry, the chemical raw material industry, and the chemical products industry.

b Inward overseas Chinese and foreign investment.

c Outward foreign investment (excluding mainland China).

d Figures in parentheses represent the ratios of overseas Chinese and foreign investment and outward investment in the chemical products industry to total overseas Chinese and foreign investment and outward investment in the same period.

did affect the government policy-making process, leading the government to propose a second period of import substitution.

3. THE STAGE OF RAPID DEVELOPMENT (1974–1979)

The Sixth Four-Year Economic Plan (1973–1976) called for making every effort to develop heavy and chemical industries (as part of the Ten Major Development Projects), in order to replace imports of intermediate raw materials and capital goods, and to increase exports. Of the policies put forward relating to the petrochemical industry, the main ones concerned plans to complete the second and third naphtha crackers.[2] These two naphtha crackers were respectively completed in 1975 and 1978, and since then each annually produced 230,000 metric tons of ethylene. The amounts invested downstream as a result of these two crackers are given in Table B-6. The findings show that investments involving twenty-three projects were made in a total of seventeen firms. The total amount invested was NT$28.97 billion, of which investments in the midstream petrochemical industry (as opposed to the upstream petrochemical industry) accounted for 81.5 percent of the total. The

TABLE B-6

Investment in the Second and Third Naphtha Crackers and Related Downstream Industries

Industry	Number of Plants	Number of Plants	Total Investment (million NT$)	Share (%)
Upstream Industry	1	3	5,362	18.5
Basic Feedstock	1	3	5,362[a]	18.5
Midstream Industry	16	20	23,608	81.5
Plastic Raw Materials	8	9	7,410	25.6
Compound Fiber Raw Materials	5	8	14,358	49.6
Rubber Materials	2	2	1,577	5.4
Detergent Material	1	1	263	0.9
Total	17	23	28,970	100.0

Source: *An Evaluation of the Ten Major Development Projects*, Council for Economic Planning and Development, 1979, p.462.

[a] The investment in CPC's 2nd and 3rd aromatics extraction units, hydro-cracking hexane unit, and coal plant are not included in these figures, and amounts to NT$3.2 billion in total.

largest amounts invested related to the manufacture of synthetic fiber raw materials and plastic raw materials, which were used to replace imports of raw materials by the textile and plastics export industries.

It was during this period (in 1973) that the first major world oil crisis took place. Skyrocketing prices of crude oil and intermediate petrochemical raw materials led government to conclude that it was important to control the supply of intermediate raw materials. The government not only adopted a low-energy price policy to support the development of the petrochemical industry. At the same time, as part of its Six-Year Economic Plan (1976–1981), it instituted a second period of import substitution. As a result, in 1976, 1978, and 1980, respectively, the government completed the construction of the upstream petrochemical industry's second and third aromatic benzene extraction units and a xylene separation unit.

Beginning in 1974, the China Petroleum Corporation (CPC) implemented its delayed adjustment pricing policy.[3] Between 1968 and 1972, CPC based its pricing policy on the mark-up principle, supplying materials according to fixed contracted prices. When the price of crude oil significantly increased in 1973, CPC at first adopted a policy that more than fully reflected its increase in costs, as can be seen in Table B-7. The prices of CPC's basic petrochemical feed stocks both before and after April 1974 reflected 80 percent and 70 percent, respectively, of the changes in oil prices. Crude oil prices continued to increase, with the result that in 1974 they were two to three times higher than in 1973. In consideration for the competitiveness of downstream exporters, the government decided to adopt a low-energy price policy to support the completion of its Ten Major Development Projects. In accordance with this policy, from October 1975 until April 1980, CPC's prices reflected only 50 percent of crude oil price change. It was the government's intention, in taking these measures, to delay upward adjustments in oil prices gradually, and thereby lessen the impact on both midstream and downstream petrochemical manufacturers.

4. THE TRANSITION STAGE (1980–1982): THE PERIOD OF PRICE DISPUTES

Following the second major world oil crisis in 1979, the prices of petrochemical raw materials increased. U.S. petrochemical firms sold large quantities of low-priced petrochemical raw materials in 1980, however, and world prices of petrochemical raw materials started to fall signifi-

TABLE B-7

Changes in CPC's Formula for Calculating the Prices of its Petrochemical Raw Materials

Period of Implementation	Formula Adopted
Apr. 1968 – Dec. 31, 1972	Fixed contracted prices
Jan. 1, 1973 – Dec. 31, 1973	$\text{Contracted Price} = \text{Base Price} \times \dfrac{c+c'}{c}$
Jan. 1, 1974 – Mar. 31, 1974	$\text{Contracted Price} = \text{Base Price} \times \left[\left(\dfrac{c+c'}{c} \times 80\% \right) + \left(\dfrac{F+F'}{F} \times 20\% \right) \right]$
Apr. 1, 1974 – Sep. 29, 1975	$\text{Contracted Price} = \text{Base Price} \times \left[\left(\dfrac{c+c'}{c} \times 70\% \right) + \left(\dfrac{F+F'}{F} \times 30\% \right) \right]$
Sep. 30, 1975 – Apr. 15, 1980	$\text{Contracted Price} = \text{Base Price} \times \left[\left(\dfrac{c+c'}{c} \times 50\% \right) + \left(\dfrac{I+I'}{I} \times 20\% \right) + \left(\dfrac{E+E'}{E} \times 20\% \right) + \left(\dfrac{W+W'}{W} \times 5\% \right) + \left(K \times 15\% \right) \right]$
Apr. 16, 1980 – Mar. 31, 1981	$\text{Contracted Price} = \text{Base Price} \times \left[\left(\dfrac{c+c'}{c} \times 65\% \right) + \left(\dfrac{I+I'}{I} \times 10\% \right) + \left(\dfrac{E+E'}{E} \times 10\% \right) + \left(\dfrac{W+W'}{W} \times 5\% \right) + \left(K \times 10\% \right) \right]$

TABLE B-7 (CONTINUED)

Apr. 1, 1981 – Nov. 30, 1981	Contracted Price $= \left[\left(\text{CPC Price} \times \frac{2}{3}\right) + \left(\text{International Price} \times \frac{1}{3}\right)\right]$

$$\text{CPC Price} = \text{Base Price} \times \left[\left(\frac{c+c'}{c} \times 74\%\right) + \left(\frac{E+E'}{E} \times 17\%\right) + \left(\frac{M+M'}{M} \times 4\%\right) + \left(K \times 5\%\right)\right]$$

Dec. 1, 1981 –	Ethylene, Propylene, Benzene, Cyclohexane, O-Xylene, P-Xylene (based on the U.S. domestic contracted price) Butadiene (based on the Japanese price)

Source: *A Study on the Pricing Structure of Petrochemical Raw Materials*, Planning Department, China Petroleum Corporation, June 1983.
Base Price = Supply price for the second quarter of each year (based on the price following the adjustment made by CPC on March 1).
c = Prior to April 1981 this was based on the price of Kuwaiti crude oil, and after April 1981 based on the average for price of crude oil imported by CPC.
E = Cost of fuel and electricity, adjusted on the basis of monthly statistics of consumer prices.
I = Average plant cost index (based on the CE plant Cost Index included in chemical Engineering's Economic Indicators).
W = Average wages (based on the daily wages for the R.O.C.'s manufacturing industry included in "Industry of Free China").
F = Production costs.
M = Materials cost index (based on the chemical industry manufacturing indices).
K = Fixed factors (= 1.0), such as when significant changes take place, either party to the contract may initiate an adjustment.
c', F', I', E', W', M' = Changes in the various factors already mentioned following an earlier adjustment.

cantly. As a result, midstream and downstream petrochemical producers worldwide were confronted with a dilemma whereby rising prices of crude oil were accompanied by falling prices of the products that they sold. In addition, the poor performance of the world economy also adversely affected downstream petrochemical producers and caused consumer markets to shrink. The result was that competition intensified and profits declined. In 1980–1981, as a result, the upstream, midstream, and downstream petrochemical industries throughout the world faced a particularly difficult situation.

It was in this context that Taiwan's government decided no longer to assist in the development of energy-intensive industries, indicating that, following the completion of the fourth naphtha cracker, there would be no construction of a fifth cracker. In addition, the government felt that the second major energy crisis, in comparison with the first crisis, had a smaller impact on both the overall rate of economic growth and on the rate of increase in prices. This smaller impact in turn made it easier for the government to raise domestic energy prices in order to curtail energy consumption. Therefore, in addition to adjusting the price of its fuel oil, the CPC from April 1980 onward raised the percentage of costs covered by the prices of its basic petrochemical feedstock to 65 percent, as shown in Table B-7. At the same time, it began making plans to increase this percentage further so that changes in costs would be fully reflected in the prices.

These changes in world markets and in the government's pricing policies resulted in conflicts of interest among the domestic upstream, midstream, and downstream petrochemical industries. For example, in 1979, as manufacturers of intermediate raw materials profited from their exports due to rising world prices, downstream manufacturers suffered from insufficient supplies of materials. This resulted in 1980 in downstream producers increasing their imports of intermediate raw materials because world prices were relatively low. Stocks held by midstream manufacturers thus significantly increased. In addition, during the second quarter of 1980, as midstream petrochemical manufacturers found that they were squeezed as a result of increases in the prices of basic feedstock and the large sales of cheap U.S. products, they became embroiled in disputes over prices with upstream manufacturers. Later, as the government implemented measures to restrict imports in order to protect midstream manufacturers, price disputes arose between midstream and downstream manufacturers. The formerly closely integrated production and distribution cooperative relationship suddenly changed into one that was antagonistic and on the brink of falling completely apart. These conflicts over prices continued to persist among the upstream, midstream and downstream petrochemical manufacturers for a period lasting several years.

Whenever the downstream petrochemical industrialists encountered difficulties, they were able, through their lobbying efforts and petitions, to obtain protection and other kinds of subsidies. As an example, in 1979, when the midstream manufacturers did not take into consideration the shortages of materials experienced by downstream manufacturers, the downstream producers combined together to present their case to the government. This caused the government to adopt policies to restrict exports of intermediate raw materials in order to maintain the already-existing production and distribution arrangements. By 1980, when the midstream manufacturers complained to the government regarding the downstream manufacturers' imports of cheaper intermediate raw materials, the government implemented measures to restrict intermediate imports. They also coordinated efforts by midstream and downstream producers to lower prices and make supplies of materials available.

In 1981, there were still several price disputes among upstream, midstream, and downstream petrochemical producers. At that time, however, the midstream and downstream sections of the petrochemical industry were able, by explaining to the government the difficulties they were facing, to cause the government to arrive at a compromise with them both. The compromise involved the upstream manufacturers lowering the prices they charged to midstream producers, who in turn lowered the prices they charged to the downstream producers. The government also instructed the China Petroleum Corporation successively to reduce its prices by adopting deferred payment,[4] by using a two-price system (whereby the agreed-upon export prices were lower than the prices charged in the domestic market), and by referring to international prices when determining local prices. In spite of these measures, however, the fortunes of the midstream and downstream producers did not change for the better. In the end, out of consideration for and in order to increase the competitiveness of the downstream petrochemical exports in October 1981, the government announced that petrochemical raw materials could be freely imported. The result of this was that the midstream and downstream petrochemical industrialists were able to procure raw materials at the prevailing international prices. Because it was not easy to transport ethylene, however, an input used by half of the midstream producers, this measure was of limited benefit. Finally, in order to resolve the difficulties facing the midstream producers, the government in December instructed the China Petroleum Corporation to supply raw materials at international rather than cost prices. In this way, this phase of price disputes in the petrochemical industry came to an end.

Strongly divergent opinions on the part of all the parties concerned with regard to just what the international prices really were was one element at the heart of the price disputes. For example, the China Petroleum Corporation believed that, since Japan, South Korea, and the European countries, like Taiwan, were all principally importers of oil, the prices that these countries charged were in effect the international prices, and that on this basis the prices that it charged itself were very reasonable. The manufacturers of intermediate petrochemical raw materials were confronted by the low prices of petrochemical raw materials, however, that had been dumped on world markets by the United States, and naturally regarded the continually falling prices of basic feedstock as constituting the international price. They also were of the opinion that the prices of intermediate petrochemical raw materials that had been dumped by the United States on the market reflected the costs of basic raw materials, and that this constituted the basis according to which the China Petroleum Corporation should calculate the prices it charged to midstream and downstream petrochemical manufacturers.

Following the relaxation of restrictions over exports and imports in October 1981, many of the intermediate petrochemical raw material producers did not promptly make guarantees to downstream producers that they would supply raw materials in accordance with international prices. Hence, downstream manufacturers imported, in some cases, more than six months' worth of the intermediate petrochemical raw materials that they needed. As a result, inventories of midstream producers significantly increased and some even had to cease production. For instance, the manufacturers of styrene monomer, ethylene glycol, and pure terephthalic acid were the hardest hit, and they had to cease operations for between one and three months. The midstream producers therefore petitioned the government to once again adjust the production and distribution system in order to resolve their production difficulties. The government, in order to rescue the midstream producers that it had in the past nurtured on two occasions, drew up new production and distribution agreements. In the case of low-density polyethylene and five other petrochemical raw materials, midstream and downstream producers from July 1, 1982, onward were required to observe the following rules:

1. Priority would be given to supplying locally produced intermediate petrochemical raw materials at international prices to downstream producers of goods for export in accordance with their needs.

2. Where local producers of these intermediate raw materials were unable fully to meet the needs of these downstream producers, the downstream producers could apply to import materials to make up for this lack. If these materials were used to produce goods to supply the local market, however, full import duties would be levied.

3. The price of intermediate materials for producing export goods should be calculated on the basis of the international cif import price. If these goods were to be sold in the domestic market, import duties and commodity taxes would be added to the cif price. Prices were to be adjusted once each quarter.[5] After these agreements were drawn up, prices within the petrochemical industry were to a large extent determined in accordance with these principles. Although different viewpoints continued to persist among upstream, midstream, and downstream producers with regard to international prices, and disputes occasionally made the headlines, most of the disputes that took place were sporadic and small.

Although it appears that the government played only an indirect role in the drawing up of these production and distribution agreements, in actual fact its control over the issue of import permits was the main reason why the midstream and downstream producers were able to reach a compromise and respect the agreements. By restricting the importation of intermediate raw materials, the government forced the downstream manufacturers to give priority to purchasing locally produced raw materials, allowing them to import only in cases where the local supply was insufficient. Furthermore, by opening up the market to imports of intermediate raw materials, the government made the manufacturers of intermediate raw materials charge the prevailing international prices for their products.

The early 1980s constituted an important turning point in terms of the development of the petrochemical industry. As the energy-intensive petrochemical industry came under attack during the second world energy crisis, it ceased to receive the government's active support automatically. Energy prices, for example, now fully reflected costs, and there were no further plans to increase productive capacity in relation to basic feedstock following the completion of the fourth naphtha cracker. The petrochemical industry also was removed from the list of strategic industries that would be given special encouragement in accordance with the Eighth Four-Year Economic Plan. As discussed in Chapter 3, it was clear that the government had shifted its emphasis away from support of the heavy-chemical industries toward the high-tech industries.

As a result of these developments, as shown in Table B-8, the growth rate of both the midstream and downstream producers was considerably lower in both 1980 and 1981 than in previous years. From 1982 onward, conditions gradually improved, but it was only from 1983 onward that the plastics industry, relatively speaking, showed any significant improvement. Furthermore, from Table B-9 it can be seen that the profits made by the upstream, midstream, and downstream sectors were significantly lower in 1980 than they had been in 1979, and the situation was even worse in 1981. In particular, the upstream China Petroleum Corporation, in order to supply lower-priced raw materials, from 1980 onward lost money on its sales of basic petrochemical raw materials. The manmade fiber industry also lost money in 1980 and 1982, and, although the other industries overall on average did not lose money, their profits were significantly reduced. There were also those that were forced to cease production and withdraw from the market.

Foreign investors also saw their former huge profits disappear and turn into losses. No longer receiving government support, they withdrew one by one from Taiwan. The U.S. company UCC withdrew from the Oriental Union Chemical Corporation, Goodrich withdrew from the Taiwan Synthetic Rubber Corporation, Gulf withdrew from the China Gulf Plastics Corporation, and National Distiller withdrew from the USI Far East Corporation. Finally, the China Petroleum Corporation, which had formerly led the development of the petrochemical industry, had become a target of public criticism and had lost some of the government support that it had in the past. Increasingly CPC's policies were used as a bargaining chip in negotiations with midstream and downstream producers who together by this time produced one-third of all manufacturing output.

In December 1979, the government's promulgation of the Regulations Governing the Imposition of Custom Duties on Twelve Major Petrochemical Products based on the Respective Proportions Sold in Local and Overseas Markets was immediately met with strong opposition from midstream petrochemical producers as well as downstream

TABLE B-8

The Growth Rate of Industrial Production of Petrochemical-Related
Industries, 1972–1994

Year	Upstream and Midstream Industry	Downstream Industry		
	Petrochemical Raw Materials (%)	Manmade Fibers (%)	Compound Resins and Plastics (%)	Plastic Products (%)
1972	14.8	39.1	28.4	19.7
1973	134.7	29.1	−3.9	12.9
1974	−21.3	3.7	−5.8	−18.3
1975	10.5	46.1	29.7	27.8
1976	97.6	20.9	45.5	31.8
1977	39.8	27.7	38.4	−14.5
1978	38.8	25.1	27.6	24.7
1979	24.7	9.3	11.8	11.9
1980	5.1	7.6	8.6	5.2
1981	3.1	5.2	−1.9	3.7
1982	18.8	91.8	100.8	1.4
1983	20.7	13.1	19.9	14.6
1984	22.0	17.8	27.8	20.4
1985	7.8	11.4	12.4	5.2
1986	11.5	18.4	27.2	21.3
1987	−2.9	9.7	10.6	13.2
1988	1.8	3.4	11.1	5.1
1989	−6.9	11.7	3.6	−1.8
1990	3.1	12.6	9.3	−8.0
1991	7.9	20.9	19.4	4.0
1992	9.9	5.4	15.0	−3.8
1993	7.1	3.2	10.1	−5.4
1994	17.3	12.0	31.2	1.2

Sources : 1972–1982: *Monthly Statistics of Industrial Production,* Taiwan, R.O.C., Department of Statistics, Ministry of Economic Affairs, No. 162, February 1983. 1983–1992: *Monthly Statistics of Industrial Production,* Taiwan, R.O.C., Department of Statistics, Ministry of Economic Affairs, No. 291, January 1993. 1993–1994: *Monthly Statistics of Industrial Production,* Taiwan, R.O.C., Department of Statistics, Ministry of Economic Affairs, No. 309, May 1995.

export-oriented producers. The midstream petrochemical producers were of the opinion that the ratio of goods to be sold in the local market determined by the government was lower than the actual proportion of goods sold in that market. The result, they believed, was that

TABLE B-9

Profits Earned by the Upstream, Midstream, and Downstream Sectors of the Taiwan Petrochemical Industry (% of Revenue or Turnover)

Sector	Products	1979	1980	1981	1982
Upstream (CPC)	Ethylene	1.41	−12.73	−10.70	−32.36
	Propylene	−10.16	−58.26	−26.30	−1.62
	Butadiene	2.56	−14.85	−4.03	−1.02
	Benzene	−9.35	−18.54	−10.20	−16.47
	Toluene	35.23	9.90	28.95	39.71
	Xylene	38.63	20.18	26.15	41.04
	P-Xylene	—	2.86	−9.55	−10.64
	O-Xylene	—	21.71	−23.80	−13.49
Midstream	Petrochemical Raw Materials	10.16	4.57	0.02	0.88
Downstream	Manmade Fibers	9.00	−1.12	2.08	−2.72
	Plastics	8.40	5.54	3.37	3.99
	Plastics Products	5.82	3.00	2.17	1.79

Sources: *A Study on the Pricing Structure of Petrochemical Raw Materials,* Planning Department, Chinese Petroleum Corporation, June, 1983. *A Survey of Industrial Conditions in Taiwan, R.O.C.*, Economic Research Department, Bank of Taiwan, 1979–1983.

Notes: In the case of the upstream sector, Gross Profit = (Turnover – Cost of Sales) / Turnover. In the case of the midstream and downstream sectors, Operating Profit = (Total Revenue – Total Expenditure) / Operating Revenue.

"—" indicates data not available.

tariff protection was reduced, making it easier for imports to flow in. Furthermore, the downstream manufacturers indicated that, although the system of export tax rebates was rather troublesome, it did in fact relieve them from paying the corresponding import duties. Following the reforms, the partial increase in the import duty that they would have to pay would mean that their costs would increase.[6] Industrialists requested several times that the government once again adopt the former export tax rebate system. In view of the way in which the export rebate system was frequently abused, however, the government determined not to go back to the old system. Instead, it resorted to the imposition of controls over imports and exports, as well as to lowering the prices of locally produced raw materials, in order to lessen the difficulties being faced by industrialists.

5. Adjustment Toward Liberalization (1983–1986)

The Taiwan authorities in the 1983 through 1986 period significantly changed the direction of their policies to encompass liberalization, internationalization, and institutionalization as explained in Chapter 3. Within the overall policy framework of the 1983 through 1986 period, the government's major policies related to the petrochemical industry included:

1. strengthening the integration of the upstream, midstream and downstream petrochemical industries;

2. ending efforts to increase production of basic feedstock following the completion of the fourth naphtha cracker; and

3. emphasizing the development of engineering plastics and special-purpose chemical products and their key raw materials rather than labor-intensive downstream industries in order to increase value added.

Thus although the government proposed policies that moved in the direction of liberalization, in actual fact it continued to implement measures whose purpose was to assist strategic industries and inhibit the growth of energy-intensive industries. Restrictions and interventionist policies that had existed in the past, such as the China Petroleum Corporation's refusal to allow the fifth naphtha cracker to be built, as well as the restrictions applying to imports and production and distribution agreements, continued. With the continued progress of liberalization efforts, however, many of these restrictions were removed in 1986.

As the economy recovered, the petrochemical industry once again began to experience rapid growth, with annual growth rates of between 10 percent and 20 percent as depicted in Table B-8. As conditions improved, however, both local and foreign supplies of raw materials began to be in short supply. At this juncture, the production and distribution agreements that had existed since the early 1980s degenerated into a series of disputes. The main issues of contention included:

1. items that were covered by the agreement did not include all intermediate raw materials, with the result that there was no consistent treatment of the various raw materials;

2. human intervention was not as flexible as the market mechanism, so that, when the market was tight, it was not possible to open the

market to imports at the right time, resulting in lost business opportunities; and

3. short-term fluctuations in prices continued to cause problems associated with the determination of international prices.

In addition to these disputes, the characteristics of the production and distribution agreements also changed. For example, as economic conditions improved, the midstream petrochemical producers no longer needed protection from imports. If the downstream petrochemical manufacturers who produced mainly for export were unable to procure low-priced raw materials as a result of the production and distribution agreements, however, their competitiveness, which had already declined, would decline even more rapidly. Thus, as time went on, the production and distribution agreements no longer served their original purpose. As a result, production and distribution agreements were abolished at the end of 1985.

As the state of the economy improved, raw material supply shortages resulted in problems associated with the proposed construction of the fifth and sixth naphtha crackers becoming more apparent. Although the fourth naphtha cracker had begun to supply raw materials from the end of 1984 on, the increased supply was insufficient to satisfy local demand. In particular, when each naphtha cracker had to in turn be closed down for annual repairs, manufacturers of intermediate raw materials had no alternative but to suspend their operations and were unable to accept new orders. In view of the government policy stance that no new naphtha crackers would be built, private-sector petrochemical industrialists proposed the idea that the private sector be allowed to construct the fifth naphtha cracker in order to resolve the shortage of raw materials. In this way they challenged the government's monopolistic approach toward the upstream petrochemical industry. Confronted with these ideas, the China Petroleum Corporation proposed an alternative strategy. It would construct the fifth naphtha cracker in order to replace the aging first and second naphtha crackers, thereby maintaining its monopolistic position while at the same time conforming to the government's policy of not increasing production capacity.

There was no agreement within the government as to which of these strategies was best. The Committee for Supervising Public Enterprises and the Ministry of Finance were of the opinion that the pricing system adopted by the naphtha crackers was inappropriate, as losses were recorded in each year. They felt that the pricing system favored the intermediate petrochemical producers too much. The Council on Economic Planning and Development, in contrast, believed that there were large economic benefits to be derived from the linkages between the petrochemical and other industries. It also believed that the losses in the industry arose because of a misallocation of costs and could thus be rectified. The Council, therefore, resolved to see the fifth naphtha cracker constructed. Finally, in 1986, the Executive Yuan approved CPC's proposal to construct the fifth naphtha cracker.

Intermediate petrochemical raw material producers continued to express their dissatisfaction with this outcome. They were of the opinion that, if the fifth naphtha cracker were to replace the existing first and second naphtha crackers, any increase in production capacity would be limited and would be unable to satisfy domestic demand. Therefore, in June 1986, four private-sector manufacturers of intermediate petrochemical raw materials (the Formosa Plastics Corporation, the China Gulf Plastics Corporation, the Taiwan Polymer Corporation, and the Taiwan Polypropylene Company Limited) jointly approached the government and once again proposed that the private sector be allowed to apply for permission to construct a sixth naphtha cracker. To everyone's surprise, this proposal was quickly approved by the Ministry of Economic Affairs, and in September of the same year the Formosa Plastics Corporation was given permission to construct the new cracker (three other applicants backed out during the course of the negotiations). This constituted a breakthrough in terms of putting an end to the monopoly that had long characterized the upstream petrochemical industry.

With the coming on stream of the fourth naphtha cracker, Taiwan had become the world's eleventh largest producer of ethylene. In terms of its ranking within the domestic economy, the petrochemical industry's share in GDP gradually increased, as shown in Table B-1. The shares in GDP of chemical raw materials, chemical products and plastic products increased from 5.8 percent, 1.3 percent, and 5.4 percent, respectively, in 1981, to 6.8 percent, 1.7 percent, and 7.0 percent in 1986. The shares of the textile and rubber industries in GDP, in contrast, declined from 9.4 percent and 1.4 percent, respectively, in 1981, to 8.4 percent and 1.3 percent in 1986.

As liberalization measures took effect, local shortages of raw materials gave way to increased imports, with the result that the proportion of petrochemical raw materials that were imported immediately increased from 14.8 percent in 1985 to 22.0 percent in 1986, as depicted in Table B-10. Furthermore, once imports were liberalized and produc-

TABLE B-10
Reliance on Imports in Respect of Basic Feedstocks and Intermediate Raw Materials in the Petrochemical Industry in Taiwan (%)

Product	1979	1980	1981	1982	1983	1984	1985	1986	1987	1988	1989	1990	1991	1992	1993	1994
Basic Feedstocks																
Ethylene	0.0	0.0	0.0	0.0	0.0	0.0	0.0	0.0	0.0	0.0	0.8	2.0	5.3	8.5	19.6	8.7
Propylene	11.6	11.7	3.1	1.6	8.2	5.2	1.2	4.1	3.3	4.3	9.7	14.0	14.6	16.8	16.0	18.1
Butadiene	4.3	0.0	0.0	0.0	47.0	0.0	2.2	12.2	17.4	30.7	28.0	40.6	45.5	53.4	55.3	52.2
Benzene	0.0	5.6	0.0	3.5	25.7	14.7	16.5	18.3	27.2	28.3	27.1	28.2	31.4	33.5	24.3	5.0
Toluene	0.0	0.1	0.1	2.1	3.2	0.1	0.2	0.7	20.2	70.6	91.2	84.9	82.9	91.6	93.4	83.5
Xylene	2.6	31.7	28.0	28.6	9.6	31.9	38.6	46.9	42.6	31.9	63.0	67.4	73.8	79.4	81.7	65.5
Subtotal	3.0	8.0	4.5	6.1	10.7	10.0	10.4	12.9	14.8	16.6	27.8	32.0	37.7	45.5	46.3	37.0
Intermediate Raw Materials																
Low-Density Poly-ethylene (LDPE)	5.7	3.4	11.4	10.7	13.0	14.9	16.4	28.7	30.0	22.1	37.7	43.5	55.5	55.1	55.7	55.5
High-Density Poly-ethylene (HPE)	39.5	36.4	22.3	35.5	54.1	15.3	6.6	8.2	20.7	24.0	30.5	26.8	43.5	45.4	48.1	47.8
Vinyl Chloride Monomer (VCM)	23.2	16.1	12.2	8.1	16.9	24.0	9.9	15.0	14.3	12.5	17.5	28.3	41.4	38.5	29.7	24.1
Polyvinyl Chloride (PVC)	2.4	0.3	3.2	2.5	0.7	0.5	0.4	4.3	9.9	11.9	13.2	11.9	14.8	14.1	17.7	17.6
Polypropylene (PP)	40.0	41.6	29.2	10.9	20.8	13.4	4.8	5.6	8.2	12.4	20.2	27.4	39.0	48.9	48.7	38.7
Styrene Monomer (SM)	6.1	51.5	39.1	39.9	3.4	0.0	0.0	35.3	40.2	42.2	48.9	42.9	58.9	64.2	65.1	70.9
Polystyrene (PS)	21.3	16.5	10.6	7.7	7.9	6.4	4.1	5.8	9.2	9.6	9.0	11.6	8.2	6.2	4.2	6.2
Methyl Methacrylate (MMA)	34.1	15.3	20.0	31.9	39.0	41.4	43.1	47.5	51.1	54.1	69.5	96.3	62.6	44.0	38.6	43.7
Melamine	63.1	78.4	33.7	35.2	33.7	11.9	36.8	26.5	15.5	11.1	11.6	4.7	16.3	44.2	50.1	45.9

TABLE B-10 (CONTINUED)

Acrylonitrile Butadiene Styrene (ABS)	81.8	77.7	58.0	35.8	28.0	22.5	18.5	20.2	20.0	17.3	16.4	16.7	16.1	18.0	18.0	17.4
Caprolactam (CPL)	48.3	35.2	31.2	26.2	29.4	33.9	24.0	36.6	46.1	51.9	48.4	47.3	50.3	59.6	69.2	61.2
Acrylonitrile (AN)	5.0	0.0	0.2	0.0	0.0	12.9	12.9	13.0	39.5	39.5	43.1	44.9	53.3	52.7	51.6	56.9
Pure Terephthalic Acid (PTA)	69.4	47.0	77.9	47.5	27.1	23.5	33.8	42.5	48.8	54.2	47.1	38.1	32.9	23.7	20.5	18.3
Ethylene Glycol (EG)	10.2	4.6	0.3	28.7	30.2	22.9	19.3	40.9	49.7	60.5	60.0	69.0	74.7	73.7	79.7	79.9
Styrene Butadiene Rubber (SBR)	14.7	19.8	6.8	8.8	7.2	6.8	10.0	10.2	18.8	17.7	25.4	28.1	34.5	44.9	44.2	39.7
Carbon Black (CB)	15.0	10.4	19.3	17.0	7.3	9.2	9.1	18.2	28.5	20.9	28.6	26.7	28.6	34.1	33.3	27.9
Phthalic Anhydride (PA)	100.0	38.5	31.3	23.6	31.8	45.8	36.7	50.6	51.4	69.4	48.3	50.3	48.4	38.7	41.1	46.9
Dioctyl Phthalate (DOP)	66.5	33.4	4.3	6.7	11.4	14.8	7.4	8.4	14.0	14.9	4.5	10.9	21.4	14.9	15.3	15.1
Methanol	25.9	15.2	53.2	78.2	97.1	100.1	76.8	79.7	83.8	87.4	85.7	84.9	100.1	101.3	92.1	94.8
Polypropylene Glycol (PPG)	69.3	25.7	9.9	15.1	11.7	60.8	12.5	27.7	40.8	54.6	50.3	42.6	6.8	12.4	35.9	34.8
Polyvinyl Alcohol (PVA)	44.0	22.7	23.2	15.8	17.3	10.1	13.3	16.2	25.6	36.8	26.5	24.0	23.4	23.9	26.4	33.3
Alkyl Benzene (AB)	2.9	9.5	0.0	1.3	14.2	14.2	8.8	10.9	19.4	44.8	9.7	7.3	28.8	10.4	6.7	5.5
Subtotal	27.1	20.0	32.2	21.6	21.3	20.9	17.3	26.4	32.1	36.3	36.7	37.6	44.3	42.9	39.9	40.2
Total	19.5	16.2	25.2	16.9	18.1	17.1	14.8	22.0	27.1	30.7	34.0	36.0	42.5	43.7	41.6	39.3

Source: Petrochemical Industry Association of Taiwan.

Notes: 1. All figures represent imports as a percent of total output of each final product or total input of each intermediate raw material.

2. Because of insufficient data, intermediate raw materials DMT and PG are not included in this table.

3. Degree of Reliance on Imports = Total Imports / (Total Output + Total Imports − Total Exports).

4. The degree of reliance on imports of Methanol is greater than 100 percent in certain years, due to methanol-producing factories being closed and production ceasing. There were still exports, however, perhaps of existing stock.

tion and distribution agreements ended, the government's ability to manipulate the petrochemical industry was greatly reduced. One result of this reduced government influence was that the private sector continued to press for the right to construct the fifth and sixth naptha crackers.

6. TRANSFORMATION OF THE INDUSTRY AFTER 1987

From 1987 onward, with the appreciation of the NT dollar against the US dollar and increasing wages due to the shortage of labor, the export competitiveness of downstream industries such as the rubber and textile industries was greatly reduced. These industries thus moved their operations offshore and restarted operations in Southeast Asia or mainland China, which reduced demand for the products of the midstream and upstream petrochemical industry. In addition, the environmental protection movement, the increased costs of using land and difficulties in acquiring land directly frustrated plans to expand the petrochemical industry during this period. The result was that the plans to construct the fifth and sixth, and also the possible seventh and eighth, naphtha crackers were delayed, further exacerbating the problems associated with raw material supply shortages. In such circumstances, midstream and downstream producers of petrochemical raw materials and products had no alternative but to rely on imports to make up for supply shortages at home. Furthermore, following the opening up of the market to imports of petrochemical raw materials, foreign petrochemical manufacturers repeatedly sold low-cost petrochemical raw materials in the local market, with the result that the proportion of petrochemical raw materials imported increased markedly. As can be seen in Table B-10, prior to 1986 the proportion of petrochemical raw materials imported was less than 20 percent. From 1986 onward that share rapidly increased, reaching a peak of 43.7 percent in 1992 and 39.3 percent in 1994.

Although the petrochemical industry in Taiwan developed mainly to serve the domestic Taiwan market, exports of petrochemical raw materials began to rise. As can be seen in Table B-11, exports of polystyrene, acrylonitrile butadiene styrene (ABS), styrene butadiene rubber, and alkyl benzene accounted for more than 50 percent of output. In particular, as indirect trade between Taiwan and mainland China began to flourish, exports to the mainland of polystyrene and ABS rapidly increased. The midstream petrochemical industries also began to export, and by 1994 exports of all kinds of petrochemical raw materials accounted for 15 percent of total output.

Prior to the 1990s, Taiwan had pursued economic growth while neglecting the environment, and the petrochemical industry was a prime example of an industry where the environment was sacrificed for economic gain. In the eyes of the public, the petrochemical complexes that had been built earlier were a major source of pollution. Those residents who lived near these complexes put up with the pollution over a long period and had no means for obtaining compensation. As national income rose, however, increased environmental awareness resulted in strong opposition to Dupont's proposed construction in 1986 of a titanium dioxide plant in an industrial zone near Changhwa. Furthermore, the protests that erupted in 1987 in relation to plans to construct a fifth naphtha cracker were on a scale never seen before in Taiwan.

Work on the construction of the fifth naphtha cracker had originally been planned to begin in 1987 in Houchin, Kaohsiung county, and to finish in 1992. This project, however, ignited the resentment of residents of Houchin who had already, over a long period, endured the pollution caused by the China Petroleum Corporation's oil refinery located nearby. Beginning in the middle of July 1987, residents began to block the western entrance to the Kaohsiung oil refinery. After several rounds of negotiations between the protestors and the China Petroleum Corporation and the government, the residents were promised that pollution controls would be strictly enforced to ensure that local environmental protection standards were met. Furthermore, it was only after the China Petroleum Corporation set up an NT$1.5 billion fund for the residents that the siege outside its oil refinery finally ended, three years after it began in October 1990. Work on the construction of the fifth naphtha cracker resumed, and the cracker was completed in 1993. After seven months of test runs, and after all the promises to protect the environment had been fulfilled, the cracker began to operate in July 1994.

The plan by the private sector to construct the sixth naphtha cracker following the completion of the fifth naphtha cracker was not only opposed on environmental grounds. It was also plagued by difficulties with regard to land acquisition and high costs associated with land use. In 1986, after it had put forward its proposal regarding the sixth naphtha cracker and various downstream industry projects, the Formosa Plastics Corporation immediately set about locating a suit-

TABLE B-11
Exports as a Proportion of the Total Output of Basic Feedstocks and Major Intermediate Raw Materials in the Petrochemical Industry in Taiwan (%)

Product	1979	1980	1981	1982	1983	1984	1985	1986	1987	1988	1989	1990	1991	1992	1993	1994
Basic Feedstocks																
Ethylene	0.0	0.0	0.0	0.0	0.0	0.0	0.0	0.0	0.0	0.0	0.0	0.0	0.0	0.0	19.6	8.7
Propylene	0.0	0.0	0.0	0.0	0.0	0.0	0.0	0.0	0.8	0.2	0.0	0.0	0.0	0.0	16.0	18.1
Butadiene	0.0	7.8	4.0	2.2	0.0	0.0	0.0	0.0	0.0	0.0	0.0	0.0	0.0	0.0	55.3	52.2
Benzene	0.0	0.0	0.0	0.0	0.0	0.0	0.0	0.0	0.0	0.0	0.0	0.0	0.0	0.0	24.3	5.0
Toluene	3.2	0.0	0.0	0.0	0.0	0.0	0.0	0.0	0.0	0.0	0.1	0.5	1.4	2.1	93.4	83.5
Xylene	15.2	14.1	16.0	2.0	0.0	0.0	0.0	0.0	0.0	0.0	0.0	0.0	0.9	0.0	81.7	65.5
Subtotal	2.3	2.2	2.1	0.4	0.0	0.0	0.0	0.0	0.2	0.0	0.0	0.0	0.1	0.0	46.3	37.0
Intermediate Raw Materials																
Low-Density Poly-ethylene (LDPE)	8.6	19.0	17.2	18.7	3.8	4.2	8.0	12.6	11.0	6.7	14.9	26.0	24.7	35.1	55.7	55.5
High-Density Poly-ethylene (HPE)	1.7	3.8	21.2	18.4	2.0	4.6	18.8	15.4	4.2	1.8	0.6	4.1	1.9	1.2	48.1	47.8
Vinyl Chloride Monomer (VCM)	0.0	0.0	0.0	0.0	0.0	0.0	0.0	0.0	0.0	0.0	0.0	0.0	0.0	0.0	29.7	24.1
Polyvinyl Chloride (PVC)	2.8	7.4	8.6	11.0	4.1	2.5	3.4	3.0	0.9	0.9	2.2	5.5	5.1	4.7	7.7	17.6
Polypropylene (PP)	7.4	2.2	0.1	8.3	1.3	0.0	6.0	8.8	0.2	0.1	7.4	10.8	6.6	9.6	48.7	38.7
Styrene Monomer (SM)	4.4	2.8	5.7	8.1	2.0	2.7	0.5	2.4	15.1	8.0	2.0	3.6	0.3	0.2	65.1	70.9
Polystyrene (PS)	5.4	11.1	12.9	11.1	5.5	8.1	9.5	10.3	11.2	28.5	39.7	30.0	51.1	53.6	4.2	6.2
Methyl Methacrylate (MMA)	3.4	5.7	12.5	14.1	0.0	0.0	0.0	0.1	0.0	0.0	2.3	23.7	11.0	19.9	38.6	43.7

TABLE B-11 (CONTINUED)

	1	2	3	4	5	6	7	8	9	10	11	12	13	14	15	16
Melamine	0.0	7.7	4.8	12.7	59.0	38.4	60.8	16.7	39.4	23.0	13.1	4.9	10.0	44.1	50.1	45.9
Acrylonitrile Butadiene Styrene (ABS)	8.0	7.2	2.0	5.3	6.9	20.2	34.9	39.4	42.1	58.8	59.1	64.3	65.8	65.8	18.0	17.4
Caprolactam (CPL)	3.4	0.0	0.0	0.0	0.0	0.0	0.0	0.0	0.0	1.1	0.0	1.7	0.8	1.6	69.2	61.2
Acrylonitrile (AN)	5.0	0.0	0.2	0.0	0.0	12.9	12.9	13.0	39.5	39.5	43.1	44.9	53.3	52.7	51.6	56.9
Pure Terephthalic Acid (PTA)	0.0	0.0	0.0	0.0	0.0	0.0	0.0	0.0	0.0	0.0	0.0	0.5	0.0	5.7	20.5	18.3
Ethylene Glycol (EG)	1.0	2.4	0.1	0.3	0.0	0.1	0.1	0.1	0.3	9.1	11.1	4.0	3.6	1.5	79.7	79.9
Styrene Butadiene Rubber (SBR)	40.1	40.4	45.0	49.4	40.7	24.5	34.3	37.0	46.2	41.2	42.5	37.2	44.1	59.0	44.2	39.7
Carbon Black (CB)	11.7	2.6	2.6	9.2	11.8	16.5	20.6	20.6	25.9	17.8	15.0	17.7	14.1	11.5	33.3	27.9
Phthalic Anhydride (PA)	0.0	0.0	0.0	0.0	11.6	7.7	8.1	4.7	4.7	0.0	5.4	0.2	2.6	1.8	41.1	46.9
Dioctyl Phthalate (DOP)	0.0	0.0	0.0	9.1	14.6	10.1	8.3	6.2	3.6	3.2	4.8	7.2	1.5	2.6	15.3	15.1
Methanol	0.3	16.6	4.1	0.4	1.7	—	0.7	0.2	1.4	23.0	3.0	4.7	104.6	—	92.1	94.8
Polypropylene Glycol (PPG)	16.3	3.4	2.9	11.0	6.3	2.0	2.6	2.3	2.4	13.2	9.3	34.0	8.8	12.3	35.9	34.8
Polyvinyl Alcohol (PVA)	54.5	61.6	72.7	67.9	72.1	63.0	60.2	68.3	77.8	84.7	77.1	74.3	70.1	71.4	26.4	33.3
Alkyl Benzene (AB)	11.2	16.8	39.8	53.0	42.0	48.2	35.4	64.2	68.8	66.0	47.5	70.0	73.0	71.8	6.7	5.5
Subtotal	5.5	8.2	7.0	8.5	5.0	4.4	6.1	7.3	7.7	10.6	12.2	13.4	15.6	18.3	39.9	40.2
Total	4.4	6.2	5.5	5.9	3.4	2.8	3.9	4.8	5.3	7.2	8.5	9.6	11.7	13.9	41.6	39.3

Source: Petrochemical Industry Association of Taiwan.

Notes: 1. All figures represent imports as a percent of total output of each final product or total input of each intermediate raw material.

2. Because of insufficient data, intermediate raw materials DMT and PG are not included in this table.

3. Inclination to Export = Total Exports / Total Output.

"—" indicates data not available.

able site on which to build the cracker. In 1987, its intention was to construct the plant at the Liche Industrial Zone in Ilan County, and the Industrial Development Bureau had already agreed to sell the required land to Formosa Plastics. The Formosa Plastics Corporation encountered strong opposition from Ilan residents, however, who were against the project on environmental grounds. After more than a year of unsuccessful dialog, Formosa Plastics was left with no alternative but to find a different site for the plant. In 1988, consideration was given to building the cracker in the Kuanyin Industrial Zone near Taoyuan in northeastern Taiwan. Once news of these plans reached the ears of Kuanyin residents, however, Formosa Plastics was immediately confronted with strong opposition to the proposed plant. In addition, the price of land in the Kuanyin Industrial Zone suddenly skyrocketed, and the Formosa Plastics Corporation appeared unwilling to accept an offer of land at such a high price. Formosa Plastics also proposed to build a harbor and applied to the government to obtain the construction rights, but permission to do this was not granted.

In response to these additional obstacles, Wang Yung-ching, Chairman of the Formosa Plastics Corporation, announced that his company was re-appraising all of its new local investment projects and considering their postponement. In addition, Wang accepted an invitation from the Chinese mainland to go there to consider the possibility of investing in the Haichang Petrochemical Complex. By stalling some huge investment projects involving between NT$90 billion and NT$100 billion and investing in the mainland, Formosa Plastics hoped to coerce the government into resolving the problems associated with environmental protests, land acquisition, skyrocketing land prices, and the need for harbor facilities.

As pointed out in Chapters 3 and 5, however, total investment in Taiwan had fallen, and the government saw the sixth naphtha cracker as an important investment project that had a significant bearing on the rekindling of private investment in Taiwan. In order to persuade the sixth naphtha cracker project to remain in Taiwan, the government in 1990 revised the Statute for the Promotion of Industrial Upgrading and allowed industrial harbors to be constructed by the private sector. The sixth naphtha cracker project also served as the first example whereby the government procured land at a high price and then sold it to the Formosa Plastics Corporation at a much lower price. In addition, the government provided different kinds of preferential tax treatment. Formosa Plastics responded by abandoning its plans to invest in the Haichang complex in mainland China. Even with the reduced price of land in the Kuanyin Industrial Zone, however, Formosa Plastics still considered the price it had to pay for the land to be too high. Finally, the proposed location of the plant was once again changed to a site in the Mailiao Industrial Zone in Yunlin County in the southwest of Taiwan, a "coastal" industrial zone where a large area of sea could be reclaimed.

During this period, environmental activists frequently surrounded petrochemical plants that were major polluters. According to statistics compiled by the Environmental Protection Administration of the Executive Yuan, there were seventy-four environmental disputes between 1988 and 1993 that involved petrochemical producers. These accounted for more than 25 percent of all environmental disputes, more disputes than any other industry. Furthermore, the "Linyuan incident," which took place in October 1988, resulted in a direct payment totaling NT$1.26 billion being made to local residents in order to get them to stop besieging the petrochemical complex. After this incident took place, it served as a model for the large compensation that environmental activists could expect to get. A large sum of money was also given to neighboring residents in the case of the fifth naphtha cracker. These examples set the stage for people all over the island living in the vicinity of a petrochemical complex to make their requests known.

This rising environmental awareness had much to do with the petrochemical industry's increasing willingness to invest in measures to protect the environment. From Table B-12 it can be seen that investments in pollution-control equipment on the part of manufacturers of chemical raw materials increased continuously after 1987, and the petrochemical industry was ranked among the top three industries within the manufacturing sector in this regard in 1992. In addition, expenditure on pollution-abatement equipment in the related petroleum and coal industry also steadily increased, with the result that in 1992 this industry was ranked first in terms of such expenditure. The environmental protection movement, however, became intertwined with claims for monetary compensation and other forms of interest group activism. Every time an election took place, the residents of the areas immediately surrounding petrochemical plants became prime targets for votes giving rise to conflicts, factory sieges, and claims for damages.

Despite these problems, the continued strong demand for petrochemical raw materials that characterized the domestic market led the

TABLE B-12

Investments and Expenditures on Maintaining Pollution Abatement Equipment in the Petrochemical and Chemical Raw Materials Industries, 1987–1992

	Year				
Industry	1987	1988	1989	1990	1992
Investments in Pollution Abatement Equipment					
Manufacturing Industry					
Amount (million NT$)	6,954	20,117	20,016	21,364	30,256
Proportion (%)	100.00	100.00	100.00	100.00	100.00
Chemical Raw Materials & Products Industry					
Amount (million NT$)	1,354	3,380	4,545	4,804	2,929
Proportion (%)	19.47	16.80	22.71	22.48	9.68
Rank	1	2	1	1	3
Petroleum & Coal Industries					
Amount (million NT$)	190	2,862	3,299	3,724	12,190
Proportion (%)	2.73	14.23	16.48	17.43	40.29
Rank	11	3	2	2	1
Expenditures on Maintaining Pollution Abatement Equipment					
Manufacturing Industry					
Amount (million NT$)	3,852	6,840	9,372	10,493	12,047
Proportion (%)	100.00	100.00	100.00	100.00	100.00
Chemical Raw Materials & Products Industry					
Amount (million NT$)	732	1,044	1,884	1,722	1,477
Proportion (%)	19.00	15.26	20.10	16.41	12.26
Rank	1	1	1	1	2
Petroleum & Coal Industries					
Amount (million NT$)	288	228	192	392	1,030
Proportion (%)	7.48	3.33	2.05	3.74	8.55
Rank	4	11	12	10	5

Source: *Report on a Survey of Industrial Statistics*, Joint Committee on Industrial Statistics, Ministry of Economic Affairs, 1994.

Note: The ranking is based on the manufacturing industry's division into twenty industries.

Tuntex Group in 1991 to offer to build a seventh naphtha cracker. Strong demand was also why the China Petroleum Corporation and eighteen other companies led by the Hohsin Group in 1993 proposed the construction of the eighth naphtha cracker. Due to problems associated with land acquisition in both cases, however, work on the seventh naphtha cracker in 1997 still remained at the environmental impact–assessment stage, and land had yet to be allocated in the case of the eighth naphtha cracker.

In addition to domestic efforts, environmental difficulties and the movement offshore of many downstream producers also led the petrochemical industry to engage increasingly in overseas investment projects. According to data in Table B-5, prior to 1986 there were only 13 cases of overseas investment in this sector. This number rapidly increased to 71 cases between 1987 and 1994. Most of the investment took place in the Southeast Asian region, followed by the United States. In addition, there were a further 715 cases of petrochemical industry investment in mainland China, amounting to a total investment of nearly US$300 million.

The government in this period also increasingly focused on the industrial upgrading of the petrochemical industry, on "quality" as opposed to quantity. The hope was that key intermediate petrochemical raw materials could be developed that would supply the needs of specialized chemical products and engineering plastics. As indicated in Table B-13, however, expenditure on R and D as a proportion of turnover in the chemical raw materials industry (i.e., the midstream petrochemical industry) tended to be less than 1.0 percent and below the corresponding rate for the manufacturing sector as a whole. Over the period from 1988 through 1992, however, the proportion increased, and by 1992 it reached 1.08 percent, exceeding the manufacturing sector as a whole for that year.

As the trend toward liberalization continued, one by one various industries and markets were opened up to the private sector, including the market for oil products and the market for basic petrochemical raw materials. This opening of markets served partially to break the monopolistic nature of these markets and led to consideration of privatizing many of the state-owned enterprises. The China Petrochemical Development Corporation was the first petrochemical industry-related enterprise to be partially privatized, this being achieved in June 1994 by selling shares that reduced the government ownership of the company to below 50 percent. Furthermore, the China Petroleum Corporation in 1997 planned to divide into nine large business departments (profit centers) and to obtain a stock exchange listing with the aim of privatizing each of these departments by the year 2001. It was also planned that the government's shareholding in the CPC in the year 2001 would not exceed 10 percent.

TABLE B-13
Industrial Upgrading in the Petrochemical Industry, 1985–1994

Year	R&D/Sales (%)				Link Indices of Labor Productivity (%)				Fixed Capital Intensity (million NT$ per thousand employed persons)		
	Manufacturing Industry	Chemical Raw Materials Industry	Petroleum, Coal Products Industries	Plastic Products	Manufacturing Industry	Chemical Raw Materials Industry	Petroleum, Coal Products Industries	Plastic Products	Manufacturing Industry	Chemical Raw Materials Industry	Petroleum, Coal Products Industries
1985	0.54	0.37	0.04	0.78	102.27	106.96	96.54	106.96	542.20	773.89	4,501.68
1986	0.47	1.07	0.14	0.39	107.35	115.94	99.67	99.68	545.45	795.16	6,341.67
1987	0.64	0.46	0.39	0.68	106.70	97.69	113.83	109.76	551.52	812.08	5,914.28
1988	0.52	0.40	0.77	0.11	105.25	101.90	98.57	99.80	607.24	921.26	6,612.35
1989	0.73	0.53	0.48	0.55	109.12	106.83	98.08	104.67	656.37	1,062.74	8,174.12
1990	0.92	0.88	0.73	0.39	107.53	108.94	85.63	120.15	730.63	1,276.30	9,195.24
1991	0.94	0.84	0.86	1.12	109.58	112.71	110.34	107.03	782.67	1,406.00	11,066.07
1992	0.92	1.08	1.13	1.57	103.80	111.61	97.74	106.01	825.31	1,420.02	12,738.34
1993	1.03	0.04	0.75	0.85	103.24	106.09	112.05	93.73	898.52	1,536.89	12,347.31
1994	1.02	0.03	0.71	1.00	103.72	116.92	98.59	97.94	940.28	1,674.83	13,540.96

Sources: *Indicators of Science and Technology*, National Science Council, Executive Yuan, 1993,1994. *Statistical Yearbook on Wages and Productivity in the Taiwan Area, Republic of China*, Directorate-general of Budget, Accounting and Statistics, Executive Yuan, 1995.

Note: The chemical and its products industry to which the statistics on fixed capital intensity relate include the chemical raw materials, chemical products, and plastic products industries.

The three major forces that interacted together to shape the development of the petrochemical industry were the government, the China Petroleum Corporation and the private-sector petrochemical enterprises. The leading role that the government played in the industry's development finally was greatly reduced by the 1990s to be replaced by increased competition within the petrochemical industry. Following the opening of the upstream petrochemical industry to the private sector, however, a large number of midstream petrochemical industrialists integrated their activities backward (some 55 percent of midstream petrochemical industrialists invested in the sixth and eighth naphtha crackers). The barriers to entry into the petrochemical industry, as a result, were in certain respects even higher than before. The trend toward large business groups in the petrochemical industry also meant that the impact that the industry could exert on the economy was continually increasing. As the petrochemical industry became more concentrated in Taiwan's offshore industrial zones, countervailing pressure from environmental activists also was likely to be significantly reduced. Preferential treatment by the government to the petrochemical industry, therefore, was no longer seen by the industry as being as necessary as it was in the earlier years. At the same time, although the need of the industry for government support was less, the capacity of the industry to bring its influence to bear on government remained considerable. The difference at the end of the 1990s was that that influence was being exercised mainly by the private sector rather than by the public China Petroleum Corporation.

NOTES

1 Li (1976, p. 36).

2 When the China Petroleum Corporation originally put forward its proposal to build the second naptha cracker, many midstream producers applied to initiate related projects. Following negotiations, there were nine industrialists intending to participate in ten projects. Then, when CPC put forward its proposal to construct the third naptha cracker, there were in all more than twenty-eight industrialists seeking to be involved in a total of thirty-eight projects. When the first energy crisis hit, however, many private industrialists withdrew and many other projects were delayed. See CEDP Executive Yuan, 1979, pp. 456–457.

3 See China Petroleum Corporation Planning Department, 1983, pp. 39–42.

4 Because the petrochemical industry was still facing difficulties, the gov-

ernment in April 1981 decided to set up a Petrochemical Production and Distribution Stabilization Fund following the CPC's 4 percent increase in its prices in March of that year. After it had commissioned accountants to examine the account of petrochemical industry participants, it was confirmed that the manufacturers of intermediate petrochemical raw materials were facing difficulties with their operations and were unable to contribute to this stabilization fund. The government thus allowed these manufacturers to submit their contributions over a period of six months. However, at the end of 1981, CPC announced that it was basing its supply prices on international prices, and that the stabilization fund was being withdrawn. These stabilization fund accounts were thus also abolished with the result that CPC effectively lowered its prices by paying the shares to the stabilization fund of the intermediate petrochemical producers. See Petrochemical Industry, Vol. 13: No. 6, p. 2.

5   See Economic Research Division, Bank of Taiwan, 1983, pp.43–44.

6   See Planning Department of the China Petroleum Corporation, 1983, pp. 86–88.

C THE ELECTRONICS AND INFORMATION TECHNOLOGY INDUSTRIES

Ying-yi Tu

1. THE BEGINNING PERIOD (1948–1960)

Taiwan's electronics industry began with the assembly of vacuum tube radios in 1948. At that time, a handful of electronic goods manufacturers imported electronic parts and tried to sell self-assembled radios in the domestic market, but the quality of these domestically produced goods could not compare with the quality of imports. Two years later, as manufacturers managed to improve product quality, the government decided to restrict imports of radios to protect this particular sector of industry. Thus, in 1950, the sale of domestic radios increased, and many assembly shops were converted into assembly factories. Gradually, some of the parts were locally produced instead of imported, but the main parts, such as vacuum tubes, could not be produced domestically.[1] As shown in Table C-1, the export of electronic goods accounted for less than 1 percent of total exports, while the import of electronic parts for the assembly of these goods accounted for 5.4 percent of total imports.

The assembly of vacuum tube radios in 1948 through 1960 can be classified as the beginning of the electronics industry, and included in the first period of the government's import-substitution strategy from 1953 through 1960.

2. THE MOVE TOWARD EXPORT TRADE IN ASSEMBLED GOODS

In 1961, Tatung Company began to import electronic components for

TABLE C-1
The Taiwanese Electronics Industry: Production Output and Import and Export Values

Stage of Development	Year	Electronic and Electronic Communications Equipment			Electronic Machinery and Equipment			
		Domestic Production (million NT$)	Share, National GDP (%)	Share, Manufacturing GDP (%)	Total imports (million US$)	Share of National Imports (%)	Total Exports (million US$)	Share of National Exports (%)
The Beginning Period	1952	21	0.12	0.95	7	3.74	0	0.00
	1955	74	0.25	1.58	14	6.97	0	0.00
	1960	219	0.35	1.84	16	5.39	1	0.61
Large-scale Assembly Period	1961	253	0.36	1.91	NA	NA	NA	NA
	1965	1,023	0.91	4.08	35	6.29	12	2.67
	1966	1,535	1.22	5.40	43	6.91	26	4.85
	1967	2,219	1.52	6.10	67	8.31	39	6.08
	1968	4,031	2.37	8.95	74	8.19	77	9.76
	1969	5,244	2.66	9.15	127	10.47	118	11.25
	1970	6,274	2.77	9.48	179	11.75	182	12.29
	1971	8,414	3.19	10.14	222	12.04	266	12.91
	1972	11,935	3.77	11.01	400	15.91	531	17.77
	1973	20,104	4.90	13.31	610	16.09	788	17.58
Attraction of Foreign Skills & Expertise	1974	21,771	3.96	12.09	756	10.85	756	13.41
	1975	19,343	3.28	10.63	503	8.45	782	14.73
	1976	25,402	3.59	10.63	755	9.94	1,277	15.64
	1977	30,656	3.70	10.81	812	9.54	1,489	15.91
	1978	43,160	4.35	12.22	1,315	11.93	2,109	16.62
	1979	49,822	4.17	11.60	1,067	10.88	2,775	17.23

	Average Growth	Change	Change	Average Growth	Change	Average Growth	Change
IT & Electronics Period							
1980	64,584	4.33	12.02	1,931	9.79	18.17	
1981	72,191	4.10	11.43	2,281	10.76	18.35	
1982	69,170	3.64	10.33	2,002	10.60	17.62	
1983	84,153	4.01	11.14	2,361	11.64	19.32	
1984	111,370	4.75	12.65	3,152	14.35	21.60	
1985	113,638	4.59	12.22	2,797	13.91	20.99	
1986	146,642	5.14	12.94	4,313	17.84	22.35	
1987	169,548	5.26	13.33	6,584	18.84	25.14	
1988	179,189	5.12	13.56	8,695	17.50	27.44	
1989	190,010	4.90	13.77	8,621	16.49	27.32	
IC Electronics Period							
1990	209,912	4.97	14.47	7,654	13.99	26.61	
1991	222,198	4.72	13.73	8,099	12.88	26.60	
1992	261,503	4.90	12.79	9,308	12.93	27.28	
1993	292,539	4.98	16.34	10,616	13.78	22.46	
1994	315,118	4.94	17.04	11,937	13.99	22.49	
Stage of Development (Years)	Average Growth	Change	Change	Average Growth	Change	Average Growth	Change
1952–1960	34.05	+0.23	+0.89	10.87	+1.65	—	+0.61
1960–1973	41.56	+4.55	+11.47	32.32	+10.70	67.04	+16.97
1973–1979	16.33	–0.73	–1.71	17.52	–5.21	23.35	–0.35
1979–1989	14.32	+0.73	+2.17	18.29	+5.61	20.63	–10.19
1989–1994	10.65	+0.04	+3.27	6.73	–2.50	2.93	–4.83

Sources: *National Income, Taiwan Area, Republic of China*, DGBAS, Executive Yuan, 1994. *Taiwan Statistical Data Book*, CEPD, 1995.

Note: "—" indicates data not available.

the assembly and production of transistor radios. In 1962, the number of transistor radio assembly factories increased to three, and these began to export their products. IBM established Taiwan's first computer company at this time, thus opening up the information technology (IT) industry as well. The broadcast of the first black-and-white television program, together with the assembly of the first black-and-white television sets, also occurred in 1962. As Table C-2 indicates, most foreign investment was in the electronics industry, particularly in the assembly of electronic goods and electronic components. The bringing in of skills in integrated circuit packaging marked the beginning of the semiconductor industry, and was also an important event in the development of the more advanced electronic components industry. The years 1969 to 1972 marked important additional milestones with the beginning of production of color televisions and electronic calculators.[2]

Following the introduction of export incentives in 1960, by 1965, this industry exhibited small but significant export sales. By 1973, the electronics share of total imports and exports had risen sharply to 16 percent and 17 percent respectively, with exports first outstripping imports in 1970. Production in this period was highly labor intensive.

Although Taiwan had the capability of supporting large exports of assembly parts, it did not shift toward importing raw materials and manufacturing its own electronic parts for assembly and instead continued to import electronic parts. Most electronic parts produced by foreign-owned factories in Taiwan were intended for sale in their mother country, not for sale within Taiwan. Parts produced by Taiwanese factories, in contrast, tended to be of inferior quality and did not meet international standards of performance. There was also some difficulty finding the skilled labor needed for the high-technology production of electronic parts, thus causing Taiwan's electronics industry to continue to rely on the import of electronic parts.

The establishment of the special export processing zone in Kaohsiung provided impetus for a sharp increase in foreign investment in electronics beginning in 1966. Table C-2 shows that the total number of foreign investments in electronics during this period totaled 260, worth US$349 million. These were equivalent to 14.08 percent of the total number of investments and 32.8 percent of the total value of investment in the electronics industry respectively, the highest percentages in any one industry. The investors included major firms such as AOL, RCA, Zenith, Philips, and Texas Instruments, among others.

TABLE C-2

Foreign Investments by the Electronics and Electrical Goods Industry, 1952–1994

Stage of Development	Year	Number of Cases	Total Amount (US$00)	Average Amount per Case (US$00)
The Beginning Period	1952–1960	2	1,043	
Totals for Period		*2* (2.33%)	*1,043* (2.93%)	*522*
Large-scale	1961	2	1,156	
Assembly Period	1962	4	851	
	1963	1	625	
	1964	2	771	
	1965	6	21,377	
	1966	22	15,381	
	1967	30	14,559	
	1968	25	26,993	
	1969	35	64,766	
	1970	33	73,832	
	1971	15	32,970	
	1972	26	19,720	
	1973	59	75,748	
Totals for Period		*260* (14.08%)	*348,747* (32.84%)	*1,341*
Attraction of Foreign	1974	37	69,652	
Skills & Expertise	1975	9	24,701	
	1976	20	72,395	
	1977	15	52,801	
	1978	25	63,495	
	1979	24	110,408	
Totals for Period		*130* (18.73%)	*393,452* (34.07%)	*3,027*

continued

TABLE C-2   (CONTINUED)

Foreign Investments by the Electronics and Electrical Goods Industry, 1952–1994

Stage of Development	Year	Number of Cases	Total Amount (US$00)	Average Amount per Case (US$00)
IT & Electronics	1980	23	108,602	
Period	1981	22	83,948	
	1982	18	70,797	
	1983	31	107,267	
	1984	42	267,652	
	1985	19	139,304	
	1986	69	231,741	
	1987	85	377,375	
	1988	37	237,329	
	1989	31	391,042	
Totals for Period		*374* *(13.93%)*	*2,015,062* *(23.17%)*	*5,388*
Adjustment Period	1990	41	377,039	
	1991	43	570,099	
	1992	46	323,308	
	1993	34	226,651	
	1994	38	296,088	
Totals for Period		*202* *(10.24%)*	*1,793,185* *(21.38%)*	*8,877*

Source: *Statistics on Overseas Chinese and Foreign Investment, Technical Co-operation,* Outward Technical Co-operation, Indirect Mainland Investment, Guide of Mainland Industry Technology, The R.O.C., Investment Commission Ministry of Economic Affairs, December 31, 1994.

Notes: 1. The period 1952–1960 saw two cases of investments, both of which occurred in 1958.

2. The percentage figures within the parentheses indicate this industry's share of total investments in the country.

Foreign investment in the electronics industry was concentrated in the areas of processing and assembly, and it brought in much-needed assembly skills. This attraction of foreign skills and expertise became the foundation for the development of the information technology (IT) industry.

3. THE PERIOD OF SKILLS IMPROVEMENT (1974–1979)

To raise the level of skills in the electronics industry, the government asked the Industrial Technology Research Institution (ITRI) to establish an Electronics Research Center in 1974 (the name was changed in 1979 to the Electronics Research and Service Organization [ERSO]). This center was charged with introducing the Integrated Circuit Demonstration Factory Plan (July 1975–June 1979). In collaboration with the U.S. RCA, the research facility brought in the CMOS Integrated Circuit (IC) technology. This technology involved a set of skills used from the beginning to the end of the entire production operation, from design and manufacturing to assembly. The move to bring in this technology cost NT$489 million, and the establishment of the model factory took four years to complete. Due to the immense success of the new technology, Taiwan became equipped with an integrated circuit manufacturing ability, an important step in the gradual shift in the character of the electronics industry from downstream assembly to upstream production.

In 1980, the United Microelectronics Corporation (UMC) was established as a spin-off organization from ERSO. It helped to disseminate the skills taught by the model factory and the expertise of the research personnel, and helped to raise the level of skills of the average factory worker. From 1980, several semiconductor production factories were set up, among which several implemented the CMOS IC technology. The others managed to adopt newer, higher technology through the transfer of human resources within the industry. This encouraged the rapid growth of the semiconductor industry. Only after this initial wave of success did the domestic-owned companies gradually expand and upgrade as well.

For downstream consumer electronic goods, this period continued to be one of large-scale assembly followed by exports. The main goods exported were still television sets and radios. In addition, Taiwan began to export newer products such as radio and cassette recorders, color televisions, record players, electronic calculators, and digital watches. As indicated by the data in Table C-3, of these new goods, the production of electronic calculators and digital watches involved the use of the new IC technology. The tremendous profitability of bringing in this new IC technology revitalized the manufacture of downstream electronic consumer goods. The IC technology was successfully applied to other areas of production as well, including the communications and

TABLE C-3

Production Output of Each Category of Electronic Product by Period

Large-scale Assembly Period

Stage of Development	Year	Radios Output (000 units)	Growth (%)	Black-and-White Televisions Output (000 units)	Growth (%)	Transistors Output (000 units)	Growth (%)	Integrated Circuits Output (000 units)	Growth (%)
Large-scale Assembly Period	1961	1	—	—	—	—	—	—	—
	1966	1,782	327	66	—	75	—	1	—
	1971	7,238	32	1,755	93	19,222	203	34,198	907
	1973	14,530	42	4,202	54	52,578	65	342,021	216

Attraction of Foreign Skills & Expertise

Stage of Development	Year	Cassette Recorders Output (000 units)	Growth (%)	Color Televisions Output (000 units)	Growth (%)	Record Players Output (000 units)	Growth (%)	Electronic Calculators Output (000 units)	Growth (%)	Digital Watches Output (000 units)	Growth (%)
Attraction of Foreign Skills & Expertise	1974	2,204	—	418	—	259	—	509	—	285[a]	—
	1979	11,611	39	1,145	22	989	31	8,752	77	6,132	85

IT & Electronics Period

Stage of Development	Year	Microcomputers Output (000 units)	Growth (%)	Integrated Circuits Package Output (000 units)	Growth (%)	Monitors Output (000 units)	Growth (%)	Computer Terminals Output (000 units)	Growth (%)	Telephones Output (000 units)	Growth (%)
IT & Electronics Period	1980	1.4[b]	—	755,005	—	39	—	0.5	—	1,758	—
	1985	909	263	1,152,125	11	3,175	52	1,107	377	11,503	46
	1989	2,670	31	2,288,709	19	7,276	23	1,959	15	16,522	9

IC Electronics	Microcomputers	Integrated Circuits Package	Monitors	Air Conditioners
Period				
1990	2,437 —	2,488,127 —	8,037 —	900 —
1993	3,775 16	4,176,475 19	12,173 15	1,176 9

[a] The figure for digital watches is based on production in 1975.
[b] 1981's data.

Sources: Taiwan Industrial Production Statistics Monthly, R.O.C., Department of Statistics, Ministry of Economic Affairs, July 1979–April 1984. Industrial Production Statistics Monthly, Taiwan Area, The R.O.C., Department of Statistics, Ministry of Economic Affairs, April 1984–April 1994.

information sectors. For example, Tatung and Toshiba Electronics began the manufacture of terminals of computers, and Taiwan International Standard Electronic Company and Siemens Telecommunication Systems Company began to produce electronic switchboards.

Even though the late 1970s was the period when ERSO brought in groundbreaking new integrated circuit technology, the effect was not felt widely until 1980, when greater efforts were made to spread this technology to locally owned companies as well. Prior to that time, domestically owned factories were still largely confined to the assembly of consumer goods and electronic components. The severe economic downturn brought about by the first oil crisis of 1973 caused the electronics industry to decline from 1974 to 1975. As can be observed from the data in Table C-1, this setback was temporary, and the industry bounced back after that. International competition, though, was stiff, and the industry did not reach the level of growth characteristic of the 1960s. The GNP share of the electronics industry, however, had already surpassed that of textiles (it was only lower than the share of textiles in 1973), and was second only to the share of the chemical industry. Exports of electronic machinery and equipment had an average growth of 23.35 percent between 1973 and 1979, which accounted for 17.23 percent of total national exports. The second oil crisis in 1979 and the resulting global economic recession did not seem to have much effect on the electronics industry in Taiwan, but the world economic recession in the 1980s did, causing a radical change in the structure and nature of this industry.

Government's attention during the late 1970s was still focused on heavy industries such as steel and chemicals, but when the National Science Conference convened in 1978 under the initiative of domestic and foreign scholars and experts, the electronics and IT industries began to receive more attention. After the conference, a Science and Technology Development Plan,[3] was drafted by K. T. Li and others and passed in 1979. This Plan led to the formation in 1979 of the Institute for Information Industry (III)[4]; the establishment in 1980 of the Hsinchu Science-based Industrial Park; the pinpointing of four key technologies (energy resources, materials, information technology, and automation); and the search for foreign experts, including the formation of an overseas-local advisory system. III and Hsinchu Science Park were major forces leading the electronics industry into a buoyant period of growth in the 1980s. The second oil crisis in 1979 also led the government to reduce its support for energy-intensive industries (particularly heavy and chemical industries) and instead to support the energy-conserving electronics, information, and other such high-technology industries.

The late 1970s were years during which the government forged closer ties with the electronics industry. Government's contributions came first in the form of setting up ERSO, which developed research in electronics technology and helped bring in and disseminate specific industry-related skills and technology in an attempt to raise the level of worker skills. ERSO also became an important source of technology and personnel for the electronics industry. Second, government established the III, which not only aided in the computerization of government departments, but also groomed experts in the information field and encouraged the use of computer information, thereby promoting the development of the IT and electronics fields among the general population. The government did not interfere in production or sales (as it did in the petrochemical industry), nor did it interfere through restrictive and protective policies (as it did in the textiles industry). Instead it provided support at the level of research and development.

Besides bringing in new technology, attracting foreign investment into the electronics industry continued to be an important part of the economic policy of the late1970s. According to Table C-2, the electronics industry continued to be the main destination of foreign investment. Each investment was, on average, 2.25 times larger in value than it had been in the previous period, and was equal to US$3 million. The investment per worker also increased from an average of NT$95,000 in 1974 to NT$144,000 in 1979. The increase in capital intensity implied a rise in skills intensity, showing a change in the direction of foreign investment. Although foreign investment continued to be the dominant force in the industry in this period, domestic firms also brought in new technology and thrived in this new environment. The foreign firms' share of exports reached a high of 93.16 percent in 1975, but dropped to 74.32 percent in 1979, signifying a strong surge in the growth of domestic industries. By the 1980s, the new technology had been transferred to those working in domestic enterprises or enrolled in technical schools. This change coincided with the inception of III, and it speedily raised the level of skills and information related to the electronics and information industries. As a result, the following two Four-Year Economic Plans, covering the period 1983 through 1990, did not place any emphasis on the continued attraction of foreign investment, but rather emphasized the importance of nationally supported research and development.

4. The Period of Information Technology (1980–1989)

During the 1980s, the environment for both domestic and foreign investment changed. Domestic industries faced the pressure of having to improve and to rise to the next level of development. National economic policy no longer focused on the heavy and chemical industries, but rather shifted attention to the electronics, information technology, and other high-technology industries. More specifically, in the field of software development, government policy emphasized bringing in technology, training personnel, and establishing a central database of industry-related information. In the field of hardware development, the emphasis was on providing facilities. The software-related measures were carried out by ERSO and the III, while the hardware-related measures were implemented by firms in the Hsinchu Science-based Industrial Park.

Because the domestic electronics industry before 1979 was still at the level of assembly production, Taiwanese-owned small- and medium-scale enterprises were reluctant to embrace high-risk, capital-intensive investments in new technology. The government, as a result, made use of the Executive Yuan Development Fund as a source of subsidies, and invited Chiao-Tung Bank, domestic-owned enterprises, and a venture capital company to co-establish and to domestically run the UMC. This facility was dedicated to the spread of the new IC technology and its research results. To ensure that this skills-transfer process was smooth and efficient, the UMC received much help from ERSO with regard to manpower training, installing and providing equipment, and furnishing its workshop. Moreover, many of the personnel of the management and operations departments were transferred over from the ERSO. The UMC thus could be said to be a spin-off company of ERSO.

This approach became an important model of government intervention in the electronics and information industries. The method began with the government's arranging a budget for the Science and Technology Development Program, and ended with the establishment of a research facility that was responsible for bringing in new skills and technology and then transferring those skills to the industry at large. Initially, the research facility sought to train personnel and workers in the new skills and technology directly. It soon, however, found the indirect method of setting up a spin-off company to deal with the transfer process of each specific skill to be far more efficient when dealing directly with a large-scale innovative industry. By 1994, three spin-off companies had been formed for such a purpose: UMC in 1980, Taiwan Semiconductor Manufacturing Company (TSMC) in 1987, and Vanguard Integrated Circuits Company (which developed sub-micro technology) in 1994. Among these three companies, UMC was the first domestic firm dealing with the production of integrated circuits. It became an important factor in the development of the IC industry by providing, together with the Hsinchu Science-based Industrial Park, a strong stimulus for the pursuit and development of IC design throughout Taiwan. TSMC was the second domestic integrated circuits firm, but was the first domestic firm involved solely in contracted IC manufacturing and not involved in designing its own product. Its super-scale IC manufacturing facility provided support for the development of many small- and medium-scale IC design industries. After this, many more medium- to large-scale IC design and production factories were set up and began to attract investments from large consortia in other sectors as well. For example, the Hualon Group set up the Hualon Micro-electronic Company. The establishment in 1994 of Vanguard led to a wave of significant investments in the domestic IC industry with 8-inch wafer technology.

To promote high technology and the development of the electronics and IT industries, the government actively tried to encourage the inflow of skills from abroad, and promoted more research and the spread of these skills to the broader population. The Hsinchu Science-based Industrial Park in particular focused on attracting more foreign and domestic capital and skills and technology into Taiwan.

The establishment of the Hsinchu Park followed the example of America's Silicon Valley. It was located close to National Chiao-tung and National Tsing-hua Universities, as well as to ERSO. This was done with the aim of absorbing high-level science and engineering personnel from the universities to support the development of high-tech factories and firms in the Park, and of gaining technical support from the research institute. As expected, with the establishment of the Hsinchu Park, many domestic and foreign firms invested in factories within the area. As of 1989, there were 105 enterprises operating within this area, and most were concentrated in computers and computer peripherals (35 firms), the integrated circuit industry (28 firms), and the information technology industry (19 firms). Among them, 12 were previously established national companies, 29 were foreign, and 64 were totally new, mostly operated by Taiwanese experts educated abroad. Up to 5 percent of profits within the Hsinchu Park were channeled to research and development, well above the figure of 1 percent for the rest of the country at that time, thus further cementing Hsinchu's role in research and development in these particular fields. From then on, through continued interaction between the firms within the Park and outside the Park and the movement of human resources between them, the technology of the electronics and IT industries gained a strong foothold in the Taiwanese economy and then spread throughout the country.

The Institute for Information Industry (III), formed in 1979, also began to play an assisting role in the electronics and IT sectors. For example, it raised industry demand by promoting the use of computers in governmental departments, and, from 1980 onward, held IT exhibitions regularly in Taiwan to increase awareness of and demand for the technology available. The III also took over the responsibility for education and training in these fields outside of the school system from the Education Ministry, and implemented the Five-Year Information Technology Training Program. From 1985 to 1992, III trained a total of almost 70,000 people, including people from the Ministry of Economic Affairs and the various industrial sectors. This strong emphasis on training human resources and promoting the IT industry increased the availability of IT and electronics experts within the country and helped this field to develop rapidly. The III was also the information and technology center for the industry, providing support for the dissemination of industry news. This was especially helpful in linking the many small-scale enterprises characteristic of the industry and providing them with a common source to evaluate the global trends in this field.

Government measures alone, however, cannot explain the rapid growth of the IT industry. In the early 1980s, for example, electronic games were immensely popular, and this provided a boost for the market. Many companies that produced such games experienced a windfall during this period. After a while, gambling games became common in toyshops, which led the government to ban the production and sale of such games. At the same time, Apple personal computers began to gain a foothold in the market. Because the parts used for the manufacture of the electronic games were similar to the parts used for the manufacture of computers, many electronic games manufacturers switched to manufacturing electronic parts for Apple-compatible computers instead. The sudden appearance of large numbers of imitation Apple computers led the Apple company to sue Taiwan through the ITC in January 1983. This in no way, however, dampened the computer industry in Taiwan, and instead led these companies to manufacture IBM-compatible personal computers. Because of low prices, reasonably good quality, and the growing popularity of personal computers in the world, the industry experienced stunning growth.

A major development in the IT industry occurred in 1981 when ERSO began photo-masking production, as well as the production of 3.5 UM NMOS Processors and microprocessors. During the period from 1981 to 1985, ERSO also developed IC skills for the manufacture of time-keeping devices, telephones, melody and speech synthesizers, memories, micro-controllers, calculators, and peripheral controllers. After these skills were transferred to the workforce, music-related integrated circuit skills led to rapid growth in related fields, while telephone-integrated circuit skills established Taiwan as the major exporter of telephones. The success of the computer-integrated circuit skills spurred the development of the computer and related industries. From Table C-3 one can observe how the output of telephones rose from 1.76 million units in 1980 to 16.52 million units in 1989. Computer-processing units and minicomputer output rose more than a hundred times in the first half of the 1980s, and in the latter half, growth averaged 15 percent to 31 percent annually. Especially after 1986, when ACER Incorporated produced Asia's first 32-bit personal computers, which had two to ten times faster processing speeds than comparable IBM personal computers, the computer output of Taiwan increased even more rapidly, and Taiwan rose to be an internationally important computer manufacturer.

The linking of the consumer electronics, computers, and communications (3C) industries with the development of the IC and information industries also gave the consumer electronics industry an opportunity to upgrade. This helped firms to produce higher quality electronic goods in greater quantities and develop new innovations such as high-resolution televisions, high-resolution video cameras, electronic diaries, and laser karaoke sets, as well as photocopiers, electronic cash registers, and other office equipment.

The electronics industry became Taiwan's leading export industry in 1987, with its export share rising by 8.44 percent during the period from 1980 to 1990. Table C-4 shows even more clearly the change in the export composition of the IT industry. Looking at the export of electronic goods and electronic parts, in 1987 the export of the former was higher than the latter. By 1988, the two were almost equal, while in 1989 the export of electronic parts was clearly higher than that of electronic goods. Further examination of the composition of electronic goods

TABLE C-4
Value of Exports of the Electronic Components Industry, 1978–1991 (US$million)

Items	Year													
	1978	1981	1982	1983	1984	1985	1986	1987	1988	1989	1990	1991
Consumer electronic goods	940	1,698	1,483	1,540	1,826	1,387	1,976	2,852	2,879	2,750	1,909	1,865
IT products	—	14	64	289	891	1,111	1,366	1,955	2,991	3,218	3,689	4,752
Communications products	45	149	178	431	356	327	520	619	638	790	804	796
Industrial electronic goods	7	13	20	48	56	80	122	216	603	246	233	224
Subtotal	1,262	1,847	1,745	2,308	3,129	2,905	3,984	5,642	6,814	7,004	6,635	7,637
Components	1,113	1,748	1,802	1,977	2,421	2,188	3,278	5,217	6,813	8,596	9,996	11,172
Total	2,375	3,622	3,547	4,285	5,550	5,093	7,262	10,859	13,627	15,600	16,631	18,809

Source: Institute for Information Industry.

Note: "—" indicates data not available.

exports reveals that consumer electronic goods were the major exports from 1980 to 1984. With the sudden boom in the IT industry, IT product exports exceeded consumer electronic goods exports in 1988. The growth in exports of IT products rose from US$14 million in 1981 to US$3.218 billion in 1989. (If electronic parts were included, the growth would be from US$106 million in 1981 to US$6.908 billion in 1989.) This change in the composition of manufactured products was reflected in the value of the kind of goods produced. According to Table C-5, consumer electronic goods had a share of 35.6 percent of the electronics industry in 1984, and data storage and processing equipment (in other words, the IT industry) had a share of only 18.5 percent. By 1989, the former had dropped to only 21.3 percent, while the share of the IT industry had risen to 32.3 percent. This trend continued into the 1990s and was an indication of the constant change and upgrading that the IT industry was undergoing.

Because industries involving high technology tend to be more risky, and because IT products tend to evolve and change quickly over time, smaller companies found it especially difficult to participate in the industry. To alleviate this problem, the government used ERSO and the III to aid the upgrading of the IT industry. It opened the Hsinchu Science-based Industrial Park specifically to foster the development of high-technology industries and to encourage greater participation and investment from the local enterprises, and it also revised economic incentives to further boost the development of the industry in general. Financially, the government provided ample funds for both loans at low interest rates and opportunities for co-partnership. This was especially designed to help capital-strapped returned scholars to establish their own firms. The UMC and TSMC, both spin-off companies of ERSO, were also important investments in the early-mid 1980s. Government reserved some share ownership in these spin-offs for the private sector, but it had to make extra efforts to get even the larger enterprises to invest small amounts of capital in these companies. For example, the government had originally invited Formosa Plastics Corporation to buy up 13 percent of the shares in TSMC, but Formosa Plastics decided to buy up only 5 percent. The investments in the ERSO's mostly capital-intensive or skills-intensive spin-off companies were thus something that the local enterprises were unable or unwilling to shoulder at that point in time.

Most of the government's funds that went to the electronics and IT industries were channeled toward the founding of ERSO spin-off com-

TABLE C-5
Electronic and IT Industry Production by Item, 1984–1994

Year	Data Processing and Storage (IT Industry)		Consumer Electronic Goods		Electronic Parts and Components		Communications Equipment		Subtotal	
	Output (NT$million)	Share of Total (%)	Output (NT$million)	Share of Total (%)	Output (NT$million)	Share of Total (%)	Output (NT$million)	Share of Total (%)	Output (NT$million)	Share of Total (%)
1984	55,779	18.5	107,618	35.6	114,641	37.9	24,269	8.0	302,307	100.0
1985	55,550	20.1	94,746	34.2	103,418	37.3	23,303	8.4	277,017	100.0
1986	80,934	22.8	109,354	30.9	134,692	38.0	29,377	8.3	354,357	100.0
1987	114,312	27.0	122,224	28.9	155,630	36.8	30,525	7.2	422,691	100.0
1988	144,243	30.7	114,383	24.4	178,487	38.0	32,009	6.8	469,122	100.0
1989	163,878	32.3	108,226	21.3	197,106	38.9	37,770	7.4	506,980	100.0
1990	194,706	35.1	89,208	16.1	224,826	40.5	46,116	8.3	554,856	100.0
1991	212,429	34.6	93,003	15.1	260,184	42.3	48,863	8.0	614,479	100.0
1992	226,083	36.1	82,077	13.1	274,003	43.8	43,388	6.9	625,551	100.0
1993	236,554	33.4	72,180	10.2	346,447	48.9	53,708	7.6	708,889	100.0
1994	270,922	33.8	72,843	9.1	406,745	50.7	52,032	6.5	802,542	100.0

Source: Industrial Production Statistics Monthly, Department of Statistics, December 1991, March 1996.

panies. There was generally no intervention in the actual operations of these enterprises. The main form of government involvement was in the area of personnel. Most high-level managers were transferred from ERSO, and the chairman was usually appointed by the head of ERSO. Since most of these personnel had few connections to the government, these two companies were guided to assume the character of a private enterprise rather than a government enterprise.

In conclusion, this period was marked by intense involvement of the government in the IT and electronics industries. Government helped in the areas of capital provision and land acquisition and in developing a legal framework. In addition, government incentives and the establishment of various resource centers boosted the industries. This latter process continued in the late 1980s, with the government's setting up of the Opto-Electronics and Systems Center in 1987 (this name was changed to Opto-Electronics and Systems Laboratories [OES]) in 1990) and the Computer and Communication Laboratories (CCL) in 1990.

5. The IC Electronics Industry (1990–1995)

From the middle of the 1980s, because the environment for domestic investment had worsened and the cost of labor and land had risen, Taiwan's labor-intensive manufacturing industries concentrated in investing in China as well as in Southeast Asia. The electronics and IT industries were unusual in that they were capital intensive as well as labor intensive, but they nevertheless led the wave of investments in regional countries. As indicated by the data in Table C-6, in the 1986 through 1994 period, the manufacturing industry that was most heavily involved in investing in foreign countries was the electronics industry (including IT). From 1986 on, the value of overseas investment in the electronics industry rose gradually and, especially in the 1990s, became dominant. Why was this so? A severe global economic downturn in the early 1990s led even internationally renowned firms to drop their prices to raise demand, creating more competition for the Taiwanese electronics and IT industries. At the same time, Taiwan firms faced rapidly rising costs within the country. This double blow led to low profits and even losses in 1992, and these industries were plunged into a deep recession. Several firms that had been on the verge of expansion domestically ended up withdrawing from the market entirely. The situation was somewhat alleviated by intervention from the government and ample aid from the national banks, but many firms also felt driven to

TABLE C-6

Outward Investments of the Electronic and Electric Appliances Industries

Year	Outside China		Within China[b]	
	Number of Cases[a]	Amount (US$million)	Number of Cases[a]	Amount (US$million)
1952–1979	17 (12.3)	5 (8.5)	—	—
1980–1985	21 (25.3)	62 (39.7)	—	—
1986	5 (15.6)	25 (43.9)	—	—
1987	9 (20.0)	40 (38.8)	—	—
1988	25 (22.7)	39 (17.8)	—	—
1989	56 (36.6)	122 (0.1)	—	—
1990	90 (28.6)	424 (27.3)	—	—
1991	85 (23.4)	209 (12.6)	42 (17.7)	32 (18.4)
1992	7 (19.0)	131 (14.8)	31 (11.7)	35 (14.2)
1993	55 (16.9)	104 (6.3)	1,190 (12.8)	445 (14.0)
1994	58 (17.9)	290 (17.9)	148 (15.8)	157 (16.3)
1952–1994	478 (21.9)	1,920 (21.6)	1,411 (13.1)	668 (14.7)

Source: *Annual Report on Foreign and Overseas Chinese Investment, Technical Co-operation, in Taiwan, Taiwanese Investment and Technical Co-operation in Foreign Countries, and Taiwanese Investment in the People's Republic of China,* Ministry of Trade and Industry Investment Survey Committee, 1994.

Notes:

[a]   Numbers within the parentheses indicate the industry's percentage share of the total number of cases of investments or total worth of investments in/outside China.

[b]   The figures for China are only for the period after official measures were taken to promote investment there. There were, however, instances of investments before that.

invest in less-developed countries as an alternative way of keeping down their spiraling costs (see Table C-6).

Overseas production of IT products continuously rose during this period. In 1993, the value of IT goods produced by Taiwanese firms overseas was 14.9 percent of total national production; in 1994, this share had risen to 20.6 percent. According to estimates of the III, the figure in 1995 may have reached 24.6 percent.

Despite the global economic recession in the early 1990s, the integrated circuits industry continued to grow after 1991. From 1991 to 1994, the overall growth rate was somewhere between 50 and 80 percent. The number of IC manufacturers grew by six in the period from 1980 to 1989, but within the five short years of 1990 through 1994, six more were added.

The first wave of investment in IC production reached its climax in 1994 because of the sub-micron investment case. Sub-micron investment was first suggested by the government in 1993. It was aimed at transferring the sub-micron production process and skills developed in the ERSO to the general industry through an experimental factory run under co-ownership of the government and private investors. As the IC industry was so buoyant at this point in time, many investors had faith in the industry's sustained development and rushed to grab this opportunity. After extensive negotiations, thirteen firms were chosen as co-partners with the government in establishing Vanguard International Semiconductor Corporation (VIS). Among the thirteen firms, the major shareholder was TSMC. Those companies that failed to gain a share in this company all pursued other investments in order to catch the IC industry at its peak and continue to maintain their own competitiveness. All these investments taken together totaled NT$470

TABLE C-7
Overseas and Local Production of IT Goods, 1992–1994

Item	Overseas Production			Overseas Production as a Percent of Total Production		
	1992	1993	1994	1992	1993	1994
Monitors	310	815 (162.9)	1,795 (120.2)	11.3	20.1	34.0
Mother Boards	184	284 (54.3)	421 (48.2)	15.0	23.9	26.6
Computer Keyboards	171	198 (15.8)	209 (5.6)	58.2	68.0	69.0
Convertible Power Supplies	122	233 (91.0)	380 (63.1)	24.4	41.3	51.6
Graphic Cards	—	136	154 (13.2)	—	29.1	32.0
Mouse	—	17	44 (158.8)	—	10.7	26.3
Others	182	8	0	4.0	—	—
Total	969	1,691 (74.5)	3,003 (77.6)	10.4	14.9	20.6

Source: Market Intelligence Center, Institute for Information Industry.

Notes: Figures in the parentheses denote the percentage growth per year; "—" indicates data not available.

TABLE C-8
Development of 8-inch Integrated Circuit Factories, 1994–1997

Firm	Item	Value of Investment (NT$billion)	Completion (expected)	Monthly Production Capability (000s)	Type of Product
Vanguard International Semiconductor Corp.	Factory 1A	18	December 1994	15	DRAM, SRAM
	Factory 1B	20	4th quarter 1996	15	DRAM, SRAM
Taiwan Semiconductor Manufacturing Co. Ltd.	Factory 3	25	3rd quarter 1995	35	OEM
	Factory 4	30	2nd quarter 1996	30	OEM
	Factory 5	25	1st quarter 1997	25	OEM
Ti-Acer Semiconductor	Factory 1B	13	June 1995	20	DRAM
Manufacturing Corp.	Factory 2	35	2nd quarter 1997	40	DRAM
United Microelectronics Corp.	Factory 3	25	September 1995	25	DRAM, SRAM, OEM
United Semiconductor Corp.	Factory 1	27	June 1996	25	OEM
United Silicon Incorporated	Factory 1	27	October 1998	25	OEM
United Integrated Circuits Corp.	Factory 1	29	November 1997	25	OEM
Nan Ya Technology Corp.	Factory 1	20	3rd quarter 1996	24	DRAM
Powerchip Semiconductor Corp.	Factory 1	20	1st quarter 1996	25	DRAM
Chia Hsin Semiconductor Corp.	Factory 2	11	4th quarter 1996	15	Memory, ASIC
Macronix International Co., Ltd.	Factory 2	30	3rd quarter 1997	30	NV Memory, Logic
Winbond Electronics Corp.	Factory 3	30	1st quarter 1997	40	SRAM, Logic
Mosel Vitelic Inc.	Factory 2	30	1997	25	DRAM, SRAM, Logic
World Wide Semiconductor Manufacturing Corp.	Factory 1	20	1997	30	OEM (DRAM, Logic)
Holtek Semiconductor Inc.	Factory 2	20	July 1997	25	ASIC
Total		470		494	

Source: *Industrial Technology Information Services Plan*, Electronic Research & Service Organization, Industrial Technology Research Institute, November 1995.

billion (Table C-7). Among them, Champ Semiconductor Corporation (CSC), Nanya Technology Corporation (NTC), and Powerchip Semiconductor Corporation (PSC) were examples of cross-industry investments. Except for VIS, the rest of the investments were mainly expansions of existing IC companies.

The cross-industry investments of business groups from other industries marked an important change in this period for IC industrial development. CSC was an expansion of the Hualon Micro-electronics Company (1987) of the Hualon (Textiles) Group; NTC was part of the Formosa Plastics Group. Even though Formosa Plastics Corporation had a share in TSMC after the company entered the market, it immediately sold off its shares in TSMC. Thus, Formosa Plastic's first real cross-industry foray into the IC industry occurred when it set up NTC. As for PSC, it was a backward vertical integration investment of the Umax business group. Among the thirteen firms that had shares in VIS, some were from the electric cable and wire industry, with others from the textile industry, the petrochemical industry, the IT industry, and the IC design industry. During this period, the IC industry proved its ability to garner a great deal of investment without the need of government incentives. In addition to the IC production industry, the LCD- and IC-related industries were also much-sought-after areas of investments among the large business groups. Even though the large value of investment and the high risks involved put them at some risk, the business groups nevertheless felt that only through this avenue could they maintain high growth in the immediate future.

According to forecasts by the VLSI Company in the United States in the mid-1990s, this wave of tremendous growth in the IC industry could last until 2002. Given this rosy forecast, many industries expanded their investment in IC production. This also led to a rise in investment in IC-related industries, including IC equipment; IC design; photomasking; and IC packaging, testing, and experimentation. In addition, China Steel Corporation signed a joint venture with the U.S. MEMC Company to produce silicon wafers used in the production of silicon chips. This made the IC production process in Taiwan more self-sufficient and more complete.

In comparison with the rapid growth of the IC industry, the consumer electronic goods industry continued to deteriorate. As shown in Table C-5, its production was worth NT$89.208 billion in 1990 (16.1 percent of the total for IT and electronics) but dropped to NT$72.843 billion in 1994 (9.1 percent of the total for IT and electronics). Although these figures were still higher than those of communications equipment, the communications equipment industry, in contrast, was in the midst of slow but steady growth. The more labor-intensive consumer electronic goods such as televisions, stereos, and so on were gradually losing their competitiveness.

To promote the development of the IT and electronics industries so as to quicken the upgrading of the general industry, the government decided in the 1990s to continue to develop new skills essential for the two industries through ERSO, the OES, and the CCL. Government also continued to concentrate its efforts in the area of developing human resources. From Table C-9, one can see that the budget that the Ministry of Economic Affairs allocated to research and development in this particular field grew yearly. The figure for 1990 reached NT$2 billion, and by 1994 it had reached NT$5 billion. In 1994, most of these funds were spent on research in digitalization and opto-electronic consumer goods, multimedia skills, computer networks, and electronic and photo-electronic components and materials. The percentage of government research funds allocated to research in the electronics and IT industries reached a high of 46.3 percent in 1991. In the years that followed, this figure was maintained above 40 percent, showing the great importance of these industries in the eyes of the government. Of all government programs designed to assist industry upgrades—whether tax credits for R and D, matching funds for the development of new products, special loan programs, special training programs for technical people, or ITRI's special budget on technology development—it was the in-

TABLE C-9

Funds Allocated by the Ministry of Trade and Industry for Research in the Electronics and IT Industries, 1990–1994

Year	Amount Allocated to Electronics and IT Research (NT$million)	Share of Total Funds Allocated to Scientific Research (%)
1990	2,083	34.10
1991	3,686	46.37
1992	4,530	41.42
1993	5,309	44.41
1994	5,153	44.16

Source: *Annual Report on Taiwanese Industrial Development*, Industrial Development Bureau, Ministry of Economic Affairs, 1990–1995.

formation and electronics industry that always got the biggest share.

By the late 1990s, most private, domestic-owned firms had grown and had the capability to invest, so capital for expansion and research was no longer as necessary as it had been in the past. Also during the 1990s, the government began experiencing serious annual financial deficits, partly because of the heavy burden of building up public infrastructure and an expanding social welfare system; this threatened its ability to continue to provide financial support for industrial development. The intermediary institutions founded by the government and aimed at providing resources for the industry also suffered a cutback in funds, partly due to decreasing support from the Legislative Yuan and even from the industry. For example, in April 1993, the proposed 1994 budget for ITRI was reduced by NT$1.5 billion from the original figure of NT$8.8 billion. Therefore, in the face of the government's financial difficulties and its desire for greater privatization in the industry, both industry-specific and other financial support began to fall.

In summary, government intervention in the development of the electronics and IT industry was unintentional and accidental in the 1970s. Although it did not actively promote this specific industry at that time, its various economic policies of import substitution, export expansion, attraction of foreign investment, and ban on electronic games production were extremely beneficial to the industry in that they provided a conducive domestic environment for rapid growth. Domestic growth was further stimulated by global developments in electronics and IT. Only when the electronics industry rose to be the primary industry in Taiwan and the second oil crisis occurred did the government consciously try to foster this industry and provide it with the resources it lacked. What was unique in its intervention was that it was mainly focused on the provision of capital for research and development, through the funding and provision of ERSO, as well as on direct investment in domestic firms. The government chose not to interfere in the actual production and sales of goods, unlike government's decisions in the case of the petrochemical and textile industries. Although the electronics and IT industries were extremely important to the government's economic plans, private firms did not make broad-based demands on the government for protectionist measures. Rather, they requested that the government protect firms geared toward innovation and original research and discourage firms engaging in the manufacture of imitation products. In fact, in 1994 many firms requested that ERSO's spin-off companies be shut down so as to ensure an environment of fairer and freer competition. The relationship between the government and the electronics and IT industries was, therefore, markedly different from that between the government and many other industries.

Notes

1   See Wan (1961, pp. 1–3).

2   See Taiwan Institute of Economic Research (1985, p. 43).

3   See Wang (1993, pp. 219–242).

4   The III was formed by the Ministry of Economic Affairs using funds from its budget and surpluses from taxes. Its duties include: (1) updating the government on the developments in the industry through regular reports on growth and economic plans; (2) providing services for the government, national, and other enterprises; (3) providing training of human resources in terms of technical skills and managerial skills; (4) bringing in foreign skills and expertise to improve software development capabilities; (5) liaising with the skills development facilities and improving the general efficiency and productivity of the industry; and (6) helping with any plans to upgrade the industry.

D Policy Regressions

Chapter 5 raises the question of whether policymakers were using instruments such as the real interest rate and the real exchange rate deliberately to generate the external surpluses of 1980 to 1986. Based on the behaviour of the policy variables and on interviews with participants, the answer turns out to be ambiguous. Assuming that the authorities did intend to use interest and exchange rates to achieve external surpluses, could they have been effective in doing so? To test this, we ran a series of regressions relating private saving and private investment to the real interest rate and other variables. The results are reported here.

Private Savings and Investment

Private savings and investment were measured as a share of GNP, S_p/Y or I_p/Y, and regressed on the current growth rate of GNP per capita, $g(Y/P)$, 1 plus the real interest rate on deposits ($1+r_d$ for savings) or loans ($1+r_l$ for investment), and the lagged dependent variable.[1] In addition, the savings regressions were augmented by two rates of dependency: the share of the population under fifteen years, and the share over sixty-five years. OLS regressions were run in logarithms and in differences of logarithms. Various lagged structures were tried. Table D-1 shows the best results from the regressions.

The saving regressions gave good results when the contemporaneous values of GNP growth and the one-period lagged values of the other dependent variables were used. The log-linear regression gives significant coefficients, at the 5 percent level or better, for all independent variables, a high adjusted R-squared, and a satisfactory Durbin-

TABLE D-1

Regression Results for Savings and Investment

Dependent Variable	Constant	$g(Y/P)$	$1+r$	Under 15	Over 65	Dependent	Adjusted R^2	Durbin-Watson
Log S_p/Y	**-4.065**	**0.050**	**0.875**	**-3.095**	**-1.601**	**0.532**	0.757	1.634
	1.084	*2.506*	*3.160*	*-3.573*	*-3.432*	*3.952*		
(TSLS)	**-4.096**	0.043	**0.924**	**-3.202**	**-1.599**	**0.552**	0.730	1.618
	-3.033	*1.766*	*3.033*	*-2.919*	*-2.735*	*3.825*		
Δ Log S_p/Y	-0.028	0.039	**0.798**	-4.459	-0.463		0.331	1.598
	-0.526	*2.194*	*3.267*	*-1.233*	*-0.205*			
	-0.003	**0.056**	**0.812**	-3.497	-1.669	**0.363**	0.537	1.792
	-0.062	*2.948*	*3.479*	*-1.001*	*-0.720*	*2.012*		
Log I_p/Y	-0.127	-0.035	**1.834**			**0.868**	0.490	1.634
	-0.834	*-1.046*	*3.495*			*4.411*		
	-0.529	**0.155**	**-3.090*			**0.435**	0.577	1.774
	-4.457	*2.996*	*-4.391*			*2.942*		
(TSLS)	**-0.534**	**0.332**	**-5.052*			**0.538**	0.334	2.046
	-3.392	*3.267*	*-4.102*			*2.269*		
Δ Log S_p/Y	0.005	**0.040**	**0.805**				0.344	1.464
	0.543	*2.275*	*3.330*					
	0.003	**0.055**	**0.812**			**0.327**	0.410	1.617
	0.351	*2.914*	*3.466*			*1.876*		
	0.003	**0.117**	**-1.320*				0.271	1.526
	0.258	*3.360*	*-2.768*					
	0.002	**0.123**	**-1.242*			**0.232**	0.287	1.673
	0.216	*3.448*	*-2.513*			*1.196*		

* Contemporaneous variable.

Notes: t-ratios appear in italics; coefficients significant at the 5 percent level appear in boldface; OLS except where noted.

Watson statistic. Adjusted Dickey-Fuller tests of nonstationarity allow us to reject it at the 10 percent level, but only barely, for the dependent variable. The ADF statistics for the dependency rates suggest nonstationarity, as is expected.

In the regressions using first differences of logarithms, the coefficients on the real interest variable were significant at 5 percent and very close to the value in the log-linear regression. The best fit in log-differences occurs when the lagged first difference of the saving rate is included, raising the adjusted R-squared to 0.54 and making the GNP growth coefficient both significant and similar in magnitude to that in the log-linear form. However, inclusion of the lagged dependent variable is questionable on economic grounds, because it implies that, in the steady state, the ratio of saving to GNP would have to change (rise or decline) at a constant rate, which is impossible over the long run.

Although the regressions generally track the course of saving well, they do a poor job of reproducing the sharp rise of saving from the late 1970s to the mid-1980s, as Table D-1 shows for the log-linear regression. From 1980 to 1986, the savings rate rose by 50 percent, while the lagged value of $1+r_d$ (i.e., from 1979 to 1985) rose by only 5.8 percent. On the basis of the coefficient of $1+r_d$, which estimates the short-term elasticity, and the coefficient on the lagged dependent variable, we can calculate the elasticity of the savings rate with respect to the interest rate over any period.[2] For the six years from 1980 to 1986, the 5.8 percent rise in the real interest rate term would have been responsible for a rise in the savings rate of only 11 percent. Coefficients from the first-difference regressions give lower estimates, accounting for a rise in S_p/Y of 7 percent at most. It appears that, although interest rate policy may have had an impact, it cannot explain much of the rise in savings rates during the early 1980s.

On the basis of the short-term elasticities in the log-linear format, the 10 percent decline in the under-15 dependency ratio would have increased the private savings rate by a third from 1979 to 1986, but this was offset by the 24 percent rise in the over-65 dependency ratio, which would have lowered the saving rate by 30 percent.

Regressions of the investment rate, using $g(Y/P)$, $1+r_l$, and the lagged dependent variable, give poorer fits than the savings regressions and have similar problems in tracing peaks and valleys. When the lagged values of the real interest term are used, they give significant coefficients of the wrong (positive) sign. Contemporaneous values of the interest variable, however, give significant, negative coefficients and, in the log-linear form, an extremely high elasticity of -3.1. The other coefficients in this format are also significant the 5 percent level and of the right sign. Although nonstationarity cannot be rejected for the dependent variable, it can be rejected at the 1 percent level for the explanatory variables. In the difference-of-logs format, the sign of the interest rate term is also significant and negative for contemporaneous values only, although the growth term gives positive and significant coefficients in all forms. The magnitude of the interest rate elasticity if much lower, however, the higher estimate being -1.3.

Using the highest available (log-linear) estimate of the interest elasticity, the rise in $1 + r_l$ of 11 percent from 1980 to 1986 can explain a fall in the investment-GNP ratio of 59 percent over six years, much more than the actual decline of 40 percent. Even the log-difference regression, which yields a much lower (and more believable) elasticity coefficient, suggests that the observed rise in interest rates could have accounted for almost half the rise in the savings rate over six years (18 percent versus 40 percent). Thus interest rate policy appears to have been more effective in influencing investment than saving in Taiwan.

EXPORTS AND IMPORTS

For exports and imports, the ratios to GNP, expressed in dollars, gave generally poor regression results. Instead, we used the more time-honored formulation of exports, E, and imports, M, expressed in current US dollars, against GNP in 1986 dollars and an index of an appropriate measure of the real exchange rate, with 1986=100. Two measures of the real exchange rate were explored, using (1) the consumer price indexes of Taiwan's main trading partners as a proxy for world prices and (2) the import or export price deflators, respectively, of Taiwan's trading partners for world prices.

As discussed in the text, the CPI-based formula is the one most likely to have been watched by policy makers, but is not the best concept to measure the impact of the exchange rate and world prices (the terms of trade) on producers and consumers of tradables in Taiwan. However, the more appropriate measure of the price signals for exports and imports, based on tradables price deflators for partner countries, behaves differently from the CPI-based measure and, in particular, shows no depreciation during the critical period from the late 1970s to the mid-1980s. Hence the CPI-based index is the only measure of the real rate that has any potential to show whether exchange rate policy might have been effective in developing Taiwan's large trade surplus. This is the one reported in Table D-2.

Five estimates of the determinants of exports are shown in the table. All are flowed. The first two, log-linear OLS estimates using the logarithms of GNP, the RER (contemporaneous in the first equation, lagged one period in the second), and lagged exports as explanatory variables, give the most believable coefficients, a high R^2, and Durbin-Watson statistic that rejects positive autocorrelation at the 5 percent level. The elasticity of dollar exports with respect to GNP is 0.4 in both equa-

TABLE D-2

Regression Results for Exports and Imports

Dependent Variable	Estimation Technique	Constant	GNP	RER (CPI)	Lag-Dependent Variable	Adjusted R² Durbin-Watson
Log E	OLS	−1.178	0.414	**0.459**	**0.836**	0.995
		−1.672	1.806	2.170	8.847	2.063
	TSLS	−1.029	0.376	0.407	**0.842**	0.995
		−1.432	1.606	1.828	8.621	2.139
	OLS	−1.166	0.400	*0.697	**0.848**	0.997
		−1.848	1.941	3.330	9.999	2.040
	Johansen Cointegration	**8.738**	**2.939**	**−4.792**		
		7.306	7.609	2.318		
	Stock-Watson GMM	**−7.246**	**2.454**	0.441		0.991
		−6.950	11.281	0.400		0.568
Δ Log E	OLS	−0.003	**2.456**	0.439		0.610
		−0.109	3.702	1.609		1.233
Log M	OLS	−1.035	0.469	*1.180	**0.751**	0.995
		−1.331	1.795	3.684	6.486	1.812
	TSLS	−0.571	0.234	*1.293	0.808	0.994
		−0.701	1.191	3.987	6.789	2.036
	Johansen Cointegration	3.516	0.933	10.110		
		0.327	0.650	0.740		
	Stock-Watson GMM	**−4.792**	**1.988**	−1.353		0.976
		12.872	8.492	−0.346		0.404
Δ Log M	OLS	**−0.102**	**4.812**	**−1.880**		0.583
		−2.711	4.968	−5.345		1.839

* In these regressions, RER is lagged one period.

Notes: t-ratios appear in italics: coefficients significant at the 5 percent level or better appear in boldface.

tions, but fails the t-test at 5 percent, though it would pass at the 10 percent level. The elasticity on the contemporaneous RER is 0.4 and on the lagged RER is 0.7; both are significant at 0.5 percent.

However, the adjusted Dickey-Fuller test does not reject the hypothesis that all variables in these regressions are nonstationary, and the Johansen test finds a single cointegration equation. The Johansen cointegration equation and an alternative specification by Stock and Watson are shown in Table D-2, along with an estimate using the first differences of the logarithms of the three variables. These regressions yield statistically significant and consistent estimates of the income elasticity that are, however, too high to be plausible; and inconsistent estimates of the real exchange rate elasticity. The only significant coefficient on RER among the three is not plausible because it is high and negative.

Thus the only estimates that make economic sense come from the log-linear regressions. The regression using the one-period lagged real exchange rate has the higher elasticity, 0.7, while the contemporaneous real rate yields an elasticity of 0.4. From 1980 to 1986, the export-GNP ratio, with GNP expressed in US dollars at the 1986 official exchange rate, fell 26 percent. Over that interval, the one-period lagged real exchange rate did not change, so it cannot be used to explain the fall in the export ratio. The unlagged real rate fell by 10 percent from 1980 to 1986, sufficient to explain a six-year rise of 18 percent in the export-GNP ratio, compared to the actual rise of 26 percent. But is this plausible? The CPI-based real export exchange rate appreciated steadily from 1976 to 1981, and only then began to depreciate for the next five years. To take these calculations at face value, we would have to assume that exporters, observing an appreciating rate in 1980, somehow foresaw the five-year depreciation that would begin a year later and based their plans on it. This seems unlikely.

The regressions are less satisfactory for imports. The log-linear regression has good statistics, but the RER coefficient has the wrong sign. Neither Johansen nor Stock-Watson regressions yield significant estimates for the exchange rate elasticity. The difference-of-logs estimates are significant and have the right signs, but their magnitudes are implausibly large. The import-weighted, CPI-based RER depreciated by 25 percent from 1980 to 1986, more than sufficient to explain the actual drop of 24 percent in the ratio of imports to GNP in 1986 US dollars. But over the same period, the 60 percent rise in GNP would have raised the import ratio by much more than the fall due to the depreciation. Thus the log-difference equation yields results that are contrary to the experience of the early 1980s.

The log-linear and log-difference regressions for imports were run with a variable indicating the tightness of monetary policy. The indicator was the residual of a regression of the money supply on GNP. These residuals were negative during the early 1980s, indicating a tight monetary policy that may have helped dampen the demand for imports. However, none of the coefficients on the money residual came close to significance.

Because the four dependent variables—savings-GNP, investment-GNP, exports, and imports—are interdependent, we reestimated the four key regressions in two-stage least squares (TSLS) to confirm the values of the coefficients, especially those on the interest and exchange rate variables. These results are reported in Tables D-1 and D-2. In the log-linear savings regressions, the TSLS estimate of the interest elasticity is slightly higher than the OLS estimate. For the log-linear investment regression, the TSLS estimate is considerable lower (more negative). These results broadly confirm the conclusion that interest rate policy could have had a large effect on investment and a much smaller one on savings. In the log-linear export regression, the TSLS estimate of the exchange rate elasticity is somewhat lower than the OLS estimate and not quite significant at 5 percent. The TSLS regression of the log-linear import equation confirms the wrong sign on the exchange rate coefficient. These estimates broadly confirm the conclusions reached using the OLS estimates.

These results are not conclusive. The best we can say from these regressions is that macroeconomic policy variables seem to work most effectively on investment and less so on savings. The strong response of exports to the real devaluation does suggest that macro policy could have been effective in generating a trade balance, but this would be more convincing if it were based on a traded-goods price index instead of the CPI index. On the basis of these results, it might appear that the authorities, had they wanted to create large trade surpluses, should have used interest rate policy to generate the savings-investment surplus and allowed trade flows to adjust, with the outside possibility that the exchange rate might have had an impact on exports.

Notes

1   We used $1+r$ because regressions were in logarithms and real interest rates were negative in some years.

2   If the regression equation is $Y = aX + bY - 1$, then the formula for a change in Y given any change in X over n years is $Y/Y = a[(1 - b^n)/(1 - b)](X/X)$.

E   Productivity and Structural Change

Some of the supporting tables for the analysis in Chapter 6 are provided in this appendix.

TABLE E-1
Growth of Labor in Taiwan: 1952 through 1994[a] (in percent)

Sector	Period									
	1952–1955	1956–1960	1961–1965	1966–1970	1971–1979	1980–1985	1986–1990	1991–1994	1952–1994
Total Economy	3.34	5.08	4.81	11.50	6.28	2.43	2.74	2.22	5.01
I. Agriculture	0.50	2.51	2.29	4.04	–3.21	–1.49	–3.05	–3.04	–0.46
II. Nonagriculture	3.82	5.51	5.24	12.71	7.32	2.91	3.48	2.70	5.72
A. Industry	4.42	7.13	5.01	13.83	8.55	2.35	2.50	0.36	5.91
Mining	0.59	8.27	2.36	1.20	–8.60	–4.49	–7.72	–12.68	–3.16
Manufacturing	4.23	7.40	4.97	14.16	9.49	2.98	1.66	–0.88	6.03
Electricity, Gas, & Water	4.45	9.32	6.44	7.54	–5.12	10.26	4.60	–10.63	3.00
Construction	6.08	5.91	5.80	16.48	9.23	–0.70	8.28	8.92	7.50
Nonmanufact. Industry	4.80	6.60	5.08	13.13	6.00	–0.02	6.60	5.03	5.85
B. Services	3.53	4.73	5.36	12.18	6.71	3.21	4.15	3.91	5.67
Commerce	0.32	4.17	5.12	16.01	8.31	3.60	3.43	4.15	6.13
Transport & Communication	7.17	5.84	5.25	11.67	7.12	0.05	3.15	2.46	5.36
Services[b]	5.01	4.89	5.55	9.71	5.84	3.52	4.97	4.03	5.49

[a] Represents total labor inputs by including estimated human capital growth. Figures are the average log growth rates over the period.
[b] Includes financial, business, social, and government services.

TABLE E-2
Growth of Fixed Capital in Taiwan: 1952 through 1994[a] (in percent)

Sector	1952–1955	1956–1960	1961–1965	1966–1970	1971–1979	1980–1985	1986–1990	1991–1994	1952–1994
Total Economy	5.70	6.04	7.78	12.76	13.48	9.31	7.91	8.87	9.57
I. Agriculture	3.70	3.33	4.44	4.54	4.20	2.52	4.84	3.36	3.89
II. Nonagriculture	6.93	7.47	9.19	15.14	14.78	9.77	8.06	9.11	10.67
A. Industry	9.82	10.62	10.82	18.75	15.67	8.40	6.33	5.88	11.36
Mining	2.69	5.63	5.94	6.31	10.16	0.08	-1.01	-14.49	3.01
Manufacturing	11.46	9.77	11.77	21.18	14.97	7.23	7.94	6.19	11.68
Electricity, Gas, & Water	42.70	27.45	14.04	17.16	18.29	10.61	3.68	5.54	16.43
Construction	0.57	0.57	0.51	8.08	11.40	10.41	5.26	6.01	6.26
Nonmanufact. Industry	7.55	11.82	9.48	14.49	17.00	10.24	3.73	5.32	10.86
B. Services	6.02	6.30	8.47	13.22	14.21	10.67	9.04	10.66	10.42
Commerce	5.32	1.19	2.06	10.19	7.48	10.25	7.99	5.52	6.52
Transport & Communication	-1.62	10.46	13.25	23.37	16.49	8.74	4.27	7.31	11.48
Services[b]	6.98	7.51	9.39	12.23	14.54	11.12	9.96	11.47	10.95

[a] Does not include estimated improvements in the quality of capital. Figures are the average log growth rates over the period.

[b] Includes financial, business, social, and government services.

TABLE E-3
Estimated Share of Labor in Total Factor Income in Taiwan: 1952 through 1994[a]

Sector	Period									
	1952–1955	1956–1960	1961–1965	1966–1970	1971–1979	1980–1985	1986–1990	1991–1994	1952–1994
Total Economy	0.741	0.741	0.741	0.741	0.741	0.739	0.732	0.749	0.740
I. Agriculture	0.644	0.644	0.644	0.644	0.644	0.663	0.701	0.742	0.663
II. Nonagriculture	0.754	0.754	0.754	0.754	0.754	0.748	0.733	0.749	0.750
A. Industry	0.690	0.690	0.690	0.690	0.690	0.680	0.663	0.699	0.686
Mining	0.886	0.886	0.886	0.886	0.886	0.885	0.881	0.840	0.881
Manufacturing	0.683	0.683	0.683	0.683	0.683	0.679	0.663	0.702	0.682
Electricity, Gas, & Water	0.273	0.273	0.273	0.273	0.273	0.292	0.243	0.275	0.272
Construction	0.842	0.842	0.842	0.842	0.842	0.842	0.810	0.789	0.833
Nonmanufact. Industry	0.711	0.711	0.711	0.711	0.711	0.683	0.663	0.690	0.699
B. Services	0.801	0.801	0.801	0.801	0.801	0.799	0.783	0.778	0.796
Commerce	0.736	0.736	0.736	0.736	0.736	0.754	0.761	0.753	0.743
Transport & Communication	0.815	0.815	0.815	0.815	0.815	0.803	0.787	0.765	0.805
Services[b]	0.843	0.843	0.843	0.843	0.843	0.836	0.802	0.800	0.833

[a] Based on the share of labor compensation in total factor income (including the imputed income of unpaid workers).
[b] Includes financial, business, social, and government services.

TABLE E-4
Growth of Gross Domestic Product in Taiwan: 1952 through 1994[a] (in percent)

Sector	Period									
	1952–1955	1956–1960	1961–1965	1966–1970	1971–1979	1980–1985	1986–1990	1991–1994	1952–1994
Total Economy	9.00	6.70	9.50	9.37	9.55	6.59	8.74	6.57	8.23
I. Agriculture	5.60	6.90	3.70	2.52	2.22	0.96	1.64	−0.09	2.64
II. Nonagriculture	10.80	6.60	11.90	10.92	10.49	7.00	9.10	6.81	9.09
A. Industry	14.80	10.50	14.50	14.77	12.31	6.86	6.95	5.09	9.86
Mining	1.60	13.30	13.60	2.40	1.88	−0.81	−0.55	3.70	3.94
Manufacturing	18.00	11.10	16.80	16.83	12.47	7.76	6.75	4.43	10.32
Electricity, Gas, & Water	14.70	20.80	14.10	15.23	11.73	8.80	7.63	6.87	10.81
Construction	12.20	5.30	4.60	10.32	14.38	1.25	8.80	8.51	8.91
Nonmanufact. Industry	12.30	6.97	9.98	9.18	11.79	3.28	7.84	7.75	8.65
B. Services	9.20	4.70	11.00	8.62	9.02	7.13	10.90	8.04	8.68
Commerce	—	—	—	7.32	9.58	7.52	10.14	8.72	7.90
Transport & Communication	—	7.20	4.60	13.70	14.15	9.11	7.79	7.05	9.23
Services[b]	—	—	—	8.63	8.05	6.55	11.86	7.93	9.01

[a] Figures are the average log growth rates over the period in real terms.
[b] Includes financial, business, social, and government services.
"—" designates data not available.

TABLE E-5
Estimated Growth of Total Factor Productivity in Taiwan: 1952 through 1994[a] (in percent)

Sector	Period								
	1952–1955	1956–1960	1961–1965	1966–1970	1971–1979	1980–1985	1986–1990	1991–1994	1952–1994
Total Economy	4.44	1.26	3.39	−1.77	1.95	2.36	4.62	2.68	2.17
I. Agriculture	3.14	3.20	0.34	−1.76	2.52	101.00	2.33	1.30	1.35
II. Nonagriculture	5.28	0.75	4.62	−1.71	1.67	2.36	4.40	2.51	2.26
A. Industry	7.81	7.97	7.43	−0.23	1.83	2.58	3.16	3.07	2.30
Mining	3.51	2.85	9.79	0.89	8.39	3.15	6.38	16.67	6.51
Manufacturing	9.98	9.88	0.50	−0.20	1.18	3.41	2.97	3.20	2.25
Electricity, Gas, & Water	−23.29	−6.08	−5.57	0.20	0.27	−1.73	3.70	7.32	−2.13
Construction	10.61	−3.33	4.48	−5.37	4.89	0.19	1.09	0.20	1.57
Nonmanufact. Industry	7.77	−0.12	4.91	−2.45	5.31	0.04	2.20	2.62	2.34
B. Services	3.80	0.02	5.96	−3.18	1.03	2.42	5.69	2.64	2.09
Commerce	4.32	1.66	2.88	−6.94	1.49	2.28	5.62	4.23	1.66
Transport & Communication	3.89	1.80	−6.80	−0.02	5.46	7.34	4.40	3.45	2.73
Services[b]	4.20	−0.63	9.84	−1.51	0.81	1.78	5.90	2.41	2.57

[a] Based on figures in Tables E-1 through E-4, where TFP growth is the residual after allowing for labor and capital inputs.
[b] Includes financial, business, social, and government services.

NOTES FOR TABLES 1-5

1. Explanation of Labor Growth (Table E-1)

Our basic approach in calculating the increase in total labor inputs over time was to estimate a translog index of labor growth that incorporates changes in the quality as well as the quantity of labor. This approach follows the technique used by Alwyn Young in his well-known analysis of productivity growth in East Asia, and readers who desire a more detailed explanation should also consult this work (Young, 1995). However, whereas Young denies that this technique results in an estimate of labor growth that includes embodied technological change, we would argue that by including quality changes, it does embody such change (see Chen, 1997).

This approach begins with the assumption of a translogarithmic value added production function, which, under neoclassical assumptions and constraints, yields a measure of the causes of growth over discrete time periods through the following equation:

(1) $\text{Ln}(Q(T)/Q(T-1)) = \phi_K * \text{Ln}(K(T)/K(T-1)) + \phi_L * \text{Ln}(L(T)/L(T-1)) + \text{TFP}_{T-1,T}$

where Q, K, L, and T denote output, capital, labor, and time and the ϕ's denote the elasticity of output with respect to each input, or, assuming perfect competition, the share of each input in total factor income. We then assume that aggregate labor inputs are similarly translog indices of subgroups of labor in accordance with the following equation:

(2) $\text{Ln}(L(T)/L(T-1)) = \Sigma_i \phi_{Li} * \text{Ln}(L_i(T)/L_i(T-1))$

where the ϕ's denote the elasticity of total labor with respect to each subgroup, or, as before, the share of each subgroup in total labor income. Practically, this means taking the average of such shares over the discrete time period in question to weight the growth of each labor subgroup.

For 1979-94, we used household labor and income survey data provided by the government of Taiwan to estimate both the work input and share of total factor income of each labor subgroup in each year for each of the eight economic sectors which comprise the Taiwan economy (see the sectoral breakdown in the Appendix tables). We began by creating seventy-two labor subgroups in each sector on the basis of sex (2), education level (6), and age (6) and then calculated the change in total number of hours worked by each group in every year from 1979-94 (although some subgroups were merged with others to eliminate subgroups with no workers, so that the actual number of final subgroups varies by sector). Yearly labor growth by sector was then estimated by weighting the growth of each subgroup (the log of the ratio of labor input in year 1 to the labor input in year 0, as in the above equation) by its relative elasticity, or share of compensation in total sectoral income.

To derive the weight, or income share of each subgroup, including paid and unpaid workers, we calculated the average hourly wage of each sector's employed workers (reported income), subgroup by subgroup, and then applied that wage to the hours worked by the unpaid and family workers in each subgroup. By summing the total "earnings" of each subgroup, we could then calculate the relative shares of each subgroup in total sectoral income.

In order to calculate the shares of each sector in total labor compensation, which are necessary to weight each sector's growth rate for the aggregated sectors and economy-wide labor growth, we summed the "earnings" of unpaid and paid workers within each sector, calculated the ratio of unreported to reported income, and then applied this ratio to the total labor income data that are readily available for each sector and year during this period. This yielded a new total labor compensation figure for each sector, adjusted to include unreported labor income, out of which the relative sectoral shares could be calculated.

For the years prior to 1979, we used a somewhat simplified version of this basic approach due to the less detailed data at our disposal. For each of the years 1955, 1960, 1965, 1970, 1975, and 1980, labor input was measured by an estimation of average monthly hours worked by each of twelve subgroups within all eight sectors. In each sector, these subgroups were formed on the basis of sex (2) and education (6) (sex and education cross-classifications for 1955-1970 were estimated from population data; cross-classifications for 1970-80 were available in labor survey data). The average monthly hours worked by men and women in each sector were then estimated from a combination of detailed survey data and sector by sector averages and used to convert employee figures into average hourly labor inputs (per month) for all subgroups in each sector.

For these earlier years, income shares were estimated by using data on average incomes cross-classified by sex and education, and by sector and sex for the years 1975 and 1980. By applying average sex/education income breakdowns to the estimated total portion of each gender's total income within each sector, we estimated the income share of each of the twelve subgroups for each sector. Since we lacked similar data for the years prior to 1975, the 1975 shares were used for each period up through 1970-1975.

For the sector-by-sector income shares, we took the average ratio of reported/unreported income from 1979 to 1981 for each sector and used it to revise the reported sectoral labor income figures as described above for the years for which we had data –1965, 1970, 1975. From the revised sector labor compensation figures, we then calculated the sectoral income shares for each of the above three years and applied the resulting shares for 1965 to each of the years prior to that.

2. Explanation of Capital Growth (Table 2)

Our basic approach in estimating the growth of fixed capital for this analysis differs from our approach in estimating labor growth in that we did not attempt to make adjustments for the quality of capital. Hence, our capital growth estimates do not include embodied technological change. However, similar to our analysis of labor growth, we estimated capital growth from the relatively early year of 1952 in each of the main eight sectors (see the sectoral breakdown in the Appendix tables) according to the following equation:

$$(3)\ K_{yr\,x} = K_{1952} + \Sigma_{1952}^{yr\,x} N$$

where K and N refer to the capital stock and net fixed capital formation. The latter, in turn, is defined for a given year by the difference between gross fixed capital formation and capital consumption in that year.

We began by estimating the existing capital stock in 1952 in each sector on the basis of a 1.5 capital/output ratio. Since yearly capital consumption within each sector was available in current prices, but not in real prices, we constructed a deflation index from data on gross fixed capital formation in current and 1991 prices and used it to express capital consumption in 1991 prices. Net fixed capital formation could then be calculated for each year and added to the 1952 capital stock estimate for each sector. From these totals, sector-by-sector growth indices were constructed, from which we derived the average log growth rates for various periods provided in Table 2. Growth rates for the aggregated sectors and entire economy were calculated from the (unweighted) capital stock totals and growth indices of the relevant sectors.

3. Explanation of Labor and Capital Income Shares (Table 3)

Calculating the respective shares of labor and capital in total factor income is a matter of estimating the former, since the two shares sum to one. For each year after 1978, the labor share in factor income for each sector was estimated by dividing the new estimate of labor compensation, revised to include the imputed income of unpaid workers (as described above in the explanation of labor growth calculations), into the sum of that estimate and capital income. Averages were then calculated for each of the relevant later periods in the analysis. Since we lacked the detailed data necessary to do similar calculations for earlier years, we used the average shares from 1979 to 1983 for these years.

4. Explanation of GDP and Derived TFP Growth Rates (Tables 4 and 5)

Sector-level GDP in constant (1991) prices are readily available from 1965. For earlier years, we estimated real GDP for each sector on the basis of sectoral shares of total GDP (again and 1991 prices) provided in Taiwan's national accounts data. With all sector-by-sector GDP figures in constant prices, we then calculated GDP growth as the average log growth rate over each of the periods in our analysis.

The estimates of average TFP growth over various periods were calculated using Equation (1) in the above Note 1, where TFP growth is the residual factor in GDP growth after accounting for labor and capital contributions. Essentially, for each sector and time period, we deducted the total labor contribution (equal to the average labor share in total factor income multiplied by the average log growth rate of labor) and the total capital contribution (equal to the average capital share in total factor income, or one minus the average labor share, multiplied by the average log growth rate of capital) from the average log growth rate of GDP. The remainder of each set of calculations comprise the estimated TFP growth figures presented in Table 5.

Selected Bibliography

A

B

Balassa, Bela, and associates. 1982. *Industrial Strategies in Semi-Industrial Countries.* Baltimore: Johns Hopkins University Press.

C

Chen Chieh-hsuan. 1991. The Economic Structure and Social Characteristics of Taiwan's SME's: A Study of Textiles, Shoe Manufacture, Machinery, and Information Industries. Doctoral dissertation Tung Hai University, Taichung, May 1991.

Chen Ts'e-yu and Mo Chi-pin. 1995. *The Interviews of S. C. Tsiang.* Taipei: Yuan-liu Press.

Cheng Hang-sheng. 1986. Financial Policy and Reform in Taiwan, China. In Cheng Hang-Sheng, ed., *Financial Policy and Reform in Pacific Basin Countries.* Lexington, MA: D.C. Heath.

Chi Schive. 1995. *Taiwan's Economic Role in East Asia.* Washington, DC: Center for Strategic and International Studies.

Chi Schive. 1987. Trade Patterns and Trends of Taiwan. In Colin I. Bradford, Jr. and William Branson, eds., *Trade and Structural Change in Pacific Asia.* Chicago: University of Chicago Press.

Chi Schive. Turning over a New Leaf: Liberalization in Taiwan. Unpublished essay.

Chiang Shih-chieh. 1985. Taiwan *ching-chi fa-chen ch'i-shih-wen-ting chung-te ch'eng ch'ang* (Lessons from the Economic Development of Taiwan). Taipei: Commonwealth Publishing.

China Credit Information Service. 1974, 1980, 1992, and 1994. *Business Groups in Taiwan.* Taipei: China Credit Information Service.

China Credit Information Service Ltd. 1992. *Taiwan Industrial Yearbook: The Petrochemical Industry.* Taipei: China Credit Information Service.

China Times. 1984. Editorial: Liberalization Should Not Be Paper Work. December 12.

China Petroleum Corporation, Planning Department. 1983. *A Study on the Pricing Structure of Petrochemical Raw Materials.* Taipei: China Petroleum Corporation.

Chiu, Paul C. H. 1992. Money and Financial Markets: The Domestic Perspective. In Gustav Ranis, ed., *Taiwan: From Developing to Mature Economy* (Boulder, CO: Westview Press.

Chou Shun-hsin. 1963. *The Chinese Inflation, 1937–1949.* New York: Columbia University Press.

Council for Economic Planning and Development. 1974. *Taiwan Statistical Data Book,* 1974. Taipei: Economic Planning Council.

Council for Economic Planning and Development. 1979. *The Assessment of the Ten Major Development Projects.* Taipei: Council for Economic Planning and Development, Executive Yuan.

Council for Economic Planning and Development. 1983. *The Development Plan for the Machinery Industry, 1982–1989.* Taipei: Council for Economic Planning and Development.

Council for Economic Planning and Development. 1989 *Taiwan Statistical Data Book, 1989.* Taipei: Council for Economic Planning and Development.

Council for Economic Planning and Development. 1995. *Taiwan Statistical Data Book, 1995.* Taipei: Council for Economic Planning and Development.

Council for Economic Planning and Development, Executive Yuan. 1969. *Fifth Four-year Plan for the Economic Development of Taiwan.* Taipei: Council for Economic Planning and Development.

Council for Economic Planning and Development, Executive Yuan. 1973. *Sixth Four-year Plan for the Economic Development of Taiwan.* Taipei: Council for Economic Planning and Development.

Council for Economic Planning and Development, Executive Yuan. 1976. *Six-year Plan 1976–1981 for the Economic Development of Taiwan.* Taipei: Council for Economic Planning and Development.

Council for Economic Planning and Development, Executive Yuan. 1979. *The Assessment of the Ten Major Development Projects.* Taipei: Council for Economic Planning and Development.

Council for Economic Planning and Development, Executive Yuan. 1981. *Eighth Four-year Plan for the Economic Development of Taiwan.* Taipei: Council for Economic Planning and Development.

Council for Economic Planning and Development, Executive Yuan. 1985. *Ninth Medium-term Plan for the Economic Development of Taiwan, 1986–1989.* Taipei: Council for Economic Planning and Development.

Council for Economic Planning and Development, Executive Yuan. 1989. *Tenth Medium-term Plan for the Economic Development of Taiwan, 1990–1993.* Taipei: Council for Economic Planning and Development.

Council for Economic Planning and Development, Executive Yuan. 1990. *1991–1996 Six-year National Development Plan.* Taipei: Council for Economic Planning and Development.

D

Department of Statistics, Ministry of Economic Affairs. 1977. *Monthly Statistics of Industrial Production, Taiwan, R.O.C.* , Taipei: Department of Statistics.

Department of Statistics, Ministry of Economic Affairs. 1983. *Monthly Statistics of Industrial Production,* No. 162. Taipei: Department of Statistics.

Department of Statistics, Ministry of Economic Affairs. 1993. *Monthly Statistics of Industrial Production,* No. 291. Taipei: Department of Statistics.

Department of Statistics, Ministry of Economic Affairs. 1995. *Monthly Statistics of Industrial Production,* No. 309. Taipei: Department of Statistics.

Department of Statistics, Ministry of Economic Affairs. *Economic Statistics Annual Taiwan Area, The Republic of China.* Taipei: Department of Statistics.

Department of Statistics, Ministry of Finance. Various years. *Yearbook of Financial Statistics of the R.O.C.* Taipei: Department of Statistics.

Directorate-General of Budget, Accounting and Statistics. 1995. *Statistical Yearbook on Wages and Productivity in the Taiwan Area, Republic of China.* Taipei: Directorate-General of Budget, Accounting and Statistics, Executive Yuan.

Directorate-General of Budget, Accounting and Statistics. 1996. *Monthly Bulletin of Statistics,* April. 22(2): 14.

Directorate-General of Budget, Accounting and Statistics, Executive Yuan. Various years. *National Income of Taiwan, the Republic of China.* Taipei: Directorate-General of Budget, Accounting and Statistics.

E

Economic Daily News. 1976. November 29.

Economic Daily News. 1978. February 23.

Economic Daily News. 1978. March 18.

Economic Daily News. 1978. July 11.

Economic Daily News. 1980. March 4.

Economic Daily News. 1981. August 14.

Economic Daily News. 1982. August 20: 3.

Economic Daily News. 1983. August 9.

Economic Daily News. 1984. April 11.

Economic Daily News. 1984. May 11.

Economic Daily News. 1984. May 26.

Economic Planning Board of the Republic of Korea. Various years. *Handbook of Korean Economy.* Seoul: National Planning Board.

Economic Policy and Economic Growth: Yu Kuo-hua's Response to News Reporter's Interviews, *Economic Daily News.* 1984. May 26.

Economic Research Department, Bank of Taiwan. 1979–1983. *A Survey of Industrial Financial Conditions in Taiwan, R.O.C.* Taipei: Bank of Taiwan.

Economic Research Department, Bank of Taiwan. 1981–1984. *A Survey of Industrial Financial Conditions in Taiwan, R.O.C.*, Vol 22–25. Taipei: Bank of Taiwan.

Economic Research Department of the Economic Construction Council. 1984. *Li-ts'u ts'ai-ching hui-t'an tong't'ong chih-shih hsin-wen kao-hui-pien* (A Collection of News Manuscripts of Presidential Instructions in Financial and Economic Discussion Meetings). Taipei: Economic Research Department of the Economic Construction Council.

Editorial. 1986. We Support the Five Scholars' Policy Suggestion of Carrying out Thoroughly Liberalization. *Industrial and Commercial Times.* September 14.

Emery, Robert F. 1991. *The Money Markets of Developing East Asia.* New York: Praeger.

Export Processing Zone Administration, Ministry of Economic Affairs. Various years. Export Processing Zones Essential Statistics (*Export Processing Zone Concentrates Monthly*, after 1992). Taipei: Export Processing Zone Administration, Ministry of Economic Affairs.

F

Fei, John C. H. 1992. Taiwan's Economic Development and its Relation to the International Environment. In N. T. Wang, ed. 1994. *Taiwan's Enterprises in the Global Perspective.* Armonk: M.E. Sharpe.

Fischer, Stanley. 1993. The Role of Macroeconomic Factors in Growth. *Journal of Monetary Economics* 32 (1993): 485–512.

Fry, Maxwell J. 1995. *Money, Interest and Banking in Economic Development,* second edition. Baltimore: Johns Hopkins Press.

G

H

Higgins, Mathew and Jeffrey Williamson. 1997. Age Structure Dynamics in Asia and Dependence on Foreign Capital. *Population and Development Review.* 23(2): 261–293.

Historical Data Compilation Committee. 1990. *History of Taiwan Annual Report, 1966–1978.* Taipei: National Policy Research Information Center.

Hsiao, F. S., 1982. The Measurement of Industry Concentration in Taiwan. *Taipei City Bank Monthly* 13(5):43–56.

Hsu Chen-kuo. 1987. *The Political Base of Changing Strategy Toward Private Enterprise in Taiwan, 1945–1955.* Doctoral dissertation, Ohio State University

Hsu Chen-kuo. 1994a. Ideological Reflections and the Inception of Economic Development in Taiwan. In Joel D. Aberbach, David Dollar, and Kenneth L. Sokoloff, eds., *The Role of the State in Taiwan's Development.* New York and London: Sharpe, Armonk.

Hsu Chen-kuo. 1994b. *Ts'ung Ho Lian te K'ou-shu li-shih kan' chi-hua tzu-yu ching-chi' kai-nian tsai da-lu shih-tai. Meng-ya yu fa-chan,* (The Study of the Initial Stage and Development of the "Planned Free Economy" with reference to Ho Lian's Oral History), a paper presented in a symposium held for the KMT's 100-year anniversary, Taipei. The original manuscript of Ho Lian's Oral History was published by Columbia University. This English work was translated into Chinese by Chu Yu-Tzu titled *Ho Lian Hui i Lu* (The Reminiscence of Ho Lian). 1988. Taipei: Chinese Literature and History Publishers.

Hsu Chen-kuo. 1995. "The Function and Content of Interest Articulation by Business Associations in Annual Gatherings" (in Chinese). *Soochow Journal of Political Science,* No. 4, January, 1995, pp. 185–216.

Hsu Song-ken and Chuang Chao-jung. 1991. *A Study on Industrial Land Use Policies in Taiwan* (in Chinese). Studies of the Modern Economy Series. Taipei: Academia Sinica.

Hsueh Li-min, Tu Ying-yi, and Wang Su-wan. 1995. *The Development and Prospect of Producer Service Industries in Taiwan-An Internationl Comparison* (in Chinese). Contemporary Economic Issues Series No. 2. Taipei: Chung-hua Institute of Economic Research.

Huang Tung-chi. 1956. Taiwan's Textile Industry. *The Textile Industry in Taiwan.* Economic Research Division, Bank of Taiwan, The 41st Taiwan Research Series: 1–18.

I

Industrial and Commercial Times (Kung-shang shih-pao). 1980. June 14.

Industrial and Commercial Times (Kung-shang shih-pao). 1982. April 24.

Industrial and Commercial Times (Kung-shang shih-pao). 1982. *Ts'ai-ching cheng-ts'e ta byan lun: Taiwan ching-chi wen-t'i yü tui ts'e t'ao-lun-hui shih-lu* (The Great Debate on Financial and Economic Policy: A Record of the Discussion Meeting on Taiwan Economic Issues and Policies). Taipei: Industrial and Commercial Times Publishers.

Industrial Development Bureau, Ministry of Economic Affairs. Various years. *Industrial Development Yearbook of the R.O.C.* Taipei: Ministry of Economic Affairs.

Industry of Free China. 1959. Vol. II, No. 4.

Industry of Free China. 1971. Vol. 36, No. 3.

J

Joint Committee on Industrial Statistics. 1994. *Report on a Survey of Industrial Statistics,* Ministry of Economic Affairs.

Jones, Leroy P. and Il Sakong. 1980. *Government, Business, and Entrepreneurship in Economic Development: The Korean Case.* Cambridge, MA: Harvard University, Council on East Asian Studies.

Jorgenson, Dale W. and Liang Chi-Yuan. Unpublished. The Industry-Level Output Growth and Total Factor Productivity Changes in Taiwan, 1961–1993. Paper submitted to the Chiang Ching-Kuo Foundation for International Scholarly Exchange.

K

Keizai Koho Center, Japan. 1981, 1990, 1991, 1995. *Japan: An International Comparison.* Tokyo: Keizan Koho Center.

Kim, Jong-il and Lawrence J. Lau, 1994. The Sources of Growth of the East Asian Newly Industrialized Countries, *Journal of the Japanese and Industrialized Countries,* 8:235–71.

Kuo Cheng-tian. 1990. *Economic Regime and National Performance in the World Economy: Taiwan and the Philippines.* Doctoral dissertation, Political Science, University of Chicago.

Kuo, Shirley W. Y. 1983. *The Taiwan Economy in Transition.* Boulder, CO: Westview Press.

Kuo, Shirley W. Y. 1993. *The Experience of Taiwan's Economic Development,* Keynote Speech, Conference on Economic Development and Trade: Spain and the Republic of China on Taiwan.

Kuo, Shirley W. Y., Gustav Ranis, and John C. H. Fei. 1981. *The Taiwan Success Story: Rapid Growth with Improved Distribution in the Republic of China, 1952–1979.* Boulder, CO: Westview Press.

L

Lau, Lawrence and Jong-Il Kim. 1994. "The Sources of Economic Growth of the East Asian Newly Industrialized Countries", *Journal of Japanese and International Economies,* Vol. 8, pp. 235–271.

Levy, Brian. 1991. Transaction Costs, the Size of Firms and Industrial Policy: Lessons from a Comparative Case Study of the Footwear Industry in Korea and Taiwan. *Journal of Development Economics,* Vol. 34, pp. 151–178.

Li, K. T. 1976. *The Experience of Dynamic Economic Growth on Taiwan.* Taipei: Mei Ya Publications.

Li, K. T. 1993. Oral History of K. T. Li. In S. L. Wang, *Oral History of Li Kuoting: The Economic Experience of Taiwan.* Excellent Publications Company.

Li, K. T. 1976. The Growth of Taiwan's Private Industry. In Tu Wen-tien, ed., *Collection of Essays on Taiwan's Industrial Development.* Taipei: Lien-chia Press. [originally published 1961.]

Lin, Che-Yueh and Tong-his Chang. 1995. "An Analysis of the Situation with Respect to the Privatization of Public Enterprises in the Taiwan Region" (in Chinese). *Industries and Finance Quarterly,* March (86): 40–51.

Lin C. Y. 1973. *Industrialization in Taiwan, 1946–1972:* Trade and Import Substitution Policies for Developing Countries. New York: Praeger.

Lin Pang-yun. 1976. A Study on the Development of Taiwan's Cotton Textile Industry. In *Collection of Theses on Taiwan's Industrial Development.* Taipei: Lien Ching Publishing Company.

Liu Chin-ch'ing. 1992. *Taiwan chan-kou ching-chi fen-hsi* (Analysis of Taiwan's Post-war Economy). Taipei: Jen-chien Press.

Lundberg, Erik. 1979. Fiscal and Monetary Policies. In Walter Galenson, ed., *Economic Growth and Structural Change in Taiwan: The Postwar Experience of the Republic of China.* Ithaca: Cornell University Press.

M

McGinn, Noel, Donald R. Snodgrass, Yung-Bong Kim, Shin-bok Kim, and Quee-young Kim. 1980. *Education and Development in Korea.* Cambridge, MA: Council for East Asian Studies.

Ministry of Economic Affairs. 1995. *Yearbook of Public Enterprises Supervising Committee.* Taipei: Ministry of Economic Affairs.

Ministry of Trade and Industry Investment Survey Committee. 1994. *Annual Report on Foreign and Overseas Chinese Investment, Technical Co-operation, in Taiwan, Taiwanese Investment and Technical Co-operation in Foreign Countries, and Taiwanese Investment in The People's Republic of China.* Taipei: Ministry of Trade and Industry.

Ministry of Trade and Industry. Various issues. *Monthly Report on Industrial Production.* Taipei: Ministry of Trade and Industry.

Ministry of Trade and Industry. Various years. *Annual Report on Taiwanese Industrial Development.* Taipei: Ministry of Trade and Industry.

Myers, Ramon H. 1990. The Economic Development of the Republic of China on Taiwan, 1965–1981. In Lawrence J. Lau, ed., *Models of Development.* San Francisco: ICS Press.

N

National Science Council. Various years. *Indicators of Science and Technology, R.O.C.* Taipei: National Science Council.

National Statistical Office. Various years. *Korea Statistical Yearbook.* Seoul: National Statistics Office.

National Statistical Office of the Republic of Korea. Various years. *Major Statistics of Korean Economy.* Seoul: National Statistical Office.

Numazaki, Ichiro. 1993. The Tainanbang: The Rise and Growth of a Banana-bunch Shaped Business Group in Taiwan. *The Developing Economies* 31 (4): 485–510.

O

P

Patrick, Hugh T. 1994. Comparisons, Contrasts, and Implications. In H. Patrick and Y. C. Park, eds., *The Financial Development of Japan, Korea, and Taiwan.* Oxford: Oxford University Press.

Planning Department, Chinese Petroleum Corporation. 1983. *A Study on the Pricing Structure of Petrochemical Raw Materials.* Taipei: China Petroleum Corporation.

Q

R

Radelet, Steven. 1996. *Measuring the Real Exchange Rate and Its Relationship to Exports: an Application to Indonesia.* Development Discussion Paper No 529. Cambridge, MA: Harvard Institute for International Development.

Ranis, Gustav and Syed Akhtar Mahmood. 1992. *The Political Economy of Development Policy Change.* Cambridge, England: Blackwell.

Joint Committee on Industrial Statistics, *Report on a Survey of Industrial Statistics.* 1994. Taipei: Joint Committee on Industrial Statistics, Ministry of Economic Affairs.

Riedel, James. 1992. International Trade in Taiwan's Transition from Developing to Mature Economy. In Gustav Ranis, ed., *Taiwan: From Developing to Mature Economy.* Boulder, CO: Westview Press.

R.O.C. Chemical Industry 1991 Yearbook. 1992. Taipei: Union Chemical Labs, Industrial Technology Research Institute and Taiwan Institute for Economic Research.

S

Science-based Industrial Park. 1994. *Statistics Quarterly* (June). Hsin-chu: Science Park Administration.

Scitovsky, Tibor. 1990. Economic Development in Taiwan and Korea, 1965–1981. In Lawrence J. Lau, ed., *Models of Development.* San Francisco: ICS Press.

Shea, Jia-Dong and Ya-hwei Yang. 1994. Taiwan's Financial System and the Allocation of Investment Funds. In A. Auerbach, D. Dollar and K. Sokoloff, eds., *The Role of the State in Taiwan's Development.* New York: M.E. Sharpe.

Shen Yun-lung, ed. 1972. *Yin Chung-jung hsien-sheng nien p'u ch'u-kao* (the primary draft of Yin Chung-jung's Biography in Chronological Order). Taipei: chuan-chi wen-hsueh Publishers.

Shieh, Samuel. 1996. The Delicate Art of Monetary Policy. *Asian Business* 32(9): 9.

Song Ha-joong. 1991. *Who Stays? Who Returns? The Choices of Korean Scientists and Engineers.* Unpublished doctoral dissertation. Harvard University.

Stern, Joseph, Ji-hong Kim, Dwight Perkins, and Jung-ho Yoo. 1995. *Industrialization and the State: The Korean Heavy and Chemical Industry Drive.* Cambridge: Harvard Institute for International Development.

Sun Ke-nan. 1998. "The Evolution and Performance of Industrial Tax Incentives in Taiwan," *Industrial Development and Policies in Taiwan,* edited by Ya-Hwei Yang. Taipei: Chung-Hua Institution for Economic Research, pp. 45–102.

Sun Ying-Che. 1996. The Division of Labor in Industrial Networking: The Example of Li-Wei Corporation. *Taiwan Economy Research Monthly* (November): 65–68.

T

Taiwan Business Bank Investigation and Research Office. 1981. *Taiwan's Textile Industry.* Taipei: Taiwan Business Bank Investigation and Research Office.

Taiwan Textile Federation. Various issues. *The ROC's Textile Annual Yearbook.* Taipei: Taiwan Textile Federation

Tatung Company, 1993. *An Introduction to Tatung Company.*

Technical Cooperation, Outward Technical Cooperation, and Indirect Investment in Mainland China, Investment Commission, Ministry of Economic Affairs. 1994. *Annual Statistical Yearbook on Investment by Overseas Chinese and Foreigners in the R.O.C.* Taipei: Ministry of Economic Affairs.

Tsiang, Suo-chieh. 1984. Taiwan's Economic Miracle: Lessons in Economic Development. In Arnold Harberger, ed., *World Economic Growth.* San Francisco: ICS Press.

Tsiang, Suo-chieh 1987. Monetary Policy under the Impact of a Persistent Huge Trade Surplus: The Experience of Taiwan, R.O.C. Taipei: Chung-Hua Institute for Economic Research.

Tsiang, Suo-chieh. 1992. *The Reminiscences of Dr. S. C. Tsiang.* Oral History Series No. 43. Taipei: Institute of Modern History Academica Sinica.

Tsiang S. C. and Wen-lang Chen. 1984. "Development toward Trade Liberalization in Taiwan, Republic of China." *Proceedings of the Joint Conference on the Industrial Policies of the ROC and ROK.* Taipei: Chung-Hua Institution for Economic Research.

Tu Chaw-his and Wen-thuen Wang. 1988. "Trade Liberalization in the ROC on Taiwan and the Economic Effects of the Tariff Reductions." Paper presented at the 1988 Joint KDE/CIER Conference, Korea.

U

United News. 1984. November 7.

U.S. Department of Commerce. 1994. *Statistical Abstract of the United States, 1994*. Washington, DC: Department of Commerce.

V

W

Wade, Robert. 1990. *Governing the Market: Economic Theory and the Role of Government in East Asian Industrializaton.* Princeton: Princeton University Press.

Wang, Sophia L. 1993. *K. T. Li's Oral History: Talking about the Taiwan Experience* (in Chinese). Taipei: Excellence Cultural Publishing Company.

Wang Yong-ch'ing. 1986. How Should We Go Our Own Way? *Industrial and Commercial News.* September 1 and 2.

World Bank. 1995. *Bureaucrats in Business: The Economics and Politics of Government Ownership.* Oxford: Oxford University Press.

X

Y

Yang, Hui-ye, Huang Ming-tsung, etc., Man-Made Fibers Manufacturing Association. 1981. *A Study on the R.O.C.'s Man-Made Fiber Industry,* Specialized Research Bulletin No. 7. First Commercial Bank.

Yang, Ya-Hwei. 1994. Taiwan: Development and Structural Change of the Banking System. In H. Patrick and Y. C. Park, eds., *The Financial Development of Japan, Korea, and Taiwan.* Oxford: Oxford University Press.

Yeh Wan-an. 1983. Taiwan's Industrial Policy: Its Formulation and Promulgation. *Proceedings of the Conference on Taiwan's Industrial Development.* Taipei: Academia Sinica.

Yin K. Y. 1973. *My View on Taiwan's Economyc.* Taipei: Council for Economic Planning and Development, Executive Yuan.

Young, Alwyn. 1995. The Tyranny of Numbers: Confronting the Statistical Realities of the East Asian Growth Experience. *Quarterly Journal of Economics* 60(3): 641–680.

Z

Index